Sewing Made Easy

NEW REVISED EDITION

SEWING *Made Easy*

BY MARY LYNCH AND DOROTHY SARA

GARDEN CITY BOOKS, GARDEN CITY, NEW YORK

Acknowledgment with thanks
is made to Simplicity Patterns and McCall's Patterns
for permission to use
many of the patterns included in this book.

Contents

Introduction   xi

1. GETTING READY TO SEW   1

    Sewing equipment. Necessary sewing aids. Sewing extras. Use
    and care of your sewing machine.

2. BUYING YOUR PATTERN   9

    How to identify an easy-to-make pattern. How to take your
    measurements for a pattern. How to select the most becoming
    pattern for your figure. Do's and Don't's of buying a pattern.

3. CHOOSING YOUR MATERIAL   21

    Meaning of pattern instructions and lay-out diagrams. How to
    choose material that will be easy to work with, that will be suit-
    able for your pattern, that will look well on you. Chart showing
    fabrics, their uses and care. Choosing interfacing and under-
    lining. Threads to match fabrics.

4. HOW TO FIT AND ALTER YOUR PATTERN   37

    Getting acquainted with your pattern. Meaning of pattern mark-
    ings. Trying on your pattern. How to make alterations in blouse
    patterns, skirt patterns, sleeve patterns, patterns for shorts and
    slacks.

5. CUTTING MATERIAL FROM YOUR PATTERN   58

    Preparing your material. Placing the pattern on the material.
    Cutting your material. Transferring pattern markings to your ma-
    terial using tailor's tacks, tailor's chalk.

6. BASTING, SIMPLE STITCHES, AND SEAM FINISHES   66

How to tie a knot for hand sewing. How to fasten machine stitching. Directions for basting: even basting, uneven basting, right-side basting, diagonal basting, basting a bias edge to a straight edge. Basic sewing stitches: running stitch, backstitch, overcasting, quick overcasting, deeper overcasting, overhanding, combination stitch. Seams and ways to finish them: plain seam, pinked seam, overcast seam, edge-stitched seam, top-stitched seam, bound seam, flat fell seam, welt seam, strap seam, slot seam, French seam, seam with edges turned in and stitched, rolled seam, machine-picoted seam, lapped seam, piped seam, corded seam, and upholsterer's seam. Tricks with seams.

7. DARTS, TUCKS, AND PLEATS   78

Darts: How to make a smooth dart. Darts used at the shoulder, at the underarm seam, at the back of the neck, at the skirt back, at the side front and back waist, at the elbow or shoulder of sleeves. Dart with gathered fullness. Double dart. Finishing darts. Tucks: how they are made and where they are used, dart tucks, pin tucks, corded tucks, narrow tucks, cross-tucks, curved tucks, shell tucks, overhand tucks, practical tucks. Pleats: how to make side pleats, box pleats, inverted pleats, fan pleats, accordion pleats, double and single kick pleats.

8. HEMS, FACINGS, BANDINGS, AND BINDINGS   89

Marking a skirt hem. Finishing a hem. Hemming by hand: quick hem, slip-stitched hem, blind hem, rolled hem, whipped hem, bias-bound hem, machine-stitched hem, narrow machine-rolled hem, catch-stitched hem, pleated skirt hem, circular skirt hem, damask hem. Facings: skirt facing, bias facing, front facing, facing for corner, shaped facing for small slit opening, facing for scalloped edge, facing for saw-toothed edge. Bandings: applied band, extended band. Bindings: how to make a bias binding, how to apply bias tape to a straight edge by machine, how to apply bias tape by hand, how to bind scallops with bias binding.

9. PUTTING YOUR DRESS TOGETHER   105

The factory method. The custom method. General rules for basting, fitting, and stitching a dress. Special fitting problems.

Shoulder pads. Sleeves: cap sleeve, kimono sleeve, long sleeve, dolman sleeve, raglan sleeve, puffed sleeve, set-in sleeve. How to make a set-in sleeve. Ways to finish sleeves. Necklines and collars: bias-faced V neckline, ribbon, silk, or rayon bound neckline, front-slashed facing, slashed neckline with collar, notched collar with lapels, collar applied with bias binding, collar trimmed with edging. Yokes. Godets. Flares. Lining a dress or skirt.

10. TAILORING TRICKS   137

Buttons: Types of buttons. Making covered buttons. Sewing on buttons. Making a button shank. Chinese loop (frog). Buttonholes: measuring buttonholes, spacing buttonholes, bound button hole, corded buttonhole, thread buttonhole, tailored buttonhole. Slide fasteners. Plackets. Snaps, tape closure, hooks and eyes, eyelet loops, fabric-covered belts. Pockets: patch pocket, slot pocket, welt pocket.

11. HOW TO BE YOUR OWN STYLIST   161

Detecting style trends. Adapting basic patterns. Skirt styles: draped fullness in front, pleated fullness in front, pleated fullness at the back, variations of back fullness, pleated skirt, flared skirt, yoke combined with pleats, curved or diagonal yoke, side-draped peplum. Necklines and waist yokes: draped V neckline, square neckline with collar, round yoke. Sleeves: ruffled sleeve, three-quarter draped sleeve, flared sleeve, long, full sleeve. Style notes for classic button-down-the-front dresses. Variations in suit styles: with pockets, with buttons and buckles, with boleros, with skirt styles. Reversible skirt.

12. BUILDING A WARDROBE   184

How to plan a flexible wardrobe. The housewife's requirements. The business woman's requirements. The teacher's requirements. The wardrobe of a receptionist, salesclerk, or hostess. How to make several different outfits from the same pattern. Five versions of a shirtwaist dress. Five versions of a suit. Completing your wardrobe. Evening and formal dresses, blouses, sports clothes.

13. YOU AND YOUR ACCESSORIES   198

General instructions on selecting hats, shoes, stockings, gloves, furs, handbags, and jewelry. Specific instructions for choosing accessories if you are tiny, if you are tall, if you are plump.

14. TAKING CARE OF YOUR CLOTHES   212

    Pointers for daily care. Pressing equipment. Pressing instructions for wool, silk, rayon, nylon, linen, velvet, corduroy, and cotton. Removing stains.

15. REMODELING YOUR CLOTHES   218

    How to select patterns. How to prepare material. Piecing insufficient material. Cutting. Suggestions for makeovers: turning a man's shirt into a blouse, cutting down an adult garment into a child's dress or coat, making a man's suit into a woman's suit, making one dress from two, remodeling an evening dress. Other remodeling possibilities.

16. GATHERS, SHIRRINGS, RUFFLES, AND HEADINGS   227

    Gathers: gathering by hand, gathering by machine, gathers to hold fullness. Shirring: shirring by hand, using a stay under shirring, shirring by machine, shirring with elastic thread. Ruffles: how to make ruffling, circular ruffles, double ruffles. Headings: gathered heading, corded heading.

17. LACE, EDGINGS, AND OTHER TRIMMINGS   232

    Lace: lace edging, lace bands and gathered lace, joining lace to a raw edge, joining lace to hemmed edge, joining lace with beading, edging on allover lace, lace inserts, joining lace inserts with edging, joining corners in lace. Hints for sewing lace. Edgings: braiding (passementeries), embroidered edgings, other types of edgings. Trimmings: allover embroidery, embroidered inserts.

18. DECORATIVE STITCHES   237

    Machine stitching for decoration. Saddle stitch. Seed stitch. Couching stitch. Outline stitch. Blanket stitch. Satin stitch. Cross-stitch. Catch stitch. Feather stitch. Lazy-daisy stitch. Chain stitch. French knots. Bullion stitch. Single hemstitching. Double hemstitching. Diagonal hemstitching. Plain fringe. Raveled fringe. Knotted fringe. Fagoting. Criss-cross fagoting. Bar or spoke fagoting. Smocking. Decorative arrowhead. Appliqué.

19. SEWING AND MENDING FOR THE FAMILY   250

    Clothes to make for the children. Clothes to make for grownups: house dresses, basket aprons, bib aprons, sewing aprons.

Turkish towel wrap. Lingerie for the trousseau. Materials for lingerie. Sewing hints for lingerie. Clothes to make for the menfolk. Mending. How to avoid slide fastener trouble. Making girdle repairs. Mending rips and tears. Use of mending tape. Reweaving problems. Darning. Reinforcing. Patching. Men's clothes repairs: sturdy patches, elbow patches, trouser knee patch, frayed sleeve, worn coat collar, relining sleeve of suit jacket, replacing trouser pocket, repairing trouser pocket, replacing torn-off buttons, underarm patch, turning collar and cuffs.

20. SEWING FOR THE HOME   273

Tea towels. Luncheon sets. Plastic tablecloths. Curtains: tailored curtains, ruffled curtains, café curtains, double-sash curtains, cottage curtains, remodeling curtains, Austrian shades, skyline shades. Draperies: how to select the most suitable material, how to make lined or unlined draperies, ways to finish draperies. Valances: covering a valance board, a buckram frame. Swag and cascade draperies. Rods and aids for hanging curtains and draperies. Dressing-table skirts: gathered, pleated. Closet accessories: shoe pockets, laundry bag, garment covers. Slip covers for chairs and sofas: suitable materials, amount required, how to take the measurements, cutting, sewing and finishing, plastic. Slip covers for studio couches. Slip covers for bedframes. Miscellaneous covers. Bedspreads. Patchwork quilts and comforters. Make-over quilts and blankets. Make-over sheets. Other household make-over hints. Lampshades.

21. CLOTHES FOR THE EXPECTANT MOTHER   322

Special considerations in buying patterns. House dresses. Play clothes. Dresses for "dress-up." Evening clothes. Coats and suits. Hats. Shoes.

22. ACCESSORIES AND GIFTS YOU CAN MAKE   328

Hints for making accessories. Bags: easy-to-make envelope bag, closed with slide fastener, lined, over-the-shoulder bag, envelope bag for evening wear, circular bag, miser's pouch. Hats: ideas for hats, headband, veiling, turban, tiered skullcap, beret, fur hats. Gloves. Collars: straight collar, Peter Pan collar. Dickeys. Cuffs: double ruffle, perfect circle, turnback cuffs, cuffs that are different. Belts: fringed sash in felt or suède, plaited belt, twisted belt of felt or suède, scroll belt in suède, grosgrain ribbon belts, other ideas for belts. Peplums: gathered peplum, overskirt, or apron peplum. Gift suggestions. Bedroom slippers. Scuffs. Toys.

23. TAILORING SUITS, COATS, AND JACKETS   364

How to choose your pattern and material. Lining material. Interlining. Interfacing and facing. Tailoring supplies. Making a tailored coat or jacket. Cutting and fitting the pattern. First tailoring steps. Interfacing and facing a casual topcoat. Interfacing and facing tailored jacket or coat. Setting in sleeves. Finishing a lined coat or jacket. Finishing an unlined coat or jacket. Lining topcoat or jacket. Interlining coat. Underarm shields for coat or jacket. Making the skirt. Working with fur.

24. MAKING ALTERATIONS IN READY-TO-WEAR CLOTHING   378

Buying for size. Shortening a skirt. Lengthening a skirt. Removing fullness at the hips. Adding fullness to a garment. Enlarging the waistline of a dress. Eliminating bagginess at the waistline of a dress. Fitting heavy or round shoulders. Fitting thin shoulders. Correcting tightness in the sleeves and underarm seams. Correcting looseness at the sleeve and underarm seams. Adjusting sleeve length. Pointers for longer wear.

INDEX   383

Introduction

The first edition of SEWING MADE EASY, published in 1950, has shown almost 200,000 women that the fine art of sewing is as valuable today as it was in their grandmothers' day. The scores of things to make for home and family described in the earlier edition have been brought up to date in this new revised edition to include all the new fabrics, styles, and sewing ideas of the last ten years. The modern woman can now practice the ever-popular art of sewing with all the advantages of the materials and techniques of the present day.

To women in all walks of life sewing is a source of lasting personal satisfaction. More than that, it is one of the most useful skills a woman can acquire. Few women can afford to buy the distinctive custom-made clothes they would like to wear, but the woman who sews can be fashionably dressed for any occasion. She can make many of the basic and costly items in her wardrobe at a fraction of their retail cost and, with the money she has saved, buy the elegant accessories which are so much a mark of the well-dressed woman.

Dressmaking is only one phase of sewing, however. In addition to making her own clothes the modern mother makes many of her family's clothes and many attractive articles for her home. For her sewing proves a profitable as well as a pleasant pastime.

Any woman can learn to sew if she has sufficient interest and is given the proper instruction. This book begins at the beginning with a discussion of the necessary sewing equipment; then progresses, step by step, through all the procedures for making a dress—from the moment the idea is conceived through the choice of pattern and material, down to sewing the last button in place. The improved sewing methods described and recommended in each section of the book insure a smooth, professional finish that clearly stamps the old "home-made" look as the result of careless workmanship. All of the material has been carefully arranged so that each procedure is explained at the time it is needed, and there is no necessity for turning to another part of the book for the information.

The art of sewing is more than the ability to cut and stitch. It is made up of many skills, each of which contributes its share to the perfect finished work. To help the home sewer achieve the smart, well-tailored look so much admired there are chapters on such relevant subjects as the choosing of suitable accessories to frame her handiwork, ideas for remodeling, and tips on the care of clothes.

The importance of style is obvious to every woman, and yet the subject is very lightly treated in most books about sewing. The reader will find that SEWING MADE EASY not only discusses the elements of style, but also shows her how she can become her own stylist by learning to detect style trends and adapting basic patterns to include the fashion notes best suited to her own figure and personality.

The many and varied aspects of sewing for the family and the home, as well as all other phases of sewing, have been given the same comprehensive treatment in separate chapters covering each subject.

The planning of this book was aimed to show the reader that learning to sew can be a pleasant experience and one in which each new project brings a growing sense of accomplishment. The instructions are clear and comprehensible. Hundreds of illustrations have been most carefully integrated with the text and have been used lavishly to insure the utmost clarity. In content and arrangement this book is useful to every woman who wants to learn to sew or to learn to sew better and more easily.

Acknowledgment of our deep appreciation is given to all those whose interest and industry helped make the book possible—to Sylvia Wiren for her illustrations, and to Celia Murray whose illustrations help to simplify the explanations of sewing procedure and add a good deal to the modern styles in this revised edition.

MARY LYNCH
DOROTHY SARA

CHAPTER 1

Getting Ready to Sew

NOW that you have decided to sew, the next thing to do is find out what equipment you will need. There is not so much as you think. You may have a sewing room if you want one, but not many women have the space. Our idea of a place for sewing equipment is a closet with shelves. We won't ask more than that, and we imagine you won't. Somewhere in the house you probably have an ironing board. Keep it near the sewing machine when you are stitching. The reason? To press your seams as you go along. Pressing speeds your sewing and is one of the secrets of that made-to-order look in clothes.

Let us list your sewing equipment in an orderly fashion, so you can see what you have on hand and how little you actually need to buy.

Iron and ironing board—You can iron on a table, but that's one way to discourage yourself at the start!

Pressing cloth—Piece of white cloth, old or new, washed to remove any starch or lint. This cloth is dampened and placed between the iron and any piece of wool which is to be pressed. A pressing cloth may also be used on heavy rayon materials which have a tendency to shine.

Shears—Good, long (8 inches long, if you're going out to buy a pair), sharp ones for cutting. A pair of small scissors is handy for cutting thread and buttonholes.

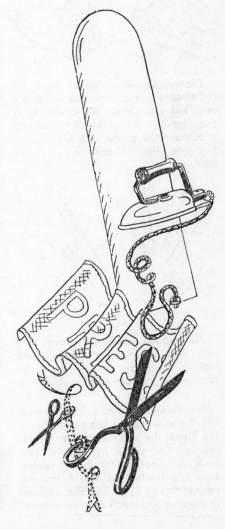

Razor blades—Single-edge, safety-razor blades. They are wonderful for opening seams, but it pays to be careful when you use them. One slip and you cut your material; two slips and you cut your thumb! Still, the razor blade is a handy gadget for the sewer.

Pincushion—Buy one of those fat red tomato pincushions. You can make one, but you should fill it with sawdust, for it is difficult to stick pins into a cotton-filled pincushion. Go ahead, buy one. The red tomato costs very little.

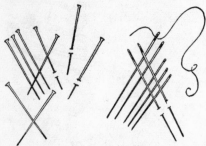

Pins—Steel are best, since they won't rust. Take an extra minute and look at the paper or the box to be certain that you are getting steel pins.

Needles—Assorted sizes. Use small ones (sizes 8–10) for fine hand sewing. The higher the number, the smaller the needle. You might like crewel (embroidery) needles for hand sewing. They are slender, but they have long, easy-to-thread eyes. Buy one package of medium and small needles assorted

(that's what the word means—different sizes in the same package), and hunt up two or three darning needles.

Tape measure—The 60-inch long, common garden variety. Not one of the little wonders which crawl back into a case just when you need it! You'll save youself minutes in measuring if you buy a tape measure with numbering on both sides beginning at opposite ends.

Yardstick—Handy for marking skirts and for drawing lines on your patterns. But as a skirt marker is inexpensive, you might get yourself one.

Mercerized thread—To match whatever you plan to sew. Buy thread one shade darker than the material because it "sews up" lighter than it is on the spool. Use leftover spools of colored thread for necessary basting.

Hint: the Don't Knows are the women who sew everything, or almost everything, with white thread.

Thimble—You'll find it handy when you must push a needle through a heavy piece of material.

Scrap basket, or box—To hold bits of thread and material.

Place to cut—A large, fairly high table is best. Have the table top bare. Beds aren't too good for cutting on—bedspreads cost money! And you have to crawl to cut on the floor. But you can use either of these places in a pinch.

Full-length mirror—Yes, we've climbed on a chair to see a hem, too, but we don't recommend it. You are better off if you can see yourself by backing away from the mirror on your bureau. You can buy an inexpensive, narrow, full-length mirror. Best buys are in secondhand furniture stores.

Material—Fabric is another name

for it. Whatever you call it, it should be becoming and something you truly like. (More about selecting materials later.)

Pattern—One which is becoming and as nearly perfect in size and fit as possible. (More about this later, too.)

Good light—Daylight is best. But if you sew at night, work under good artificial light.

Common sense—In large doses. This is one of the virtues which makes sewing simple.

Money—As much or as little as you

care to spend. One of the reasons for sewing is to save money, but you will not save money by buying poor material. If you have a small amount to spend, haunt the remnant counters until you find a short length of good material which has been reduced for a quick sale.

Time—Don't try to make your first dress in one afternoon—not many of us can go straight through from pattern to party in one fell swoop.

Patience—Don't spoil the fun by doing something silly, such as failing to read the instructions with the pattern, or sewing something so carelessly that it comes apart the first time it is washed.

SEWING EXTRAS—Have as many sewing extras as you can, for they do make the details of sewing easy. But don't think you must buy all the fancy gadgets at the notion counter when you first start to sew. Our favorite gadgets are:

Skirt marker—The kind that forces air into a chalk container when you press the rubber bulb and marks a line around the skirt as you turn.

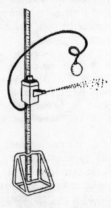

Pinking shears—Used to trim inside seam edges to prevent fraying. They should never be used for cutting anything but material.

Sewing cabinet—Neat, pretty, keeps all your equipment in one place.

But there is nothing wrong with shoe boxes and suit boxes for storage.

Tailor's chalk—It is inexpensive and much quicker and easier than the tailor's tack. This is used to mark pattern perforations.

Tailor's ham—You can make it yourself. It looks like a cross between a big shoulder pad and a baby football. It is made of two circles of unbleached muslin or other heavy material stuffed with cotton. It is held beneath the top of a sleeve, or the curve of an armhole, to make pressing easier.

Sleeve board—To press sleeves without a crease. A sleeve board is shaped like a tiny ironing board.

Treated pressing cloth—Lint free. Has chemicals in it to help you do a professional pressing job with the cloth wet or dry.

Dress form—Very helpful when you must do your own fitting. Dress forms, like pinking shears, are investments for the serious sewer. There are different kinds of dress forms on the market. If you sew just for yourself, you can get a dress form that is exactly your size. But if there are others in the family for whom you sew, or who are sewers themselves, you can buy an adjustable form which can be made to suit all sizes and shapes of figures. The form can be expanded or taken in wherever necessary and can also be made shorter or taller.

Another type of form is made of large metal links which resemble a chicken-wire fence. It is made like a sleeveless jacket coming to the bottom of the hips and left open all the way down the front. Put the form on over your slip, and then with your hands

it takes a lot of skill in front of a long mirror to manipulate the wire links to your body.

THE USE AND CARE OF YOUR SEW-ING MACHINE—There are some people who enjoy sewing by hand, and of course there are certain fine stitches and finishing touches which should be done only by hand. But a sewing machine should be part of every home sewer's equipment. If you do not have a machine of your own, perhaps there is someone near by who has one which you can share.

If you are buying a sewing machine, select one that is made by a well-known, reliable firm. Then you will be able to buy attachments to fit your machine, and if broken parts occur with years of use, they can easily be replaced.

A treadle (foot-operated) sewing machine will give satisfactory service, but an electric sewing machine is much less tiring to operate. If you live near a branch shop of a sewing-machine company, you may be able to purchase a reconditioned machine which is in perfect working order. Or, if you now have a treadle machine, you can have it converted to electricity by the addition of a motor; but this must be done by someone who is expert, and it is best to consult the branch shop or agent of the sewing-machine company if you decide to do this.

These branch shops also offer sewing lessons, and they rent machines to home sewers on a weekly or monthly basis. In some of these shops they make arrangements to permit sewers to bring in their material at certain hours during the day and stitch on their machines for a very small charge per hour.

In order to keep your machine in good condition, you need to remember these three rules:

mold the wire to fit your figure. Remove it carefully, place it on the stand which comes with it, and you have your own figure molded into shape. It is best to have someone help you with this, as

Keep the machine clean. A hairpin, a soft brush, and the habit of covering your machine when it is not in use are usually all that is required.

Keep the machine oiled. The frequency of oiling depends somewhat on the use you give your sewing machine. It is best that you follow the instruction book on this, until you learn from your own experience how often you should oil it. After you have oiled it, wipe off the excess oil and stitch away on a piece of flannel or other absorbent material to soak up any extra oil before you start to sew on a piece of good material. You will be wise not to oil your machine at a time when you plan to use it, as there is danger of some oil spattering on your material. When you are in doubt about oiling, consult the instruction book which comes with the machine when you purchase it.

Know the possibilities of your machine. Those attachments which came along with it were made to be used. They are simple to operate and will help you to save time and to produce finer and more professional-looking sewing. Our favorite attachments are the buttonhole maker and the cording foot. The buttonhole maker attachment makes buttonholes from about one fourth to one inch long in practically no time at all. With a little adjustment it can even make longer buttonholes. The cording foot attachment is used to stitch covered cord welting or slide fasteners in place.

Side issue, but important: When children want to use the sewing machine, it is far safer for you to show them how to use it than to have them experiment on their own when you are not around. They are apt to hurt themselves as well as damage the machine or the material on which they are stitching.

When you buy your machine, ask for demonstrations of threading the machine, putting in the needle, winding and inserting the bobbin, regulating the size of the stitch, and the use of the attachments which accompany it. Practice all these operations on the machine before you buy it. Then do the same thing at home. Do a little practice stitching, using the attachments, too, so that you will understand their operation.

If you are miles from a sewing-machine shop, ask your county extension agent, home demonstration leader, 4-H Club leader, the home economics teacher in the nearby school, or a neighbor, for assistance. And if you don't have any of these near by, you can still turn to the instruction book and follow it patiently.

Learn the names of the most important parts of your sewing machine so you can identify them. They are usually shown on a diagram in the instruction book.

Practice stitching on a double thickness of a piece of material before you actually start your first sewing project. You can draw straight lines on the sample piece of material with pencil or tailor's chalk. After you have threaded the machine, and before you start your practice stitching, make a check to be certain that the thread from the needle and the thread from the bobbin are both pushed away from you toward the back and are under the presser foot of the machine. If you do this for every line of sewing you start, your threads will never form a tangled knot. You should have at least 6 inches of thread extending through the needle and under the presser foot when you start to sew.

Start your sewing on the straight line which you marked as a guide. The presser foot of the machine must be down when you sew, to hold the material firmly in place. When you come to the end of a line and want to turn a nice square corner in your stitching, leave the needle in the material, raise the presser foot, and turn the material at right angles to the line. Then lower the presser foot and continue to sew as before. To end your sewing, stop with the needle raised to its highest point, raise the presser foot, and push the material away from you, under the presser foot and toward the back of the machine. Pull the two threads (from the needle and the bobbin) and cut them off, leaving about 2 inches, which will be sufficient to tie. Also leave a 6-inch end of thread through the needle and the bobbin hole, so that you won't have to re-thread the needle with every new line of stitching you start.

If your machine is stitching correctly, the upper side of the stitching and the underside of the stitching will both look alike, and the upper and the lower threads will pull evenly when you draw them under the presser foot and away from you.

If loops of thread form on the underside of the stitching (this is apt to tear the material, or break the needle), it may mean that your machine is not threaded correctly, or that the upper tension is too loose. The machine instruction book will tell you how to regulate the tension properly.

For some types of material you may want to use a short machine stitch and for others you may prefer a long stitch. This is also important when you have many thicknesses of material and have to adapt the size of the stitching accordingly. The instruction book will show you how the length of the stitch can be adjusted. The average is usually 12 to 14 stitches to the inch.

When you are satisfied with the way your first rows of practice stitching look, you should continue to practice a few rows more, until you can make the rows of stitching an even distance apart. The best way to do this is to use the width of your presser foot as a guide. That is, make each new row of stitching exactly the presser foot's width beyond the last row you stitched. Also practice turning corners and finishing a line of sewing with sufficient allowance for tying the ends of the thread neatly and securely.

When you have mastered straight stitching, you may proceed with the "plus" features which are now part of most machines. There is the zigzag attachment that can produce many kinds of decorative stitches, including edgings and borders for play clothes, children's clothes, curtains, and other household articles. Some of the new machines also enable you to darn stockings and socks by means of special attachments. When you buy your machine, these features will be explained to you by the salesclerk. Or you may learn to operate them by studying the manuals which the manufacturer furnishes with the machine. Here, too, as with plain stitching, you should first practice on pieces of leftover material until you feel that you have perfected your skills.

Are you satisfied with your own progress? Have you practiced your way to perfection? Is there space in a convenient spot in your house to accommodate you and your sewing in comfort? Have you the necessary equipment and perhaps some of the little extras? Then you are ready to sew!

CHAPTER 2

Buying Your Pattern

THE success of any sewing venture depends in large part upon the pattern you select. Unless you are an experienced sewer, you will want to buy your pattern before you buy your material. There are several reasons for this:

1. The pattern envelope lists the amount of material you need to buy for the style you want, in your size, so there will be no wasted material.

2. The pattern envelope also lists the notions: the thread, slide fasteners, buttons—all the things you need to give your dress a perfect finish.

3. The pattern envelope has suggestions for materials which will look especially well when they are made up in the pattern you have bought.

EASY-TO-MAKE PATTERNS—If you are making your first dress, you should look for a pattern that is easy to make. There are two ways to recognize easy-to-make patterns:

1. They are marked easy-to-make on the pattern envelope,

or

2. They have very few pattern pieces. The number of pattern pieces is shown on the back of the pattern envelope. An easy dress pattern might have only four or five pieces—a front waist, a back waist, a front skirt, a back skirt, and a sleeve.

This is an **easy-to-make dress pattern.**

It has **four pieces:**

FRONT   BACK

This is an easy-to-make blouse pattern.

It has three pieces:

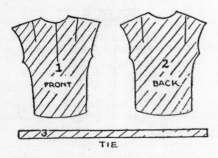

EASY-TO-MAKE DETAILS—These are easy-to-make details to watch for if you want a very simple pattern. Naturally, you will select only those which are becoming to you.

Cap or kimono sleeve—Cut in one piece with the blouse, and does not have to be set in separately.

Collarless neckline—May be round, oval, square, or pointed. Pointed is hardest of this group to make but is easier than putting on a collar.

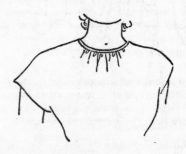

Gathered or four-gored skirt—Skirt and waist joined at normal waistline without set-in waistband.

HARD-TO-MAKE PATTERNS—This is a dress pattern which is not easy to make, for it has nineteen pieces. It is a good pattern but should not be a "first dress" for the beginning sewer.

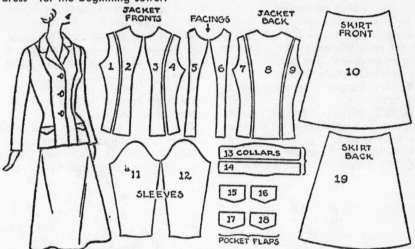

JACKET FRONTS   FACINGS   JACKET BACK   SKIRT FRONT 10

1 2 3 4 5 6 7 8 9

11 12 SLEEVES

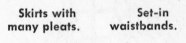
13 COLLARS
14

15 16

17 18
POCKET FLAPS

SKIRT BACK 19

HARD-TO-MAKE DETAILS—These are hard-to-make details which the beginning sewer should avoid when choosing a first pattern. They are good in style but a little tricky. Save these to try on your second dress.

Long, tight sleeves which must be fitted at the elbow.

Skirts with many pleats.

Set-in waistbands.

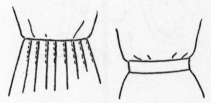

Fussy necklines.

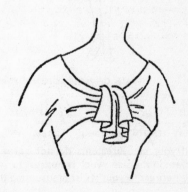

HOW TO TAKE YOUR MEASUREMENTS FOR A PATTERN

1. Wear a good girdle and brassiére when taking measurements.

2. Take measurements over dress.

3. Hold tape snugly but not tightly. Do not make allowance for seams or ease in movement. The pattern measurements will include these.

4. Most important measurements to take are:

A. BUST (measured around the fullest part). Be careful not to let the tape slip down in back.

B. WAIST (at the smallest part).

C. HIP (about 7 inches below the waist). This is not always the largest measurement in inches. If the lower hip is very large, always buy a pattern with a gored skirt to flatter the figure.

D. SLEEVE LENGTH (measure the underarm from the hollow to the wrist). This measurement is important only if you are making a dress with long sleeves.

E. BACK LENGTH OF DRESS (from bone at the back of neck to the hem). Pattern allows for hem.

Check your bust, waist, and hip measurements with the standard measurements given on this chart. Chart shows standard sizes used by all pattern companies.

SCALE OF MEASUREMENTS FOR WOMEN'S AND MISSES' PATTERNS

SIZE	10	12	14	16	18	20	40	42	44	46
BUST	28	30	32	34	36	38	40	42	44	46
WAIST	24	25	26½	28	30	32	34	36	38	40
HIPS	31	33	35	37	39	41	43	45	47½	50
SLEEVE LENGTH (underarm)	16¼	16½	17	17½	18	18	17¾	17¾	17½	17½

If your measurements do not agree with the ones on this chart, buy a dress pattern in the size which is nearest to your bust measurement, a skirt pattern in the size nearest to your waist measurement.

HOW TO SELECT THE MOST BECOMING PATTERN FOR YOUR FIGURE—

Generally speaking, there are five different types of figures. Before you go out to buy your pattern, look into your full-length mirror, study your own figure, and appraise it frankly. You will find that even though your figure does not fit every standard measurement it can be classified under one of these five general types:

Are you average? One way to check this is to check your actual measurements (bust, waist, hip, back length from the neck to the hem) with the standard measurements for your height, as shown on the back of any good pattern envelope, or on the chart. The average figure ranges from 5 feet 3 inches to 5 feet 6 inches. This type of figure can wear almost any style, so long as it is kept in proportion to the figure.

Right   Wrong

Are you short? If you are less than 5 feet 3 inches, you are called short. You may be short and plump, or you may be a tiny, perfect doll. But these Do's and Don't's for dress and pattern buying apply to all small figures.

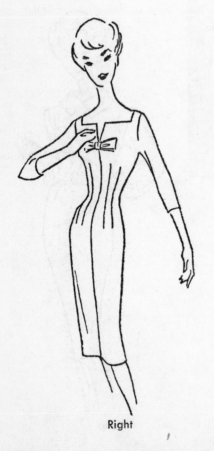

Right

Wrong

Are you tall? If you are 5 feet 7 inches or over, you are counted tall. Tall women are lucky, for they can wear the striking, unusual clothes shown in the fashion magazines.

Right

Wrong

Are you top-heavy? If your bust is large in proportion to your waist and hips, wear clothes with darts under the arm and on the shoulder to give fullness over the bust. Sleeves should end above or below the bust. An easy-fitting top will conceal the heavy lines of your bust and show off your nice trim hip line. No frilly collars unless you want to look matronly.

Right   Wrong

Are you pear-shaped? That "hippy" look is the saddest thing in life for some of us. But you can choose patterns which will conceal it. Always wear your skirts slightly flared, smooth-fitting from the waist to the fullest part of the hip, where the skirt then spreads out to hide the fact that you spread out! Have any decorations or trimming at the top of your dress, so that the hips will not attract attention.

Right

Wrong

WHAT ARE YOUR FIGURE FAULTS?

No shape up there? There are always a few subtle ways of "building up" where you need to look larger. Try the addition of a ruffle or two on a crisp white blouse. If you feel that this is a serious figure problem, then it might be advisable to wear a padded brassière. (Be sure that the material used in the pads does not irritate your skin.)

Thick through the middle? You are the one who should avoid wide belts, fancy belts, and large buckles. It is best for you to wear a narrow belt made of the same material as your dress, or perhaps a narrow leather or suède belt of a matching color. Buy your patterns with long, slender front closings, which carry the eye up and down and away from the waistline. These create optical illusions which are helpful to a better appearance.

Short neck? Buy a pattern with a V, a deep U, or a keyhole neckline. You are the type who cannot wear fussy trimmings or frilly collars, and certainly no flowers at the neckline and no Peter Pan or high collars.

Want your arms to look more beautiful? No little puffed sleeves or short tight or capped sleeves for you. Choose a pattern which permits you to cut the sleeves full length, or, if you feel you want them shorter, then cut them slightly above or slightly below the elbow.

Long neck? If your neck is too long or too thin in proportion to your figure, then you can soften the line by buying patterns which include small, close, high-fitting collars and necklines. Patterns which have separate collars are good, as are those which call for trimming high on the neckline.

Broad shoulders

Wrong

Right

Broad shoulders? While some fashions favor the broad shoulder, which gives you a head start on those whose shoulders are too narrow, you must

avoid shoulder padding which is apt to make you look like a football player. Use little or no padding, and enjoy the advantages of your good shoulders.

Narrow shoulders? They can be built up to better proportion by good shoulder pads, which you can either make or buy. Before you finish your dress or coat be doubly sure that the padding on the shoulders is just right for you. Another good idea for you is to choose a style which calls for shoulder ruffles. Of course, these are more suitable for summer clothes or on dresses intended for dressier occasions. Beware of the raglan or the dolman sleeves—they are not for you! Leave those to your broad-shouldered sisters.

A consoling thought when you buy your pattern, and when you try to adjust it to your own body, is that hardly anyone has a perfect figure for the pattern—there is usually some adjustment which has to be made before the actual cutting and sewing take place. Here again are the Do's and Don't's of buying a pattern:

DO

1. Buy an easy-to-make pattern.
2. Buy your pattern by measurement, not by your size in a ready-to-wear dress. (More about this later.)
3. Buy a style which is becoming to your figure. (More on this later.)

DON'T

1. Buy a pattern with many pieces.
2. Buy a pattern which is much too large or too small for you.
3. "Guess" instead of measuring for the size pattern you need.
4. Buy a pattern which is not meant for your figure.

CHAPTER 3

Choosing Your Material

BEFORE you allow yourself to look at materials, take time out to read the helpful information on the back of your pattern envelope.

In addition to the chart of body measurements and corresponding pattern sizes which you used in buying your correct pattern size, you will find:

1. Charts to show the amount of material required—the yardage: see the chart below.

2. A list of all the small articles, such as thread, slide fastener, and buttons, needed to finish the dress. These small things are called notions. Buy them when you buy the material so that the colors will match perfectly and you will have everything at hand when you are ready to sew.

3. Some patterns give suggestions for suitable materials.

The chart below is taken from the back of a pattern envelope.

Note: Additional yardage is required when the material is not pre-shrunk, when stripes must be matched for nap materials and plaids, and for extra seam allowance if material is likely to ravel easily. These additional requirements will be shown in separate charts.

MATERIAL REQUIRED—WITHOUT NAP OR UP-AND-DOWN DESIGN

SIZES	12	14	16	18
STYLE I—DRESS WITH THREE-QUARTER SLEEVES				
39" material	3	3	$3\frac{1}{8}$	$3\frac{1}{4}$ Yds
41" material	$2\frac{3}{4}$	$2\frac{7}{8}$	$3\frac{1}{8}$	$3\frac{1}{4}$ Yds
54" material	2	$2\frac{1}{4}$	$2\frac{1}{4}$	$2\frac{3}{8}$ Yds
STYLE II—DRESS WITH SHORT SLEEVES				
35" material	$2\frac{1}{2}$	$2\frac{5}{8}$	$2\frac{7}{8}$	3 Yds
39" material	$2\frac{1}{4}$	$2\frac{1}{4}$	$2\frac{1}{2}$	$2\frac{5}{8}$ Yds
41" material	$2\frac{1}{4}$	$2\frac{1}{4}$	$2\frac{3}{8}$	$2\frac{1}{2}$ Yds
RIBBON FOR BELT				
2" wide	2	2	$2\frac{1}{8}$	$2\frac{1}{8}$ Yds

STYLE I OR II
TRIANGULAR-SHAPED SHOULDER PADS—$\frac{1}{4}$ yard of 35" muslin, or purchase pads.

Style 1   Style 2

Many patterns have two or more views and can be made in more than one way. A long-sleeved dress requires more material than a dress with short sleeves, so there are different yardages for Style 1 and Style 2.

Materials come in different widths, so the yardage is given for the usual widths of cloth. Cottons, silks, linens, and rayons are from 35 to 45 inches wide; woolens are usually 52 to 54 inches wide.

Home sewers also come in different sizes! Be sure to check the size of your pattern in the view you intend to make

and the width of the material you plan to use. You must know these things in order to purchase the proper amount of material.

Look at the chart once more. To be sure that you understand how to find the amount of material needed for a dress, suppose you are making Style 2 in a 39-inch material and that you wear a size 16:

1. Find the heading "Style 2, Dress with Short Sleeves."

2. Look down the list until you see "39-inch material."

3. Follow the dotted line to the right

until you find the yardage listed under size "16." For this pattern, it is 2½ yards.

The amount of material required for any clothing differs
    with the pattern style used,
    with the width of material,
    with the size.

Buy exactly the yardage indicated, except when your material is plaid, or striped, or has a pile. For any of these materials allow ⅓ yard more unless the pattern includes a separate chart for "materials made up and down" or for "materials with pile." If there are special charts for these materials, no additional allowance will be necessary.

The reason for the extra yardage, of course, is that there are cutting problems involved in the use of these materials.

Plaids and stripes must be matched at all seam joinings.

"Up-and-down" materials are those which have designs all going in the same direction. Materials with a "pile" (or nap) are those such as velvet or corduroy. Both of these materials must be cut with the top of every pattern piece laid in the same direction, as shown in the following illustration:

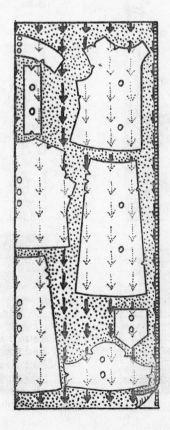

If the pieces are laid with the tops going in different directions, as shown here, the dress, or coat, or skirt will appear to have been cut from two different shades of the same material.

Unless you are liberally endowed with patience and are not easily discouraged, it would be better not to choose one of these fabrics for your first attempt at sewing. Why try to make sewing seem like work? Do it the easy way!

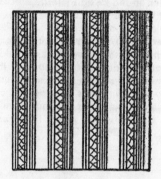

Stripe   NO!

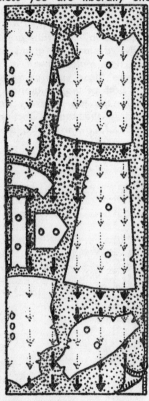

Not for beginners

Up-and-down   NO!

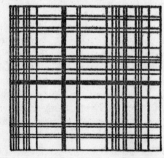

Plaid   NO!

Pile   NO!

The easiest material for a beginner to cut and sew for a first dress (from the viewpoint of fabric design) is a small allover print. There is no need to worry about matching the design and any little imperfections in your work will be hidden in the design itself. The allover print will also tend to conceal the over-simple lines of the dress and make it appear much trickier than it actually is.

Either of the two types of fabric design shown below is easy to use and will produce satisfactory results.

For the beginner

Geometric Print

Small Flower Print

Now that you understand the instructions on your pattern and why it is wise to choose a material that will be easy to work with, you are ready to buy your material. You may buy it in your favorite department store, or make your choice from a mail-order catalogue. The important thing to remember is that you must choose the material. Don't let the material choose you! Keep in mind your pattern, your coloring, your figure, and the occasions when you want to wear the dress.

A becoming material is of a color which looks well on you. You can discover your best colors by "trying on" colors—that is, holding them up to your face to see how they look. If you intend to wear the color in the daytime, look at it in bright daylight. If the color is to be worn in the evening, see how it appears under artificial light.

Generally speaking, every girl or woman can wear some shade of every color. Not everyone can wear every shade of every color. The right choice of color can bring out your good points and can soften any part of your figure which you would like to make less noticeable.

Dark colors, for example, will make the pleasingly plump even more pleasing and quite a bit less plump! Small touches of bright color near the face put sparkle into it. Bright color—an entire dress of it—will attract attention to you. You might try it if you are tiny and afraid you'll be overlooked.

We have purposely omitted including a standard color chart in this book because we feel that color charts are usually misleading. There are so many shades of hair and eyes, so many skin tones, that it is no longer possible—if indeed it ever was—to group women accurately into four or five color types. Pick a color that complements your skin, your hair, and your eyes. Then match your cosmetics to that color.

A becoming material is also one which "hangs well" on your figure. You know that some materials are stiff and stand out from the body. Other materials are soft and cling to the body. The stiffness, the gloss or shine, the bulk or thickness must all be considered when you buy your material.

If you are of average height and weight, you can wear almost any fabric, stiff or clinging, thin or heavy, crisp or soft. But if you are one of those pretty women with ten pounds more than you really need, you might guide your fabric buying by the following suggestions.

Don't wear:
Taffeta—plain or moiré—it is too crisp to fall gracefully on your figure.
Extra-heavy silk or rayon faille.
Satin, used as a blouse, skirt, or entire dress—its sheen will make you appear larger than you actually are.
Woolen materials which are heavy, thick, or rough. This includes bulky tweeds.
Cotton materials, such as organdie or denim. Organdie, although sheer, is amost as stiff as taffeta, and denim has a stiff, heavy texture.

Do wear:
Rayon, silk, or thin woolen crepe.
Satin as a trimming—tie, yoke, cuffs.
Smooth-surfaced woolens, such as flannel, gabardine, or suède cloth.
Cotton materials, such as lawn, muslin dimity, linene, seersucker, piqué (if it is not too heavy), and other firmly-woven materials of medium weight.

Plaids or stripes—We have already suggested that you do not choose a plaid or striped material for your first dress. But later on, after you have become a more experienced sewer, you will probably want to use one of these materials. Patterns which can be made up attractively in these designs will include a special layout to help you in cutting the material. If the pattern you have chosen does not include this special layout, you would be wise to reconsider the advisability of using a striped or plaid material for that particular pattern. After you have had some practice in cutting out and putting together several dresses of these designs, you may be able to work without a special layout, but you will always be

much more certain of your results if you continue to follow detailed pattern instructions and omit any guesswork.

Pattern in many pieces—We agreed that your first dress pattern should have as few pieces as possible, but as you progress with your sewing you will, of course, want to try patterns made up of more pieces. For these patterns a plain-color material is often the wisest choice, since it will show up the fine details of your sewing.

Material with nap—If you plan to use corduroy or velveteen, or an up-and-down print design, be sure to select a pattern that includes a layout for these materials.

Border prints—Buy a border-print material only if one of the pictures on your pattern shows the pattern made up in a border print:

All border prints must have a special pattern layout, so the border can be used as decoration for the dress. After you have done quite a lot of sewing you will enjoy planning ways in which you can use a border-print material. But it is not a wise choice for a first dress.

Pleats—There are two kinds of pleats, pressed and unpressed. They are exactly what they seem to be. A dress which shows a pressed pleat on the pattern envelope calls for a fairly crisp material—one which will hold a pleat when it is pressed. Firmly woven cotton, linen, linene, most rayon crepes, and wool crepes are materials which will take pleating well. Unpressed pleats are soft folds of material used to give fullness and held in place at the top by stitching. Unpressed pleats do not have a sharp line creased in with an iron. Almost any material will take unpressed pleats, although they are inclined to stand out from the body if the material is stiff or crisp.

Softness (gathers and folds)—If the dress is to be full and draped yet follow the lines of the figure, a material such as jersey should be used. If there is to be fullness at the neck or shoulder, where gathers and folds are frequently a part of the design and decoration of the dress, then the material chosen should be thin enough and soft enough so that the fullness will look soft also, not thick and bunchy. Don't think of using jersey for a first dress! Ask the saleswoman if you have any doubts about the suitability of a fabric for the pattern you have chosen.

In buying your material, remember the occasions on which you expect to wear the dress.

Don't allow yourself to be tempted by the sight of yards of lovely fabric which was never meant for you or your activities. You wouldn't buy satin to wear when you wash the baby.

But you have seen other women, who look like this

buying material which looks like this

with a result which will look like this

Oh no!

You will find that you have a great deal of leeway in choosing a fabric, but you must still be guided by your own good judgment as to whether it is suitable for your purpose.

Silks, rayons, satins, taffetas, and velvets are used primarily for dressier occasions, although certain types of rayon, such as acetate, Bemberg, or shantung, are also used for street and sportswear.

Cotton today may be bought either in untreated fabrics which require pressing after they are washed, or in "drip dry" materials which are finished in such a way that they need little or no pressing.

Because of its washability, cotton remains first choice for house dresses and sportswear. For summer afternoon and evening wear, however, organdie, dimity, lawn, or voile are cool and appropriate. Piqué, which was once considered suitable only for sportswear, is now popular for evening dresses and even for wedding gowns.

Woolens, such as flannel, gabardine, serge, or tweed, are appropriate choices for suits, coats, and tailored dresses. But some woolen crepes are so sheer that they can be used for afternoon dresses, evening dresses, and frequently for summer wear.

Here are a few points to consider in buying your material. If your dress is going to get hard, everyday wear around the house, or if you want it to be of a light color, you will save money by choosing a washable material. If it is to be used only for party wear or is of a color which will not show soil easily, it can be of a material which has to be dry-cleaned.

Spend as much money as you can on your material, for cheap material— poorly woven, badly designed, imperfectly dyed—is a bad investment. Why waste all your interest and good work on a piece of material which is not worth your time and effort? If you do not have much money to spend, look over the remnant counters for a piece of good material that has been reduced for clearance. Open up the remnant before you buy it to be sure there is no tear, discoloration, or imperfection of design. In most cases you will find that this is just a short length which has been left from a large bolt.

Always read the label on the material you plan to buy. It will give you all the necessary information on shrinkage, percentage of wool, rayon, or silk, and color fastness. This is an important step in buying any kind of material. Some rough-textured rayons, for instance, look and feel so much like wool that the only way to be sure is to read the label.

To sum up, here are the Do's and Don't's of buying your material:

DO

1. Always take your pattern with you when you go to buy your material.

2. Buy only the amount shown on the pattern envelope for your size in the style and the view you have decided to make.

3. Buy all trimmings and notions, such as slide fastener, buttons, thread, snap fasteners, bias tape, et cetera, when you buy the material.

4. Remember the purpose the dress is to serve in selecting the material.

5. Always read the label.

DON'T

1. Guess at the amount needed to make your dress.

2. Wait until later to buy the little things you will need to finish the dress.

3. Yield to the temptation of some material which is lovely but unsuited to your purpose.

4. Buy any material without knowing to what extent it is guaranteed.

It includes those materials most commonly found on the market today. In addition there is a short glossary of terms preceding the chart to help those sewers who are not familiar with specialized trade usages.

FABRIC CHART

This excellent chart, compiled with the aid of Professor B. R. Koenig of the Philadelphia Textile Institute and the Fabric Editor of McCall's Patterns, gives you in concise form some helpful information about fabrics and their special uses. It includes those materials most commonly found on the market today. In addition there is a short glossary of terms preceding the chart to help those sewers who are not familiar with specialized trade usages.

FABRIC AND COMPOSITION	SPECIAL FEATURES	USES OF FABRIC	HANDLING AND CARE
ACETATE Acetylated cellulose	Does not shrink or stretch. Resilient. Resistant to moths, mildew. Can be made color-fast, water-repellent, and resistant to crease. Must be heat-treated for permanent pleating, embossing, or moire, since it has low melting point.	Blouses Coats Draperies Dresses Lingerie Menswear Suits	Dry-clean unless labeled washable. If washable, wash quickly in warm water and mild suds. Do not wring; let drip dry to avoid wrinkles. Iron while still damp.
ACRILAN acrylic fiber	Resilient, lightweight, strong. Resistant to moths, mildew, sunlight, abrasion. Quick-drying. May be waterproofed and permanently pleated.	Blouses Coats Dresses Linings Suits Upholstery	Wash in warm water and mild suds. Let drip dry. Iron with warm iron, if needed.
ARNEL triacetate fiber	Low absorbency, soft hand. Fairly strong. May be permanently pleated. May be made water-repellent, resistant to fumes and fading.	Blouses Children's wear Curtains Dresses Lingerie Sportswear Suits Uniforms	May be washed and ironed just like cotton. May be dried in automatic dryer. Needs little or no ironing.
CORVAL cross-linked rayon (cellulose)	Soft hand, good absorbency. Lightweight, warm, long-wearing, wrinkle-resistant. Has worsted texture.	Blouses Children's wear Menswear Skirts Slacks	Dry-clean unless labeled washable. If washable, use warm water and mild suds. Drip dry, iron with warm iron if necessary.

Fiber	Properties	Uses	Care
COTTON vegetable fiber	Durable, moth-proof, static-free. Good absorbency. Resistant to abrasion, heat. May mildew. Can be dyed in wide range of color, and can be made colorfast in most of them. Can be made water-repellent, fire-resistant. May be treated for resistance to creasing, and to need little or no ironing.	Accessories Blouses Children's wear Coats Curtains Draperies Dresses Lingerie Slip Covers Sportswear Suits	A 100% cotton fabric needs no special care; it can be washed in hot water, ironed (on wrong side) with hot iron. Can also be starched. If fabric is resin-treated (to make it drip-dry or "no-iron"), wash it in warm water and use warm iron for touch-ups. If cotton is combined with synthetic fiber, follow washing directions for synthetic material.
CRESLAN acrylic fiber	Dyes in wide range of colors; is colorfast to light, perspiration, laundering. Mothproof, nonallergic, mildew-resistant. Lightweight, drapeable, holds shape, resistant to wrinkles and stains.	Coats Dresses Rainwear Robes Slacks Sportswear Suits	Wash in warm water and mild suds—then drip dry. If touch-up ironing is needed, use low heat.
DACRON polyester fiber	Retains size and shape. Resistant to moths, mildew, wrinkles. Strong, with little stretch. Can be made to resist pilling and static. Can be permanently pleated.	Blouses Curtains Draperies Dresses Lingerie Pillows Shirts Suits	Wash in warm water and mild suds—then drip dry. Needs little or no ironing.
DARVAN nytril fiber	Soft, resilient, has luxurious hand. Can withstand high temperatures. Retains crease. Resistant to moths, mildew, wrinkles. May be made water-repellent and anti-static.	Coats Dresses Shirts Skirts Suits	Wash by hand or in machine in hot water. May be dried in automatic dryer set at medium heat. Needs little ironing, at low heat.
DYNEL modacrylic fiber	Has resilience and bulk. Dyes well. Resistant to moths, mildew, flame. Resists matting and wrinkles. Retains pleats and shape. Can be napped or brushed. May be treated to have either soft or hard hand. Nonallergic.	Draperies Dresses Fleecy coats Lingerie Menswear Suits	Dry-clean unless labeled washable. If washable, use warm water and mild suds—then drip dry. If ironing is needed, use low heat.

Fiber	Characteristics	Uses	Care
FIBERGLAS glass fiber	Resistant to flame, sunlight, chemicals, moths, mildew. Wears very well.	Curtains Draperies Home furnishings Window screening	Avoid excess rubbing in use or in laundering; read instructions on label. Curtains may be hand-washed, blotted dry in towel, and rehung within a few minutes; no ironing needed.
KODEL polyester fiber	Strong, resilient. Resistant to chemicals, weather effects wrinkles and pilling. Low absorbency. Can withstand high temperatures. Can be permanently pleated.	Coats Menswear Suits	May be washed in hot water if desired. Needs little or no ironing, but for touch-ups will take hotter iron than most synthetic fibers.
LINEN vegetable fiber from flax	Easily bleached, has good absorbency after bleaching. Durable, lustrous, resists soiling. Has interesting texture. Dyes well, can be made color-fast. Resistant to stains, crease, mildew. Can be made water-repellent.	Coats Draperies Dresses Sportswear Suits Upholstery	Washable, but read label for special instructions. Iron on wrong side while fabric is damp. Resin-treated linens should be washed in warm water, ironed with warm iron. Linen blended with synthetic fibers should be handled according to directions given for the synthetic.
NYLON man-made fiber from carbon, hydrogen, nitrogen, oxygen	Very strong; resists abrasion, flame, moths, mildew. Low absorbency, dries quickly. Fairly elastic. Can be permanently set for size and shape.	Blouses Children's wear Curtains Lingerie Shirts Skirts Sportswear Upholstery	Wash in warm water, by hand or machine; wash white nylon separately. Do not wring; may be dried in automatic dryer, but drip dry for fewer wrinkles. If touch-up ironing is needed, use low heat.
ORLON acrylic fiber	Gives warmth without weight; has luxurious hand. Durable, wrinkle-resistant. Low absorbency. Resistant to moths, mildew, sunlight, fumes.	Blankets Coats Dresses Sweaters Suits	Washes easily, but read instructions on label; drip dry (dries quickly). If touch-up ironing is needed, use iron at very low heat.

Fiber	Properties	Uses	Care
RAYON — regenerated cellulose	Some long-wearing, others less durable. When wet, fibers are weakened. Feels cool (except spun rayon). White rayon retains whiteness. Drapeable, good absorbency, but relatively nonresilient.	Accessories Blouses Children's wear Curtains Draperies Dresses Household furnishings Lingerie Play clothes Suits Table linens	Some are washable; read label for instructions. Iron on wrong side with warm iron, but check instructions on label for exact temperature of iron.
SILK — animal fiber from silkworm cocoon	Long-wearing, warm, resilient. Good absorbency. Can be shaped easily. Some silks are increased in body by addition of metallic salts; read labels.	Accessories Blouses Coats Curtains Draperies Dresses Household furnishings Lingerie Suits	Some are washable; read label for instructions. Iron on wrong side while fabric is damp, using moderate iron heat.
TOPEL — cross-linked rayon (cellulose)	Soft, has luxurious hand. Has silky texture, good absorbency, and warmth. Takes dyes well.	Blouses Children's wear Dresses Shirts Sportswear Uniforms	In general, a "wash and wear" fabric, needing little or no ironing. If blended with other fiber, follow washing instructions for blended fiber.
VICARA — natural polymer from corn	Has luxurious hand, very good absorbency. Resilient, drapeable, nonallergic. Resists pilling, is resistant to moths and mildew.	Children's wear Dresses Menswear Sportswear Suits	Dry-clean unless labeled washable. If washable, do so by hand with warm water and mild suds. Iron with low heat.

VINYL PLASTIC
synthetic film, transparent

Nonporous, does not absorb moisture. Film itself is soft; when coated on fabric, it is stiffer.

Aprons
Bathroom curtains
Food covers
    Household items
Kitchen accessories
Raincoats
Shower curtains
Slip covers
Table covers

Washing and ironing uncertain; read instructions on label. Wipe with damp cloth to clean; shake out and let dry to remove wrinkles. In sewing, put tissue paper under fabric and machine stitch through it.

WOOL
animal fiber from sheep

Resilient, but retains ironing. Gives warmth, has good absorbency. Attracts moths, but may be treated against them; subject also to mildew.

Light weight:
Baby clothes
Blouses
Children's wear
Dresses
House coats
Medium or heavy:
Bathrobes
Coats
Hats
Purses
Scarves
Slacks
Suits

If not labeled preshrunk, shrink material before cutting to sew. If not labeled washable, dry-clean. Brush after each wearing. Iron with steam iron or use damp pressing cloth over material. Use moderate heat. Always clean woolens before storing, and if wool has not been treated, protect against moths.

ZEFRAN
acrylic fiber

Lightweight, warm, durable. Wrinkle-resistant. Retains pleats and crease. Dries quickly.

Dresses
Shirts
Skirts
Slacks
Suits

Dry-clean unless labeled washable. Wash in warm water and mild suds— then drip dry. If touch-up ironing is needed, use low heat.

GLOSSARY

Abrasion—Surface wear or rubbing: a fabric that is "abrasion-resistant" does not show surface wear or is not affected by rubbing.

Absorbency—The ease, speed, and amount of liquids that a material will absorb or take up: a fabric that has "good absorbency" or "high absorbency" will take up moisture easily and quickly. (A 100% cotton fabric is a good example.)

Drapeability—The characteristic of a fabric that hangs or falls into folds readily. Some fabrics are more "drapeable" than others.

Fiber—An individual strand, the component of yarn. It is also called a filament, but fiber connotes a strand of specified length and filament connotes indefinite length. Yarn is, of course, the term for a number of fibers or filaments twisted together to form one continuous strand to be used in making textile materials or fabrics.

Hand (also, handle)—The feel of the material: textile experts describe a material as having "a soft (or hard, or luxurious, or coarse) hand."

Pilling—The tendency of loose ends of fibers to roll up and make little balls of fluff on the surface of the material, especially at points where the material has been rubbed.

Resilience—The ability of a fabric to spring back to its original texture after being crushed or subjected to pressure: wool, for example, has good natural resilience.

Static-free (or, resistant to static)—Used to describe material that is free of static electricity or its effects.

CHOOSING INTERFACING AND UNDERLINING

There is no reason for a garment to have a "homemade" look. The home sewer may purchase the same interfacings and underlinings used by the best couture houses or manufacturers. The pattern makers also use this same high-quality construction, but they have simplified the cutting and sewing instructions so as to make it an easy matter for you to put the best workmanship into your garment in the simplest possible way.

The purpose of interfacing is to give the garment crispness or "body," to maintain permanent shaping, and to offset extra strain on the fabric in such places as under the buttons or buttonholes.

The purpose of underlining is to give "body" to lace or other lightweight fabrics and to prevent bagging or "sitting out" in a slim skirt made of any weight material.

The information telling which interfacing and underlining you should choose is usually contained on the back of the pattern you buy. The salesclerk can also help you to decide which is most suitable for the garment and fabric you are using. The following lists give the trade names for the two major types of interfacing:

WOVEN INTERFACING

ARMO—A hair canvas woven of various blends of goat hair, wool, cotton, and rayon. Used mainly for coats and suits. It is guaranteed preshrunk for dry-cleaning, and is crease- and wrinkle-resistant. It comes only in natural color.

ARMO FINO—Same as above, but is the heavier weight used in winter coats and heavy suits. It contains more goat hair and, therefore, is too scratchy for use on lightweight garments.

FORMITE—A sheer canvas woven of various blends of hair, wool, cotton, and rayon. Used mainly for dresses and sportswear. Guaranteed washable and dry-cleanable. Has a permanent resilient finish. Will not crush or stain; is odorless.

SIRI—A lightweight woven interfacing and underlining used mainly for dresses, blouses, and any other garment which needs shape retention without too much stiffness. Washable and dry-cleanable. Will not scratch if worn next to the skin.

STA-SHAPE—A tailor's canvas which comes in various weights. Suitable for coats, suits, and dresses. Washable and dry-cleanable. Crease-resistant. Controlled shrinkage. It is guaranteed for the life of the garment.

NONWOVEN INTERFACING

INTERLON—A lightweight porous material. Washable and dry-cleanable. Comes in various weights which makes it suitable for interfacing dresses, sportswear, coats, suits. Retains body for the life of the garment.

KAYAB—Has an open-work effect, which gives it a built-in air-conditioning feature. It is porous. Washable and dry-cleanable. Will not shrink. Comes in various weights, suitable for dresses, sportswear, suits, coats.

PELLON—Comes in two types: (1) regular or all-straight which means the "grain" is straight in any direction, and (2) all-bias which means the "grain" is bias in any direction. Washable and dry-cleanable. Crease-resistant. Porous and fast-drying. Comes in various weights, suitable for dresses, suits, lightweight coats.

UNDERLINING

Choose a soft lightweight silk, rayon crepe, or taffeta, depending on the sheerness of the material of your garment. China silk and Siri (which is mentioned in the foregoing list) are often used. A cotton or nylon net is sometimes used for underlining a dress or blouse of lace or chiffon where "body" is desired without loss of the material's softness. Underlining is not used in the same way as interfacing: it is sewed together (as one) with the material of the garment itself.

CHOOSING THREADS TO MATCH FABRICS

The color and weight of thread depends, of course, on the color and weight of the fabric you buy. However, it is good to use the best type of thread for your material in order to get finest results. Generally, materials are classified as animal, vegetable, or synthetic fibers. Animal fibers are mainly silks and wools. Vegetable fibers are linens and cottons. Synthetic fibers are the man-made ones, such as acetate, Acrilan, rayon, nylon, Orlon, Dacron, Vicara, Fiberglas, or Saran.

Sometimes your material is a blend of two or more fibers. In such a case, the label will give the exact percentage of the fiber content. You can then match your thread according to the dominant fiber.

For animal-fiber fabrics use silk thread.

For vegetable-fiber fabrics use mercerized cotton thread.

For synthetic fabrics use nylon thread, with the one exception of Fiberglas, for which use cotton thread.

When materials are blended, choose threads as follows:

1. A synthetic blended with cotton or linen (for example, nylon and cotton) calls for nylon thread.

2. For blend of vegetable and animal fiber (for example, cotton and silk), use silk thread.
3. When two or more synthetic fibers are blended (for example, Orlon and nylon), use nylon thread.
4. If two animal fibers are blended (such as silk and wool), use silk thread.
5. A synthetic blended with wool or silk (such as nylon and wool) calls for silk thread.

SIZES AND TYPES OF THREAD

Thread sizes come in letters A and D, and numbers from 8 to 100. The higher the number, the finer the thread.

Sizes 50 and A are considered the same. Sizes 60 and over are finer than A, and sizes 40 and less are coarser than A.

Aside from the various colors and sizes in mercerized cotton, silk, and nylon threads, there is also a silk buttonhole twist (size D). This is used for making hand buttonholes, for sewing on buttons, and for decorative hand-finishing on suits, coats and dresses.

Glazed button-and-carpet thread, which is extra coarse, is used for heavy hand sewing, such as fixing carpets or upholstery, repairing heavy work clothes, and sewing on heavy buttons.

Elastic thread (covered in woven nylon or cotton) is available for hand- or machine-sewing. It can be used to do quick shirring; to hold in waistlines on knitted garments, pajama pants, and dirndl skirts; and to help you in whatever other uses you may resourcefully devise in your sewing. See page 228 for directions on how to sew with elastic thread.

CHAPTER 4

How to Fit and Alter Your Pattern

HERE you are, with a pattern in your hand and a piece of material on the table. And you're trying to decide what you should do next, in order to put the two together to make a dress! You think—that is what you do! Sit down in a comfortable chair with your pattern, a piece of paper, and a pencil.

Look at the pictures on the front of the pattern envelope. There are two of them, aren't there? You have already decided which one to use, because you bought exactly the amount of material needed for it, as listed on the yardage chart on the back of this same pattern envelope.

There are two general types of patterns: one in which the markings are done with perforations and one in which the markings are printed on each pattern piece. Both types of markings are interpreted in the same way.

Now take your pattern pieces from the envelope. On the back of the envelope you will find a diagram listing each pattern piece by name. If yours is a printed pattern, the name of the piece will also be printed on every piece of tissue. That is, the back waist will be marked "Back Waist," the

front skirt will be plainly marked "Front Skirt." If your pattern is not printed, it will be necessary for you to write the name on each piece you are going to use. This will take a few minutes, but it will save confusion later. You can find the name of the piece by comparing the shape of the piece of tissue with the drawing of it on the back of the pattern envelope. You may pick up a piece of pattern lettered "B." From the diagram on the back of the envelope you can see that "B" is marked "Back Blouse." So you write "Back Blouse" on that piece of pattern. Mark every piece of pattern you will use.

To know which pieces of pattern you need for the style you have selected, look for the diagram of the pattern pieces on the printed instruction sheet, or primer, which is included with your pattern. The diagram will look similar to that shown on the following page.

Circle or mark with a colored pencil the diagram showing the layout plan for the style you have chosen.

You may also find the pattern pieces

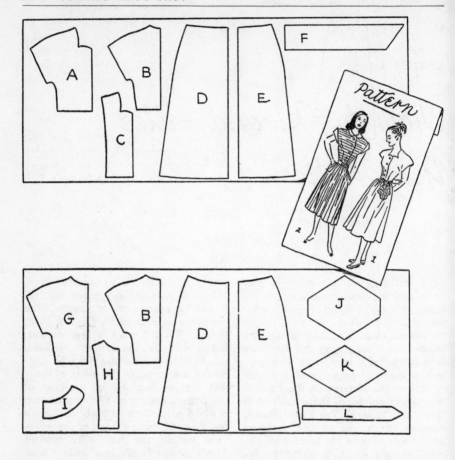

needed for your particular dress listed below the diagram, like this:

PIECES USED

STYLE   I—A, B, C, D, E, F, G, H
STYLE II—C, D, E, F, G, K, L, M

To simplify the explanation for you: you may find that the pattern has two sleeves or two front blouses. One will be marked "Style I," the other will be marked "Style II." If a pattern piece is marked by name only, such as "Skirt Back," that piece is needed for both Style I and Style II. If you have de-

cided to make Style II, separate all the pattern pieces marked "Style I," pin them together, and put them away until your dress is finished. By keeping out only the pattern pieces you need for the style you are making, you will always be sure that you have the right pieces.

Do all these pieces have the correct names either printed on them or written on by you? Yes? Then you are ready for the next step.

Most patterns which are easy to make have very few pieces. The usual pieces are:

Skirt back

Sleeve

Pattern pieces are usually given for only half the dress (or skirt, or suit— whatever you are sewing). This illustrated skirt shows the reason for it:

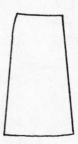

Skirt front

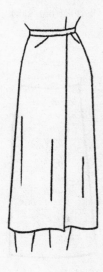

Blouse back

Both sides of the skirt are exactly alike, so it would be unnecessary and confusing to put two separate front skirt patterns in the envelope. The same thing is true of the blouse and the sleeves.

Sometimes you will find a pattern in which the two front skirt pieces or blouse pieces are not exactly alike. In this case you are given two separate pattern pieces, one for the left side, one for the right side. They will look something like these sketches:

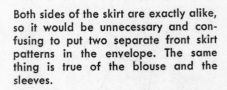

Blouse front

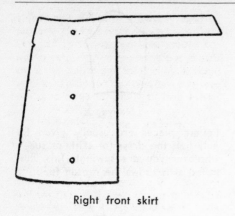

Right front skirt

Left front blouse

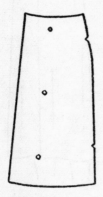

Left front skirt

Right front blouse

Pick out the main pieces of your pattern—the front and the back blouse, the front and the back skirt, and the sleeve. You will see that each piece has many little circles printed on or punched out of the tissue paper. Along the edges of the pattern pieces you will see places where three-cornered pieces have been printed on or cut out of the tissue. These little circles and triangles have definite meanings for you when you cut out your dress and when you sew. If you buy a printed pattern, you will find the meaning explained on each piece.

The printed primer or set of instructions included with your pattern is your guide for cutting and sewing. The purpose of this primer is to help you, step by step, in the making of your dress. Because you may have some questions about these markings, we are going to tell you a little about them.

Finished dress

—three together. Double or triple notches are designed to help you put the pieces together correctly. For example, a sleeve pattern is wider at the back than it is at the front, so there are two notches at the back of the sleeve and only one at the front. The

two notches in the sleeve match the two notches in the armhole of the waist back and the single notch matches the notch in the armhole of the waist front. Thus the sleeve fits into the armhole of the waist as it should.

NOTCHES—A notch is the three-cornered piece either printed on or cut out of the edge of your pattern. Notches show where pieces of the pattern are to be joined together. One printed pattern has the notches printed and numbered, so that you match notch 6 with notch 6, notch 4 with notch 4, and so on. On some pattern pieces you

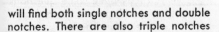

will find both single notches and double notches. There are also triple notches

PERFORATIONS—A perforation is usually a circle punched out of a pattern. You will also find patterns with square perforations. Perforations may be in two or three different sizes, ranging from small to large on the same piece of pattern. Your primer of sewing directions will tell you exactly what each perforation means when you come to it, but these are the best-known uses for perforations:

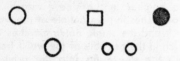

1. Perforations about ½ to ¾ of an inch from the notched edge of a pattern piece mean that you are to stitch together the matching pieces of your dress along the line marked by these perforations. The distance between the edge of the pattern and the row of perforations is called the seam allowance. Whenever two pieces of pattern are to be joined together, there will be a seam allowance. The seam allowances on a printed pattern are indicated by a printed line.

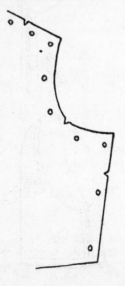

2. Perforations are also used to mark the allowance for the hem or the facing of the neck, sleeves, or side opening of a dress.

3. Other perforations show how the separate pattern pieces should be placed on the material for cutting. (If you are using a printed pattern, you will find these directions on each pattern piece.) When two or three large perforations in a straight row are used near a notched edge, as shown below,

or three perforations appear together like a group of cannon balls, it means that this edge of the pattern is to be placed on a straight fold of the material. You remember that we said many

pattern pieces come in halves, like half the back blouse and half the front skirt. Since most back blouses, for example, are cut in one piece, the pattern piece for one half of the back blouse must be placed on the fold of the material. After the back blouse is cut and the pattern removed, the whole back blouse will be in one piece when the fold of the material is opened up. That is, it will if you follow your pattern directions for cutting. Cutting, of course, is another story which we shall go into a little later.

4. Two or three large perforations in a straight row in the middle of a piece of pattern mark the grain line for that piece of pattern. Many people call the grain line the "straight of the goods." Both terms mean the same.

TRYING ON YOUR PATTERN—After
you have examined the pattern pieces
you are going to use and have identi-
fied the markings, the next step is to
"try on" your pattern. There are two
reasons for doing this: to see how well
the pattern fits and whether you will
have to make any alterations. A pattern bought in the size nearest your
body measurements should not need
many. Always try to make as few
changes in the pattern as possible, for
too much alteration is likely to spoil the
original design of the pattern.

If possible, stand before a full-
length mirror when you try on your pattern. And if you can have someone to
help you, so much the better.

First pick out all the front pieces of
your pattern—the front blouse, the
front skirt, the inset front yoke or belt,
if there is one.

Pin these pieces together according
to the pattern markings. If you have
followed our advice and selected an
easy-to-make pattern, you will not have
many pieces to pin—perhaps only one
pattern piece for the front blouse and
one for the front skirt. But if you have
several pieces in your blouse, or in your
skirt, pin all of them together, matching
the notches. If the notches which are
supposed to match do not seem to
meet, you may need to crease in a
dart, or fold the tissue pattern into little
gathers. The pattern markings and the
pattern direction sheet will help you to
decide where darts and gathers belong
in your particular pattern.

In pinning the pattern pieces together, take the exact seam allowance
that you will take later in sewing. This
is usually a half inch, but it may vary
with different patterns. Your printed
seam line or the perforations are your
guide. Place pins about one inch apart
in the direction of the seam. For example, the direction of a side seam is
downward toward the floor. The pins

for this seam should be pointed down
and parallel to the edge of the piece
of pattern. When you have all the front
pattern pieces pinned together, you
will have one half the entire front of
your dress.

Next pin the back pattern pieces together in the same way.

Pin the side seams, joining the front
half of the pattern to the back half.

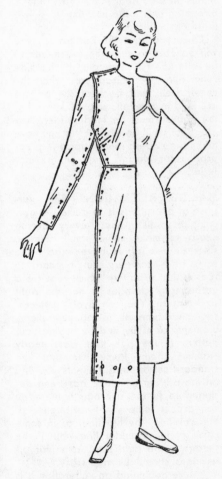

You are now ready to try on your
pattern. The center front of the dress
must be held, or pinned, to the center

front of your figure. (You can think of the center front as an imaginary vertical line dividing you into two equal parts.) The center back of the pattern must be held, or pinned, to the center back of your figure. The waistline marked on the pattern must be held even with your own waistline.

Pin the sleeve together and try it on for length. (Collar, cuffs, and other small pieces usually do not require alteration unless the neckline or sleeve is greatly altered.)

Once you have the pattern on, you will be able to see where it needs to be altered. For example, if the side seam allowance disappears when the center front and back of the pattern are held in position, you will know that the pattern must be made wider. Any alterations will be made after you have taken the pattern pieces apart in preparation for placing them on the material.

MAKING ALTERATIONS—The purpose of alterations is to make the garment fit well. Almost every person needs to make some small change, since no two of us have exactly the same body contours. But it stands to reason that a pattern which requires a great many changes is not the right size pattern. You can avoid unnecessary alterations by taking your measurements carefully and by buying your pattern in the size that most nearly matches them. Remember that the standard set of measurements you find on the pattern envelope has been designed to fit the average figure. You can expect some slight variations—at the waistline, the hip line, or in some cases at the shoulder line—but if the pattern is the right size, no major alterations should be necessary.

Before beginning any alteration it is a good idea to recheck your own measurements with the pattern allowance for each piece. This may seem like a lot of unnecessary work, since you have already taken your measurements before you bought the pattern, but this remeasuring pays dividends in a well-fitted garment. It is much easier to see why the pattern looks large at the waist when you measure the pattern piece (making allowance for the seam) and find that your own waist is two inches smaller than the pattern piece. So take the time to recheck your measurements with the pattern measurements—it will save time in making alterations.

There are two kinds of pattern adjustments: pattern alterations, which are made at the time the material is cut out, and fitting alterations, which are made after the garment has been basted together. Some pattern alterations are made by altering the pattern piece itself, others by making the necessary allowance in cutting the material.

In general, if a garment must be made wider than the pattern piece, the alteration is done when the material is cut out. If it is to be made smaller, the alteration is made when the garment is fitted. The exceptions to the latter are a one-piece or princess-style dress with no seam at the waistline, slacks, shorts, and any alteration in the skirt length.

It seems unnecessary to point out that all pattern alterations should be made carefully. Yet we have seen—and we are certain that you have too —women who seemed to run wild as soon as they picked up a pair of scissors, slashing the pattern here, adding an inch here, whacking off an inch there. The result was exactly what you would expect—a badly fitting, unattractive garment which clearly reflected the careless and haphazard way in which it had been fitted and put together.

Remembering these four simple rules will help you to make your pattern alterations in the right way:

1. Make your alterations along the outside edges of the pattern wherever possible. There are a few alterations which are made by slashing and spreading the pattern pieces, but they are somewhat more difficult to make, and we suggest that you use them only for sleeves, a one-piece dress, and slacks or shorts.

2. Make all alterations to increase the size of the garment before cutting your material. There are two ways to do this:

a. Pin tissue paper to the edge of the paper pattern, mark the amount

Whenever you add width to a pattern, remember that ¼ inch added to each of the 4 sides means an increase of 1 whole inch in the width of the garment.

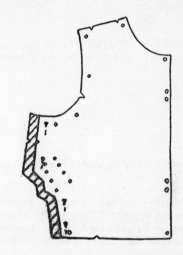

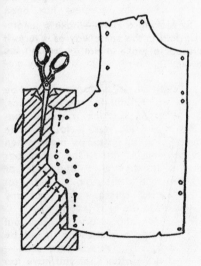

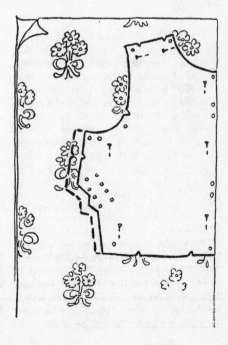

to be added on the extra tissue, and then cut the new pattern line which you are to follow; or

b. Mark the amount to be added along the edge of your pattern in pencil. Then pin or chalk mark this additional width on the material at the edge of your pattern piece before you cut into the material. The second method is quicker; the first is safer for the beginning sewer.

3. Make all alterations to decrease the size of the garment (with the exception of the skirt length, a one-piece dress, shorts, or slacks) when you are fitting the basted garment prior to the final stitching.

4. When in doubt, be guided by your pattern direction sheet or primer.

Terms used in pattern alteration

TO FIT—To hold a single pattern piece up to your figure, at the place where it belongs, or to pin several sections of the pattern together for the same purpose.

TO ALTER—To make any changes in the pattern so that it will fit better. Alterations may be made by adding pieces of paper to the pattern to make it larger. In a few cases an alteration is made by folding the pattern to make it smaller. Most alterations are made before the pattern is placed on the material for cutting. Slight alterations, such as taking in a side seam a fraction of an inch, can be made after cutting, when the garment is fitted to your figure. Pattern pieces may be altered in any of the following ways:

By Spreading—Slash or cut a piece of pattern, and then spread it until it fits your measurements. The spread is retained by pinning the two slashed edges to another piece of paper, which holds them apart. A slash can be used to make a pattern longer or wider.

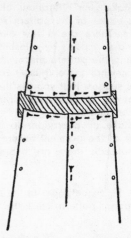

By Making a Pleat—Make a lengthwise fold in the same way as a tuck. It is used to make a pattern piece narrower.

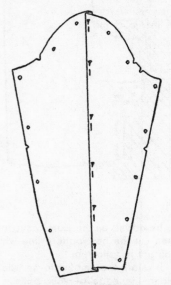

By Making a Tuck—Fold a piece of pattern horizontally and then crease it again so it can be pinned flat. A tuck is three thicknesses of pattern tissue. It is used to make a pattern piece shorter.

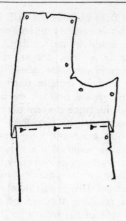

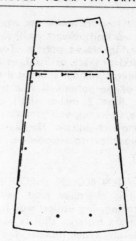

By Tapering—Take away fullness from the side of a garment by increasing the seam allowance. The new seam line is begun at the depth needed and slanted outward gradually, until the new line joins the original seam line.

Blouse or waist alterations—Check the blouse length and width carefully (a) by comparing the measurements given on the back of the pattern envelope with your own measurements taken accurately with a tape measure, and (b) by holding the pattern piece in position to see how well it fits your figure. Also check to see what seam allowance has been made.

TO LENGTHEN BLOUSE—Length can be added to the bottom of the pattern, both front and back, when cutting out the garment. If the pattern is in several pieces, be sure to lengthen each piece.

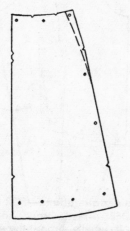

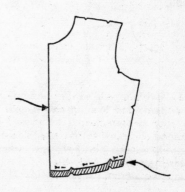

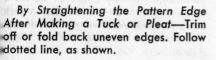

By Straightening the Pattern Edge After Making a Tuck or Pleat—Trim off or fold back uneven edges. Follow dotted line, as shown.

Be careful to mark notches or any other pattern markings found on the lower edge of the blouse pattern. You can safely add as much as 2 inches to the blouse length without spoiling the proportion of the pattern. If your pattern is more than 2 inches short at the waistline, however, you probably have the wrong size pattern. The illustration shows you how to lengthen a blouse properly.

TO WIDEN BLOUSE THROUGH THE BUST—This alteration must be made in the cutting. The easiest way to do it is to cut the material slightly wider at the underarm seam, tapering the additional width from its widest point under the armhole down to nothing at the waistline, where the underarm seam ends. When you widen the waist at the underarm seam, be careful not to make the armhole larger. By cutting slightly outside the pattern line, as shown in the sketch, you can keep the armhole to its original size. Follow the dotted line indicated in the drawing. Notice that this line is tapered from the original shoulder line, which is cut exactly as shown in the pattern. In making changes like this in a pattern, mark all notches carefully on the material so you will have a guide for putting your blouse together. A beginning sewer should not attempt to use a pattern which needs more than ½ inch added width.

TO WIDEN BLOUSE AT THE WAIST-LINE—This is another alteration which must be made in the cutting. If your waistline is 1 inch larger than the waistline measurement given in your pattern, add ¼ inch to each side of the blouse at the bottom, on both the front and the back pattern pieces. You may need more or less than 1 inch. To find how much width you must add to each side seam of the blouse, subtract the waist measurement given for the pattern from your actual waist measurement. Divide this number by 4. Add the resulting fraction of an inch to each side of the front and the back blouse at the waistline. All this extra width is allowed at the lower end of the side seam and tapered to the armhole. It is a simple alteration to make, since it does not affect the size of the armhole.

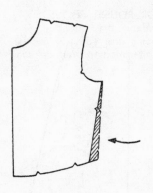

Shoulder alterations—FOR BROAD SHOULDERS—The broad-shouldered person is usually broad through the back at the shoulder blades but may have a small bust and waistline. Compare your shoulder measurement with that given on the back of the pattern. If additional width is needed, the al-

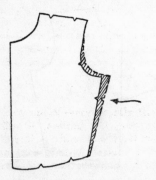

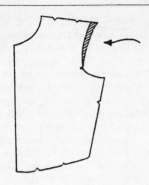

teration is made as shown in the illustration. Be sure to mark all the notches directly opposite the original notches in the pattern. Taper the cutting line in gradually and down to the underarm seam. You may need to cut out the underarm slightly when the dress is fitted before the sleeve is set into the armhole.

FOR ROUND SHOULDERS—If your shoulders are rounded, as many women's are, you will need to make this alteration in your pattern. At the

part where your shoulders are the heaviest, make a horizontal cut in the pattern, tapering it to the edge of the armhole, as shown in the illustra-

tion. Spread the pattern at the slash and insert as wide a piece of tissue paper as necessary to give a smooth, comfortable, and well-fitting line across the shoulders. Pin this extra piece of tissue in place between the slashed pieces and use the altered pattern piece as your cutting guide. Note that this alteration is made in such a way that the size of the armhole remains the same. Unless you have a full bosom, you will probably have to make a corresponding adjustment in the blouse front. This is done by taking a horizontal tuck in the pattern across the bust line.

All of the above alterations are made in the pattern or in the cutting operation. There are other alterations which may be necessary—shortening the blouse, making the blouse smaller at the waistline, making the blouse smaller under the arm, making adjustments for narrow shoulders, sloping shoulders, square shoulders. These are best made in the fitting and are described in Chapter 9, "Putting Your Dress Together."

Skirt alterations—When you try on a skirt or skirt pattern, it will look longer than it actually is if you look down at yourself. Instead, look directly across at your reflection in a mirror.

TO LENGTHEN SKIRT—Cut the skirt of the garment longer at the bottom than the pattern pieces. Be sure to follow the curve of the original hem line exactly. If you don't, your skirt may

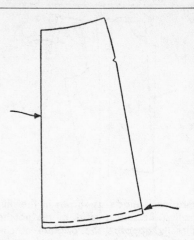

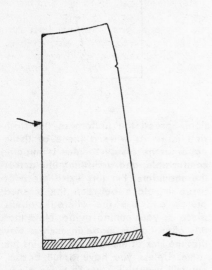

hang in points. Remember, however, that the pattern for even the straightest-looking skirt has a slight curve at the bottom.

TO SHORTEN SKIRT—If your pattern is only slightly long, you can trim off the extra length of material when you mark the skirt for hemming. But if the skirt pattern is entirely too long when you hold it up to yourself in front of your mirror, decide how much you should shorten it, and measure that distance from the distance of the bottom of the pattern, marking it with pins or with a chalk line. Place the pins or mark with chalk every inch, so that the new hem line will follow exactly the curve of the hem line in the pattern. Be sure that you allow 2 inches for a hem, just as the original pattern did. Since

this is the pattern which you will use for yourself not only now but in the future, it seems sensible to cut any extra length off the bottom of the skirt pattern and use that as your guide later on. But bear in mind that if you cut 3 inches from the hem of the skirt pattern in front, you must cut off the same amount from the skirt back.

When marking the pattern for cutting, always measure from the old hem line to the new one, never from the top of the skirt to the hem line. The reason for this is that measurement from the top of a skirt to the bottom does not always allow for correct recutting of the curve at the bottom of the skirt.

TO LENGTHEN OR SHORTEN A SKIRT WHICH IS IN SECTIONS—Find the most becoming length for your figure, including a 2-inch allowance for hem, on one piece of the skirt pattern. Then add or take off length as needed. If you must add 1 inch to the piece you try on, it will be necessary to add 1 inch to every other piece of the skirt pattern. If you need to shorten the piece, remember to shorten all other pieces of the skirt pattern exactly the same amount. See drawing.

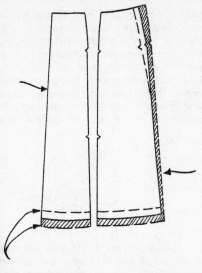

pattern on the material and measure down from the original hem line, marking the new hem line on the material itself. Be sure to add the extra length to both the front and the back skirt pieces. Or you may prefer to pin tissue paper or newspaper to the bottom of the skirt pieces and mark the new hem line on that. After the new hem line has been marked, cut along on the line, so that the pattern piece is exactly the right length to cut out in the material. The latter is probably an easier method for the inexperienced sewer.

TO WIDEN SKIRT ALL THE WAY DOWN THE SIDES—This alteration is often incorrectly used by beginning sewers who actually need only to make the skirt larger at the waistline. If you

TO SHORTEN OR LENGTHEN A CIR-CULAR FLARED SKIRT—*To Shorten*—Measuring from the original hem line, mark the exact distance to be cut off with pencil, pins, or chalk. Mark or pin at 1-inch intervals. This will give the new hem line the exact curve of the original hem line. Cut along the marked line.

To Lengthen—There are two ways to lengthen a skirt. You can place the skirt

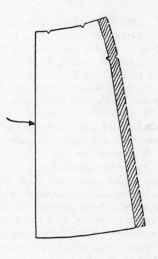

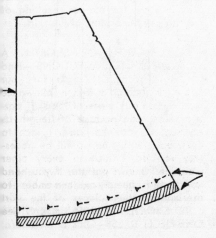

feel that you do require the full width, pin a paper extension to the outside edge, as shown in the illustration. But remember that the proper proportion of a skirt is lost if fullness is added where it is not needed. Also, a skirt which is widened all the way down

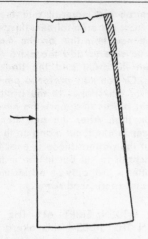

when extra fullness is needed only at one place will tend to make your figure appear wider than it actually is.

TO WIDEN SKIRT AT WAISTLINE—This alteration is easily made by adding one fourth the extra width which is needed at the waistline to the side seams of both the front and the back skirt pieces at the top. Gradually taper this extra width in to the original seam line. If your hip measurement corresponds to the hip measurement of your pattern, you can taper the extra fullness in above the hip line. If your waist and hip measurements are both slightly larger than those given on the back of your pattern envelope, you will need to extend the tapering line below the hip, to cover the widest girth of the figure. You will also need to make the skirt larger at the waistline if you made the blouse wider at the same place. Ordinarily, the bottom of the blouse and the top of the skirt will have exactly the same amount of extra width added at each side.

Princess or other one-piece dress alterations—The princess-style dress is particularly attractive on the woman

with a well-proportioned figure. But if your figure isn't exactly perfect, you can still wear a princess-style dress by making the necessary adjustments. The general procedure is a little different from that in the regular two-piece dress in that there is no seam at the waistline and the pattern is fitted by making adjustments above and/or below the

waistline. Below are the two alterations most frequently made in one-piece dress patterns.

TO SHORTEN PRINCESS (OR OTHER ONE-PIECE) DRESS—This is an alteration which must be made before the pattern is placed on the material for cutting. Pin the waistline of the pattern to your waistline. Make a tuck straight across the pattern above the waist and another below the hip to take out the extra length. Then pin the fold down flat to the pattern. If the skirt is very full, and you are short, you can reduce the amount of flare in the skirt by shortening it slightly. Every piece of the pattern must be shortened exactly the same amount, and be sure to leave the 2-inch hem allowance which most patterns provide.

are pinned to your waistline. If the pattern is too short, you will need to lengthen it in three places. Cut and spread the pattern, as shown in illustrations, above the waistline and below the hip line. Length can also be added at the hem, as shown. The "spread" pieces of pattern are then pinned to

TO LENGTHEN PRINCESS OR OTHER ONE-PIECE DRESS—This alteration is also made before the pattern is placed on the material for cutting. Fit the pattern pieces together and try them on your figure. Make certain that the pattern markings for the normal waistline

an insert of tissue paper. This will make each piece the correct size for your figure. Every piece of pattern must be lengthened exactly the same amount in order to make the hem line even.

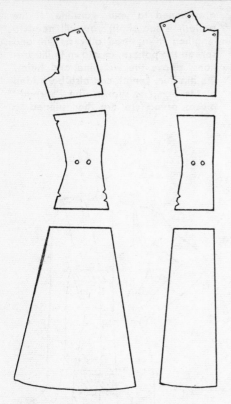

by splitting the pattern piece between the waistline and the crotch and spreading it as shown in the sketch. Length in the legs can be added by spreading the pattern piece below the crotch. If you are quite tall, you

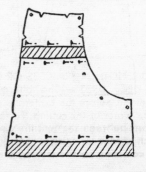

Shorts and slacks alterations— Shorts and slacks (like skirts) are made wider or narrower at the side seams. They may be too long or too short both in the leg and between the waistline and the crotch. Occasionally they will be long or short in only one of these places. The back seam from the waistline to the crotch is always longer than the front seam, in order to allow for ease in sitting.

TO LENGTHEN SHORTS OR SLACKS —Hold the side front pattern piece to your figure while you are wearing panties or a sports girdle and panties. If the pattern fits too closely in the crotch, the garment will be uncomfortable. For greater ease add length

may want to add length both in the upper leg and at the bottom. Spread the pattern piece for the back exactly the same width as the front.

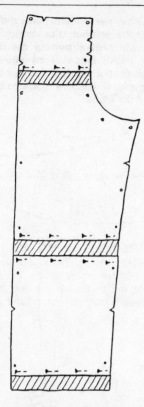

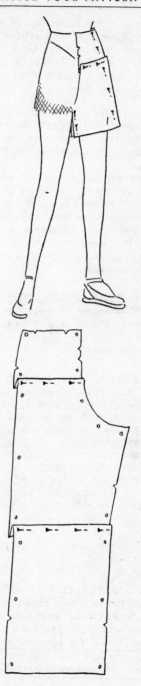

TO SHORTEN SHORTS OR SLACKS
—Try on the side front piece as de-scribed above. Take a tuck across the

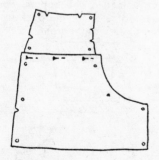

pattern between the waistline and the crotch to take up extra length. The pat-tern can also be shortened by making tucks across the upper leg or at the bottom. Remember to take the same size pleat in the pattern back as you took in the front. The back pattern piece is always supposed to remain longer than the front.

Sleeve alterations—Even though every other part of your pattern fits perfectly, the sleeves sometimes need adjustment. They're either too long or too short.

Every well-fitting sleeve is about 1 inch larger than the matching armhole, so don't think there is something wrong with your sleeve pattern when you discover this 1-inch difference in measuring. The extra inch of fullness is meant to be eased in to allow freedom of arm movement.

TO SHORTEN OR LENGTHEN SHORT SLEEVES—Neither of these alterations is difficult. Simply add 1 inch to the bottom of the sleeve pattern, or take it off, as necessary.

TO MEASURE PROPERLY FOR LONG, TIGHT SLEEVES—When you make a garment with long, tight sleeves, you need to fit your sleeve pattern with special care. Compare the measurement of your bent arm from the point

where the sleeve joins the shoulder seam to the wristbone, as shown in the sketch. The sleeve pattern should be about 1 inch longer than your arm measurement. Hold the sleeve pattern to your arm, with elbow markings at the bend of the elbow.

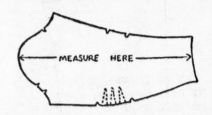

MEASURE HERE

TO FIT LONG SLEEVE TO LONG ARM—Slit the pattern horizontally above and below the elbow. Pin paper beneath the spread. If the arm is very long, length may also be added at the wrist.

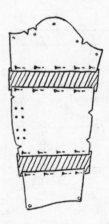

TO FIT LONG SLEEVE TO SHORT ARM—Take tucks across the pattern above and below the elbow. Pin the tucks to hold them in place for cutting.

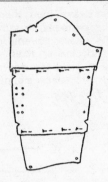

also be made slightly deeper than the seam allowance given in your pattern. It can be done while fitting the garment and will usually be used whenever the side seams of the blouse are made deeper.

TO FIT SLEEVE TO HEAVY ARM— Cut and spread the pattern as shown.

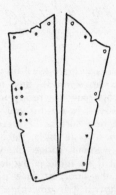

TO FIT LONG OR SHORT SLEEVE TO THIN ARM—Take a narrow pleat (about ⅛ inch) the full length of the sleeve pattern, as shown. This altera-

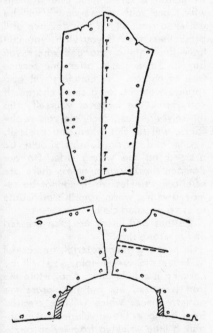

This, of course, will increase the size of the sleeve at the top and will necessitate increasing the size of the armhole as well. (See alteration for making blouse wider at bust.) Both of these alterations must be made in the pattern before cutting the material.

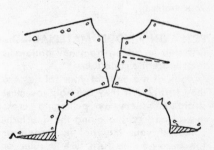

tion is made before the garment is cut out. If necessary, the sleeve seam can

CHAPTER 5

Cutting Material from Your Pattern

NOW that you have tried on your pattern and have made any necessary adjustments, you are ready to cut out your garment. To do this you will need a flat cutting surface. Preferably this should be a large table, since it is the most convenient space on which to work. But if no table is available, you may use the floor, or, in a pinch, the bed, although it is advisable to place a large piece of plywood or similar lightweight board over the bed to keep the material even and to avoid cutting the bedspread.

Collect all the things you will need—straight pins, shears, a yardstick or tape measure, tailor's chalk, or threaded needles for making tailor's tacks—and put them in a convenient spot near where you plan to cut out your material.

PREPARING YOUR MATERIAL—The first step in cutting from any pattern is to prepare the material.

Look at the ends of your fabric. Are they straight? If they are not, you must straighten them by pulling a cross thread and cutting along the line indicated. If your material is corded or too heavy to be torn, use a ruler or yardstick and draw a chalk line across the material to serve as a cutting guide.

Material which is wrinkled should be pressed before it is cut. All woolen materials should be dampened evenly (a small sponge is fine for this) and pressed under a pressing cloth with a warm iron, to shrink them. Even woolens which are sold as pre-shrunk will be easier to work with if you dampen and press them first. If you wish, you can have the material sponged where you buy it. Some stores offer this service free of charge. Dry cleaners will also sponge woolens for a small charge. If you shrink the material yourself, clip the selvedges at 2-inch intervals so the fabric will lie flat when you press it.

Silk and rayon fabrics should be pressed on the wrong side. Do not dampen these fabrics unless there are stubborn wrinkles which cannot be removed with a warm iron. It is advisable to use a pressing cloth.

Cottons and linens are also pressed on the wrong side.

In pressing your material, be careful to leave the center fold; you will be needing it a little later. And, while the iron is warm, but not hot, press the pattern pieces which will be creased from being in the envelope and probably a little wrinkled from trying on.

PLACING THE PATTERN ON THE MATERIAL—Fold the material right side out for cutting, making sure that the selvedge edges are even. Pin the pattern firmly to the material, using plenty of pins and lifting the material as little as possible when inserting them. Make certain that no pattern corner is folded under and that the material is smooth beneath the pattern.

Cutting a pattern piece off-grain—that is, turning or tilting a piece of the pattern just a little to get the pattern section on the material without piecing it—is one sure way to ruin your garment at the very beginning. If any pattern piece is cut off-grain, the garment will never hang the way it should. It is just as wrong in a plain material as it is in a print or stripe, because the all-important grain line, which is indicated on your printed pattern by an arrow—and on other patterns by a series of perforations—has been put there to act as a guide for making your dress hang correctly. This marking must always be laid parallel to the straight of the goods.

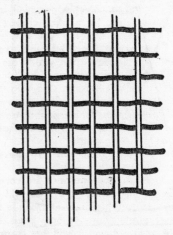

To help you understand what "straight of the goods" is we must tell you something about the way in which material is woven. Most materials have two sets of threads combined in a plain weave. The lengthwise or warp threads are the threads which mark the lengthwise (up and down) grain of the material. The threads which run cross-wise are called filling threads. Haven't you seen a clerk in the yard-goods department tear a piece of material after she has made a little cut to start it? The clerk tears the material on the crosswise or filling threads, to be certain that it is straight. A torn edge is always a straight edge. There are a few materials, such as chiffon, which must be cut, because they will pull when torn. The threads of the material can never be woven crooked. Sometimes the material is pressed crooked before it leaves the mill, but it can never be woven off-grain.

To place a piece of pattern on the straight of the goods, you must see that all perforations which mark the grain line for that piece fall on the true lengthwise grain. One way to be certain they are correctly placed is to measure the distance from the perforations to the firmly finished lengthwise edge of the material, called the selvedge. The distance from the top perforation to the

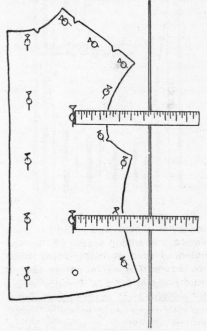

selvedge should measure exactly the same as the distance from the bottom perforation to the selvedge. On a printed pattern piece the top and the bottom of the arrow should be the same distance from the selvedge.

The illustration shows how the paper pattern is placed on the material. Even though the outer line of the pattern is not straight, the perforations lie on the "straight" of the material. Note how simple it is to keep the evenly measured distance from the edge of the material.

If the material has a stripe or a design which makes a straight line, this line can be used as a guide for laying your pattern perforations on the straight grain of the material.

Allow ½ inch for seams. Press the seam open on the wrong side when you finish stitching and the piecing will be practically invisible.

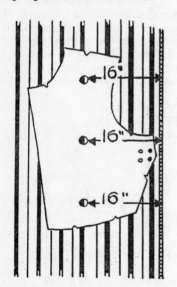

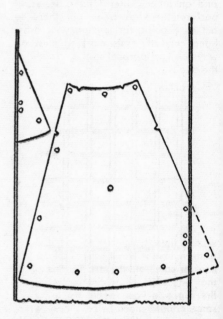

Piecing at bottom of skirt—Occasionally it is necessary to add a small piece of material in order to fill out the outline of a pattern piece. This is called piecing, and is done by stitching a small piece of material in place before the pattern is cut out. If you find that you must piece, do it carefully, matching the design on a print or stripe.

Most cottons, rayons, silks, and linens are approximately 39 inches wide. Woolens average 52 to 54 inches in width. Your pattern will probably show layouts for both fabric widths. If by chance you have chosen a 54-inch fabric which does not have a pattern layout for that width material, the pattern pieces must still be placed according to the grain line, as shown in the layout you are given. Place all your pattern pieces on the material before cutting, to be certain that you have enough material and know how the pieces should be laid.

Occasionally you will find that you must cut a piece once, then lift that cut piece of material with the pattern still pinned to it, place it again, and cut a

through two thicknesses of material; but in others the diagram will indicate that the sleeve pattern is to be laid on a single thickness of material. Where this is the case, the second sleeve is cut by turning and reversing the pattern piece as it is laid on the material.

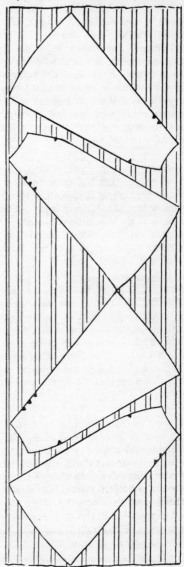

second time. If you are to do this, your pattern layout sheet will show dotted lines or some other marking to indicate that you must allow the material and the space in your layout for using the same pattern piece twice. Pieces which are cut double—that is, through two thicknesses of material at the same time—are not pieces which are cut twice.

Sleeves are excellent examples of pattern pieces which require careful laying out in order to avoid cutting both sleeves for the same arm. In some patterns the sleeve is cut out once,

Careful attention to the position of the notches and other pattern markings will help you to lay out the sleeve pattern correctly.

You have made any alterations within the pattern before you placed it on the material. If you must cut a pattern piece wider or longer, allow material for this when you pin your pattern pieces. Remember to allow for increased width or length on every pattern piece affected. For example, in a skirt which is to be made longer, every piece of the skirt pattern will require an additional few inches of material so that the new length will be even all around.

You will always waste a little material when you cut out a pattern in a plaid or a stripe. It is important to take the extra few minutes required to place the pattern on the material exactly as indicated on the pattern layout, for it has been designed so that the stripes or plaids will match perfectly.

Pattern layout for striped bias skirt—The following two illustrations serve as examples of a completed skirt in striped material—one shows an excellent result because the pattern was laid out properly, and the other shows a badly finished job because of unstudied and careless laying out of the pattern.

A very narrow pin stripe or a tiny check can be treated as a plain material; but larger stripes or plaids must be cut so that the darts will not interfere with the design and so that the large stripe or line of plaid will be centered in the back and front.

There are many possible stripes and plaid combinations from which to select. Some of them are difficult to

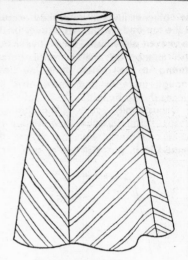

Right

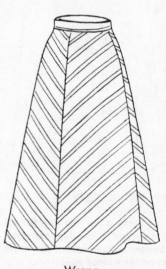

Wrong

handle. Remember the advice in Chapter 3 and don't make your very first dress a striped one!

When you cut an uneven plaid, use a pattern layout for material with a nap. An uneven plaid is one in which the colors or lines do not repeat evenly at the top and the bottom. For instance, an uneven plaid might have lines in this order: red, navy, green—red, navy, green. An even plaid would have the

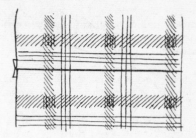

Right

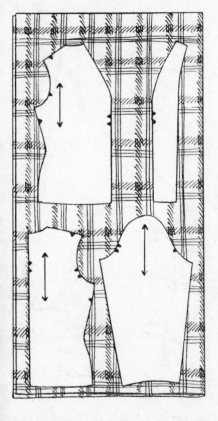

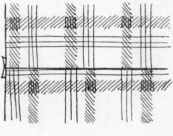

Wrong

lines reversible, so that the top and the bottom of the plaid would be alike. An example of this might be a plaid in red, navy, green—green, navy, red.

When you cut two pieces which are supposed to be exactly alike, be certain that the stripes match. Match the stripes before stitching by basting the pieces together. To get the best results this basting should be done from the right side. See right-side basting, in Chapter 6.

Cutting your material—Cut your material with long, clean strokes of your shears. Do not take short, hacking, choppy strokes, and don't let your shears or scissors bypass those notches along the edges.

Cut the notches out, as shown, not in, so there will be no danger that your shears will cut too deeply into the seam allowance. Cut every notch as you come to it. Be sure to cut double and triple notches where you find them.

Do not allow for seams. There is a seam allowance on your pattern.

Transferring pattern markings to your material—When you have finished cutting, mark the center front and the center back of your garment with

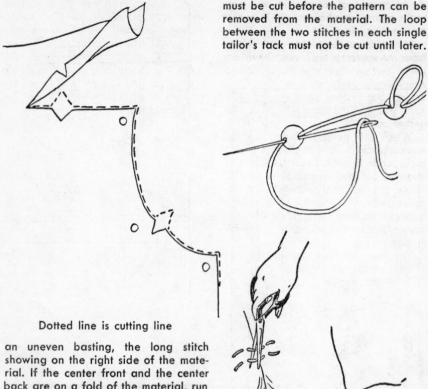

Dotted line is cutting line

must be cut before the pattern can be removed from the material. The loop between the two stitches in each single tailor's tack must not be cut until later.

Clipping tailor's tacks

an uneven basting, the long stitch showing on the right side of the material. If the center front and the center back are on a fold of the material, run your basting down this fold. If they are not on a fold, take tailor's tacks through the perforations which indicate the center front and the center back.

TO MAKE TAILOR'S TACKS—Use double thread, unknotted, in a color which will contrast with your material. Take a single stitch through the perforation, bringing the needle back to the right side of the material. Take another stitch, leaving a 1-inch loop of thread on the right side between the two stitches, as shown. Cut this thread, leaving a 1-inch end. By leaving a loop of thread between tacks you can mark several perforations which are close together at the same time without cutting the thread between each tailor's tack. These loops, of course,

Indicate all pattern markings with tailor's tacks. These markings will usually be perforations, either printed or punched in the pattern pieces. They will indicate where darts, tucks, and pleats are placed. They may also be used to show where pockets are supposed to go. There will be one to mark the top of the sleeve. If you are in doubt as to the meaning of any pattern marking, check your pattern primer or direction sheet.

Never, never remove a pattern piece from the material until you are absolutely certain that you have marked every single perforation or other symbol on that pattern which you need to help you put the garment pieces together correctly.

When the pattern pieces are removed, you will need to cut any tailor's tacks made through two thicknesses of material before you can start to sew. To do this pull the pieces of material apart gently and clip the tailor's tacks between the thicknesses of material, as shown. The marking threads will remain in both pieces.

You can save time by marking some of your perforations with tailor's chalk. To do this, take a small "stitch"

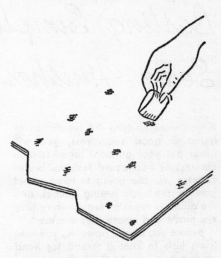

on the other thickness of a double piece of material. (For a single thickness you will need to mark only the right side.) Tailor's chalk is best used to mark perforations which are to be used early in the sewing, since it will rub off. Use tailor's tacks for more permanent markings.

Tailor's chalk markings

through the perforation with a pin. Rub the chalk over the pin at the perforation. Turn the material over. Rub the chalk over the pin where it shows

The next step is to put your dress together. But before you can do that, you must learn something about the basic sewing stitches and various seam finishes that can be used to assemble a garment. You should also know how to make the darts, tucks, or pleats that your pattern will require. The next few chapters—6, 7, and 8—contain all the information you need about these subjects. In Chapter 9 we will go ahead with the dress you are working on and give you step-by-step instructions on how to put it together.

CHAPTER 6

Basting, Simple Stitches, and Seam Finishes

IF you want to earn the reputation of being a good seamstress, you will never put your garment together in a careless or haphazard fashion. In this chapter you are going to learn about basting, the basic sewing stitches, and the different types of seams—how they are made and where they are used.

Before you begin, however, you must learn how to knot a thread for hand sewing and how to finish the ends of machine stitching, for without this information your sewing will be wasted effort. Doing each of these things neatly is as much a mark of fine sewing as are carefully taken stitches.

HOW TO TIE A KNOT FOR HAND SEWING

1. Hold the end of the thread between the thumb and the first finger of the left hand.

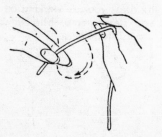

2. Use the right hand to bring the long end of the thread completely around the first finger. Continue to hold down the end of the thread with the thumb and the first finger of the left hand.

3. Roll the short end of the thread away from you, pushing the loop off the end of the first finger.

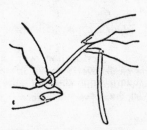

4. Pull the loop between the thumb and the finger to form the knot. Practice several times until you achieve a smooth, small knot with every attempt.

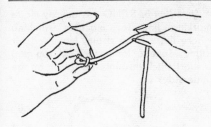

TO FASTEN MACHINE STITCHING—

There are two threads in the usual machine stitching.

1. One of these threads is the upper thread, which comes through the eye of the machine needle. The other is the bobbin thread, with an end on the underside of the machine stitching. These threads are fastened on the under (or bobbin) side.

2. Pull the bobbin thread gently until a small loop from the upper thread appears on the underside of the material. Insert a pin in this loop and draw the upper thread to the underside of the material.

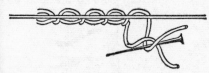

3. Tie the two ends of the thread in a square knot and trim the ends close to the knot.

BASTING—Basting is used to hold material together before the final stitching, and is done by hand with a needle and thread. It is a series of long or long and short stitches which are removed after the seam is stitched by machine or finished by hand.

Must you baste? The answer is up to you. After you have been sewing for a time, you will find that you can sometimes pin straight seams together and stitch them by machine without basting first. But when you are a beginner at sewing, you will be wise to follow the pattern directions exactly. If they say "baste," you baste! Every sewer, experienced or beginner, is wise to baste the side seams of a garment for fitting, because these are the places where changes most frequently need to be made. And ripping out a machine-stitched seam is certainly more work than taking out a temporary basting.

Directions for basting—Pin the seams together before basting, placing the pins at right angles to the edges of the material, so that you can baste without jabbing yourself.

Use a slender needle and a thread about 24 inches long of a different color from your fabric. This is a good way to use odd pieces of thread.

Thread the needle and knot one end of the thread.

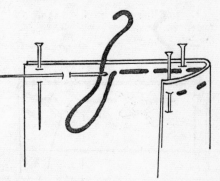

Keep the stitches going forward. Do not take any backstitches. (A row of backstitches will not pull out easily when you want to remove the basting thread.)

Fasten the basting thread with two or three backstitches placed side by side, not one on top of the other. The backstitches can then be flicked out with the point of the needle and the entire basting thread removed with one pull from the knotted end.

When basting long seams, work on a flat surface, such as a table. It will be easier to keep the seams straight.

Types of bastings—EVEN BASTING—Used as a guide for fitting or stitching. Work the needle in and out of the material, making each stitch about a half inch long.

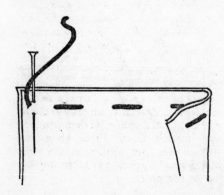

UNEVEN BASTING—A quickly made marking line for machine stitching where there is no strain. Not used for fitting. Take a long stitch on top and a short stitch through the fabric on the underside.

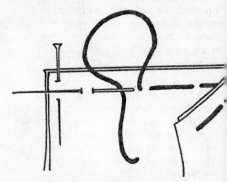

RIGHT-SIDE BASTING (often called SLIP BASTING)—Used to mark the seam line when stripes must be matched. Turn under the seam allowance on one piece of the material. Crease. Pin on top of the other piece of the material, matching the stripes perfectly. Run the threaded needle through the fold in the upper piece. Bring the needle out, then take a small stitch in the under piece of the material. Right-side basting is also used to mark

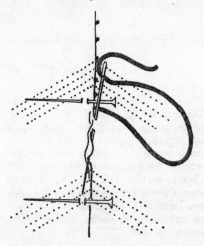

any changes in seam lines after the clothes have been fitted. (Clothes are fitted right side out because both sides of the body are not always alike.)

DIAGONAL BASTING—Take a slanting stitch on top with a straight stitch on the underside. Used when two or more thicknesses of heavy material are to be held together. Never used as a guide for seam allowance or for fitting.

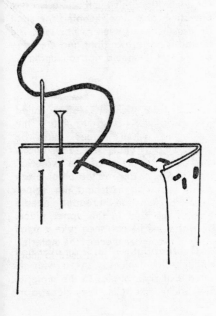

BASTING A BIAS EDGE TO A STRAIGHT EDGE or BASTING AN EDGE MARKED "EASE"—Keep the bias edge, or edge to be "eased," on top, facing you. Pins placed close together make this basting fairly simple, because the pins can be used to adjust fullness evenly. This basting is used when sleeves are basted into the armscye (armhole), and frequently in basting collars to V necks, and in other places.

BASIC SEWING STITCHES—You can sew a fine seam by hand or by machine. Hand stitching is used for finishing hems, necklines, sleeve edges, and for decorative touches on well-made clothes. Hand stitching is not so strong as machine stitching, so it is not often used for seams in dresses. However, hand stitching may be used for seams in children's clothes and for dainty underwear.

If you are left-handed, your needle will probably be going in the opposite direction from that shown in the drawing; that is, if you find it easier to sew from left to right and not from right to left.

Pattern directions will instruct you to use one or more of the following seams or seam finishes:

Running stitch—This is the first, the basic sewing stitch. It is the stitch you used when you made your first doll's dress and is called running stitch, because the expert sewer can fill the entire needle with stitched fabric before removing the needle from the fabric. Use thread not more than twenty-four inches long, since a longer thread may knot or tangle. Knot the thread at one end. Sew with a single, not double, thread. Work the needle in and out of the fabric, taking straight, even stitches, about 15 or 18 to the inch. Fasten the thread at the end with 3 small backstitches taken one on top of the other.

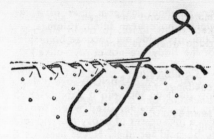

Backstitch—This stitch is taken just the way it sounds—backward. Fasten the thread and take one running stitch forward. Then insert the point of the needle in the beginning of that stitch and bring it through the material the length of a stitch ahead of the first one. If an entire seam is stitched, there will be one backstitch for every stitch forward. A backstitch can also be taken every few inches to strengthen a running seam.

Deeper overcasting—Usually used for decoration, this overcasting is done one stitch at a time, keeping the slant of the stitches as even as possible. The thread is not drawn tight and the edge of the fabric should not roll under.

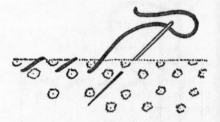

Overcasting—This is most often used to finish raw edges to keep them from raveling. It is a slanting stitch made by bringing the needle through the fabric from the underside and continuing to work the thread over and under the edge. Each stitch is taken from the underside and at an equal distance from the preceding one.

Overhanding—This is an over-and-under stitch which is taken with the needle at right angles to the material. The stitches are taken very close to the

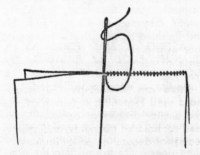

Quick overcasting—This is the same stitch but is taken closer to the edge of the material. The needle is worked over and under the material and two or three stitches are taken at one time before the thread is drawn through the fabric. The thread should be kept loose. This stitch is used on soft material and may roll under the edge a little.

edge of the material and as close together as possible. The overhand stitch is used for joining two flat pieces of material, and the thread should be kept rather loose, to avoid making a ridge when the seam is pressed.

Combination stitch—This stitch combines the running stitch and the backstitch and is used for strong, hand-sewn seams. Take three or four running stitches forward and then a backstitch. Repeat this for the length of the seam, taking a backstitch every time the thread is drawn through the fabric.

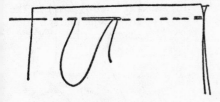

SEAMS AND WAYS TO FINISH THEM
—Too often the home sewer will spend time and effort in selecting the proper pattern, the right material, and the most suitable trimmings, and then ruin the finished appearance of the garment by crooked or unfinished seams. It is true, of course, that careful basting and seaming take more time than hastily "running-up" a dress, but both of these are essential in turning out an attractive, well-fitted, and long-wearing garment. More than that, by giving careful attention to the small details and finishing touches you will increase your own pleasure in sewing and the sense of accomplishment which it can give you.

There are three types of seams: those used in putting together dresses and similar articles of apparel, those used for tailored garments, and special seams for decoration or for lingerie.

Dressmaker's seams—PLAIN SEAM —The stitching of two pieces of material together on the wrong side after

they have been basted or pinned. It is usually done by machine but may also be done by hand. The bastings are then removed and the seam pressed open.

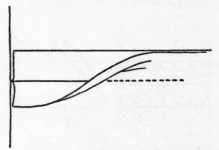

PINKED SEAM—This is actually a plain seam with pinked edges. Pinked edges are the quickest finish for any firmly woven fabric. If you use pinking shears in cutting out your material, all that will be necessary is to do the required stitching. If you do not have pinking shears, the edges may be pinked by cutting a saw-toothed edge with your regular shears. Unless the material is very heavy, hand pinking may be done on double thicknesses of material before the seam is pressed open. All seams should be pressed open after they have been pinked.

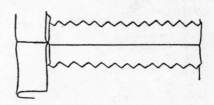

OVERCAST SEAM—This is a finish used by fine dressmakers. It is a stronger finish than pinking and is especially good for finishing edges of materials which ravel easily. Overcast all raw edges, taking the stitches about

⅓ inch apart. Ordinarily the seam edges will be overcast separately and the overcast seam pressed open. A few seams, such as that for setting the sleeve into the armhole, will be overcast together. (See page 124.)

it easier to adjust gathers and bastings. If additional seam strength seems desirable, a plain seam can be taken first and then top stitched on the right side.

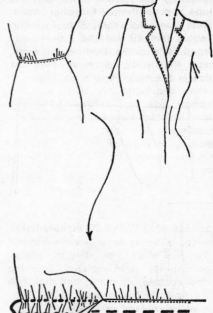

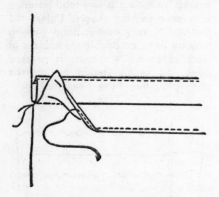

EDGE-STITCHED SEAM—A good way to finish long, straight seams on fabrics such as rayon, silk, cotton, or lightweight woolens is to turn under the raw edges and machine stitch close to the folded edge, as shown in the illustration. A bulky woolen material can be finished by edge stitching without turning under the edge.

TOP-STITCHED SEAM—This seam is used in two ways: to join waists and skirts, and for decoration. A plain seam on the wrong side of the material can also be used for joining a waist and a skirt, but most beginning sewers find that using the top-stitched seam makes

A top-stitched seam is made by turning under the seam allowance along one edge (in a waist and skirt joining, turn under the seam allowance on the skirt top). Baste or press down this seam allowance. Place the basted edge along the line marking the seam allowance of the other piece and baste the two pieces together, keeping the basting slightly away from the folded edge but near enough to be used as a guide line. Then, with the right side of the material facing you, stitch the two pieces together, keeping the line of stitching as close to the edge as possible.

Tailored seams—BOUND SEAMS —Used for finishing unlined coats or jackets. For a firm binding use bias tape to cover the raw edges of seams. Press open the seam. Then to make certain that the binding will be fastened in a single stitching, fold the tape slightly off center so that one side is one-eighth inch wider than the other, and baste into place with the narrow side of the tape facing up. Machine stitch close to the edge of the binding on the upper side, using the basting as a guide line. Remove the basting threads and press the seam again.

measure more than ⅓ inch between the two rows of stitching.

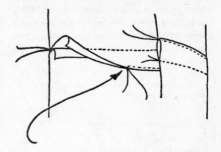

This seam can also be finished by hand and is used in this way when making infants' clothing.

WELT SEAM—Used for women's tailored shirtwaist dresses and tailored blouses. Stitch a plain seam on the wrong side of the material. Trim ⅛

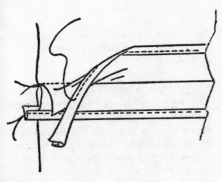

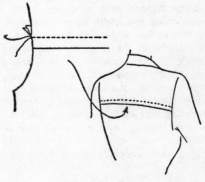

Seams in lightweight materials can be bound in the same way, using flat silk or ribbon binding and folding it off center, as explained above.

FLAT FELL SEAM—Used on men's shirts, boys' trousers, and on women's strictly tailored blouses and shirtwaist dresses. Stitch along the seam allowance on the right side of the material. Trim one edge to ⅛ inch from the seam. Then turn under the other raw edge and top stitch it flat to the material. The finished seam should not

inch off one seam edge and press the seam to one side, with the trimmed edge underneath. Fold under the raw edges and baste into place. Then turn the material and make a second stitching on the right side. This second row of stitching should be ¼ inch from the first row and should hold the seam allowance flat.

STRAP SEAM—Used as a decorative tailored finish on unlined coats and jackets. First stitch a plain seam on the right side of the fabric. Then trim the edges to ¼ inch and press the seam open. Cut a bias strip of material more than twice the width of the seam allowance, turn the edges under, and press. Place this bias strip over the

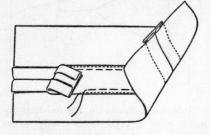

seam and baste in place. Then finish by stitching along both edges on the right side of the garment.

SLOT SEAM—Another more decorative seam finish for tailored garments. Cut a straight strip of material more than twice the width of the seam allowance. Run a basting thread down the center of the strip. Then baste the seam of the garment on the wrong side, but do not stitch. Press the seam open and turn the material to the right side. Center the fabric strip under the seam so that the folded edges meet the line of basting, and baste the strip in place. Then, working from the right side, stitch carefully along each side

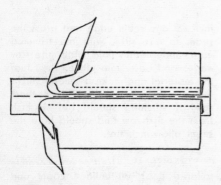

of the seam about ¼ inch from the center line. Remove the bastings and press.

Special and decorative seams—FRENCH SEAM—Once used as an inside seam for dresses but now used largely for children's clothes, sheer blouses, aprons, and underwear. Stitch a plain seam on the right side of the material ¼ inch from the edge. Trim the seam to ⅛ inch from the stitching and turn the material to the wrong side, creasing sharply along the seam

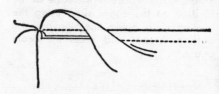

line. Baste flat along the crease and then stitch by hand or machine ⅛ inch from the fold.

SEAM WITH EDGES TURNED IN AND STITCHED—A quick version of the French seam, though not so strong. Make a plain seam on the wrong side of the garment. Then turn the raw edges in and stitch by hand or machine, as shown in the illustration.

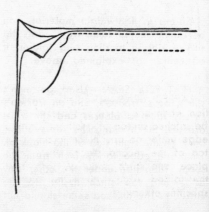

ROLLED SEAM—A finish for very sheer materials, especially for organdie or batiste blouses. Stitch a plain seam by hand or machine. Then trim the seam allowance to within ¼ inch of the stitching. Roll the edges of the material toward you with the raw edge under and finish.

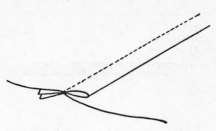

MACHINE-PICOTED SEAM—Used on very sheer materials, such as fine net, or any seam not subjected to strain. Using the machine hemstitcher, stitch along the seam line. Then cut through the center of the hemstitching to form a picoted edge.

PIPED SEAM—Used for decoration. Baste a folded piece of bias material to the right side of one of the pieces to be seamed. This bias fold should extend ⅛ inch inside the seam line. Baste. Place the second piece to be seamed on top of the bias fold and machine stitch along the seam line. When the seam is turned to the right side, the bias fold will extend between the two pieces of material. To be most effective the bias material should be of a contrasting color. (Practice on a sample piece first, and if you learn to hold the bias material evenly as you sew, you may be able to stitch a piped seam without basting.)

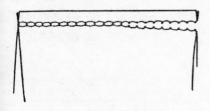

LAPPED SEAM—Used for decoration when one piece of material is to be stitched on top of another. Turn the edge under on one piece, place it on top of the second piece, baste it in place, and stitch about ¼ inch from the folded edge, unless the pattern specifies otherwise.

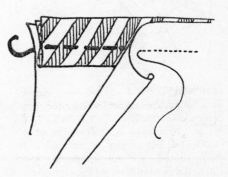

Wrong side

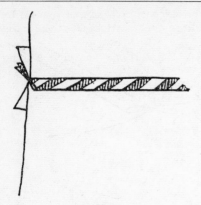

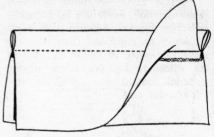

Right side

CORDED SEAM—A piped seam with a piece of cotton cable cord inserted in the fold of the bias material before it is stitched in place. Corded seams of the same material are frequently used for bedspreads, dressing-table skirts, and similar articles. Made of a contrasting color, they are especially attractive for slip covers.

should be done about ¼ inch from the turned-in seam, although a wider allowance may be made if it seems more desirable. When this type of seam is used, no additional trimming or cording is necessary.

TRICKS WITH SEAMS

1. Clip curved seams from the outer edge toward the stitching, so they will lie smooth. Be careful not to clip the stitching.

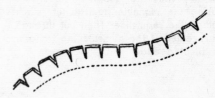

2. Press open one seam before you stitch a second seam across the first one.

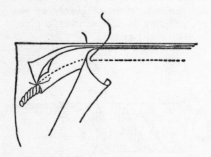

UPHOLSTERER'S SEAM—A simple and attractive seam finish for slip covers and cushions. This is actually a French seam taken in reverse. The seam is stitched first on the wrong side and then turned without trimming and stitched a second time on the right side. For best results the second stitching

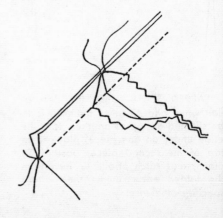

3. Before stitching, place soft paper under thin, soft materials, such as chiffon, and under bias seams. This paper

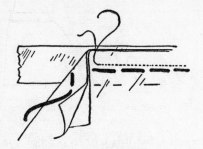

is placed between the sewing machine and the material, to prevent the material from stretching. Tear the paper away gently when the seam is completed.

4. When stitching a bias edge to a straight edge, always work with the bias edge on top, so that you will be able to adjust the fullness as you stitch.

5. Flat skirt or rayon seam binding stitched to the top of a skirt before it is joined to the waist of the dress will keep the waistline from stretching and

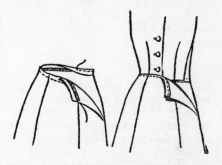

losing its shape. Taping the seams of loosely woven woolens will also help to keep them from stretching.

CHAPTER 7

Darts, Tucks, and Pleats

DARTS—A dart is a triangular fold of material stitched wide at one end and tapering to a point. A double dart (most often used at the waistline) is a diamond-shaped piece of material folded and stitched, as shown in the illustration, with one long point at each end of the fold.

to make, but it is best to practice one or two sample darts before trying them on your garment.

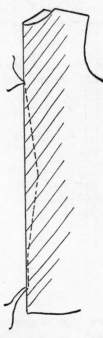

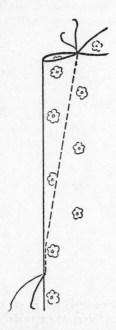

Darts are used to shape clothes by controlling fullness, or removing it where it is not needed. They are easy

The trick to making a smooth dart is this: Match the perforations outlining the dart and baste along the line indicated, beginning at the top or wider part of the dart.

Press the dart.

Then stitch, bringing the stitching toward the fold at a point ½ inch from the place where the dart must end.

Stitch this final ½ inch straight along the folded edge of the dart.

Leave the threads at least 3 inches long when you cut them.

A dart made like this will be perfectly flat and smooth after it has been pressed.

It will not have the unsightly pucker often seen in a dart which has too rounded a point.

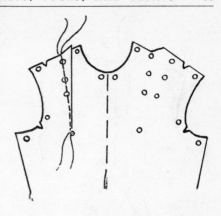

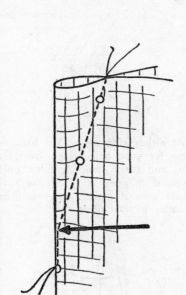

A dart tuck is sometimes used at the shoulder in place of the dart. A dart tuck is not stitched to a point but takes up the fullness for the entire length of the dart.

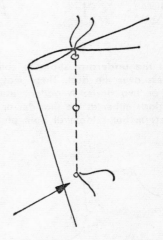

Darts are most frequently used in these places:

At the shoulder to give fullness to the bust. Sometimes two small darts are used rather than one large one. Your pattern will show you the darts you should use for your garment.

At the back of the neck, or at the back shoulder, to provide freedom and ease of arm movement. These darts are usually smaller than those used elsewhere in the garment.

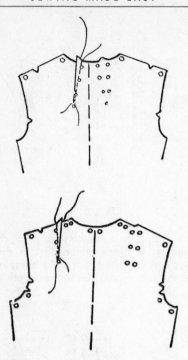

At the elbow or at the shoulder of long, fitted sleeves. Darts are used to adjust the fullness at the shoulder and to give elbow room.

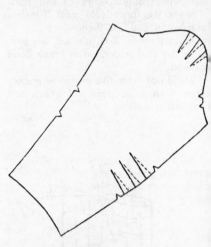

At either side of a skirt back to allow for ease and fullness over the hips, and for a smoothly fitted back waistline. A gored skirt, with the back cut in several places, can be fitted smoothly without darts.

At the underarm seam to control fullness over the bust. There may be one or two darts. A pattern usually has darts either at the shoulder or the underarm but seldom at both places.

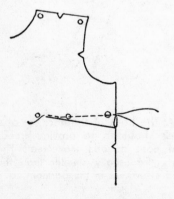

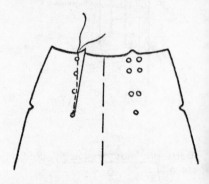

At the side front and the side back waist to control fullness at the waistline. Several small darts are more effective here than one or two large ones.

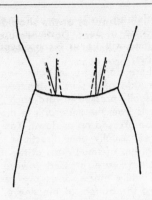

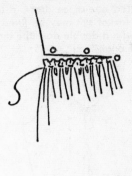

A dart with gathered fullness is sometimes used **at the side front of a skirt,** either at the waistline or slightly below it. See illustrations.

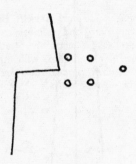

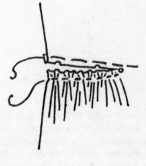

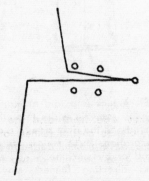

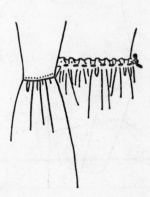

A fitted one-piece dress, a coat, or a long jacket suit may be fitted **at the waist** with a double dart (the diamond-shaped one).

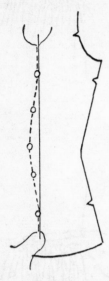

Although darts are used primarily for fitting purposes, they may also be used for decoration. When used in this way, the darts are made on the right side of the garment and the threads at the points are pulled to the wrong side and tied.

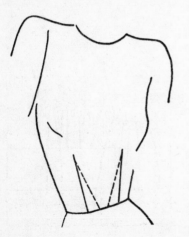

Finishing darts—Careful attention should be given to finishing darts so that they will be as inconspicuous as possible.

Where darts are in pairs—one on either side of a skirt or blouse—they are usually pressed toward each other.

Darts from the underarm to the bust may be pressed up or down. Your pattern will usually give directions.

A group of small darts at the top of the sleeve are pressed toward the back, while elbow darts are pressed toward the bottom of the sleeve.

Double darts and some large single darts are slit along the folded edge toward the point, the open seam pressed flat and the edges overcast, as illustrated.

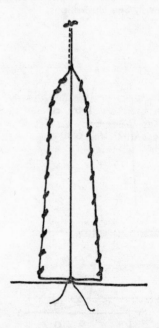

TUCKS—A tuck is a fold of material, usually the same in width throughout, often made on the right side of a dress for decoration. Tucks may be stitched by hand or by machine.

Tucks directing fullness may be

evenly spaced or spaced in groups. If they are to be used in your dress, your pattern pieces will have special perforations or other markings to indicate the correct spacing, and your pattern direction sheet will give exact instructions for stitching.

The dart tuck, often used to give fullness over the bust, is shown in the section on darts in this chapter. Rows of dart tucks, or any tucks which are used to control fullness, should always be ended in an even line.

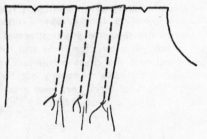

Pin tucks are the tiny, dainty tucks often used on baby clothes and on blouses. When baby dresses or blouses are especially fine, the tucks are often handmade. They are made with very short running stitches and take up only a few threads of material.

For a fine finish on dresses of firm material, **cording** is sometimes stitched into rows of decorative tucks so they will stand out. This can be done by hand or by machine.

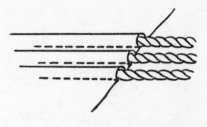

Use the cording foot for machine stitching and turn the ends of the cord to the back of the fabric, fastening each end securely.

Vestees are sometimes finished with rows of **narrow tucks** pressed flat. When these rows of tucks run crosswise as well as up and down, the decoration is called **cross-tucking**. Stitch and press all the tucks that run up and down. Then mark, stitch, and press the crosswise tucks.

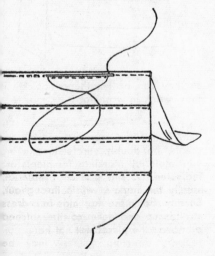

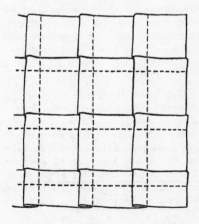

Curved tucks are used on circular skirts. To make such tucks requires easing in the fullness on the underside. Baste the outside edge of the tuck first, then adjust the fullness evenly and bast the inner seam of the tuck before stitching.

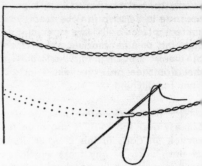

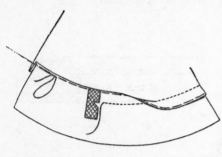

Shell tucks are used both for shortening and for decoration on fine underthings and baby clothes. The shells are first marked with pencil dots—usually ¼ inch deep and about ½ inch apart.

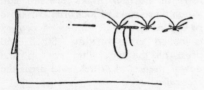

Crease the tuck between the dots and take two overcast stitches through each set of dots, drawing them tight. If the tucks are being used for decoration, contrasting thread is effective.

Overhand tucks are another type of decoration used on curved lines or scallops on baby clothes and other dainty garments. As with the pin tuck, only a few threads of material are taken up. The tuck is creased and overhand stitches taken over the edge of the fold. Marking the width of the stitches will help to keep the tucks even.

Many mothers of growing girls run handmade tucks in the skirts or the hems of dresses for a practical reason —as the girl grows, the tucks can be released and the dress made longer without the trouble of taking out the hem. "Practical tucks" are also made in hems of curtains on the wrong side,

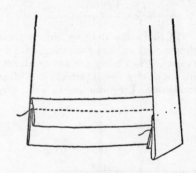

so they can be lengthened quickly if they shrink in washing.

PLEATS—When your pattern calls for pleats, be doubly careful in marking your material. Markings for pleats are indicated on the pattern piece and should be marked with tailor's tacks. Be sure that those markings fall on the straight up and down of the material, otherwise the pleats will not hang correctly.

Lay the material flat on an ironing board to pin and baste the pleats. Do not press pleats at the bottom until after the skirt is hemmed. When rows of pleats are stitched, the stitching should end on an even line.

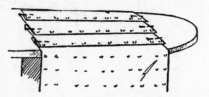

There are six main types of pleats:

1. Inverted pleats, which are the reverse side of box pleats, with two side pleats folded to meet each other on the right side and stitched as shown, to hold the pleat in place.

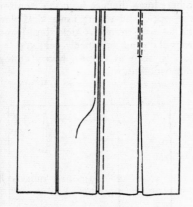

2. Side pleats, in which the fold of the material is turned to one side. If there is a seam beneath a side pleat, it is not pressed open, but is turned to one side. Side pleats are often graduated in size, so that they are deeper at the top of an all-pleated skirt to make it fit smoothly at the hip and waistline.

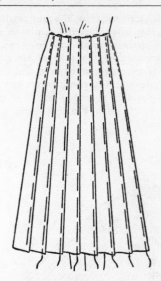

3. Box pleats, which are two side pleats, side by side, turned away from each other.

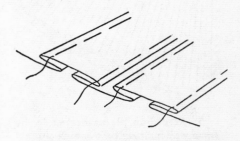

These first three types of pleats may be used singly or in combination. Box pleats and side pleats are often used together in a skirt. A wide box pleat will come at the center front and the center back, with side pleats over the hips. Pleats such as these are sometimes called by other names. For example, rows of very small side pleats close together are called knife pleats.

4. Fan pleats, or sunburst pleats, are a series of narrow side pleats which are wider at the bottom than at the top, since they are made on a perfect circle of material. They are most often used in the skirt of an evening dress of crepe or chiffon and can be very lovely. You can prepare the material for this pleating, but it is usually better to have the job done professionally.

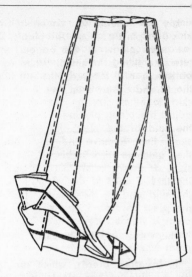

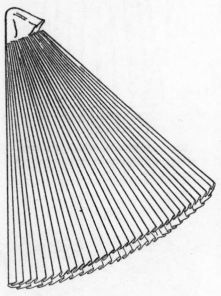

5. Accordion pleats are made the same way but may be done on straight (not necessarily circular) material.

Your pleated skirts will hold their line without frequent pressing if you give the pleats a razor-sharp line by edge-stitching them on all the folds. The edge stitching will appear to be a continuation of the stitching which fastens the pleats to the upper part of the skirt. Hem the skirt before you do this edge stitching and continue the stitching only to the top of the hem. Fasten the ends of the machine threads on the wrong side of the skirt.

6. A kick pleat is used to give fullness to a skirt at the knee while retaining a smooth, unpleated hip line. Some skirts have kick pleats only in the front; others have them in both the front and the back; still others have kick pleats at the side seams. A kick pleat is most suitably used in closely textured materials, such as crepes, heavy cottons and woolens.

There are two kinds of kick pleats—

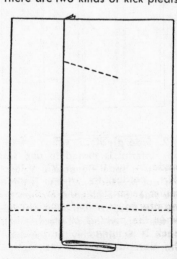

single and double or set-in. A single kick pleat is a wide side pleat, and allowance for it is made in the skirt pattern by making the seam wider at the bottom than at the top. Machine stitch the seam of the pleat, then baste the skirt together. Try on the skirt and adjust the pleat, pinning it flat so that the fold of the pleat lies along the seam line. Remove the skirt, baste, then machine stitch again on the right side, as shown in the illustration. Pull the thread ends to the wrong side of the skirt and tie them neatly to keep the pleat securely in place. After the pleat is stitched down, turn under the hem, first snipping the seam of the pleat where it meets the hem, so that the seam may be pressed open and lie flat within the hem. The edges of the seam are finished with an overcast stitch. This single pleat may also be

A double or set-in kick pleat looks like an inverted pleat at the bottom. The front section is cut in the same way as the single kick pleat. Then a

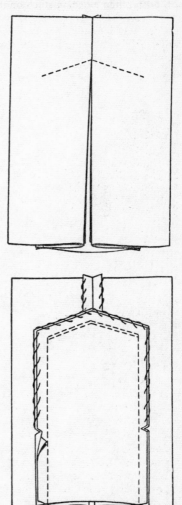

made in the front or the back of a skirt, particularly where there is a center seam down the skirt. The sewing procedure is the same, except that when the pleat is in the front or the back it is turned so that the fold of the material faces to the right.

separate piece is cut for the back of the pleat, preferably pointed at the top. To make the pleat, stitch down the seam of the skirt as far as the seam extensions. Baste the separate back piece to these extensions and machine stitch, joining this seam to the first in an inverted Y. Try the skirt on again and pin the two pleats into an inverted pleat. Baste, then machine stitch on the right side, as shown in the illustration, bringing the threads inside and tying them neatly and securely. Finish the pleat at the hem line in the same way as described for the single kick pleat.

CHAPTER 8

Hems, Facings, Bandings, and Bindings

THE difference between the homemade look and the professional appearance of the sewing you do often depends on the care that is taken with such details as the hem, a row of scallops, or a binding. These are the finishing touches which not only add to the appearance of your garment but also reflect unmistakably the care and fine handiwork which went into them.

HEMS—Your skirt pattern has a line of perforations about 2 inches from the bottom of the pattern piece. These perforations show you where the material should be turned up to allow a 2-inch hem, but you will be wise to try on the dress or the skirt when it is almost finished, before you start the hem. Wear shoes with the heel height you expect to wear with the dress. If the hem line allowed on the pattern is not a becoming length for you, re-mark the hem line.

There is no one "correct" length for a hem line. You may hear someone say, "They are wearing skirts 12 inches from the floor this season," or, "They say evening skirts are shorter, above the ankle." Forget what "they" say. The right skirt length for you is the length which looks best on you. You may lengthen your skirts if hems are longer; you may shorten your skirts a

little if hems go up, but always be guided by what is becoming to you rather than by the dictates of fashion.

Marking a skirt hem—The easiest way to mark a skirt hem is with a skirt marker. It is an inexpensive sewing aid and a wise investment. With it you can quickly mark your own hem, without help.

If you do not have a skirt marker, and do have someone who can help you to mark your hem, ask her to do it like this:

Put on a dress which you think is a becoming length.

Ask your helper to measure with a yardstick the distance from the floor to the hem line of this dress.

Change to the dress or skirt with the unmarked hem.

Ask your helper to mark the bottom of your skirt with a row of straight pins placed parallel to the bottom of the skirt and the same distance from the floor.

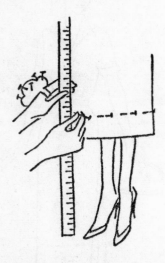

Do not remove the pins. Using additional pins, turn up the material below the row of pins and look again to see if the length is even and becoming. The finished and pressed hem will look slightly longer than the pinned hem line.

If you must mark your own hem and have neither a skirt marker nor an assistant to help you, do it this way:

Wearing the dress with the unmarked hem, stand beside a table which is lower than the fullest part of your hips.

With pins or chalk mark a line where your skirt meets the table top. Remove the dress.

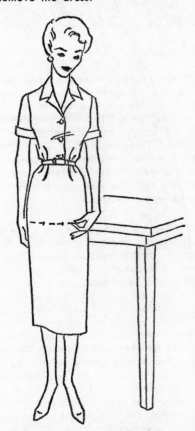

Choose a dress whose length you think is right for you and match the waistlines of the two dresses exactly.

Measure the distance from the pinned line on the unmarked skirt to the hem line of the other skirt.

Place a second row of pins this same

distance below the first row of pins in the unfinished skirt. This will mark the hem line.

Leaving these pins in place, turn under the material which is below the

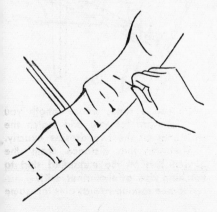

newly marked hem line. Then try on the skirt again to see that the length is even and becoming.

Finishing a hem—Baste close to the fold, leaving the raw edge free to trim and press. Most hems are about 2 inches wide. A very full skirt may have a narrower hem; a skirt for a growing girl may have a wider hem, which can be let down.

Decide the hem width you want and make yourself a hem gauge by notching a piece of cardboard to measure that width.

Holding the gauge with one hand to check the width, trim the hem to the desired width, being careful to cut only the edge of the hem, not the material beneath the fold.

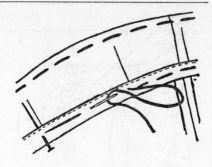

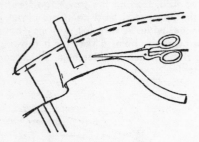

Machine stitch flat silk or rayon seam binding on top of the raw edge of the hem. The seam binding should cover the raw edge and extend beyond it. This is the usual hem finish for all but very sheer fabrics. No seam binding is used on sheer fabrics, because it is visible from the right side of the garment.

HEM BY HAND—Take a stitch in the fold and another in the material beneath the fold, keeping the thread loose and catching only a few threads, so the stitches will not show on the right side of the garment. Quick or blind hemming can be used for applying flat seam binding. (See below.) To finish a hem without seam binding, fold under the raw edge 1/4 inch. Press or machine stitch along the fold, and finish with one of the following hemming stitches.

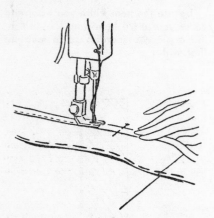

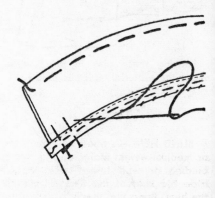

With a section of the hem flat on a table, baste the hem of the skirt. Make tiny pleats if there is too much fullness in the hem. Several small pleats are better than a few larger ones, since the latter may cause the hem line to sag.

QUICK HEM—Take slanting stitches, catching only a few threads of the material beneath the fold.

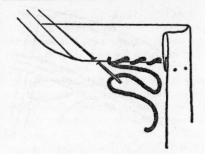

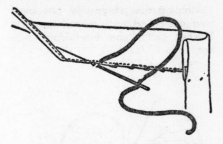

SLIP-STITCHED HEM (invisible)—Hide the knot of the thread beneath the hem. Slip the needle ¼ inch under the fold of the hem. Bring the needle out. Pick up a thread or two of the material beneath the hem. Slide the needle back into the fold. Repeat.

ROLLED HEM—Used on very wide or circular skirts. It is also used to finish the edges of ruffles, scarves, and in other places where a fine, narrow hand

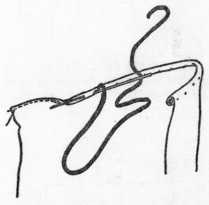

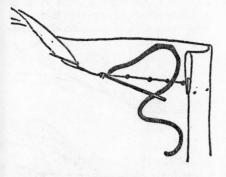

BLIND HEM—A good hem for light or medium-weight materials with seam binding or with turned-under edge. Hide the knot of the thread beneath the hem. Bring the needle out close to the edge of the fold. Pick up one thread in the skirt, taking a straight stitch directly beneath the edge of the hem. Slide the needle into the fold ¼ inch, catch one thread of the fold, and bring the needle out close to the edge. Repeat.

finish is desired. Machine stitch ⅛ inch from the raw edge. This gives body to the material and makes it easier to roll the edge. Take small slip stitches, rolling the material between the thumb and finger of the left hand as you sew. The tighter you roll, the narrower your hem will be.

WHIPPED HEM—A narrow hem, somewhat like the rolled hem. The raw edge is not machine stitched. Sometimes suggested for use on underwear, although a rolled hem is generally better for this purpose. The needle is inserted on one side of the material and brought out on the other side.

Slanted thread is carried (whipped) over the rolled edge of the material. Stitches should be even and fairly tight.

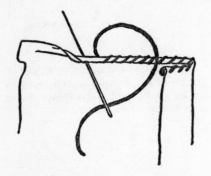

BIAS-BOUND HEM—Used for coats and jackets—especially for those which are unlined. Bind the hem with bias-

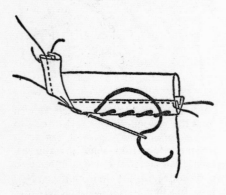

fold tape, covering the raw edges of the hem just as you would bind a seam with tape. Keep the wider half of the bias tape on the underside of the hem when machine stitching the tape to the hem so that the stitching will catch both edges of the tape. Blind stitch or slip stitch the folded edge of the bias-bound hem in place.

MACHINE-STITCHED HEM—Generally used only on edges of firmly-woven fabrics, although it is sometimes used to give a flat hem finish to a bulky wool suit. It may also be used on long, very full skirts, such as evening dresses, where hand hemming is frequently a waste of time. A machine-stitched hem is usually thought to cheapen the appearance of a garment if it is used indiscriminately. Turn under the raw edge and press. Turn the skirt to the right side. Machine stitch several even rows on the right side. Raw edges of fabrics which ravel easily should be covered with seam binding. Baste the seam binding over the raw edge before turning the skirt to the right side for the final rows of stitching.

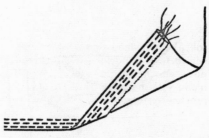

NARROW MACHINE-ROLLED HEM—A hem finish which can be used to advantage in many places. It is practical and quick for hemming edges such as those of aprons, but it should never be used to hem skirts, since it will give a cheap look to the garment.

The best method for making a narrow machine-rolled hem is to turn under the raw edge 1/8 inch to the wrong side. Press. Turn the edge a second time as you stitch it on the machine. This second turn should also be about 1/8 inch. The machine stitching should be very close to the edge of the second

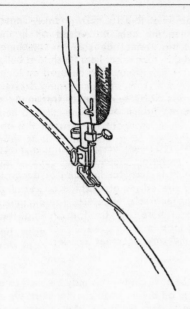

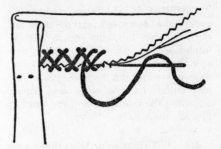

PLEATED SKIRT HEM—The seams at the edges of the pleats must be pressed to one side, not pressed open, so that

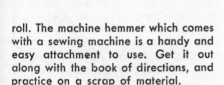

roll. The machine hemmer which comes with a sewing machine is a handy and easy attachment to use. Get it out along with the book of directions, and practice on a scrap of material.

CATCH-STITCHED HEM—This is more than a hemming stitch. It is used to finish hems of heavy, firmly woven materials which do not ravel, and is also used to fasten linings in coats and jackets, and to hold facings in place. The edge of the material is usually pinked before catch stitching, to make certain that it will not ravel. Catch stitches are backstitches, each taking up two or three threads of the fabric— one stitch in the hem, the next in the skirt or body of the garment. The third backstitch is again taken in the hem, and the fourth in the skirt. These alternating stitches give a zigzag appearance to the sewing thread.

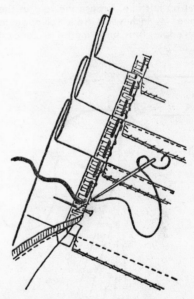

the edge of the finished pressed pleat will be knife sharp. Ordinarily, all skirt seams are pressed open. Where there is a seam at a pleat, clip the seam at the place where the hem will be stitched to the skirt. The portion of the seam which will be inside the hem should be pressed open before hemming; the seam above the clipped place should be pressed to one side. Overcast the clipped edges of the seam so they will not fray into the stitching.

CIRCULAR SKIRT HEM—To distribute evenly the extra fullness of a flared skirt, gather the raw edge of the turned-up hem, adjust the gathers, and sew bias tape over the gathered edge before sewing the hem in place. Or turn under the raw edge and baste, adjusting the fullness along the basting thread, then hem.

DAMASK HEM—For tablecloths and napkins. To be certain that the linen is cut on the straight grain of the cloth, pull out one thread across the width of the material from selvedge to selvedge. Cut on this line. Crease the fold of the linen ⅛ inch wide from selvedge to selvedge. Turn once more, to conceal

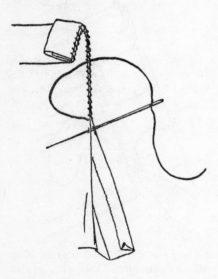

the raw edge in the hem. Final hem width should be ¼ inch. The hem is creased toward the right side exactly at the hem line. When hemming, point the needle toward you. Take a small, straight stitch which catches both the hem and the folded material at the hem line. The stitches over the top of the folded ridge should be slanting

and the thread drawn fairly tight. When the hem is pressed open, the stitches cannot be seen on the right side.

FACED HEM—See **skirt facing** in the section which follows.

FACINGS—A facing is a shaped piece of material, matching or contrasting, which is used for finishing or decorating the edges of clothing or curtains, luncheon sets, et cetera. The examples given here will be for clothing, but facings are applied in exactly the same way on other articles.

Skirt facing—This may be used as a hem on a very wide circular skirt. On a short skirt, such as that worn with a skating outfit, a shaped facing of a contrasting color can be applied on the right side and used both for the hem and for decoration.

Using the bottom edge of the skirt as a guide, and having the skirt length ½ inch longer than you wish it when finished, cut a band curved to fit the skirt edge. Allow ½ inch for any joining seams. Cut the facing 1 inch wider than you want the finished band to be. Stitch the facing by machine to the edge of the hem, with a seam allowance of ½ inch. Press the facing back on the skirt at the stitching line. Press down a ½-inch seam allowance at the top edge of the facing. Stitch this edge to the skirt by hand or edge stitch it by machine.

If the shaped facing is turned to the wrong side of the skirt and used for a hem, the top edge should be caught down with a hand-hemming stitch, slip stitch, or blind stitch. If the shaped facing is turned to the right side of the skirt and used for decoration, stitch the upper edge by machine.

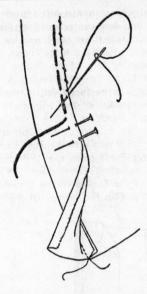

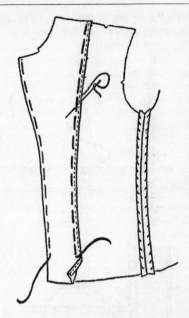

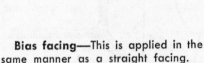

Bias facing—This is applied in the same manner as a straight facing.

coats and suits which are to be lined), or (b) turn under the raw edge of the facing, stitch edge by machine, and

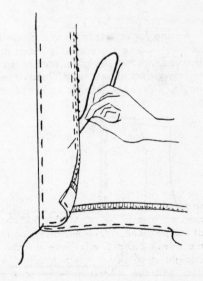

Front facing—This may extend from the neck to the hem of a coat, dress, or jacket. If it goes from the neck down, it is attached to the front opening before the collar is put in place. With or without a collar, a complete front facing is always applied before the hem is turned, since the hem is usually the last part of a garment to be finished. Pin the facing in place to see that it matches the edge it is to fit, then stitch it right side down on top of the right side of the garment. Turn the facing to the wrong side of the garment. Press exactly on the seam line, making a knife-creased edge. Following your pattern directions, either (a) catch stitch the raw edge of the facing to the garment (this is for facings in

then slip stitch the facing to the garment. The hem should be turned in under the facing at the lower edge and the facing tacked at the corner.

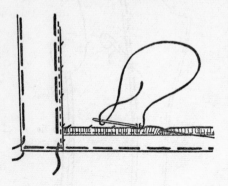

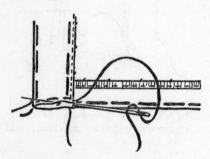

Facing for corner (making a mitered corner)—Corners are usually faced or banded with two straight pieces of material which must be neatly joined at an angle. This neat joining is called a mitered corner and is often found on V necks and square necks. Place the facing, right side down, on top of the right side of the garment to be faced. Leave a triangular fold of the facing at the corner. Pin or baste the facing in place, so that it is perfectly flat. Crease the extra material at the triangle of the facing. Machine stitch diagonally across the facing at the corner. Cut away the triangle to 1/8 inch from the stitching. Press open the 1/8-inch seam which remains. Then stitch the inner edge of the facing to the garment by machine. Clip the corner at the inside

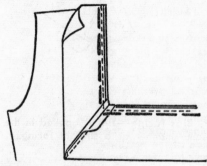

edge, so that the facing will turn over smoothly and lie flat at the corner. Be very careful that you do not nick a thread of your stitching when you clip. This "clipping at corners" is a trick for

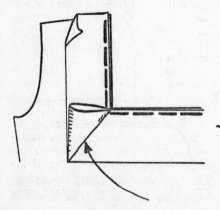

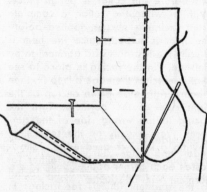

making any facing with curves or angles lie smooth. Next, turn under the raw edge of the facing, press it, and edge stitch it by machine before slip stitching or blind stitching it to the dress. Here's another trick to remember: When you catch facings to the inner edge of a dress by hand, do it lightly. If you take many, many, short, tight stitches, the dress will look tugged and pulled and worked over.

Shaped facing for slashed openings—For neck and sleeves. See Chapter 9 for instructions and sketches.

FACING FOR SMALL SLIT OPENINGS—These slits may be used for scarves and sometimes for belts. Place an oblong piece of material twice as long as the opening is to be and half as wide as it is long on top of the marked opening. The right side of the patch should face the right side of the garment. After the patch is pinned in place, mark the opening on the wrong side of the patch with a pencil. Stitch an oval opening not more than ¼ inch wide with a point at each end of the pencil mark. Slash on the pencil mark. Turn the facing through the slit to the

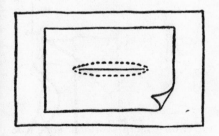

wrong side. Press. Press the raw edges under and edge stitch by machine. Fasten each corner of the facing to the garment with 2 stitches taken with a

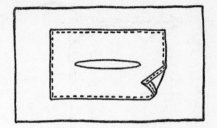

needle and unknotted thread. Leave the thread ends long enough to tie together in a square knot. This is called tacking. It holds firmly without giving that sewed-down look.

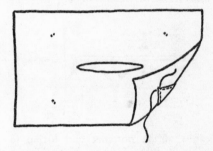

FACING FOR A SCALLOPED EDGE—This type of facing is often used as an edge on necks and sleeves. It is also used for household decoration on linens, et cetera. If you have no pattern, make your own by cutting paper scallops in a set of 3 exactly alike. Cut a facing strip of straight or bias material, matching the grain of the facing material with the grain of the cloth of the edge to be faced. For most purposes you will probably find that you are facing a straight edge. Place the facing right side down on the right side of the edge to be faced. If the facing must be pieced, do this before marking the scallops. Mark the scallops by placing the pattern on top of the facing and tracing around the pattern with pencil or chalk. Stitch along

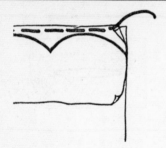

ment. Suggestion: If you want your scallops to be deeply rounded, not shallow, make very deep curves on your paper pattern.

the pencil or chalk curves. Leave the needle in the material and raise the presser foot of the machine to swivel around corners. When all the scallops have been stitched, trim the

FACING FOR A SAW-TOOTH EDGE
—Cut a saw-tooth pattern of paper and mark it on the facing as you would for scallops. Stitch by machine, turning

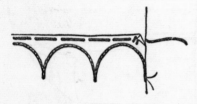

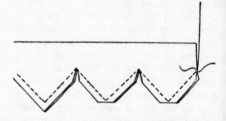

edges of the garment and facing to within ¼ inch of the stitching. Clip the corners and curves so that the facing will lie smooth and flat when it is turned to the wrong side. Press. Press

all corners sharply, leaving the needle in the material when you raise the presser foot to turn the material. The

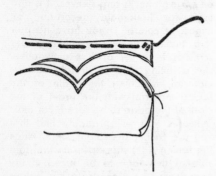

under the unfinished edge. Edge stitch this unfinished edge by machine. Then slip stitch or blind stitch it to the gar-

secret of a sharp saw-tooth edge is to clip the facing at the corners and to clip off pointed tips of the teeth, so they will lie smooth when turned.

BANDINGS—Bandings serve the same purpose as facings, except that they are not always used at the edge of a piece of material. A banding may extend beyond the edge, or it may be used as a flat decoration far from the edge.

Applied band—Used for decoration. Crease the seam allowance to the wrong side of the band. Press. Pin the band in place on the material and edge stitch on each side by machine,

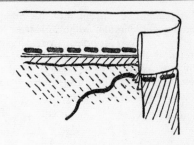

Press all raw edges. Edge stitch on the right side of the material. This holds all raw edges firmly in place and makes a neat finish for the banding.

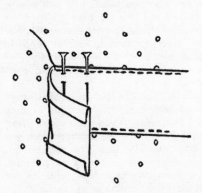

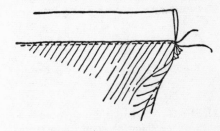

or slip stitch by hand. If the banding is narrow or if it has a pointed or curved edge, it is sometimes helpful to cut a matching piece of cardboard and press the seam allowance over this for a sharp, clear outline.

Extended band—Fold the band in half, right side out. Pin the raw edges of the band to the raw edges of the material, right side of the material up. Stitch the three edges together ¼

Another extended band—This is applied in exactly the same way that you sew a band to the top of a separate skirt. Pin one edge of the right side of the band to the wrong side of the garment. Stitch. Turn under the remaining edge of the band about a half inch to the wrong side. Press. Pin this pressed edge to the right side of the garment, just covering the first row

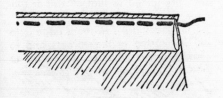

inch from the raw edges. Open.

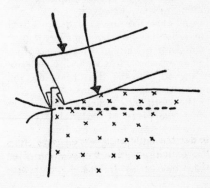

of stitching. Be certain that the band lies flat and smooth, without ripples. If there are any ripples, you have stretched the band in pressing or in pinning. When the top edge of the band is perfectly flat, edge stitch it to the garment by machine.

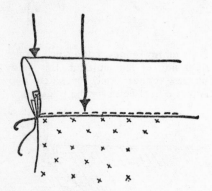

BINDING—Binding is usually a narrow strip of matching or contrasting material used to conceal the raw edges of a piece of clothing or an article of household use. Binding may also be used as a trimming. Most bindings, in order to fit smoothly and to turn easily around curves and corners, are bias bindings. Bias binding, often called bias tape, or bias fold, comes in cotton, rayon, or silk, and can be bought in many colors at most stores. Do not confuse bias binding with the flat seam binding used to finish hems, however.

An attractive and pleasing effect can often be had by trimming a garment with a binding of self material. This is especially true when the material is striped, for the bias trimming will show the stripe at a slant.

The word bias indicates the way in which the piece of material is cut to make the strips for the binding.

To find this bias grain of cloth, fold the selvedge edge of the material at right angles to a straight crosswise thread of the material. The folded edge of the triangle you have made is the bias grain of the material.

If you will take this folded edge between your two hands and pull gently, you will see that the bias grain of the material stretches very easily. It is fine for stitching around curves and in other places where a straight piece of material would be too stiff and awkward.

From this bias fold mark off straight strips with a ruler. Most bias binding is 1 inch wide. If you want wider strips, mark them twice the finished width you want, plus ½ inch for two seams. Cut these strips as long as possible. Cut them one at a time, and do not trim off the slanting ends.

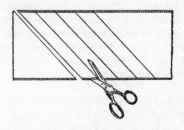

Join the bias strips on the straight of the material, as shown in the sketches. If material is striped, be sure that the strips are joined so that all stripes run in the same direction.

To make a bias fold, press ¼ inch on each raw edge of the joined strips toward the center.

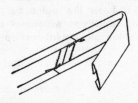

This bias tape is now ready to be used for binding seams or the edges of aprons, dresses, or curtains.

To apply bias tape to a straight edge by machine—If bias tape must be joined (as when binding an arm-hole or a pocket), estimate the amount of tape needed by stretching it very slightly around the outer edge of the place to be bound. Allow about ½ inch for seams. Cut the tape on the straight of the material—that is, diagonally. Join the two ends of the tape, a wide end to a narrow end, as you did when making the bias tape from

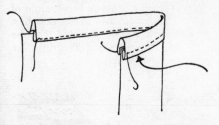

the short bias strips of material. Pin the completed circle of bias tape around the opening which it fits. The under

part of the bias tape should be slightly wider than the top—that is, the fold should be slightly off center. This is to make sure that both sides of the tape will be caught in the stitching. Edge stitch on the right side where the bias tape joins the garment.

To apply bias tape by hand—If bias tape is to be applied by hand, it is opened flat and placed right side down on the right side of the material to be bound. Stitch by machine about ¼ inch from the edge. Turn the bias tape over the edge of the material. Hem down on the underside, using a quick hemming or slip stitch. Hand hemming should cover the first row of machine stitching on the underside. This method of applying binding is much used for finishing underwear.

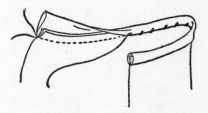

To bind scallops with bias bind-ing—The best type to use for this pur-pose is the narrow binding. You can use ready-made binding or cut strips not more than 1 inch wide. Ready-made tape must be open to its full 1-inch width. Pin the tape right side down to the right side of the scallops. Stretch the bias binding tightly when pinning it in the points which come between each scallop. Ease the bias binding when you pin it to the curves. Then baste the binding, as it will be much easier to stitch in this way than if you rely on the pins.

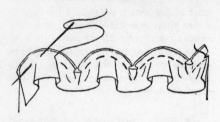

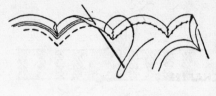

Stitch by machine in the same way as you would apply a scalloped facing. Then clip the corners and curves from the raw edges in toward the stitching. Turn the bias binding over the edge to the wrong side of the scallops and hem the binding by hand. At each point between the curved scallop make a crease in the binding and take an extra stitch there to hold that crease. This will keep the point flat. Press carefully, and you will have a professional-looking bound scallop.

CHAPTER 9

Putting Your Dress Together

FACTORY METHOD OR CUSTOM METHOD—If you are the average home sewer, you will be wise to eliminate experimentation at first in putting together the pieces of your dress, coat, suit, or whatever garment you are making. It is much better for you to follow exactly the directions which are given step by step in the pattern direction sheet or primer. When you have become entirely familiar with pattern directions, you can begin to try your own short cuts in sewing.

There are two distinct ways of putting a garment together after it has been cut from the paper pattern. One is the method usually followed in factories, where there are no fitting problems and where the most important factor is speed in production on a large scale. The other way of putting a dress together is known as the custom method, and is followed by the fine shops where clothes are made to the exact measurements of the women who order them. In the custom method the clothes may be fitted several times before the actual sewing and finishing are completed.

Factory method—Every dress factory has its own methods and each differs somewhat from the others. In general, however, the steps are as follows:

The entire front of the dress is put together. The front of the blouse and the front of the skirt are assembled separately and are then joined together.

The entire back of the dress is put together—first the back of the skirt, then the back of the blouse. The two sections are then joined together.

The front and the back of the dress are then stitched together at both shoulder seams.

The neck is finished completely.

The sleeves are sewed flat into the armhole; that is, before the lengthwise seams have been stitched.

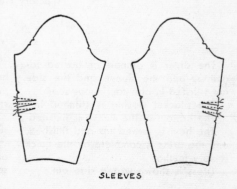

SLEEVES

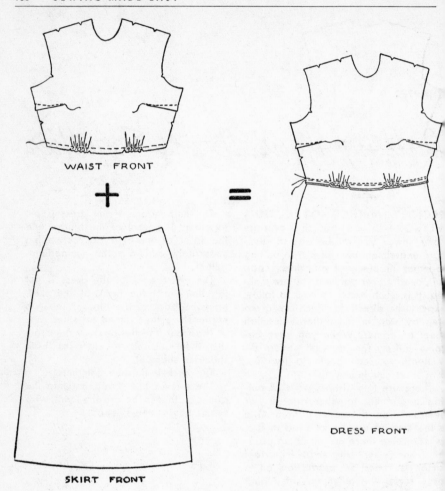

WAIST FRONT

+

=

SKIRT FRONT

DRESS FRONT

Factory method

The dress is pinned or basted together, and the sleeve and the side are stitched in one continuous seam.

The placket closing is stitched in.

The bottom of the sleeve is finished.

The hem is turned up and finished, and the dress is complete by the quick factory method.

Dress is shown wrong side out.

Custom method—Dressmaking houses, too, differ in their methods and procedure. The following sequence of steps is most frequently used.

Construction is done on flat pieces, such as a yoke.

The front of the blouse and the back of the blouse are each completed separately. The front and the back of

WAIST BACK

SKIRT BACK

DRESS BACK

Factory method

the blouse are then basted together at the shoulder and underarm seams, and the final stitching done after proper fitting.

The front of the skirt and the back of the skirt are each completed separately.

The front and the back of the skirt are basted together at the side seams. They are stitched together after proper fitting.

The top and the bottom of the dress are then basted together and fitted on the person who is to wear the dress.

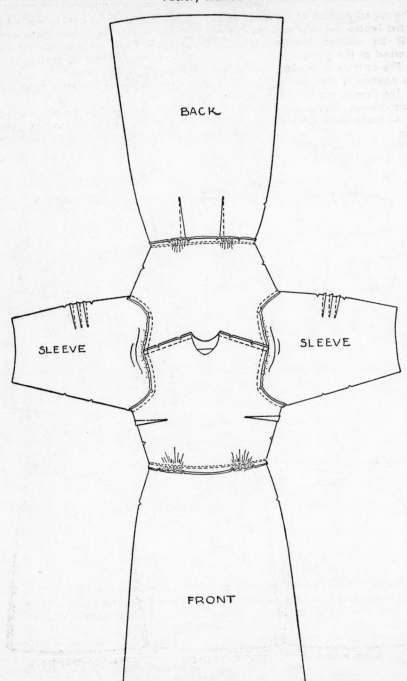

BACK

SLEEVE

SLEEVE

FRONT

The correct position of the seam at the waist (where the skirt and the blouse will be stitched together later) is marked at this fitting.

The armhole is checked, to see that its position is right for the figure.

The sleeves are fitted into the armhole, pinned, then basted.

All basted parts get their final stitching.

The length of the hem is marked at the last fitting. This is best done when the entire dress has been stitched and is ready for the final determination of the length of the dress.

Clothes should be fitted right side out.

Since speed is the only advantage of using the factory method to put a dress together, it should be used only

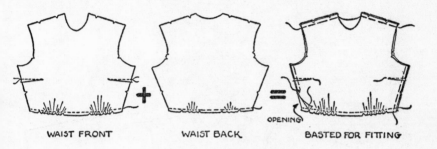

WAIST FRONT   WAIST BACK   BASTED FOR FITTING

Custom method

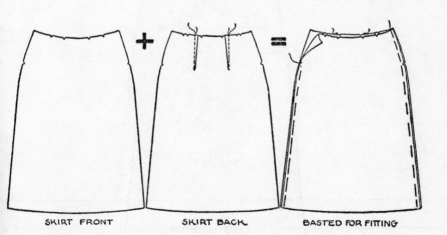

SKIRT FRONT   SKIRT BACK   BASTED FOR FITTING

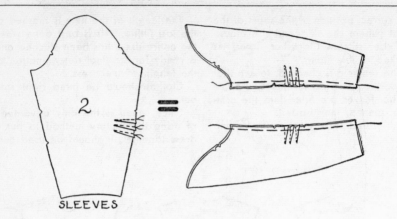

SLEEVES

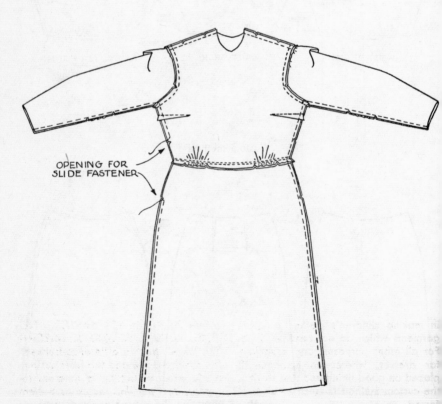

OPENING FOR
SLIDE FASTENER

Custom method

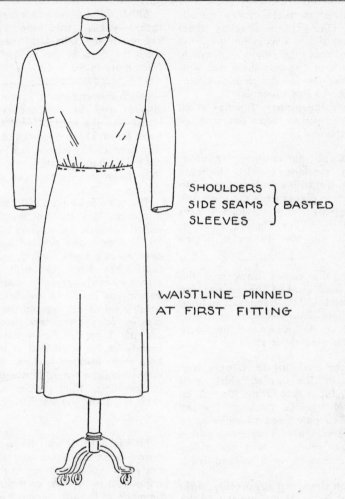

SHOULDERS ⎫
SIDE SEAMS ⎬ BASTED
SLEEVES ⎭

WAISTLINE PINNED
AT FIRST FITTING

Custom method

in making children's clothes or other garments which do not require fitting. For all other purposes, and especially for dresses, where the emphasis is placed on good fitting and fine sewing, the custom method is much to be preferred.

GENERAL RULES FOR BASTING, FITTING, AND STITCHING A DRESS— You know now the difference between the factory-made and the finer custom-made ways of putting a garment together. You will find that your pattern direction sheet combines both methods but advises you to use custom methods mostly. The pattern direction sheet or primer should always be your final guide whenever you have a question, because that direction sheet was written especially for the one particular garment you are making.

Usually the pattern direction sheet will advise you to follow this order of construction:

Mark all perforations or other pattern markings which indicate sewing directions before removing the pattern pieces from the material. Markings are made with tailor's tacks or with chalk. See Chapter 5 for instructions on how to make tailor's tacks.

Baste the center back and the center front lines of the garment on the material. If the garment is to hang well, these lines must be perfectly straight up and down on the figure when the garment is fitted.

Pin and baste all darts, tucks, and seams in the waist, skirt, and sleeves for a first fitting. Do not do the final machine stitching. Do not press. You may need to make some slight change before stitching, and it is always easier to take out a few bastings than to rip a stitched seam.

Try on the waist separately, right side out, or baste the waist and the skirt together on the wrong side for a right-side fitting. Always put the shoulder pads in place before trying on the blouse, for the pattern has made allowance for them. If you have a simple slashed neckline opening, you may need to stitch your shoulder seams, finish the neckline with a facing, and slash the neck opening so that it will be large enough to slip over your head, before you can try on the waist.

Stitch, finish, and press any darts, tucks, yokes, and the shoulder seams. If the skirt has been fitted, stitch the darts in the skirt when you stitch those in the waist.

Stitch the underarm seams of the sleeves and the side seams of the waist and the skirt after they have been fitted. Leave openings at the left side seam or any other place indicated on the pattern direction sheet for a slide fastener or other type of dress closing.

The seam finish used will depend on the fabric. Most pattern directions for materials which are not very sheer call for ½-inch seams pressed open and overcast to prevent fraying, unless the fabric has been cut with pinking shears. Always press a seam open before you join it to another. Seams which meet or are crossed are usually pressed open separately before they are put together. There are a few seams—at the waist and at the armhole, for instance—which are not opened but are turned in one direction for pressing. Your pattern direction sheet will show you which seams these are.

Fit the skirt, if you have not already done so. Press and stitch all darts and seams. In fitting, any needed adjustment in the skirt or waist should be made at the side seams. Be careful not to fit the skirt too tight.

If the neck has not been finished, finish it now. The type of finish and the point in the sewing procedure where the neckline is finished are determined by the pattern you use.

Stitch the skirt and the waist together. Tie a tape measure or a string around your waist to mark your normal waistline for this fitting. The seam should come beneath the tape. Be sure to wear the foundation garment for your fitting that you expect to wear beneath the finished dress.)

There are two ways of joining a waist and a skirt. You may prefer to baste the skirt and the waist together on the wrong side with a plain seam. Or you may want to baste down the seam allowance at the top of the skirt and then pin the skirt on top of the waist. After the skirt is fitted, it is top stitched or edge stitched (see Chapter 6) to the waist from the right side. Using the top-stitch method makes the waistline easier to fit, but the seam must be stitched carefully to avoid catching unwanted material.

Pin and baste the sleeves to the armholes. The sleeves had already been separately basted and fitted on the arm before the underarm seam was stitched and pressed open. Try on the dress with the shoulder pads pinned in place. Stitch the sleeves into the armholes. Press over a rounded pad or tailor's cushion.

There are, of course, many types of sleeves, but the most frequently used is the plain sleeve set in the plain armhole, without any apparent fullness. Actually, any plain sleeve of this type is about 1 inch larger than the armhole opening into which it is supposed to fit smoothly. This extra inch of fullness allows for freedom in moving the arm. Do not cut off this extra fullness. It is supposed to be "eased" into the armhole opening. If you have matched your pattern markings carefully and have the correct sleeve in the correct armhole, you will come out all right. Specific directions for inserting sleeves will be given later in this chapter.) Sleeves may be finished at the bottom as soon as the correct length is known.

Finish the openings in the dress.

This may be a slide fastener or placket at the waistline. Or it may be a front-buttoned closing, in which case you may possibly want to finish the front closing before you stitch the side seams of your dress. Here again your pattern direction sheet will be your final guide as to which step should be taken first.

Mark the hem line in the skirt. Have the side opening closed, wear the belt if the dress is to have one, and the shoes you plan to wear with this dress when the hem line is measured. If the skirt is cut on the bias grain of the material, or if the material is a knitted one such as jersey, the hem should be marked, trimmed, basted, and allowed to hang for a day or two before it is finished. A second fitting will show up any dips in the hem line caused by sagging material.

Most finished hems should be about 2 inches wide. Unless the material is very sheer, hems look best when finished with the rayon tape called seam binding. It is almost a rule that all well-made clothes are hemmed by hand. The few exceptions—including wide-skirted evening dresses and underwear—may be machine hemmed, but the finer garments will always be finished by hand with a narrow rolled hem. In an inexpensive, ready-made garment the manufacturer tries to imitate the hand hemming which he cannot afford. It costs you only time, so hem by hand and have the very best finish for your clothes. Specific directions for hemming are given in Chapter 8.

Give the completed garment a final pressing, even though you have been pressing as you go. If the garment is made of woolen material, you will be wise to have the final pressing done by a good tailor.

Hang your finished garment on a good hanger. It can be a lovely satin-padded wooden one that you have covered in your spare moments or it can be a plastic or wooden one shaped to hold your clothes in place. The thin wire hangers which come from the cleaner's, however, will tend to poke ridges in the shoulder lines of your clothes. Don't use them unless you must. And if you must, wrap the wire with tissue paper until the top of the hanger is well padded.

ALTERATIONS IN FITTING A BASTED DRESS

—Few figures are perfect. If you have chosen your pattern in the correct size and style for your figure, as suggested in Chapter 4, and if you have made minor alterations needed in your pattern, your fitting will be a smooth one. Occasionally you will find one of these fitting suggestions helpful. They may also be needed for adjusting ready-made clothes to your figure.

Rules for fitting

1. The best-fitted foundation you can buy is never an extravagance. Wear for your fitting the foundation you intend to wear with the dress.
2. Wear for your fitting the shoes you intend to wear with the dress.
3. Always wear a dress right side out for fitting, with the shoulder pads in place.
4. Be certain that the center front and the center back lines are marked on the dress with long bastings. Pin the center front and the center back of the dress to the center front and the center back of your slip at the waistline.
5. Do all fitting in front of a full-length mirror if possible.
6. If possible, have someone help you with the fitting.

There are actually two kinds of fitting problems: those that may occur because of figure irregularities and those that are routine pattern adjustments made at the time the garment is fitted.

For convenience, both types of problems have been grouped together, since both are adjusted in the fitting of the garment.

If center front and back bastings of skirt slant to one side—This is caused by a slight difference in the size of the hips—a common figure fault. Let out the side seam at the larger hip, or pin the seam deeper on the opposite side until the basted line hangs straight. Rebaste along the pinned line for stitching. Alteration will usually be needed on the one side only.

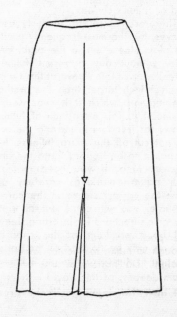

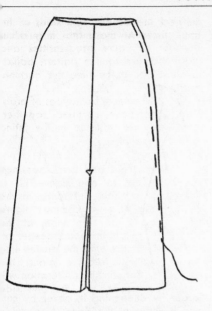

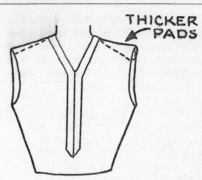

If there are slight wrinkles from the **neck to the underarm**—These are corrected by the use of proper shoulder pads. Do not attempt to take the shoulder seams deeper if the pattern has made allowance for shoulder pads. Simply make the pads thicker.

If center front and back bastings of blouse slant to one side—One shoulder may be slightly lower than the other. Both shoulders can be made to appear alike by use of a thicker shoulder pad for the low shoulder. Test

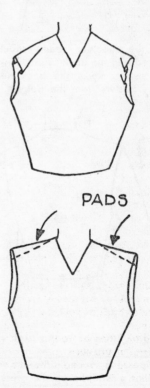

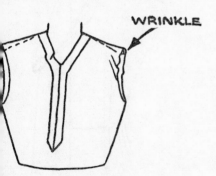

the pad until you have one thick enough to make the center lines hang straight. Do not make one shoulder seam deeper, as this would only make the figure fault more noticeable.

If the blouse is baggy at the lower back—This should not happen if the blouse pattern has been carefully fitted, though you may find it in ready-made clothes. The side seams

and the shoulder seams should be opened and the back raised. Pin-fit the side seams. Recut the back neckline and shoulders from the pattern.

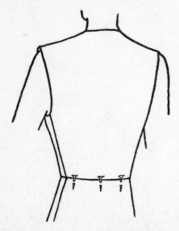

If the neckline is too high or too tight—Do not cut a new neckline on the figure. Mark one side with tailor's chalk or pins. Take off the dress. Fold

the neck in half. Cut both sides at the same time. Always make a neckline

larger by deepening it, never by cutting it wider at the sides. A too-wide neckline will gape where it should hug the neck.

If there is gaping at the back of the neck—Take several small darts before finishing the neckline. This alteration can also be used when the back is slightly wide at the shoulders.

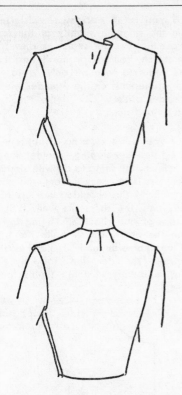

ing all the way around. The normal waistline is at the point where the body curves in most, the place where your hands rest when you attempt to encircle your waist.

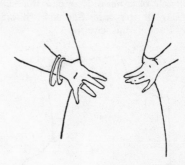

If your back waistline is slightly shorter than the pattern, don't think you are deformed. Many women find this to be true. It is a simple thing to shorten the waistline in one place when fitting the garment, and this is the alteration you should make rather than to shorten the entire blouse.

If the blouse is too large through the bust—If the blouse is long enough the underarm darts can be made deeper. Correct choice of shoulder pads and brassière will also do much to eliminate the unattractive hollow which sometimes appears between the shoulder and the bust line on a figure with a large bust.

If the blouse is too long—The safest way to shorten a blouse at the waistline is by fitting before the skirt is stitched to the blouse. But a word of caution is in order: One of the most common mistakes of the home sewer is to make a waistline too short. Before you cut off any material, be certain that the waist actually needs shorten-

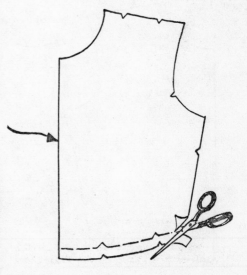

If the blouse needs to be made smaller at the waistline—Pin the side seams deeper. Gradually taper the pinned line out until it joins the original seam line at the underarm seam. When you make this alteration in the blouse, you will also need to make the skirt smaller at the top. See skirt alteration later in this chapter.

If you have narrow shoulders—Trim the armhole slightly at the top, across the shoulder seam, as shown in the sketch. You will probably find that it is better to take off only ¼ to ½ inch at the most on the shoulder width. Shoulder pads will build the shoulder line up and out.

If you have sloping shoulders—Unless the very sloping shoulder line is in fashion, the thing to do with sloping shoulders is to conceal them with padding. Build the shoulder line up with pads until the dress fits well. If it is a case of one shoulder's being lower than the other, simply build the pad up on that side until it matches the opposite shoulder line. This, by the way, is a very common figure fault.

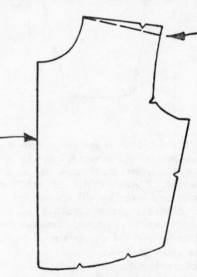

Occasionally fashion will accent the sloping shoulder line. When this happens, the woman whose shoulders slope naturally has an advantage. She can simply make the shoulder seam wider at the outer edge, toward the armhole. This tapering seam should not be more than ¼ inch deeper than he original seam allowance. A deeper shoulder seam may mean that about ⅛ inch must be trimmed away from the armhole directly beneath the arm at the underarm seam.

If you have square shoulders—A shoulder line can be squared by making the shoulder seam slightly deeper at the neck and tapering the seam from the neck to the armhole. You can make this seam ¼ inch deeper than

If the blouse must be made smaller under the arm or down the entire side seam—The blouse is fitted so that it looks and feels well by pinning the underarm seam deeper. When this is done, the armhole must be recut, because the deeper underarm seam will make the armhole smaller and at the same time make the underarm seam wider than the sleeve seam at the point where the two seams meet.

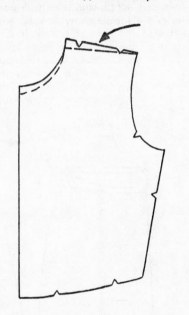

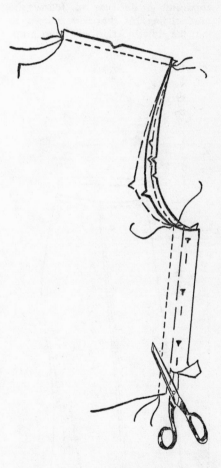

he seam allowance without making a noticeable difference in the size of the neck opening. If the seam is taken deeper than this, however, you may need to increase the size of your neck opening, since you will be making the neck opening smaller when you take in the shoulder seam. Do not widen the neck opening. Cut it deeper at the center front, following the original neckline.

If the skirt needs to be made smaller at the waistline—Pin the side seams of the skirt deeper from the waist to the hip line or below. Taper the new seam line so that it will join the original seam smoothly with no ripples.

If the skirt must be made narrower all the way down the side seams—Pin the side seams deeper all the way down, but not so tightly that you will be unable to walk and sit comfortably. Be sure to follow the original lines of the skirt pattern so that the adjusted skirt will hang properly.

If the skirt side seams swing forward—Shorten the skirt slightly at the back waistline, until the side seams hang straight. This "take up" will be widest at the center back and taper away to nothing at the sides.

If the skirt side seams swing toward the back—Shorten the skirt slightly at the front waistline until the side seams hang straight.

When this adjustment is made, the raised part will be widest at the center front and will taper away to nothing at the sides.

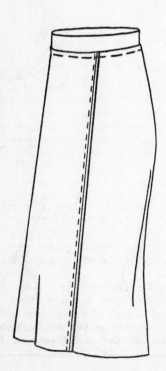 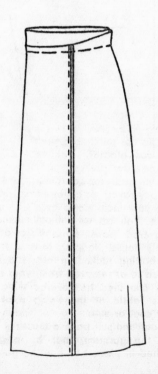

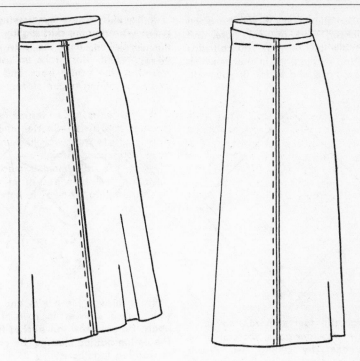

SHOULDER PADS—Some patterns include directions for making shoulder pads. A beginning sewer might be wise to use purchased pads in a small size for blouses, medium size and thickness for dresses, and larger and heavier pads for coats and suits. You can buy rayon- or cotton-covered pads from your local stores or a mail-order house. You can also buy inexpensive uncovered pads at a dressmaker's supply house. Padding (layers of cotton batting tacked in place) can be added to or removed from these pads. They can then be covered with your dress fabric or the lining fabric of your coat or suit.

Coat and suit pads are usually built into the garment; that is, they are stitched in place between the garment and the lining. However, dress shoulder pads should only be tacked, so that they can be removed before you send the dress to the cleaner or before the dress is washed. (Yes, cotton wash dresses should also have pads. The shoulder line is important in any type of dress.)

Pin the pads in place for a fitting. Tack them in the finished garment according to directions given in the pattern primer. Shoulder pads should extend slightly beyond the shoulder—about ¼ to ½ inch for a regulation triangular shoulder pad—and slightly more than half the pad should be placed in front of the shoulder seam.

No one can tell you exactly the type of shoulder pad to buy for your particular need without seeing your figure and your shoulders. If you have an experienced clerk at your store, she can usually advise you. You can also be guided by the pads in clothes which you now have and which fit you well.

Stitch the squares together twice— once near the unfinished edges and the second time ½ inch from the edges.

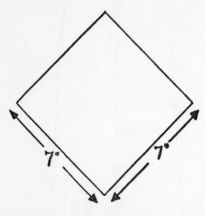

If you still feel you want to make your own shoulder pads, you can make simple ones by cutting two 7-inch squares of washed muslin for each

Baste through the muslin and filling with 1-inch stitches in rows 1 inch apart. Do not draw the stitches tightly. The cotton batting must not be crushed or wadded together.

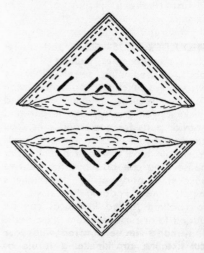

pair of pads. Put a 1-inch layer of cotton batting between the two pieces of muslin. Thin out the cotton to almost nothing ½ inch from the outer edges of the square.

Cut the square diagonally to form two triangular shoulder pads.

Take a small dart, as shown, on the underside of the pad, to make it cup over the shoulder. Cover the pad with the dress material and tack it in the dress.

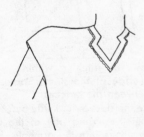

Long sleeve, cut in one with the front and the back of the dress, is one that is loose under the arm. The shoulder seam helps to give it shape.

SLEEVES—A tricky sleeve or cuff may add an interesting touch to your clothes, but until you are an experienced sewer it is best to select a pattern which calls for the simplest type of sleeve.

Cap sleeve is simplest to make. It is merely an extension of the armhole. It should not be fitted too closely or it may pull under the arm.

Dolman or bat-wing sleeve is an exaggerated sleeve style, popular every few years, but not flattering to the very short figure or the one with a heavy bust line. It is set into a wide, loose armhole and tapers to the wrist.

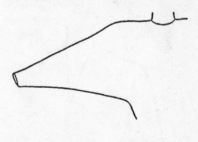

Kimono sleeve is a longer version cut like the cap sleeve. It is usually rather loose under the arm. It may or may not have a shoulder seam. The underarm seam should be clipped at the curve to prevent its puckering.

Raglan sleeve is used frequently in sports clothes. It is not a good style for the figure with a heavy bust line, since it adds breadth to the figure. The sleeve and the shoulder are cut in one piece, as shown in the illustration. Clip the seams at the curve, so they will lie flat.

Puffed sleeve is sometimes called dirndl sleeve when it is short. A long, full version with a tight-band cuff at the wrist is called a peasant sleeve.

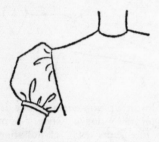

Set-in sleeve is the most commonly used and most generally becoming. It can be short, long, or an in-between

length. A set-in sleeve which is cut in two pieces is often used in coats and suits.

HOW TO MAKE A SET-IN SLEEVE—
Stitch the underarm seams after the

basted fitting. Remove the basting. Press open the seam.

Stitch the darts if the pattern shows them. If there are no darts, loosen the upper tension of the machine and run

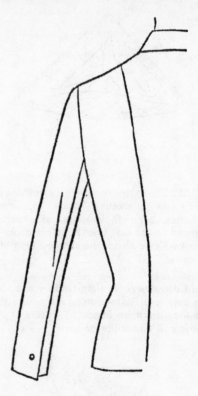

two rows of stitching within ½ inch of the edge of the sleeve, across the top, between the notches.

Have the sleeve right side out. Working from the wrong side of the dress, slip the sleeve into the armhole. Match the right sides of the material together and pin at the underarm seam. Check to see that the notches correspond, so you will be sure to have each sleeve in the correct armhole.

Pin the sleeve in the armhole at the notches, placing the pins at a right angle to the edges of the material.

If there are notches or perforations to match the sleeve top with the top of the armhole, put a pin there.

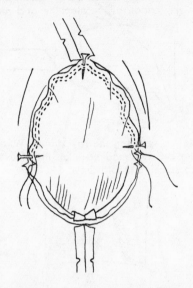

Gather the two rows of machine stitching by pulling the bobbin threads gently until the top of the sleeve fits the top of the armhole. (The sleeve is about 1 inch larger than the armhole.)

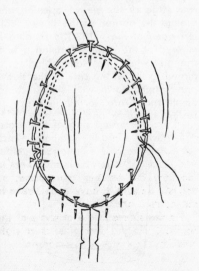

Pin all the way around the armhole, using plenty of pins and working always with the sleeve held toward you.

Baste the sleeve in place, still with the sleeve held toward you. Unless the pattern picture shows fullness in the form of darts or gathers at the top of the sleeve, your basted sleeve should look perfectly smooth in the armhole. There should be no little pleats or puckers.

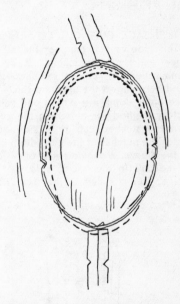

Stretch the armhole rather tightly as you stitch the sleeve in by machine.

Do not remove the gathering threads unless they show. Overcast the edges of the seam together, then press with the seam turned toward the sleeve. Shrink out any fullness at the top of the sleeve with a damp pressing cloth. A tailor's pad or cushion is the most convenient base for pressing.

Ways to finish sleeves—The sleeve finish varies with the material and the style of the dress. The most popular ways to finish sleeves are:

PLAIN HEM—Usually about 1 inch wide. The sleeve may also be finished with seam binding. It is used for short or long sleeves.

TURNBACK CUFF CUT WITH SLEEVE —Made from a wide hem of 2 or 3 inches. After the hem is finished, the double fold of the material is turned back to the right side of the sleeve to form a cuff. This may be pressed or tacked in place.

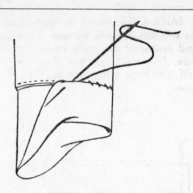

TURNBACK CUFF CUT SEPARATELY —This type of cuff can be stitched in place entirely by machine, or by a combination of machine stitching and hand hemming. If the machine stitching is carefully done, it is a neat and satisfactory method for attaching the cuff. Turn the stitched cuff right side out. Match the notches of the cuff with those of the sleeve. Machine stitch one side of the cuff to the wrong side of the sleeve. Turn the cuff to the right side

sleeve, covering the raw edges. When the cuff is turned back on the sleeve, no stitching should show.

TIGHT SLEEVE OPENING FACED WITH SEAM BINDING—The silk or rayon binding is stitched on top of the raw edge of the sleeve opening and around the portion of the sleeve seam left open at the wrist. The binding is mitered at the corner, forming a neat triangle when the seam binding is turned to the wrong side of the sleeve and caught down with slip stitching. Small snaps are sewed in place to fasten the seam opening.

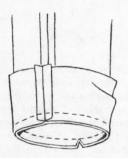

of the sleeve and turn under the raw edge of the cuff. This will cover the first seam. Hand hem or machine stitch the turned-under edge of the cuff to the

BAND CUFF—Used on dresses and on soft and tailored blouses. Stitch the end seams of the cuffs on the wrong side. Turn right side out. Press. If the cuff is to have a buttonhole, it is made now.

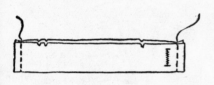

Roll the hem at the sleeve opening.

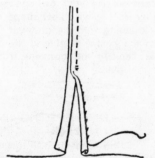

Pin the cuff to the sleeve, with the seam on the right side. Gather the sleeve to fit the cuff. Baste. Stitch by machine. Turn under the seam allowance on the remaining edge of the cuff.

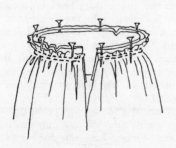

Pin this turned-down edge on top of the seam joining the sleeve and the cuff and edge stitch the cuff to the sleeve.

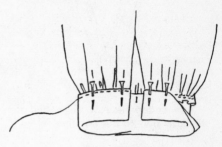

NECKLINES AND COLLARS—There may well be two or three correct methods for finishing a particular neckline. You will learn by experience which method is easiest for you and best for the neckline on which you are working.

Bias-faced V neckline—Baste a bias strip, ¾ inch wide, right side down, on the outside of the neckline.

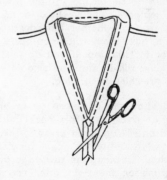

Miter the bias to form a point at the V of the neckline, as shown. Turn the bias facing to the wrong side.

Turn under the raw edge and slip stitch invisibly to the neckline.

If the front neckline of the dress is cut on the bias grain of the material, as is often the case when the front of a V-necked dress is gathered or draped, the facing for the neckline should be cut on the straight grain of the material. Always hold a narrow neck facing, whether bias or straight grain, quite firmly when you baste it in place for stitching. If you do this, the neckline will lie flat and smooth without stretching or gaping.

Ribbon silk or rayon seam binding at neckline—This neck finish is used on silk or rayon dresses. The ½-inch-wide ribbon or seam binding is stitched flat along the raw edge of the neckline on the right side. You may need to make a small pleat in the seam binding at the shoulder seams so it will lie smooth when turned, since seam binding has no "stretch" to curve around corners. Miter the ends of the

seam binding or ribbon at the point of the neckline. Turn the seam binding to the wrong side of the garment. Then tack or slip stitch it in place, catching only a thread of the material, so that the stitches are invisible on the right side of the garment.

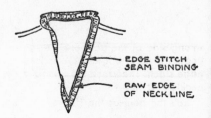

To cut a shaped facing without a pattern—Make your own paper pattern by tracing the exact shape of the neck opening with the garment folded down the center front and the center back. Remove the garment from the traced outline.

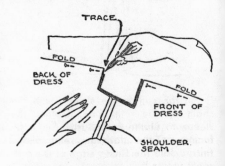

Cut the facing with the center front and the center back lines on a fold of the material. Join the front and the back neck facing pieces at the shoulders. The stitching line for these joining seams should be traced from the shoulder seams of the garment, so that the finished facing will fit the neckline smoothly.

Place the facing right side down on the right side of the garment. Pin. Baste. Stitch. Turn the facing to the

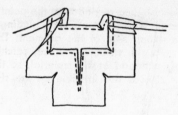

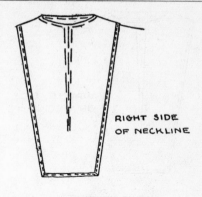

RIGHT SIDE
OF NECKLINE

wrong side of the garment. Press. Turn under the outer edge of the facing and edge stitch. Then tack the facing to the neckline at intervals.

Slash the opening.

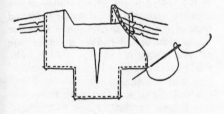

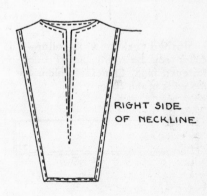

RIGHT SIDE
OF NECKLINE

Front slashed facing—Cut the facing on the straight grain of the fabric. Join the facing on the shoulder seam unless it is cut in one piece. Turn the outside edges of the facing to the wrong side and edge stitch. (This can be done later if you wish.) Baste the right side of the facing to the right side of the neckline, matching notches. Baste the opening and stitch around the neck. Continue around the mark for the opening, stitching this in a deep, narrow V with the point at the bottom of the opening and just wide enough for a pair of scissors to slash to the very point.

Turn the facing to the inside.

Tack the facing to the garment at the corners. Slip stitch the facing to the garment around the back of the neck. Do not hem all around the facing, for even the smallest stitches will be visible on the right side of the dress.

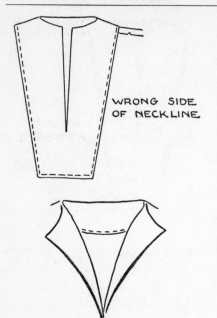

WRONG SIDE
OF NECKLINE

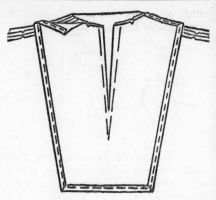

Slashed neckline with collar—This collar can be worn turned back or fastened high, Chinese fashion. Stitch the ends of the collars.

Pin the lower edge of the collar at the center back to the center back of the neckline. Baste the lower edge of the collar to the neckline from one end of the facing to the other; that is, from shoulder seam to shoulder seam, around the back of the neck. Clip the upper side of the collar ½ inch deep at the shoulder seams. Insert both thicknesses of collar between the neckline and the facing. Pin. Baste. Stitch the collar and the facing to the neckline in one continuous row of stitching around the neckline.

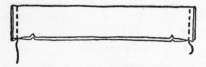

Turn right side out. Press.

Make the facing as directed above, but stitch only around the front opening. Slash. Turn. Press. Check the collar size to see that it fits the neckline exactly.

Turn the facing to the wrong side of the garment. Turn the seam up into the collar. The upper side of the collar will be left free from shoulder to shoulder across the back neckline. Turn this free edge under. (The ½-inch deep clipping will enable you to do this.) Slip stitch along the seam line where the under collar is joined to the neckline.

to match the center back of the collar to the center back of the neckline and

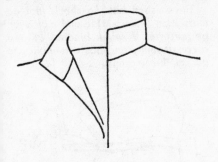

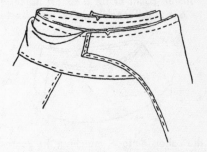

Notched collar, where turnback front facing forms lapels—The collar is prepared, placed, and stitched exactly as the slashed neckline with collar with two exceptions: no separate facing is needed, since the front turnback

to match all notches, so that the lapels will each extend an equal distance beyond the ends of the collar.

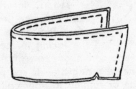

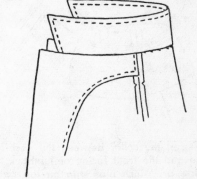

makes the facing and, in addition, the collar does not reach to the edge of the front facing. It is very important

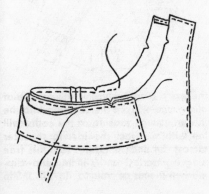

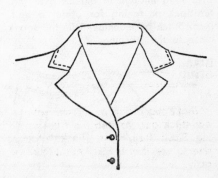

Collar applied with bias binding —The binding may be cut from self material according to directions given in Chapter 8. This bias method of applying a collar can also be used for a notched collar or for a collar attached to a slashed neckline. Pin and baste

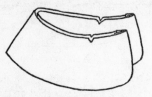

the collar in place, matching the center back of the finished collar to the center back of the neckline, matching all notches.

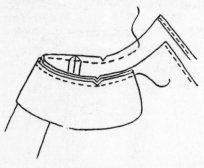

Insert the collar between the neckline and the front facing or turnback. Baste a ¾-inch bias strip on top of the collar wrong side up. Cut this bias strip long enough to extend over the turnback or facing for about a half inch. Stitch by machine. Trim the seam close to the stitching.

BIAS
STRIP

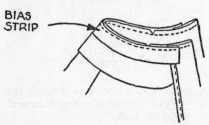

Turn the facing or turnback to the wrong side. Turn under the strip and slip stitch it to the neckline.

The finished binding should not be more than ½ inch wide and may even be narrower. A wider binding will not curve smoothly and has a tendency to pucker the neckline.

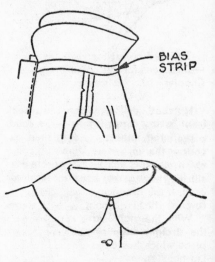

BIAS
STRIP

Collar with edging—If you plan to add lace or ruffling to your collar, be certain that you make an allowance for

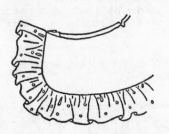

the extra length which it will add. This allowance will be twice the width of the trimming; that is, a 12-inch collar with a 1-inch wide ruffle will be almost 14 inches long after the ruffling is inserted and stitched between the two pieces of collar.

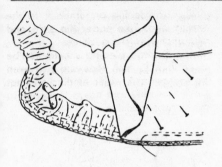

garment right side out and finish by top stitching very close to the pressed seam line.

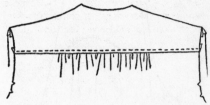

Tailored collar for suits and coats —Directions for this collar are given in Chapter 10, "Tailoring Tricks."

YOKES—You'd make a yoke the same way as you would stitch a gathered piece of material to a straight piece. Loosen the upper tension of the machine slightly. Run a straight row of stitching along the edge to be gathered. If the distance is long, make two rows of stitching about ⅛ inch apart.

With the right sides together, pin the straight edge of the yoke to the piece which has been stitched, matching notches.

FLARES—A flare is fullness. Your pattern may have a flared skirt or a flared peplum. Pattern pieces are usually cut to allow for some flare in the skirt. The amount of flare depends on the type of dress and the fashion of the moment. If you are the average woman, you will take a skirt which has a flare starting at the widest part of the hips.

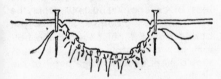

Pull up the bobbin thread to form gathers.

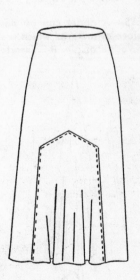

Gather only enough for the two pieces to fit together; then stitch the pieces together by machine. Press, turning the seam toward the neck. Turn the

A gentle flare is kind to your figure and never gives your skirts that "cupped" or "seated" look.

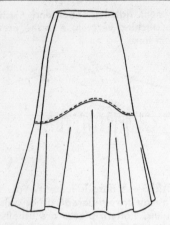

A two-piece skirt can be flared. For variety, the flare is sometimes set in or added on to a skirt. Inserts and circular flounces are two devices used to give a flare. These may be seamed on the wrong side, or top stitched, as your pattern suggests. To make inserts and curved flounces lie smooth, clip all curved seams on the wrong side.

GODETS—A godet can be described as a piece of material which is shaped like a wedge of pie. It is inserted in a

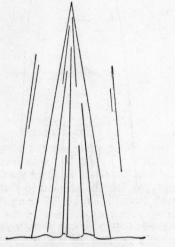

seam or slash, usually in the skirt or

sleeve, to give fullness.

Pin and baste the godet in place from the wrong side of the garment, starting the basting at the point of the godet and basting downward toward the bottom. The seam at the point of

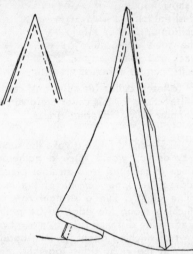

the slash will be very narrow. If the godet is cut on the bias, it should be basted in place and allowed to hang for a day or two before stitching. If the bias piece sags, rebaste it from the point toward the bottom. Stitch as you basted from the point toward the bottom, in two separate seams. The seams should meet exactly at the point of the slash.

To fan-pleat a godet, divide the finished and hemmed godet into a number of overlapping side pleats at the bottom. These pleats taper to nothing at the top.

LINING A DRESS OR SKIRT—To insure a fine, professional fit with dresses made of sheer or lightweight materials, you can line the entire garment. You may want to line just the bodice or skirt. The finest dressmakers and manufacturers turn out some of their best clothes with linings stitched right into them.

If the garment is of lace or other sheer material like chiffon, it should be lined with a solid-color crepe or taffeta. The lining can be either the same color as the dress or skirt or a contrasting color if you want it to "show through." If a sheerer look is desired for the sleeves in a lace or chiffon dress, they should be lined with the same color net. The facings for neck and sleeve edges, or collar and cuffs, can be either of the same fabric as the garment or of the same color net.

Tailored dresses and skirts of sheer wool and jersey are often lined with same color crepe or taffeta. Crepe, being soft, is good where there are gathers or fullness, while taffeta lends itself better to straight lines. Dressy clothes of soft crepe may also be lined to give them body and good fit. Here, too, you choose a lining which will best suit the material and style of the garment. The sleeves are usually not lined, as that would make them bulky.

When choosing a lining, make sure that it has the same washing or dry-cleaning qualities as the material in the garment. It would be sad indeed to have the lining shrink or fade. You should also be sure to get the lining in a crease-resistant fabric, as its purpose is to give a sleek look to your garment.

Cut the lining from the pattern in the same way you cut the garment. For a straight, or fairly straight, line skirt, it is desirable to treat the material of the garment and the lining as one piece of fabric. The lining, however, should be cut shorter at the hem than the outer skirt in order to avoid unnecessary bulk when turning up and sewing the hem. For a gathered or full skirt, it is best to handle the outer material and the lining separately at the seams. Baste lining and fabric together at the waistline and handle as one fabric when joining the skirt to the bodice.

The illustration shows only the front of the skirt, since the same principle is used for the back of it. After cutting, lay the right side of the lining on the wrong side of the skirt material. The reason for doing this is that if the garment is of a sheer fabric, the lining will show through. You will notice that in the illustration the lining is cut shorter than the outer material, since the skirt is straight. Baste in the lining at the waistline, seams, and bottom of the skirt. If the skirt has darts at the waistline, baste and stitch the darts through the outer material and the lining. The placket and the fastening (slide or snaps or whatever you use) are also sewn with the two thicknesses of materials together.

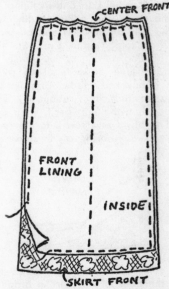

To finish the lower edge of a straight line skirt, try on dress, mark hemline, and trim the lower edge of the lining up to the hemline marking so that you don't have to turn up the lining. Keep lining basted down. Turn up the hem and baste ½ inch above the hemline. Be sure you include the lining in the basting so that it will stay flat when you sew the hem. Stitch your seam binding to the edge of the hem, and hand-sew the binding to the skirt. The lining should have a good fit at the hem and not pucker.

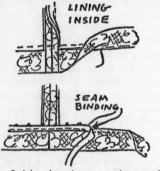

To finish the lower edges of a gathered or full skirt and its lining, try on the dress and adjust length. Turn up the hem on the skirt and baste ½ inch from folded edge. Finish the hem with binding, sewing as you usually do with the type of material of which your garment is made. Turn up the lining so that it is about ½ inch shorter than the skirt itself. Then proceed to baste and sew it in the same way you would ordinarily finish a hem.

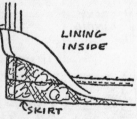

In some cases you may want to line only the back of the skirt in order to avoid "sit down" wrinkles. Or you may prefer to line the skirt only part way to the hem. In that case, the lining will serve to give a smoother look to your skirt over the hips, and should end just below your hipline. Do not turn under and sew a hem on this lining, since the fold may leave a ridge. Instead, use pinking shears to cut off the lining at the desired length.

To line the bodice of a dress, baste the lining to the outer fabric all around. If you are also going to line the sleeves (only in lace or very sheer garments), baste the net to the sleeve all around. If darts are indicated, they should be stitched through the outer fabric and the lining together. Then proceed to put together the front and back and sleeves (lined or unlined) as you would ordinarily sew a dress or blouse. Retain the basting around the neckline and the edge of the sleeves, until you finish them with facing, collar and cuffs, or whatever trim you wish to use. Also retain the basting at the waistline until the bodice is joined to the skirt.

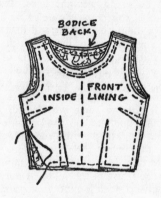

CHAPTER 10

Tailoring Tricks

THOSE little finishing touches which you give your dress, coat, or jacket often mark the difference between the smart, professional appearance of a garment and the amateurish, "home-sewed" look. Among the tailoring details which show up the work of a fine seamstress are buttonholes, buttons and other fastenings, plackets, and pockets. The time and effort spent in making each of these exactly right, instead of "just about," will always prove more than worth-while in the finished appearance of any garment.

BUTTONS—Buttons are used for decorative as well as utilitarian purposes, and you will find many types of buttons to choose from. The right selection for your particular dress or jacket depends not only upon the style of the pattern you have chosen but upon such things as the texture of the material, whether the garment will be dry cleaned or laundered, et cetera.

Fabric buttons are best on clothes which will be dry cleaned, since the metal molds used for fabric-covered buttons may rust when subjected to water. Some types are easy to make at home, especially with one of the button-covering kits now available. But in many cases it saves both time and effort to have the buttons made by a professional, and since the cost is usually minimal, it is well worth it. If there is no button-making concern in your neighborhood, consult the fashion magazines or the classified telephone directory for the addresses of firms which cover buttons. Mail them the fabric, directions, and money. The material required will, of course, vary with the size and number of buttons needed. It is also a good idea to order three or four extra buttons to replace any that may be lost.

Variations of fabric buttons include:

Flat, round buttons covered with the same material as that used in the dress.

Fabric covered with a matching or contrasting fabric rim.

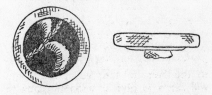

Fabric covered, with satin-stitch design in self-colored or contrasting lozenges in satin-stitch embroidery. It is usually best to have these buttons

made professionally and add the embroidery yourself. These buttons add
beautiful detail to a soft dressmaker
suit or coat in wool.

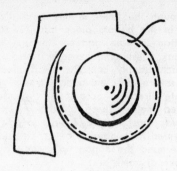

the mold and sew it in place with
stitches taken across the back of the
mold. Then cover with the circle of
fabric, drawing the gathered thread

Fabric covered, hand stitched. They
are used on tailored clothes. You can
buy molds and cover these buttons
quite well at home.

tight, as shown in the illustration, so
that the surface of the button will be
smooth. Fasten the thread, then cut

a smaller circle of fabric, turn under
the edges, and sew to the back of the
button, covering the raw edges of the
other fabric covering.

To make a covered button buy
wooden molds in the size needed and
use a soft, firm material, such as out-
ing flannel, to pad the buttons. Cut
each pad slightly smaller than the
mold. Cut the fabric covering for the
button a little larger than the button
mold and run a gathering thread
around the edge. Place the pad over

Another mold you can buy to make
fabric-covered buttons consists of two
pieces of aluminum. The bottom piece
has a shank in it, and both pieces
have holes punched in them for you to
sew through. You cover the top piece
with fabric and attach it by sewing

through the holes in the mold. Then fit in the bottom piece and sew the button to your garment through the shank. These molds come in a package which usually contains eight pieces in several different button sizes. Complete directions accompany the packaged molds. These aluminum button molds are rustproof and are not harmed in laundering or dry-cleaning.

Among the buttons you can easily make at home are:

Black walnut made from pieces of the shell cut cross-grain and waxed or shellacked. Suitable for woolen dresses, since they are not washable.

Crocheted—You can buy or make them. To make: Crochet over a wooden curved-top disk or button mold. A small ball of yarn is also a good base, but do not use beans, as they may mold or attract mice. Best used on clothes which have to be dry cleaned.

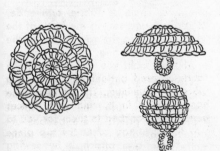

Ball buttons—These are best made by professionals; but in a pinch you can make them at home by covering old-fashioned shoe buttons with a small circle of fabric gathered and fastened to the shank of the button. Rows of these are very decorative for fastening a dress down the front, or they can be used for wrist openings. Fabric loops instead of buttonholes are generally used with ball buttons.

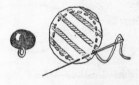

Fabric-covered ball buttons. For best appearance have these very small.

Self-fabric bias-cord buttons, rolled and tacked into flat disks. The thread used on these buttons should be

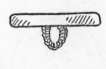

a perfect match. The shanks for attaching these buttons are made of thread loops.

Following are the kinds of buttons which are not made at home, but which you will see on sale in stores:

Wood—These can be bought in the natural state or varnished. For tailored dresses and suits. But a word of caution: Wooden buttons lose their beauty if washed.

Clear glass—Flat-disk or ball button. This type of button has the same uses as the pearl button, but it is often dressier.

Braided leather—Used on sports coats and suits.

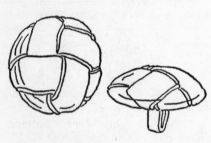

Silver or gold-colored metal—Good for nautical look in jackets, coats, and for rather tailored woolen dresses. Can also be used very effectively on simple silk or linen clothes which have to be dry cleaned.

Bone—Usually has a slight rim and holes for the thread. For sports and casual woolen clothes.

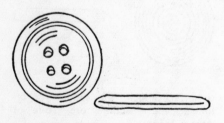

Pearl—May be flat disk or have holes for the thread. For summer dresses, blouses, children's clothes.

Flower, vegetable, animal shapes, and painted or enameled designs—Best used on plain fabric rather than prints. These buttons are usually washable, but be sure to inquire when you buy them.

Unusual old or antique buttons—
Worth saving if you have them. Worth
hunting if you want a special-type button for a dress. (Old buttons also make
wonderful earrings if you have only
two of them, or if you have two more
than you need for your dress.)

Plain buttons in novel shapes—
Can be used on plain or figured materials, in matching or contrasting colors.

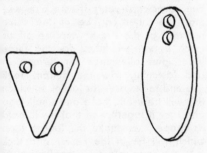

SEWING ON BUTTONS—You are
wise if you make a thread shank for
almost any button. A thread shank is
a necessity when you are sewing a button on thick material. The extra space
allowed by the shank is needed for the
overlapping of thick layers of material
where they are buttoned together.

Some buttons, of course, are made
with shanks.

**Cut-steel, mirror, rhinestone, and
other jeweled buttons—**Use these
only on plain materials and for clothes
designed for most dress-up occasions;
for example, cut-steel buttons on a
black velvet dress for late afternoon or
evening wear. When used, elaborate
buttons should be the only trimming on
the dress.

To make a thread shank, sew the
button over a pin, as shown. Use single
thread, with the knot on the underside

of the button or concealed between two layers of material. Take at least 6 or 8 stitches through the holes in the button. Remove the pin. Wind the thread around the stem of thread left beneath the button. Fasten the thread

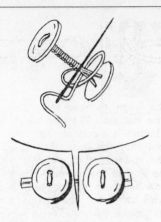

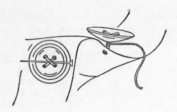

in the underside of the garment and cut (do not pull and break off).

A small button can be stitched to the underside of the garment when the large button is being sewed to the upper or right side. This serves the same purpose as the thread shank. The but-

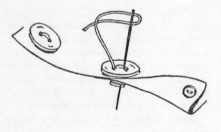

ton stay is sometimes used on women's coats; rarely on any other type of women's clothes. It is more often used on men's clothes.

You can link two buttons together to use for cuff links, or to join a neck opening, by covering the threads which join the buttons together with blanket stitching.

While the Chinese loop fastening (or frog) is not a button in the literal sense, it actually serves the function of a button, so it is included here. It is simple to make. Buy a narrow but firm braid, in cotton, silk, or rayon, depending upon the material of your dress, or ready-made covered cord. If neither of these is available, you can cover cord yourself with bias tubing. The latter can be of the same material as the dress. Measure off as much as you will need for the three loops plus allowance for turning in and fastening over the button. Tack one end to the dress or jacket on which this will be used. Make one small loop and tack it together so that it will hold its shape, then make the longer loop which will be in the center and tack it in the same place as the first. Now make the third loop on the side opposite to the first one, and tack it. Make the last loop—the one used to fasten the button—so that it extends outward enough to go over the button. Bring the end of this loop back to the original starting point, tuck it in neatly so that no raw edges show on the surface, and carefully fasten it down. Now with a thin needle and single thread, on the wrong side, take small running stitches all around the design

of the loops, to keep them down flat on the material. The side which holds the button is made in the same way except that the loop that holds the button is brought together, as shown in the illustration. You may use a long, narrow button, or even a round button. But to carry out the Chinese idea further make the vertical bar yourself, using a matchstick or other piece of wood, and covering it with fabric. If you use wood, however, you may not be able to use this frog on washable clothing.

BUTTONHOLES—There are three types of buttonholes: the bound buttonhole, the thread or worked buttonhole, and the tailored buttonhole. The type you use on your garment will depend upon its style and the fabric. In most cases you will be guided by the directions on your pattern.

Measuring buttonholes—To determine the correct size for the buttonhole, place a button on a scrap of

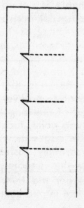

material and mark the width with pins, then practice making one or two buttonholes on this scrap material before you begin to make them in the garment itself. One word of caution: In making buttonholes, always be careful not to pull or tug the material so that the buttonholes will be stretched out of shape and spoil the appearance of your garment.

Spacing buttonholes—Your pattern will have perforations to mark the position of the buttonholes, but a pattern alteration may have thrown the original

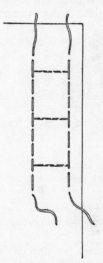

spacing out of line, so it is wise to re-mark them, making sure that the spaces between them are even. A cardboard gauge with notches, such as that shown in the illustration, will be helpful in marking the buttonholes correctly.

When you have determined the correct position, mark them with tailor's chalk or a row of long basting stitches.

Bound buttonholes—These buttonholes may be used on practically all fabrics, except those which are sheer or very light in weight. They are made on a single thickness of the material, which may or may not be reinforced.

The advantage of a bound buttonhole is that it adds an air of quality to the clothes which you sew at home. It is an indication that care was given to the dress, or the coat, or the jacket, and it adds just that difference between the outfit that is turned out in the "mass-production" factory and the one that is made just for you.

With thread—preferably of a different color, so that you can see it better —mark the position of the buttonhole on the garment. It should be the length of the diameter of the button. Baste a strip of fabric, either straight or true bias, over the outside, with the right side of the strip facing the right side of the garment. The strip should be at least ¼ inch wider than the buttonhole mark on each side. Be sure to baste through both layers of fabric.

Baste a line through from mark to mark.

Machine stitch ⅛ inch on each side of the mark and across both ends.

Cut between the two rows of stitching; then clip the corners at each end.

Cut through the strip of facing material.

Push the material through the slit, to bring it to the wrong side.

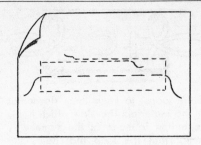

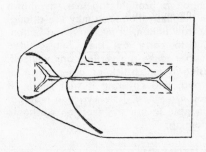

Form a little pleat at the ends on the wrong side. Press flat.

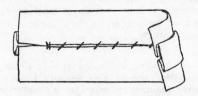

If the buttonhole is not to be faced, sew the binding flat and overcast the edges.

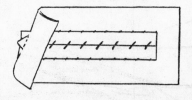

If the facing is to be applied, slash the facing under the buttonhole, clip the corners, turn in and hem the edges.

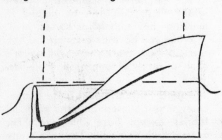

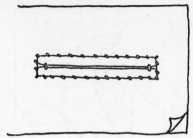

The right side of the finished bound buttonhole should look like this.

CONTRASTING   BINDING—Bound buttonholes are sometimes finished with a harmonizing or contrasting color. Bias tape is rather narrow, but folded bands of bias material can be used as shown in the two-piece bound buttonhole. To make this type of buttonhole:

Baste or mark the position of the buttonhole with chalk.

Baste two pieces of folded bias material, or material folded on the straight grain of the cloth, as shown. Have these pieces at least ½ inch longer than the marked opening. Stitch along the basted lines. Do not stitch across the ends.

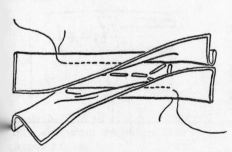

Lift the pieces and cut the buttonhole. Slit diagonally (like little arrowheads) at the corners.

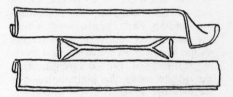

Turn the stitched pieces through the opening to the wrong side of the buttonhole.

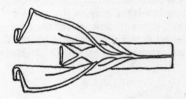

Stitch together the ends of the binding and clipped triangle at each end of the buttonhole. The folds of the binding will meet like lips at the center of the buttonhole.

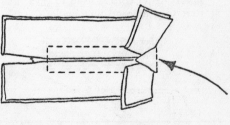

Press the finished buttonhole.

Here are a couple of hints on making good buttonholes with a contrasting binding. First, choose a material of the same or as nearly the same texture as the garment on which you are working. Then use two different-colored threads to make the buttonhole—one for basting, which is bright enough to be seen easily, and one of the same color as the binding for finishing the buttonhole.

CORDED BOUND BUTTONHOLE—
Made the same way as the buttonhole above, except that a cotton cord is inserted in each folded strip before the strips are basted and stitched in place.

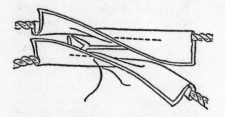

The lips of this buttonhole have a padded, rounded appearance. A corded buttonhole is generally used only on tailored woolens. Occasionally a very small cord is used to give firmness to a tailored buttonhole.

Slit opening made like bound buttonhole—Two bound buttonholes, one

placed about 1 inch above the other, can be used as an opening through which to run scarf ends or a tie.

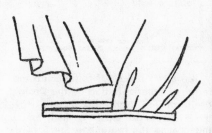

Thread buttonhole—A thread buttonhole is also called a worked buttonhole. Any worked buttonhole is harder to make than a bound buttonhole, but there are some garments for which it is more suitable than a bound buttonhole. It is the correct finish for boys' and men's clothes and for a woman's strictly tailored suit. Small and dainty thread buttonholes are also used on children's dresses and on blouses.

Mark each buttonhole, using pattern markings or gauge. Baste the layers of material together and baste around the buttonhole before you cut. If the material has a tendency to ravel, you can run a single row of machine stitch-

of the buttonhole to whatever depth seems desirable and the thread brought under the point of the needle as shown. Either mercerized cotton or buttonhole twist may be used.

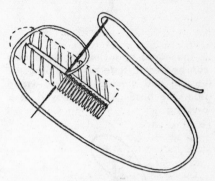

Buttonhole stitches are taken close together, so that you cannot see the fabric showing between the stitches, but they do not overlap. The depth, or bite, of the stitches is determined by the size of the buttonhole and the type of fabric used. Naturally, a large buttonhole on a heavy fabric will have stitches which go deeper into the material than those in a tiny buttonhole on a lightweight fabric.

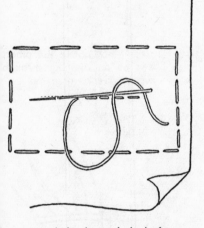

ng around the buttonhole before you cut the opening. The stitching must be done so that it will be very close to the cut.

After you have marked the buttonhole, basted around the place to be cut, and made the cut, your next step is to overcast the cut edges so they will not ravel. Overcasting also provides "body" for your buttonhole stitch.

The buttonhole stitch resembles the blanket stitch, but differs in that it has an extra ridge of thread called a purl. The needle is inserted under the edge

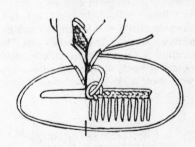

The ends of the buttonhole, which bear the greater strain, should be finished with a group of stitches worked fan-shape. Make a bar tack of blanket stitching at the opposite ends.

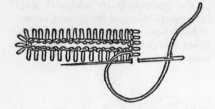

The edges of a finished buttonhole can be basted together with diagonal basting and pressed from the wrong side. The bastings are removed after pressing.

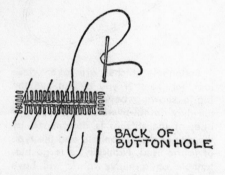

BACK OF BUTTON HOLE

Tailored buttonhole—A tailored buttonhole is often seen on men's suits and on coats of heavy material for men and women. It differs from an ordinary worked buttonhole in one way. Before the tailored buttonhole is cut, a hole is punched at the end which will get the greater strain. The hole can be punched with a special stiletto, with a crochet hook, knitting needle—anything that is sharp and round.

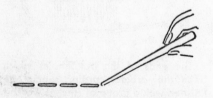

Most buttonholes will be horizontal, such as that shown in the illustration,

but on blouses, children's clothes, as well as in any place where pattern

directions call for them, you can make vertical buttonholes. Vertical buttonholes have a bar tack at each end.

A strand of thread or buttonhole twist is usually tacked around a vertical buttonhole opening and stitches are worked over it.

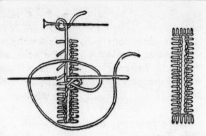

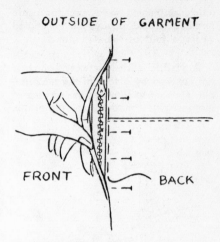

OUTSIDE OF GARMENT

FRONT   BACK

SLIDE FASTENERS—Follow the specific directions given with your slide fastener or in your pattern direction sheet. Buy the size and type of slide fastener suggested for your pattern. Skirt fasteners are open at one end. Dress slide fasteners are closed at the top and the bottom. Slide fasteners for jackets can be separated at the bottom. Slide fas-

very close to the metal edge of the fastener. If you don't have a cording foot, use your regular machine presser foot, with one "prong" of the "fork" sliding on the ridge of the metal.

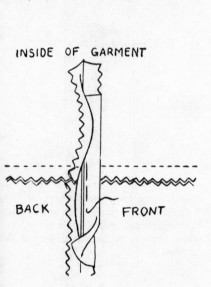

INSIDE OF GARMENT

BACK   FRONT

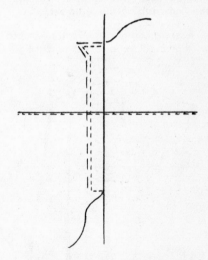

eners should always be closed when they are stitched in place. If you have a cording foot—a presser foot with one "prong" of the "fork" removed—use that to stitch in your slide fastener, for your machine needle can then run

If your side opening for a slide fastener comes at a place where the seam is narrow, you will have to add a bias facing to the edge of the seam and turn it under, as shown, before you baste your slide fastener in place for machine stitching. A fastener for a side opening should always be concealed under a fold of the material.

A visible slide fastener, which is not covered by a fold of the material, but is meant to show on the surface of the garment, is made of colored plastic

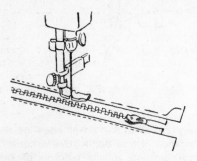

or metal. Since it is used for decoration as well as for closing an opening, you may buy one to match or contrast with the material of the garment.

A separating slide fastener, such as that used for a jacket or cardigan

sweater, may be concealed by a fold of the material or it may be visible. Follow the directions with the pattern or slide fastener. Always turn the ends of the slide fastener tape to the wrong side of the garment and tack firmly into place. Never trim off those ends.

Slide fastener at the neck—If the slide fastener is inserted in a faced neck opening, the neckline is first finished according to pattern directions and the fastener is stitched in like this.

Join the front and the back neck facings at the shoulder seam. Press open the seam. Baste the facing to the neck and to the center front or the back, wherever the slit opening is to be.

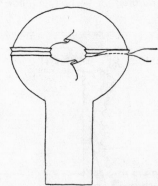

Stitch around the place to be opened in a long, very narrow V. This V should be about ½ inch wide at the top and taper down to a point, just wide enough to be slit open, at the bottom.

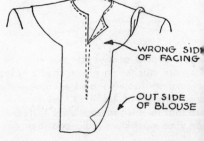

WRONG SIDE OF FACING

OUTSIDE OF BLOUSE

Slash between the stitching—that is, down the center of the V.

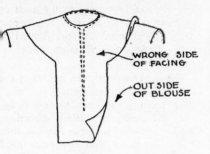

WRONG SIDE OF FACING

OUTSIDE OF BLOUSE

Clip the neck seam so that it will lie flat when the facing is turned. Turn the facing. Baste flat.

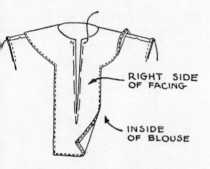

RIGHT SIDE OF FACING

INSIDE OF BLOUSE

Turn the raw edges of the facing and edge stitch. Press the facing.

Pin the closed slide fastener in the faced neck opening from the right side. The edges of the opening should meet to conceal the fastener. Turn under the

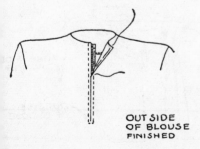

OUTSIDE OF BLOUSE FINISHED

edges of the fastener tape at the top and baste the fastener in place, then remove the pins and stitch the fastener, using a cording foot if you have one.

PLACKETS—Dress placket, snapped —Prepare two bias strips 1 ¼ inches wide and 1 inch longer than the dress opening. Working from the right side, place one strip along the front edge of the dress opening, right sides facing, and stitch along the seam allowance indicated. Turn to the inside. Press, then turn the raw edge under ¼ inch and catch stitch in place.

Place the second strip right side down about ⅛ inch in from the opposite edge of the placket and stitch, allowing ¼ inch seam allowance. Turn to the inside and press. Crease facing in half, turn under the raw edge, and catch stitch in place.

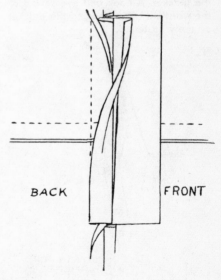

BACK   FRONT

Turn under the raw edges of the bias strips and whip them together at each end of the placket, keeping them flat.

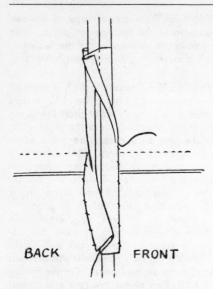

BACK   FRONT

Sew snaps at equal distances apart, placing the ball sections on the front of the placket. A hook and eye sewed at the waistline will help keep the placket securely fastened.

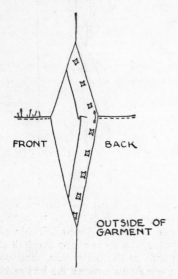

FRONT   BACK

OUTSIDE OF GARMENT

Skirt placket—This is made like the dress placket, except that bias and

straight facings are stitched in place before the belt or the waistband is

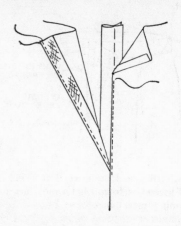

stitched to the skirt. The skirt band and the top of the facings are caught in one seam. After the waistband is folded

and stitched as shown, the back of the belt should first be stitched to the skirt, with the seam on the right side. Then

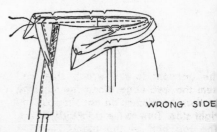

WRONG SIDE

the second row of stitching can be edge stitched on the right side of the skirt.

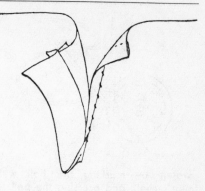

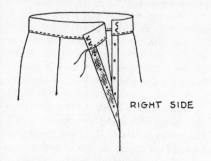

RIGHT SIDE

Placket in a slash—A placket opening must sometimes be made at the neck or in some other place where there is no seam opening. To make this type of placket opening, slash the opening as deep as you need to have it. Then cut a straight strip of matching material twice as long as the slashed opening and about 2 inches wide. Stitch one edge of this strip to the outside of the slash, with the right sides of the material together. The machine stitching should be about ¼ inch from the edge of the slash and should taper to a point at the end of the slash. Turn

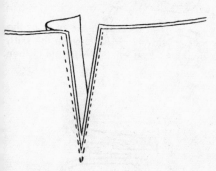

the garment to the wrong side and hem the free edge along the stitching so that the stitches do not show on the right side. Turn to the right side. Press. The top half of the placket will lie

flat against the garment; the lower half of the placket will extend so that snaps can be added.

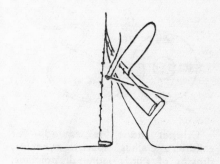

OTHER FASTENINGS—Snaps, hooks and eyes, and thread loops are used by all home sewers. They are listed here as tailoring tricks because they are among the other tiny details of fine finish which a good home sewer, like a tailor, never neglects, because she knows they are important for the perfection of her masterpiece.

Snaps—The section with the socket corresponds to a button as to position. It is usually sewed on the left side of a garment. The section with the ball corresponds to the buttonhole, and goes on the right side. Place the ball section of the snap in position and sew it in place. You can place the socket ac-

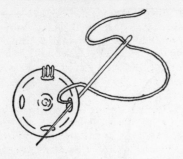

curately by marking the ball with tailor's chalk and pressing the ball to the facing piece of the material. The chalk will mark the correct position for the socket portion of the snap.

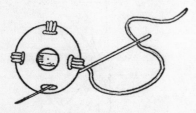

Gripper snaps (not sewed)—For children's clothes, sportswear, shirts, dresses of sturdy material, pajamas, slip covers, dressing-table skirts, and other clothing or house furnishings that need strong fastening, there are snaps which are attached with a few quick strokes of a hammer. These are bought in kits containing five or more snaps, depending on their size, and include a metal bracket, socket, and stud tools. Directions on the kit tell you how you can easily attach the snaps to the garment or household article. Refill kits of the gripper snaps are available. They are strong, rustproof, and can be washed and dry-cleaned.

Velcro tape closure—This looks like two pieces of velvet ribbon with the pile (the nap) sides laid face to face. However, the pile is different

on each tape; one is rather flat and the other is fuzzy with little burrs on it. Their threads interlock when they are pressed together by your fingers to form a fastening, and all you need to do to open it is to pull the two tapes apart gently, with the same motion as that of peeling a banana. Velcro (a trade name) is made of nylon and is bought in a package or by the yard. It comes in many colors and in five widths—from 5/8 of an inch to 2 inches. The directions that come with it tell you how to sew it flat on the garment. This tape should not be used on any sheer fabric and cannot take the place of all hooks, snaps, or slide fasteners. However, it has a useful place on the fronts of sports jackets, on the beltlines of wrap-around skirts, and on maternity dresses, where it allows for easy adjustment of the waistline. It is also an aid in making such items as dressing-table skirts and slip covers.

Hooks and eyes—The hook corresponds to the buttonhole in position

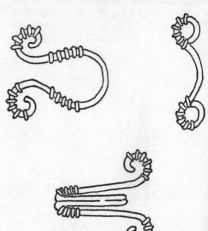

and the eye to the button. Sew them as shown. It is important to fasten the hook under the curved section, to hold this firmly in place. Use single thread knotted at one end and start on the wrong side of the material. Fasten the thread with three small stitches.

Thread loop for eyelet, for button, for belt carriers—Make an eyelet with four to six single threads, blanket stitched together. The eye of the needle

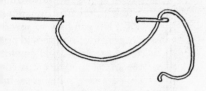

is the best part to use when making the blanket stitch. See illustrations. If you

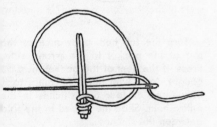

know how to crochet, you may prefer

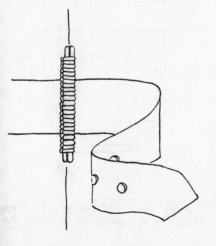

to crochet the two threads into a chain stitch for a stronger loop. Leave a thread at each end of the loop long enough to thread into a needle for tacking the loop in place. This is also known as the **bar tack.**

Narrow fabric belt with fabric-covered buckle—The cost of having this done by a commercial concern is minimal, but you may prefer to make the belt yourself. In either case it is advisable to have the buckle covered by a professional. If you plan to launder the dress you are making, you would be wise not to use a covered buckle, since the frame used by most manufacturers is seldom guaranteed to be rustproof.

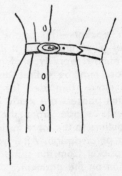

Material for the belt should be cut on the straight of the goods. It should be twice as wide as the finished belt and have sufficient allowance for lapping over. If it is not to be lined, the belt should be stitched on three sides with a ¼ inch seam, leaving one end open, then turned and pressed before the raw edges of the open end are turned in and whipped.

If the belt needs stiffening, cut a strip of belt interlining ½ inch narrower than the belt strip. Lay in position on the wrong side ¼ inch from one edge of the belt strip and fold down the seam allowance. Baste, then fold the belt in half over the interlining. Turn down the raw edge and baste the two edges of the belt together. Machine stitch the belt on the right side, keeping as close as possible to the edge of the belt and making certain that the stitching catches the interlining.

POCKETS—Pockets can be both useful and ornamental. Here are several types of pockets, which begin with a simple-to-make pocket and become progressively more difficult. These are pockets which may well be used in changing the appearance of the original pattern style. Your pattern direction sheet will describe a pocket planned for the outfit, and you should follow the general directions for making it.

Patch pocket—This is the easiest pocket of all to make, yet it is adaptable to almost every type of garment. Its purpose may be entirely utilitarian but it is more often used for decoration. Patch pockets are made in every conceivable shape from the simple square outline to the more intricate detail of a petal design. After you have cut the pocket from the pattern, mark its position on the garment.

Turn under the top edge of the pocket ¼ inch. Edge stitch by machine.

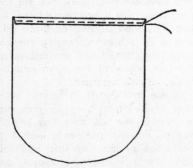

Turn under the side seams of the pocket ¼ inch and baste close to the folded edge, so that a curved pocket will round out smoothly and evenly.

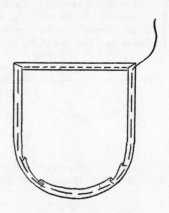

Turn the full hem allowance at the top of the pocket to the wrong side. Press. If the hem of the pocket must be caught down with hand stitching, take only three or four tiny stitches in the entire hem. Slide the thread in the fold between the stitches.

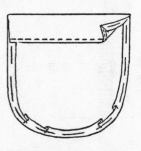

Edge stitch the side edges of the pocket to the dress.

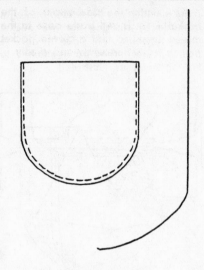

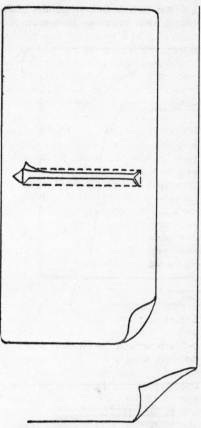

Slot pocket—Made exactly like a bound buttonhole. This pocket is often used as a handkerchief pocket on a woolen dress.

Mark the place where the pocket is to go and baste the fabric over the mark, right sides together. The size of

Pull the pocket through the slit to the wrong side. Stitch across the ends of little clipped V's.

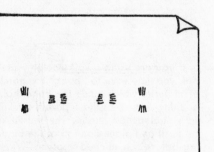

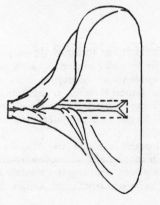

the pocket opening is determined by the length of the stitched oblong.

Stitch before cutting, then cut and slash the corners, as shown.

Seam the top and the bottom of the pocket strip together as shown.

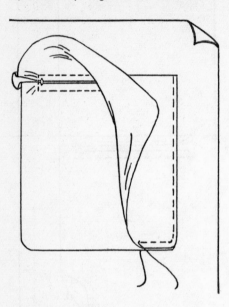

Stitch around the finished pocket on the right side.

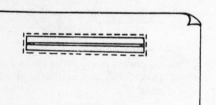

Slot pocket for tailored garments —Pockets in bulky materials, such as heavy woolens or corduroy, do not make up smoothly when a self-fabric pocket lining is used. For these materials it is better to use lighter material for a lining.

The pocket is made as described above up to the point where the bound buttonhole-type opening is completed. Then a separate pocket of muslin or some similar firm, lightweight material is made by stitching the two pocket pieces together, right sides facing. The pocket is not turned but is stitched to the opening, as illustrated.

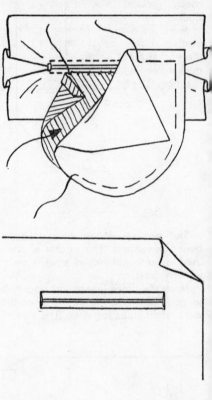

If you are using a soft woolen material, you may want to "back" the patch of material which binds the buttonhole opening as well as the separate pocket with unbleached muslin. The muslin is cut to fit and placed on top of the binding before it is stitched in place. When the pocket itself is made, the muslin is placed on top of the wrong side of the pocket, then stitched in place when the pocket pieces are stitched. The purpose of the backing is to keep the pocket from sagging or stretching out of shape. The illustration shows the finished pocket opening from the right side.

Welt pocket—The welt pocket is used on tailored garments such as coats, jackets, woolen skirts, and slacks.

Mark the pocket opening with long basting stitches but do not cut it. Cut the pocket piece 1 inch wider than the pocket opening and twice the depth of the pocket, plus 1 inch for seam al-

ment, matching the two lines carefully. Baste the markings together, then stitch ¼ inch on each side of the basting and across the ends. Slash to within

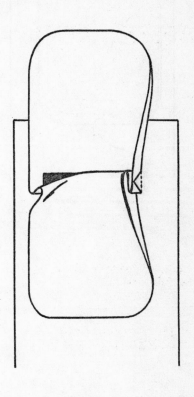

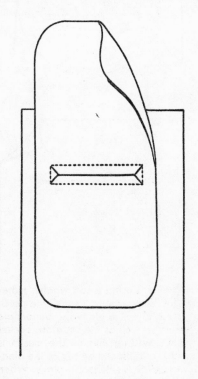

½ inch of the end, then diagonally to the corners.

Pull the pocket through to the wrong side and make the welt by folding the lower section of the pocket so that it exactly meets the pocket opening. Stitch the welt in place, double stitching across each end for added strength.

Fold down the upper part of the pocket and stitch the pocket together. Overcast all raw edges.

lowance. With tailor's chalk draw a line across the pocket piece 1 inch above the center. Place the piece right side down on the right side of the gar-

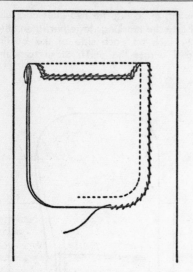

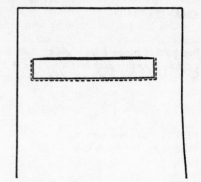

The illustration shows the finished pocket from the right side.

CHAPTER 11

How to Be Your Own Stylist

KEEPING in step with style can be an adventure. But there is a difference between being fashionably dressed and being a slave to fashion. The style-conscious woman does not accept every fashion fad *in toto*, whether it is becoming or not. She learns where to look for changing style trends and then adapts them to best advantage to her own figure. Thus she becomes her own stylist and is able to give her clothes that subtle "something different" which is so important in achieving a distinctive appearance.

The woman who makes her own clothes has several advantages over the woman who must buy the style nearest to her requirements and then pay to have it altered, or who must pay the high cost of having a couturier design her wardrobe. Not only can she wear clothes which would be far beyond what she could afford to buy, but she has the added satisfaction of knowing that they are designed for her figure alone, not for a general category of women's figures.

A woman who decides to be her own stylist must do three things: she must learn what style notes to look for and where they first appear; how to adapt fashions to suit her own figure; and how to use a basic pattern. Needless to say the fashionable woman is also one whose clothes fit the occasions for which she wears them. In the following chapter you will learn what points to consider in planning your wardrobe to suit your mode of life. So for the present we need consider only the factors we have just mentioned.

New fashion notes appear in various places. The shoulder line is probably one of the first. For several years shoulder lines were square and well padded. This style was gradually replaced by a softer, rounded shoulder which emphasized the natural shoulder line. Occasionally you will find a fashion trend toward sloping lines, and at one time gathers and fullness at the shoulder were in vogue.

Sleeve styles change, too, though perhaps not so radically as shoulder lines. Certain sleeves, such as the long, fitted sleeve, can usually be found in any season, but others, such as the dolman, the puff, the bell sleeve, or the bracelet or three-quarter length, may be popular for only a season or two. Watch for new sleeve styles.

Changes in skirt styles are always a fashion note. They range from slim, straight skirts to draped fullness concentrated at the front or the back, or soft flares, peplums, and flounces. They may be pleated or gored, and may in some seasons be quite plain.

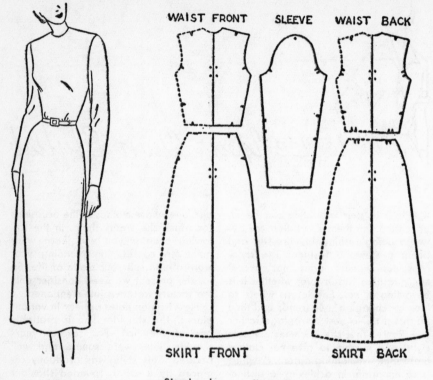

WAIST FRONT   SLEEVE   WAIST BACK

SKIRT FRONT   SKIRT BACK

Simple dress pattern

Necklines, too, will change from high and rounded to deep plunging V's, but these are fashions which the wise home sewer is especially cautious about adopting. Surprisingly few women, for instance, find a square neckline becoming.

Although the natural waistline has proved to be the most popular throughout the years, an occasional fashion trend accents the high, pinched waistline or the other extreme of the long torso with the waistline encircling the hips.

All of these are separate fashion notes which go to make up the general silhouette of a new style. You will seldom see them one at a time, but rather in combination. For example, a rounded shoulder line introduced one season may be featured again the following season, but the sleeve style may have been changed and the skirt fullness moved from the front to the back.

Any fashion-conscious woman knows where to look for new styles in clothes. They first appear, of course, in fashion magazines, then in shop windows, newspaper advertisements, and so on. Even women's magazines can be a gauge for fashion, for they are quick to adopt the latest style in their illustrations as well as on their fashion pages. Motion pictures also play a part in set-

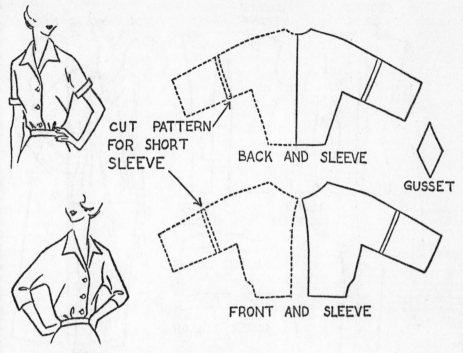

CUT PATTERN FOR SHORT SLEEVE

BACK AND SLEEVE

GUSSET

FRONT AND SLEEVE

Simple waist pattern

ting styles, though many of the styles shown are too extreme for everyday wear.

The easiest way to begin your adventure in styling is to clip pictures of styles that appeal to you—a dress, a sleeve, a neckline, or even a cuff. Collect these pictures in an envelope and then, before you actually adopt them, study them in relation to how they will look on you.

In Chapter 2 we discussed the problems of choosing the right pattern for your figure. In learning to style your own clothes you must remember these same points and adopt only those features which are becoming. For example, if the current fashion is for a square padded shoulder line but you happen to have naturally square shoulders, padding is not for you; it will only exaggerate the shoulder line all out of proportion to the dress. If the deep plunging neckline is in vogue but you have a long neck, then it would be better for you to modify the neckline to becoming proportions or to concentrate on fashion notes which accent the skirt or the sleeve. When you become your own stylist, you are able to use only the fashion notes which enhance your appearance.

All of these things apply to you, whether you are sixteen or sixty. The mature woman has just as much right— indeed it is almost her duty—to be as fashionably dressed as a younger woman. And gone are the days when a certain number of years meant she must automatically adopt lavender-sprigged designs. Today her wardrobe

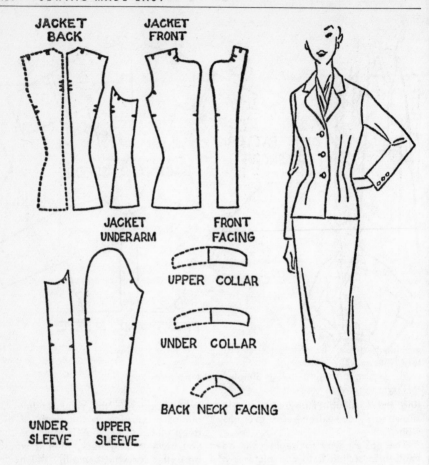

JACKET BACK

JACKET FRONT

JACKET UNDERARM

FRONT FACING

UPPER COLLAR

UNDER COLLAR

BACK NECK FACING

UNDER SLEEVE

UPPER SLEEVE

Jacket pattern

problems are basically the same as the younger woman's: suitability for the occasion and becomingness to face, figure, and coloring.

As we have already pointed out, to be your own stylist it is essential to learn how to adapt a basic pattern. For best results we suggest that you get three basic patterns to work with:

1. A simple dress pattern consisting of a waist, a skirt, and a long, fitted sleeve.

2. A waist pattern with a dolman and a cap sleeve.

3. A jacket pattern for a suit or a two-piece dress.

When you have fitted these paper patterns to yourself and made any required alterations, your next step is to cut a pattern of muslin or some similar cotton fabric. It will probably prove well worth your while to cut two muslin patterns in each style—one consisting of whole pattern pieces, just as when

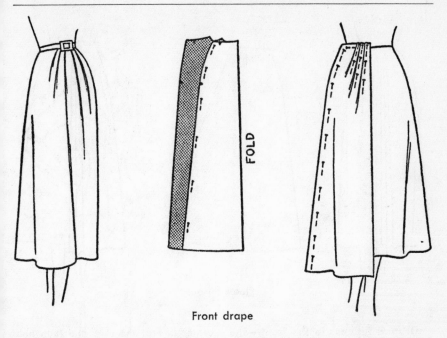

FOLD

Front drape

making a dress, the other in half-pattern pieces. The former is easier to work with in adapting and visualizing the styles you wish to adopt. The latter is easier to work with in the cutting process. Don't forget to include markings for the darts and notches. Label each piece of pattern so you will know what it is. After you have fitted the pattern to your figure, pin the pieces of each pattern together with a safety pin. Or put the pieces of each pattern into a large envelope and mark it for identification. When this is done you will have made a workmanlike start toward becoming your own stylist.

One of the major pattern companies now makes a basic dress pattern, in misses and junior sizes, of viscose and acetate (not paper) so that you can pin, baste, and try it on before you cut into your fabric. Alterations can be stitched in place on this basic pattern, and it can be used over and over again. Of course, the cost is higher

than for the usual paper pattern, but it is worth it if you want well-fitted dresses with your own original touches.

Adapting basic patterns—If you can draw at all, make a rough sketch to help you in visualizing the complete costume you want to make. But for the most part you will be able to achieve the desired results by following the pattern adaptations described below. In doing so, however, remember to do your experimenting with the pattern before you cut your material—that is the reason for using a muslin pattern.

SKIRTS—Too often the skirt is neglected while all the interesting detail is concentrated on the blouse or the sleeve. Proper attention to the skirt of a dress often turns an otherwise ordinary style into a distinctive costume. Separate skirts which are worn with blouses as cocktail and evening dresses are especially adaptable to individual treatment.

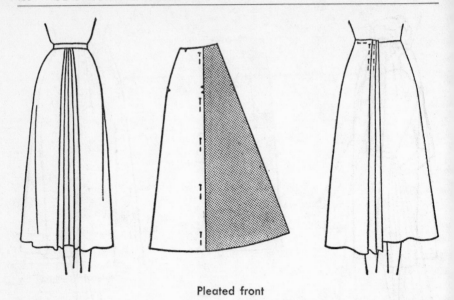

Pleated front

Draped fullness in the front—The back of the skirt is cut from the basic skirt pattern. Adjust the muslin front skirt pattern to include the allowance for the tucked front by pinning an additional width of paper to the side. Hold the extended pattern in place and pin the tucks in place as far as the center front. Then remove the pattern, mark the position of the tucks, and remove the pins. Then, using the altered pattern as a guide, cut the front in one piece with no center seam.

Sew up the side seams of the skirt. Leave the center front plain for about 3 or 4 inches across. Then pin the tucks on each side, and baste and stitch at the waistline. The tucks are more attractive if they are not pressed flat.

Pleated fullness at the front—The back of the skirt is cut from the basic pattern. The front, however, requires additional width for making the pleats. Pin a piece of tissue paper along the center line of the skirt and then hold the pattern in place at the waistline. Fold the pleats toward the center—three on each side of the center line will usually give a becoming fullness—beginning at a point 2 or 3 inches from the center front and making folds in the muslin pattern as well as in the paper extension. Pin the pleats in place as far as the center front, then remove the pattern and cut the new center front line in the paper extension. Unpin the pleats after marking their position, and place the pattern extension on a fold of the material. Cut the insert for the pleats in one piece. Then cut the half pattern of muslin from single thicknesses of the fabric to make the side pieces of the skirt.

Stitch the insert to the skirt side pieces, then stitch the skirt front to the skirt back. Try on the skirt and pin the pleats in place as you did on the pattern. Remove the skirt and baste the pleats into position. Stitch down each

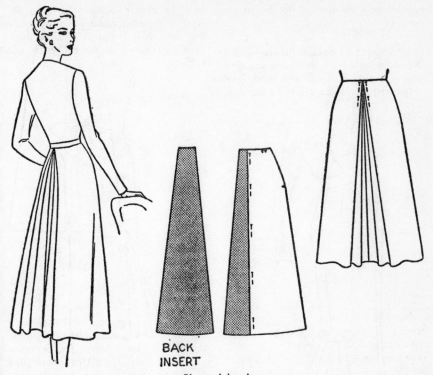

BACK
INSERT

Pleated back

pleat for 3 or 4 inches, and leave enough thread to pull through to the wrong side and tie. Stitch across the pleats at the top. This is a separate stitching from the one which will later join the waist to the skirt. Depending upon the effect you want to achieve and the texture of the material, the pleats may be pressed the full length of the skirt or left unpressed to fall into folds.

Pleated fullness at the back—The front of the skirt is cut from the basic pattern. The back of the skirt will hang and fit better if it is cut in three pieces —two wider ones for each side of the back and one narrower one for the center piece from which to form the pleats.

Using the basic half-skirt pattern as a guide, pin a paper extension to the center back line, as shown in the illustration. Make pleats in the paper extension until you have the desired fullness. (Note that the muslin center back will be on top of the last fold of fullness.) Then cut out the skirt back pieces from the material, placing the paper insert on a fold, the side gores on a single thickness.

Stitch the skirt back pieces together, then pin and baste the folds into position, as shown in the illustration. When you are satisfied that the fullness is evenly adjusted and hangs well, stitch 3 or 4 inches down the sides of the pleats to hold them in position, then across the skirt back, before stitching to the waistline. This type of pleated fullness may be pressed flat or left unpressed.

Variations of back fullness—Using the same style note as above you may vary the way in which the back inset is finished off. If you are tall enough or

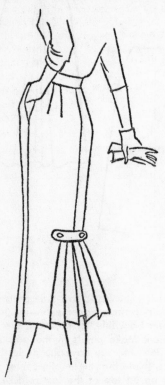

face in one direction. To give the inset a smooth-looking finish, cover the seam with a flap of double thickness and put a button at each end of the flap.

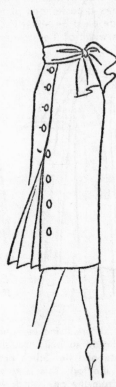

slender enough to wear this well, and if you are one of those young-at-heart people who like an extra fillip in your clothes, make a pleated inset at the bottom of the skirt, starting it about 6 to 8 inches above the knees. Do not cut this inset from a bias material. It is very easy to cut an extra straight piece of fabric and make either four or six pleats. Place two pleats (for a total of four) or three pleats (for a total of six) on each side, facing them toward the center back, so that all pleats do not

A more sophisticated way of finishing the back of the skirt is to pleat the back insert and then sew buttonholes all the way down the left side, with buttons to correspond down the right side. Close the top three or four buttons, to give a flatter line. The insert may be made of the same material as the dress or it may be in a contrasting color or design.

Pleated skirt—Whether you want your skirt to be pleated only in the front or in both the back and the front, the method of adapting the basic pattern is the same. Working with the skirt half pattern, pin a paper extension to the center front line, as explained on page 166. Then fold the skirt front into box and side pleats. The illustration here shows a center box pleat with a single side pleat on either side. In figuring the width of the extension, work

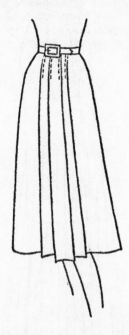

form of flared skirt is the simple circular flare. In some instances it may prove practical to buy a separate flared skirt pattern, but your basic skirt pattern can be altered to make a flared skirt. If you plan to do this, cut a paper pattern, for in this case paper will be easier to work with than muslin.

Lay the skirt pattern flat on the table and slash it as indicated in the illustration. Then spread the slashes until you feel there is enough fullness. Note that the fullness is inserted below the hip line. Slip a piece of paper beneath the basic pattern and pin the slashed pieces to it, so that the altered pattern will be a solid piece from which to cut.

out the complete insert in paper, then fold the paper insert in half and cut the insert on a fold of the material. The side pieces of the skirt are cut on a single thickness.

Stitch the insert to the side gores of the skirt. Stitch the skirt front to the skirt back and try on the skirt. Pin and baste the pleats in place, then remove the skirt and proceed to finish laying the pleats. In Chapter 8 you will find detailed information on how to finish your pleated skirt.

Flared skirt—Flares are sometimes set into skirts, but the most popular

Make the alteration in the skirt back in the same way, matching the fullness; then cut both of the altered pattern pieces on a fold of the material. If the pattern has been properly altered, the flare will fall along the bias grain of the fabric. For additional information on making flared skirts, see Chapter 9.

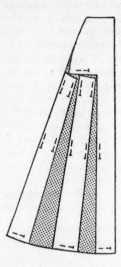

Yoke combined with pleats—If you want to retain the flat hip line yet have a pleated skirt, it can be accomplished with a yoke. The depth of the yoke should be in proportion to your

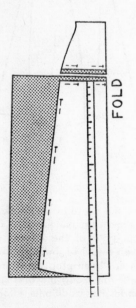

height, and it is best to keep the yoke line a little high rather than to bring it down too low. Hold the basic skirt pattern up to you. Decide where the yoke is to end and put a mark there. Then with a tape measure or ruler, from the bottom of the pattern up, measure the same distance all around. Cut the front and the back yokes from a piece of paper, using the marked basic pattern for guidance. Allow 1 inch at the bottom of the yoke for the seam.

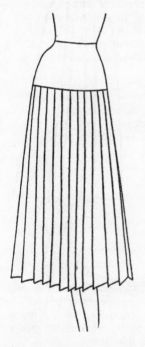

To make the pleated section of the skirt, you will work with the lower section of the skirt pattern—the part below the line marking the yoke line. Place the pattern on a fold of the material just as you would do if you were cutting the complete skirt pattern. Then extend the width of the skirt at the side, as shown in the illustration. Be careful not to change the general line of the pattern piece. Twice the width of the pattern piece is usually needed for making the pleats.

If the skirt is to be pleated in the back as well as the front—and this is usually the case—make the same alteration in the skirt back. Measure and pin the knife pleats in place as described in Chapter 7. Then baste the pleated section to the skirt yoke and edge stitch the yoke to the lower section.

Curved or diagonal yoke—This type of yoke is best used only on the front of the skirt. To make the necessary alterations in the skirt front, use the full-width muslin pattern as a guide.

First mark off the line which the yoke is to follow. Cut a paper pattern of this yoke, adding an extra inch for seam allowance.

The next step is to make a full-width paper pattern of the lower skirt section —the part below the line marking the yoke. Lay this paper pattern on a larger sheet of paper and slash, as shown in the illustration. Pin the separate pieces in place on the large sheet of paper so that the altered pattern will be a solid piece from which to cut. Note that the first slash is made a few inches beyond the center front and that the slashes are made at equal intervals. Add an extra inch for seam allowance at the top of this skirt section and don't forget to follow the curved yoke line in making the extension. In cutting your material, if you find that you have to piece it a little at the side, it can be done so that the seam will fall under a pleat.

Stitch the side seams of the skirt, then pin and baste the pleats in place and finish the skirt as described in Chapter 8.

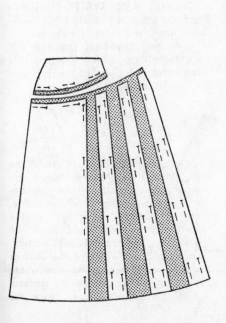

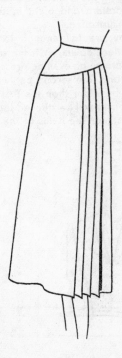

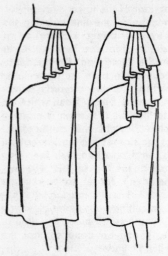

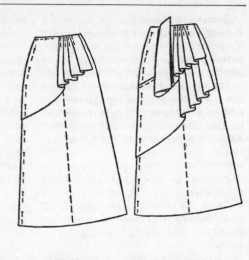

Side-draped peplum—A soft, draped peplum will often add an interesting touch to an otherwise simple skirt. The side-draped peplum is worn only across the front of the skirt. Cut a paper pattern and pleat it, as shown in the illustration.

If you are tall enough to wear a double-tier peplum, or if the peplum is to be worn on an evening dress, make a second one. The second peplum will, of course, be wider than the first and the two peplums will be stitched together at the waistline. The hems of the peplums can be rolled or finished with flat ribbon binding. In Chapter 22 you will find additional information on making peplums.

When you are satisfied with the drape of the peplum, cut the material and pin and baste the folds in place.

NECKLINES AND WAIST YOKES—The focal point of a dress is the neckline, since it is a frame for the face. It is important, therefore, that the line be a flattering one, and any time and effort spent in finding just the right one for you is seldom wasted.

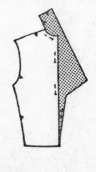

Draped V neckline—If you like a V neckline and want to use a draped V, it can be done with your basic blouse pattern, and is usually more becoming than the plain V neckline.

To make the necessary alteration, use a paper pattern of the blouse front and add a paper extension, as shown in the illustration. The other blouse measurements will remain the same.

Cut the blouse in two separate pieces. The notched line of the pattern extension indicates the center seam of the blouse.

Seam the ends of the back facing (the short projection above the neckline) together. Slip the piece over your head and turn in the facing, pinning it in place temporarily. Arrange the drape of the neckline by making soft pleats meeting at the center front. Pin each pleat separately. When you have arranged the material to fall in soft, flattering folds, tack the pleats down carefully and then unpin the turned-in facing. Remove the blouse front and baste the center front and the shoulder seams. Stitch these seams, then baste and stitch the back facing to the back neckline. Turn in the facing and slip stitch.

Square neckline with collar—If you look well in a simple square neck-line, this variation may be desirable.

The blouse is cut from the basic pattern, the only alteration being in the neckline. Try on the whole muslin blouse pattern and have someone help you mark the new neckline with colored chalk. When you have the proper proportions, remove the muslin pattern and mark the same line on the blouse half, then cut out on a fold of the material. This will insure your getting both sides of the neck alike. The collar is made from a bias fold of material. Fold the bias band in half lengthwise and baste the edges. Pin the band around the cutout neckline, pleating it at the corners, as shown in the illustration. Baste bias binding around the edge of the neck and stitch, then turn the binding to the inside of the neckline and slip stitch.

Round yoke for blouse—The basic dolman and cap sleeve pattern is suggested for use in making this style, since the round yoke lends itself most gracefully to the drop shoulder. However, a blouse with a set-in sleeve may also have a yoke inserted.

This is a simple pattern adaptation. As in the case of the square neckline, hold the muslin pattern up to yourself and mark off (or, better still, have

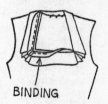

BINDING

COLLAR

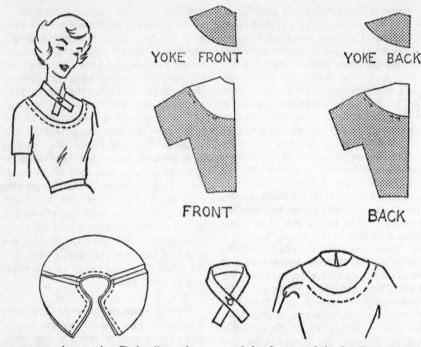

YOKE FRONT   YOKE BACK

FRONT   BACK

someone else mark off) the line where you want to set in the yoke. It is a better style to extend the yoke around the back, too, although some people prefer to insert it only in the front.

When you have decided what the shape and the depth of the yoke should be, cut a paper pattern for half of the front yoke. Do the same for the back yoke, add 1 inch for seam allowance, then lay both the front and the back yokes on a fold of the material for cutting. This is done so that both sides of the yoke will be alike. In some cases it may be desirable to cut the yoke on a double fold of material so that the second thickness of material can serve as a facing for the neck as well.

The pattern for the lower section of the blouse is altered in the same way, a paper pattern being cut for that part below the yoke line plus 1 additional inch at the top for seam allowance

and the front and the back pieces laid on a fold of the material for cutting.

Join the yoke at the shoulder seams. Do the same on the lining, then baste and stitch both together at the neckline; turn to right side and press. Stitch bias facing of fabric around the top of the lower blouse section; turn it in and baste it to the raw edge. Join the yoke to the lower section and baste through all thicknesses of material. Machine stitch. If you have pinking shears, trim the raw edges. Otherwise leave the raw edges so that there will be no bulky appearance where the yoke is joined to the waist.

You will find additional information on necklines and yokes in Chapter 9.

SLEEVES—By making a change or two in your basic long-sleeved pattern you can cut any type of set-in sleeve. The important factor here is to get the

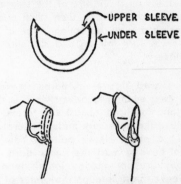

UPPER SLEEVE
UNDER SLEEVE

proper armhole fit by following the basic pattern closely at the top. The remaining portion of the sleeve may be finished in any way you prefer.

Ruffled sleeve—This can be made with one or two ruffles. If you use two, the bottom ruffle should be cut a little longer and wider.

Three-quarter draped sleeve—Cut the sleeve to whatever length you desire and wider than the original pattern at the bottom.

Make a row of running stitches up the center of the sleeve four inches,

Roll the hems of the ruffles. Baste them together at the top and sew into the armhole, leaving the underarm free, as shown in the illustration. Cut a bias facing about 1 ½ inches wide. Sew this facing to the under portion of the armhole and turn to the inside. Turn up a ¼-inch hem, then slip stitch the facing into place.

and then another row ¼ inch on each side of this center row. Pull the threads of the three rows of stitches into gathers until it measures about 2 ½ inches. Fasten the threads. Hand stitch a piece of seam binding over the

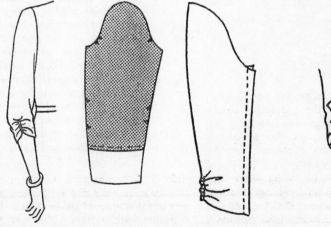

gathers on the inside of the sleeve to hold them in place, then stitch a bias facing around the bottom edge of the sleeve. Turn this up and slip stitch in place.

Flared sleeve—A flared sleeve in a long or three-quarter style is a dramatic touch to almost any dress. To make the necessary pattern alteration, cut a paper sleeve pattern. You will not have to mark the sleeve darts, for they are not needed in this type of sleeve. Slash through the center of the pattern to a point about 6 inches from the top. To add the desired width for the flare, slip another piece of paper under the pattern and spread the slash, pinning the pieces together, as shown in the illustration. Add a little at the sides for extra fullness.

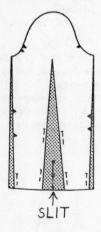

SLIT

When this alteration has been made, measure the paper pattern to your arm and determine how long you want the sleeve to be. Cut off at this point, leaving an allowance for the hem.

Finish the hem by facing with a bias binding, turning up, and slip stitching. An effective finish can also be obtained by addition of a turned-back cuff.

Another way of finishing this type of sleeve is to make the flare a slight one, slit it at the bottom, and finish it with a fabric or braid facing mitered at the corners, as shown in the illustration.

Long, full sleeve—Cut a basic sleeve pattern from a piece of paper and slit it all the way through the

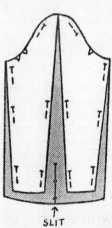

SLIT

center vertically. The additional width is at the bottom with 2 extra inches

llowed in the pattern. Cut a straight
and for the cuff.

If the sleeve is to be three-quarter
length or shorter, do not cut it off
without first trying the paper pattern
on your arm and marking off the

length. Remember to leave an additional 2 inches at the bottom so you
can get a full puff when the sleeve is
gathered into the cuff.

To set the sleeve into the armhole,
stitch the sleeve seam; then run a
double row of basting across the top
of the sleeve. Pull the threads until the
sleeve fits the armhole. Apply the cuff
band.

**Directions for sewing sleeves and
cuffs**—No matter what kind of sleeve
or cuff you choose as the style feature
of your costume, it will not look well
unless it is properly set into the armhole. In Chapter 9 you will find suggestions and instructions on sleeves
and cuffs. Chapter 22 also contains
additional information on cuffs.

BOLERO WITH DOLMAN SLEEVES—
A bolero, in the dressmaking sense, is
a shortened jacket. The one shown in
the illustration is made from the basic

blouse pattern with dolman sleeves. It
is not necessary to fasten it with buttons and buttonholes, unless you prefer
to have a way of closing the jacket.
The center fronts may be cut straight
or with rounded corners.

Make the pattern for the bolero by
pinning a paper extension to the muslin
pattern and cutting as shown in the illustration. You will also need a facing
for the side fronts of the bolero. Try
on the altered pattern before cutting
out the material so that you will be sure
the bolero is the right shape and length
for your figure.

Baste the facings to the bolero, right
sides facing, then stitch. Turn them
right side out and press. Then slip stitch
them in place.

Contrasting color and design are

often used effectively as the facings
for the bolero. If your jacket is navy,
try a pale pink, or a colored print facing.

**BUTTONED - DOWN - THE - FRONT
DRESSES**—The buttoned-down-the-
front dress is a perennial style for many

women. As a rule this dress can be worn by any type of figure. But unless a new fashion note is introduced occasionally into this classic dress, it is apt to become boring not only to the beholder but to the wearer of the dress as well.

Classic style—This can be made by altering your basic dress pattern. The back of the dress is cut from the basic pattern. Add a paper extension to the front waist and skirt muslin patterns, measuring it carefully so that the addition in width will be uniform in both sections of the pattern. This will be the overlap needed for the buttons and buttonholes. Cut out the pat-

tern on two thicknesses of material but not on a fold of material.

Turn the front facings to the wrong side, allowing the necessary overlap. (When finished, the buttons should mark the center front line.) Baste and press the facings into place, then put the dress together. Mark the buttonholes and work them. You will find information on making buttonholes in Chapter 10.

Variations of buttoned-down style—You do not have to use buttons all the way down the front of the skirt. An effective style is one in which the dress is buttoned to the waist only and the skirt is straight, flared, or pleated.

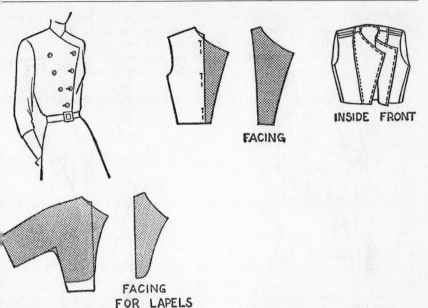

FACING

INSIDE FRONT

FACING
FOR LAPELS

Another way to use the buttoned
waist is to vary the way the buttons
are placed. It may be straight double-
breasted, in which case you should allow a much wider fold to turn under
both sides of the waist.

Or it may be buttoned in a triangular form, as shown in the above sketch.

To make this alteration on the basic
waist pattern, add a triangular extension of material, also cut a facing
to go under the additional material extending 1 or 2 inches into the shoulder
seam. This variation in style can be
combined with almost any type of skirt.

Another way of using the buttoned-
down-the-front style, and at the same
time adding a new style note, is to extend the button closing only halfway;
some styles feature buttons to the hipline, with the lower part of the closing
seamed together. This is worn with
or without a belt. Others use a
different treatment: The top part of
the waist is finished as a slit opening
and the buttons used from that point
to the waistline. The illustration shows

a further adaptation of this idea with the waist made on the basic drop-shoulder pattern and the button decoration carried out on the pockets.

Not too much can or should be done to change the basic design of the jacket. But here are some suggestions if you are looking for new style features and how to adapt them.

Pockets—Pocket styles often set the

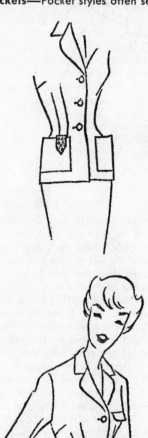

VARIATIONS OF SUIT STYLES—The same basic jacket pattern can be used for a tailored or a dressy suit, depending on the material and the type of trimming used. A two-piece dress

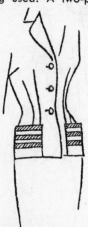

with an unlined jacket may also be made from the basic jacket pattern as well as a separate jacket to wear over a dress of contrasting material.

ew fashion note for jackets. The accompanying illustrations will give you
new ideas for pockets, and in Chapter
0 you will find complete information
or making them.

Buttons and buckles—If you
prefer to omit pockets but still want to
give your costume a touch of in-
dividuality, use a different type of
closing. Buttons may also be used as
a style note. While you will undoubtedly have some new and original
ideas of your own, these sketches will
give you some suggestions.

Simulated pockets are made by
crossing two bands diagonally. Make
them double thickness in the same or
a contrasting material.

the same length; or you may prefer
to graduate their length, making the
top band the longest.

Double-thickness bands of fabric
make effective jacket closings. Sew a
buckle on each end of the band on
the left side. On the right side make

Stitch three or four narrow bands of
contrasting fabric or closely woven
braid horizontally across the front of
the jacket. If the jacket is of lightweight material, use grosgrain ribbon.
Do this stitching before the facing or
lining is put in. The buttonhole is made
through the band, and the button may
be covered in the same material as the
band or the jacket. All bands may be

an eyelet with a buttonhole stitch in each band to hold the prong of the buckle. The bands are stitched down at the opposite ends and about 1 inch in from the edge. They must be left loose enough to allow for buckling.

SKIRTS—The skirt style of a basic suit can also be varied. If the suit is a tailored one, the skirt can be made with inverted pleats, box pleats, or a combination. For a simple two-piece jacket dress make a simple flared skirt.

REVERSIBLE SKIRT—Here is a way to enjoy two skirts in one. You can use two different colors or designs as long as the materials are of the same texture and weight. Use your basic

skirt pattern, and cut the two front pieces with an allowance of about 5 inches extra at the center front of each piece. Cut the two pieces of material exactly alike. Trim the two bottom fronts in a straight or rounded manner. Sew each skirt separately, first stitching the darts to make it fit at the waistline, then stitching the seams. Try on skirt to make sure that it is the exact length from the floor that you want, as there is no hem to be made and no allowance of material is needed. Put the two skirts together, with the wrong side (the seams and darts inside) facing. Pin all around, then baste ¼ inch in from the edges. Baste a 1-inch folded flat braid binding over the entire edge. There will be ½ inch of braid on each side. Stitch braid. Try on skirt, lapping right front over left. Sew three hooks-and-eyes or stitch tape closure (Velcro) at the waistline as a fastening, making sure to do this very neatly so that it looks well on either side of the reversible skirt.

CHAPTER 12

Building a Wardrobe

THE desire to be smartly dressed for every occasion is inherent in every woman who takes pride in her appearance, but, unless they have unlimited means, few women are able to realize such an ambition.

The budget-minded woman plans her wardrobe for maximum flexibility: she buys accessories that can be worn with several outfits; she learns the secret of changing the appearance of a basic dress; she chooses her clothes with an eye to the type of life she leads. But, if she must buy all her clothes, she must still limit her wardrobe to what she can afford.

The woman who sews knows no such limitation. Her wardrobe can be far more complete, for she makes her clothes for less. With the money she saves by doing so she can buy the expensive accessories that other women must pass by.

HOW TO PLAN A FLEXIBLE WARD-ROBE—No matter what her activities are, the wise woman plans a flexible wardrobe—one in which each outfit can be worn in more than one way. She knows that the size of her wardrobe is not nearly so important as the number of occasions for which she can be well dressed.

The following are some general hints on ways of building a flexible wardrobe:

Plan accessories that are not limited to a single outfit. When you buy a hat and a bag to match, choose a colo and style that will look well with severa items in your wardrobe. Select you shoes in the same way. A pair o patent-leather sandals may be just the right complement to your new spring print, but how will they look with you suit? Suède pumps might be a wise choice.

Choose the general style that yo feel is most becoming to you and make the bulk of your everyday clothes along those lines. If you are the tweedy type then most of your clothes will be the casual variety—nubby woolens, sepa rate skirts of corduroy or tweed sweaters or wool jersey blouses, o classic fly-front dresses. Silks and luxury blended fabrics, along with sheer woolens, will be saved for very special occasions, and even they wil be of the quiet, dull-finish materials though not necessarily in subdued tones. If you are the classic tailored type who feels more at ease in a chi black woolen suit with a crisp white blouse, you will ignore the tweeds and choose the more sophisticated fitted coat, the smoother-weave materials and the dressmaker suits. You, too, wil dress up in silk, rayon, synthetic blends or sheer wool. But you can also wea the higher-sheen fabrics—satin or sil and satin combined, brocade, or taf feta.

Always include a basic dress or two in a dark solid color. It can be black dark brown, navy, dark green, or ox ford gray. If its lines are simple and the neckline unadorned, it can be converted in a twinkling into three or four different-appearing dresses simply by a change of accessories—a gold belt, a necklace or scatter pins, a set of frilly cuffs, a fetching collar, or a bright-colored scarf. Most of these you will be able to make yourself, so that the cost of including a complete set of accessories is minimal.

One of the most versatile garments you can have in your wardrobe is a well-fitted, untrimmed sheath dress of straight lines, with no sleeves and a fairly low neckline. It may be worn belted or unbelted as you prefer, and whichever way looks best for your figure. The sheath is most useful in black, although you may prefer some other solid dark color. It should be made of lightweight wool, crepe, faille, or velveteen. You can "dress it up" or "dress it down" by your accessories. In the daytime you can wear it with a sporty jacket, while in the evening you can carry a fur, a satin stole of a bright contrasting color, or one of those lovely sheer "sari" scarves of delicate colors with gold thread designs woven in. A black velveteen sheath dress may be made to look very dramatic by the addition of a wide white lace collar (the lace wide enough to form little caps over the bare shoulders). A heavy cotton Venetian lace is best to use. Another glamorous way to treat a sheath is to have one bright color accent—a wide sash with two loops over one hip, or a satin cummerbund. This is good only if you have a small waistline. The sheath can be an "around the clock" dress if you wear it during the day as a jumper with a simple blouse underneath it; then remove the blouse for late-day or evening functions and add your dress-up accessories.

Plan several outfits that can be mixed or matched: two-piece dresses that can be interchanged, boleros or jackets that look well with more than one dress, and so on. This is an excellent way to remodel clothes and get added wear from them. Chapter 15 will give you suggestions and information on ways for getting the maximum wear out of your clothes.

YOUR CLOTHES AND YOUR ACTIVITIES—Most women know the types of clothes that their jobs require, but they are often uncertain how to budget their clothing expenditures. If time is a factor to be considered, plan to buy your suits, coats, and bags, and make the rest of your clothes—blouses, house dresses, accessories, and dressier clothes.

The woman whose occupation is "housewife" always has a supply of gay-colored cottons that can be kept fresh and clean without any trouble. She may also wear sweaters and skirts during colder weather. But her wardrobe requirements are by no means limited to these. She must be well dressed for her social activities as well —for bridge luncheons, club meetings, social calls, and that occasional evening in town. Like every other woman she can benefit by the judicious use of accessories to vary the appearance of her outfits. They can do much to eliminate that "same old dress" look. The housewife is perhaps luckier than many women whose occupations take them outside the home in that the hours in which she can sew are not confined to one period of the day. She can usually arrange her housekeeping duties so that she has the time to make almost every item in her wardrobe.

The business or professional woman usually prefers suits or simple tailored dresses or suit dresses, but frequently she must go directly from business to an early dinner date. The solution to this problem is a quick change of accessories. She can wear a simple dark two-piece suit of dark, lightweight wool and change the top to a dressy blouse for after-office hours.

Still another way of handling the five-o'clock-date problem is to wear one of the increasingly popular office-to-date dresses which consists of a dress and a long-sleeved jacket to match. Worn with the jacket, the dress looks like a two-piece suit. When the jacket is removed, the dress becomes a perfect short-skirted late-day dress.

The business woman who travels or wants to spend her week ends in the country must also plan to include practical sportswear. It is for her that the new three-piece outfits have been designed. These consist of a tailored skirt, jacket, and slacks to match. She can combine the jacket and slacks, add a smartly tailored cotton blouse, and be suitably dressed for the country estate. Or she can slip on a T shirt or short-sleeved sweater and be ready to "rough it."

The teacher's clothing problems are unique among all other women's. The keynote of her wardrobe *must* be variety. Unlike the business girl, she cannot wear the same suit two or three successive days, even with a different blouse each day. Her pupils' critical eyes demand a more apparent change if she is to hold their interest. Color is also a prime consideration. Black-and-white combinations do not impress pupils nearly so much as colorful all-over small print designs or a two-tone color treatment. One of her mainstays is the mix-match dress and she plans it with as many variations as possible. Discretion usually requires her to dress conservatively for school and social functions, so she saves her secret urge to dress with a flair for her "at-home" attire.

Receptionists, hostesses, and sales-clerks frequently have a different problem. Their positions require them to wear dressy clothes all day, and they generally welcome the opportunity to relax in clothes that are casual and comfortable. They are the women whose wardrobes include a goodly number of basic dresses which they vary with accessories. In their case, these accessories frequently include several pieces of tastefully-chosen jewelry—pearl chokers, a single large "conversation-piece" brooch, earrings that are different—but they also need dozens of collars, attractive cuff sets, unusual belts, et cetera, all of which they can make at a fraction of the purchase price.

PATTERN POSSIBILITIES—The woman who is designing a flexible wardrobe soon learns to see in a pattern, not only the dress she intends to make, but all of the other ways in which she can use or adapt that same pattern as well.

A typical example of a pattern so simple and basically so good in design that it can be adapted for every activity from playing a game of tennis to acting as bridesmaid.

You might use this simple shirt-waist dress pattern to make a very short version in crisp white piqué to wear for tennis. Later on you might make it in black linen, with big white pearl buttons, to wear over matching shorts for a beach or play dress. With this you could wear a big rough straw hat or a bright bandanna around your head and black cotton *espadrilles* on bare feet.

A more conservative version could be made in lawn or a cotton print for daytime wear. A dress like this could be worn for shopping, visiting, or almost anything, depending on your selection of material and accessories.

This same dress could be made in pastel linen to wear with a big shady black hat and black or white gloves to a summer wedding.

especially if the belt were made of pastel or black velvet ribbon to match the ribbon on a picture hat. For a fall wedding the same pattern could be made up in glowing chrysanthemum colors of cotton velveteen.

Done in black silk, this pattern would be the perfect late-day dress. The front could be closed with a row of rhinestone buttons.

**Shirtwaist Pattern
Adapted to Tennis Dress**

You could even be a bridesmaid in a dress like this. Made full length, in cotton surah, it would be particularly attractive in an all-white wedding,

Shirtwaist Pattern Made up as After-noon Dress

Shirtwaist Pattern: Full-length Formal and Cocktail Dress

A suit pattern, like a dress pattern, has infinite possibilities for variations in the basic style which will make it suitable for many different occasions.

For summer, the suit shown might be made up in white crease-resistant linen, with pearl or self-covered buttons, and worn with white, black, brown, or navy-blue accessories.

It would look equally well in cotton oxford, twill, or needlepoint piqué, in white or pastel colors, made with short sleeves.

You might decide to make this suit

up as a two-piece dress in printed shantung or surah.

To adapt this suit so that it can be worn for almost any summer occasion, make the top of white piqué with three-quarter-length sleeves and use silver,

Basic Suit in White Linen

If you prefer you could trim the neckline, front, and bottom of sleeves with braid binding. It would also be attractive with a pearl necklace and washable white gloves. For a distinctive style note add fabric buttons covered in the same material as the dress.

For summer mornings, a short-sleeved version of this two-piece dress, made in polished cotton, printed no-iron cotton, or a miracle mixture, would make a smart outfit in which to do the marketing. Such materials require no trimming except perhaps a few white pearl or colored buttons of a simple design.

Basic Suit Pattern as Evening Dress

Basic Suit as Two-piece Dress

gold, or white pearl buttons. Make the skirt of black linen or piqué. For an extra fillip, add black gloves, shoes, and hat.

The same pattern could also be made into a dinner suit. Make it in

Basic Suit with Short Sleeves

black or a jewel-toned faille with long sleeves and fabric-covered buttons. In this variation it can be worn to an afternoon club meeting or to church on Sunday. By adding a small party hat and wearing high-heeled black pumps, you will have an outfit that is suitable for an evening in the finest restaurant or theater.

There is also an evening version of this pattern. Cut the skirt floor or ankle length, and make the jacket of a plain or contrasting material. Choose a glamorous fabric like brocade for the jacket, and make it with long or three-quarter sleeves for the distinguished elegance of the covered-up look. The skirt can be made from velvet, faille, or crepe, in black, brown, dark green, or some other dark rich color.

Although all the variations suggested here for this pattern are for the suit dress, you can also make this same pattern in any of the usual suiting fabrics—twill, worsted, flannel, or gabardine. For more casual wear, corduroy is also a suitable fabric. For late fall or winter a fur collar could be added to this type of suit. Chapter 23 gives directions on how to cut and sew fur.

COMPLETING YOUR WARDROBE—

To be really complete, a wardrobe must enable you to be well dressed for any occasion. We have already discussed your clothes and their relationship to your activities, but there are some extras that any complete wardrobe should include. Among them are

Two-piece Evening Dresses

dinner dresses, cocktail suits and evening gowns, sportswear, and a supply of blouses. All of these are made according to the same procedures outlined for making a dress, but since they frequently present special material problems, we have included information that applies specifically to these parts of the wardrobe.

EVENING AND FORMAL DRESSES—

Dinner and cocktail dresses and evening gowns and suits are customarily made of such luxury fabrics as satin, peau de soie, brocade, taffeta, moiré, velvet, lamé, faille, and lace. Sheer materials for these gowns include chiffon, net, lace, and organdie. Fine cottons, jersey, and fine woolens are also popular materials for formal wear.

Gowns of these materials can be trimmed with sequins, rhinestones, lace, net, or ribbon, or they may be made up unadorned. As with any other type of dress it is wise to use trimming with a sense of discrimination, for an evening gown heavily loaded with sequins is in just as poor taste as a daytime dress so trimmed.

The past few years have seen a trend toward the two-piece evening dress. This type is particularly practical for the woman who cannot afford to make a new gown for every formal function.

Black is the most popular color for the skirt. It can be made in heavy crepe, tissue faille, moiré, satin, or some other similar heavy-textured material. It can be floor length or the more popular cocktail length.

The blouse can be made in brocade, satin, velveteen, lace, or lamé. For summer-wear polished cotton, needlepoint piqué, sheer cotton, or linen is a suitable material.

Evening sweaters can also be worn with an evening skirt. They are made of wool blends, such as Orlon or banlon, and may be trimmed with bead

Office Dress

work, embroidery, lace appliqué, ribbon, braid, or even a fur collar. The fur may be sewn to the sweater or attached to it by snaps.

Another type of evening gown is the simple sleeveless one. It can be adapted for a cocktail gown or for formal wear. Make it up in heavy crepe or satin and wear it with a filmy lace or chiffon scarf or stole thrown across the shoulders. A bolero jacket in lace or brocade will completely change the appearance of the dress.

A short-length evening dress that is often a lifesaver to the woman who works is the dress shown in the illustration. Make it in heavy crepe. Wear it with appropriate daytime accessories; then make it formal for the evening hours by removing these accessories and tying on a lace apron. It can be made with or without the peplum and tied with a matching ribbon fastened to the apron as a belt. It may be worn with the lace apron tied in front or in back, whichever you prefer.

BLOUSES—Few wardrobes ever have too many blouses, for the occasions on

Tailored Blouse

Office Dress Converted for Evening by Adding Lace Apron

which they can be appropriately worn are almost limitless.

In the section above we described their use for evening wear. Here we will be concerned with their possibilities for daytime functions.

There are two general styles: tailored and dressy. The illustration shows how both styles can be made from the same pattern, and one or two blouse patterns are often all that

Overblouse

Dressy Blouse

are needed to make a complete supply of blouses. Vary the patterns by changing the collar style or shape of the cuff, adding bands or using tucks.

Tailored shirts are smart in cotton, silk broadcloth, rayon or silk crepe, surah, and Dacron and cotton shirtings. Dressy blouses are made of such sheer materials as nylon, batiste, eyelet embroidery, organdie, or thin silk.

Choose a style that is becoming. Short-waisted women sometimes prefer the overblouse. If you are one of these, remember that it must be fitted more

closely at the waistline than the usual shirtwaist style. Women with large figures should avoid satin or large-print designs. Their best choice is a solid color or allover print with fabric-covered buttons of the same material. Small figures should select patterns that include frills. Contrasting or unusually shaped buttons can also be used effectively.

SPORTS CLOTHES—For vacations or for relaxation well-fitted sportswear is an important part of the average woman's wardrobe. Unlike other fashions, styles in sportswear do not change from season to season, and, if the pattern is chosen carefully and made up in good material, there is no reason why the garment should not remain smart looking for two and sometimes three seasons.

As a rule sports clothes are designed for comfort, and it is wise to remember this when fitting any article of sportswear.

If you are making a vacation wardrobe, choose your materials with an eye to the laundry facilities available at the place you are visiting. If they are inconvenient, drip-dry cottons or the miracle-fiber blends are practical materials to use for your play clothes.

Dress Without Jacket

Linen, arnel, sharkskin, piqué or shantung can be used for spectator sports clothes.

For cold weather, corduroy, flannel, and tweeds are good choices.

The type and amount of sports clothes you make depend on how much need you have for them, whether you spend your vacations in quiet spots or fashionable resorts, and whether you enjoy your sports actively or as a spectator. Basically, however, a sports wardrobe includes:

Bathing suit made of wool knit jersey, cotton, or sharkskin.

Beach robe or shortie coat made of terry cloth, sharkskin, poplin, or seersucker.

Denim sports skirt to wear with shirtwaists, sweaters, or T-shirts. Faded blue is generally the preferred color, although recently darker and brighter shades have been used.

Skirt of printed cotton to wear with peasant-tailored blouse.

Woolen or corduroy skirt to wear with cotton or wool flannel shirtwaists, sweaters, and jackets.

A sleeveless jacket or vest is useful, too, to wear over a long-sleeved sports blouse. Make it from the same jacket pattern, but bind the armholes instead of setting in the sleeves.

Cardigan sweater of solid color, to wear on a cool day.

A collection of blouses, T-shirts, pullover sweaters, scarves, all carefully selected so that they are interchangeable with the several skirts and jackets.

Casual dresses of classic lines, buttoned-down-the-front, or the fuller skirt styles can last from year to year. If you've always wanted a bright-colored dress but your job requires conservative clothes, choose a brilliant hue for your casual dress.

Dress With Stole

Dress With Jacket

Jackets of colors to contrast with skirts. Use an easy-to-make pattern and make an unlined jacket in a cardigan style.

Play suits, which consist of one-piece shorts and a separate skirt to wear over them, are easy to cut and sew. One pattern is all you need, and you can vary the details and the materials to make any number of suits. Use cotton or sharkskin material if you are very active. A printed polished cotton, or piqué, is suitable for a play suit if you plan to wear it just for relaxation. Worn with the skirt, it can be counted an additional dress in your wardrobe.

Sunback dresses are popular items in sportswear. Make them with matching boleros and use them interchangeably; for instance, a striped dress with a striped bolero can be interchanged with a solid-color dress with a solid-color bolero. The dress can also be attractive worn without a jacket but with a gay-colored contrasting scarf tied over the shoulders in a soft knot. You might even sew a stole of the same material as the dress, or of contrasting fabric. A sunback dress with matching jacket in shantung or sharkskin or a fine linen may be worn even in the city.

Slacks, shorts, overalls, pedal pushers, and ski pants are included in sportswear. Denim, corduroy, and flannel are good for slacks and their shorter version, the pedal pushers. The weight of the material depends on whether you want to wear them for lounging at home or for a summer or winter vacation in the country. Use wool, of course, for ski pants; denim or corduroy for overalls. Any material—from cotton broadcloth to wool—is suitable for shorts. Rayon material is not generally recommended for women's sports pants, either long or short, since it will neither wear so long

nor hold its press so well as other materials.

The same blouses, sweaters, jackets, and accessories you wear with your sports skirts may also be used with the slacks and shorts. You will need heavy sweaters or jersey pull-over blouses to wear under a ski jacket, and it should, of course, have a hood. Patterns for both the ski jacket and the pull-over blouses are easily obtainable.

Hot-weather items in sportswear include the halter and the bare midriff, and they are easy to cut and sew, but choose the pattern carefully, for not all styles are becoming to every figure.

CHAPTER 13

You and Your Accessories

ACCESSORIES do so much to add to or detract from the appearance of any outfit that any discussion of sewing would be incomplete without some consideration of the various accessories and the factors you should keep in mind when selecting them. Many of them you will be making; others must be purchased, for obviously you cannot "make" shoes, stockings, or furs. Yet the discrimination you use in combining all of these items can enhance or ruin the effect of a beautifully finished garment. The accessories are the frame for the clothes you wear; it is important to choose the right ones.

Some of the problems in choosing the right accessories are common to all figure types and we shall discuss them first. Later we will take up the points that apply specifically to you.

GENERAL INSTRUCTIONS

On buying hats—When you try on a hat, be sure to see how it looks on you when you are standing. Many a hat which looks well when you are seated proves to be too small or too large for your face and figure when viewed in a full-length mirror.

Your hat usually looks best if the color is repeated in some other part of your outfit. That is, the hat may be the same shade as the trimming of the dress, or it may match the gloves. It may look very well if it exactly matches the dress or coat in color. Never, never buy a hat in a color which *almost* matches something else!

Buy hats that can be worn with several outfits. If you wear casual sports clothes, your hats should be simple straws, felts, or fabrics. If you love soft, pretty clothes, your hats can be of velvet, feathers, and flowers, though you can also wear the plainer hats. A simple rayon or wool crepe dress can be made suitable for almost any occasion, from work to a wedding, by merely changing the hat worn with it. One simple, adaptable dress and two hats usually prove better than two dresses and one hat.

If you "can't find a hat" it may be that you actually do have trouble in getting just the right hat, or it may be that what you need first is a new hair style. But don't buy just any hat. If you do not trust your own millinery taste, take along a friend in whose judgment you do have confidence.

On buying shoes—Buy good shoes. Cheap shoes are poor economy. Two pairs of school or business shoes, or house shoes, worn on alternate days, will outlast one pair worn every day, plus a second pair bought only after the first pair is worn out. Your only shoe economy may be in buying inexpensive evening slippers, for they do not undergo the strain of everyday use and are bought for appearance rather than durability.

Wear shoes, not bedroom slippers, with your housedresses. Do this both for your feet and for a neater appearance. Bedroom slippers are not made for all the walking a woman does in carrying on her household duties.

Keep your shoes in good repair and polished. Runover heels, besides being a sign of poor grooming, are bad for your feet.

Good taste in shoe styles is based on the following points:

The spectator pump is correct with all spectator sports clothes, woolen dresses, tweed suits, and most tailored suits. The spectator has a built-up leather heel or a wooden heel covered with leather. Two-tone spectators (brown and white, or black and white) are worn with summer clothes and on some college campuses all year round. The standard spectator pump does not have a very high heel. Two-tone spectators are worn on city streets in summer, but as a rule they don't look well with city clothes.

In the strictest fashion sense a white or light-colored shoe is not worn on a city street. The reason for this is sensible—city streets soil the shoes and thus spoil the freshness of their appearance.

Good-looking oxfords or low-heeled shoes are in perfect taste for street wear. Teen-age and younger girls can wear loafers, sandals, and saddle oxfords for street wear because their clothes are the casual type. But the woman whose clothes are dressy, even when they are in the sportswear class, would do well to avoid wearing loafers or saddle oxfords in the city.

The most generally becoming dress shoe for all types of feet and all types of figures is the opera pump. It may have a spike heel or a baby French heel. It may have a round throat or a V throat. It may have a small buckle or bit of stitching or it may be perfectly plain. The opera pump may be bought in kid, calf, satin, suède, reptile, linen —almost any fabric or leather.

Those pretty red or green high-heeled kid sandals are intended to be worn only with special outfits, for afternoon parties or for the evening. They are not made to wear to work every day. But you can wear polished dark red or green spectators anywhere your suit can go.

On stockings—Your legs will look best in the stocking shades worn by the majority of girls and women. A very "different" shade will make your legs noticed. After all, the most beautiful legs in the world would look out of place wearing bright purple stockings to church.

On buying gloves—Glove size is measured in inches. The measurement is taken around the palm of the hand, at the base of the fingers. If your hand measures 6½ inches, you wear a 6½ glove. Many women like to buy gloves slightly large.

String gloves are a heavy-ribbed short glove in wool, cotton, nylon or rayon. Yellow, beige, or natural color gloves are worn with sports clothes and riding clothes. Woolen gloves or mittens are fine with sports clothes. They are especially smart in black for a woman and in bright colors for teenagers.

Double-woven fabric is a cotton material made especially for gloves. It is very thick and smooth and can hardly be distinguished from suède leather. It is also more practical than leather, for it can be washed.

Chamois can mean either the natural creamy yellow color which is popular for gloves (regardless of the material used), or it can actually mean the chamois leather.

Kid, glacé kid, and glacé are terms used to describe thin, smooth-surfaced leather gloves. Fine kid has a gloss but is not usually so rich and luxurious looking as suède.

Pigskin is exactly what it says. Pigskin gloves are worn with sports, tailored, and casual clothes. Ostrich, reindeer, and capeskin are also used for everyday wear.

Suède and mocha are soft, velvety leather. Doeskin is similar but usually not so fine in quality. Some doeskin gloves will wash, but white doeskin becomes yellow after a few washings, and most leathers tend to stiffen with washing. Black suède is lovely but is likely to "crock," that is, to rub off on your clothes and hands.

On buying and caring for furs—
Nothing looks so cheap as a cheap fur coat. If you want fur, whether it be in a muff or a coat, spend the money you have on the best grade of an inexpensive fur rather than on a poor grade of an expensive fur. The average shopper knows so little about furs that it is wise to buy only from a well-known, reliable fur dealer. Bargains in fur coats are bargains only if the customer can judge what she is getting for her money. In deciding what kind of fur to buy, remember that you cannot expect a coat made from fragile, delicate fur, such as squirrel, to wear as well as a sturdier fur, such as raccoon.

Never put furs near direct heat, for the skins will dry or crack. Hang wet furs to dry them. When they are dry, shake them. Do not brush furs.

If possible place your fur coat in cold storage during warm weather.

If possible pull up your fur coat when you sit down, especially when you drive a car.

On handbags—We have already pointed out that when buying an inexpensive bag it is wise to choose a good fabric rather than a poor leather. Consider the excellent plastics which look like patent leather and which do not crack so easily. Buy light-colored bags only in washable or wipeable coverings. Practical, long-wearing leathers are calf, cowhide, pigskin, lizard, ostrich, and alligator (if not pieced). You can also buy or make attractive casual bags in felt.

An inexpensive bag with a covered metal frame usually looks better than a similar bag with a visible metal frame. Clear lucite or plastic closings are inexpensive and more attractive than cheap metal ones. A good leather bag will outwear two fabric bags and is worth repairing. Very fine leather bags are leather lined.

Clean out your bags regularly—it is amazing how many things you carry which are of no further use and which help to destroy the neat, trim look which your bag should have inside as well as out.

Leather bags should be cleaned with saddle soap. Incidentally, the use of this same saddle soap will prolong the good life and good looks not only of your leather bags, but of your shoes, belts, and luggage as well.

Comments about jewelry—Jewels are the ornaments which are designed to attract attention and to enhance the loveliness of a girl or a woman. There are fashions in jewels which change as all fashions do. But there are also classic—styles which never change—in jewels. They can be worn any time in any place. Here are some of them:

A simple pearl necklace, single or double strand, of a length to fill the neckline of a daytime dress. This always looks well on any girl or woman, of any age or size.

A small locket, cross, or star on a thin gold or silver chain worn by a little girl or a young woman.

A wrist watch, either the sports or the dress-up type.

A simple gold bracelet.

Any pieces of old-fashioned jewelry for which you have a sentimental attachment. Try to think up new ways in which to wear these. For example, two or three old pins, or watch safety clasps, can be pinned to the lapel of a suit or the neck of a sweater. A larger pin or brooch can be fastened to a plain hat or used to hold a scarf in place.

Popular pieces of jewelry, which are apt to change with the change of fashion, include earrings, chain necklaces, many silver bangle bracelets worn together, charm bracelets in gold or silver, and for the hair there are silver or gold bobby pins and barrettes. Gold- or silver-coated plastic or jeweled buttons are in style every so often.

Anklets are also included in the jewelry category, but they are really not a practical ornament for the average woman. An anklet is made of a thin gold or silver chain, and it is usually worn as a fad by very young girls. As a word of caution to them: only the young girl with extremely slender legs and ankles should attempt to wear any kind of anklet.

Jewelry, like every other accessory item in an outfit, has to be worn sparingly. No well-dressed girl or woman would try to wear all her jewelry at one time, even though her pieces are very beautiful. If you possess a set of lovely jewelry, do not wear the complete set all at once. For instance, if you have earrings, necklace, a pin, and a bracelet all matching, it is better to interchange them than to don them all at once. At one time, depending upon your outfit and the place you plan to wear it, you can accent your costume by the earrings, pin, and bracelet. At another time you might wear the necklace and earrings. And on still another occasion you can wear the necklace and the bracelet by themselves, or just the earrings and the pin, or the pin and the bracelet.

You, of course, are the best judge of the type and amount of jewelry you should wear: it is largely a matter of personal taste and preference together with a sense of style, and this you will develop as you gain experience in planning your wardrobe.

Now that you have some general information on buying accessories you are ready to consider them in relation to your own particular figure.

IF YOU ARE A WEE BIT!

Your hats—ON THE STREET—A fairly small-sized hat is best. One which has upsweeping lines will make you appear taller, but a tall quill or ornament on a hat with "down" lines will only make you look short by contrast. Wear a plain hat with a medium-width brim such as a ribbon-banded summer straw, but do not buy a huge cartwheel. Wear a brimmed hat straight on your head, or tilted slightly back, but never wear your brimmed hats down over the eyes.

SUNDAY BEST—Observe the same rules as above. Tiny hats of flowers or of feathers were made for you, but remember that they are only for best. They look out of place with a tweed sports suit.

FORMAL—If your dress is simple, with no decoration of its own, you can wear a flower or a jewelled comb in your hair. But if your dress is made of print material, or it has trimming on it, then you do not need a hair ornament.

If You Are a Wee Bit

Right

Your shoes—ON THE STREET— Some of the smartest street shoes are spectator pumps, which come in colors to match your dress or coat. Shoes in a matching color tend to make you appear taller. If the spectator pump with the built-up leather heel is too plain for most of your clothes, then you can wear a simple pump with a covered heel of medium height. Very high heels for street wear have a tendency to make you look unbalanced. Bright-colored shoes are fine for sports and for parties but they usually make you look shorter.

SUNDAY BEST—The same rules as given above apply here. To go with your dressiest daytime outfit, wear a perfectly fitting pump with a high heel. You can buy this in suède, either in brown or black. For weddings and to wear with dinner dresses you can attach a small cut-steel buckle to this same pump. It will add a touch of true elegance for a festive occasion.

FORMAL—Silver or gold sandals with high heels are always a safe choice, but of course these are to be worn only with complete evening dress. If you wish, you can wear colored

Wrong

slippers to match your dress. If you cannot get them in the same color, buy white satin or faille slippers and have them dyed to match.

Your stockings—SOCKS—These are to be worn only with your flat-heeled shoes. Since you usually wish to look taller than you are, you will probably wear your flat shoes only for sports. Never wear socks on the street in a city, unless you are in your teens. And never wear socks anywhere if you are in doubt and if you feel that they might possibly look out of place.

STOCKINGS—A neutral tone—that is, a beige rather than a bright orange tone—will make you look taller. Gray is also a neutral tone, although it is not always in fashion, and you will have to use care in selecting it. Black stockings, because they are rarely worn, attract attention to the wearer. However, a sheer black or a sheer very dark gray stocking is in good taste for the more dressy outfits.

COLORED STOCKINGS—The hand-knitted woolen stockings in bright colors, or very long socks, are fine for the teen-age girl in the cold winter months. Colored nylon or fine cotton-mesh stockings are sold as high fashion every few years. If you have sufficient courage and possess a pair of exceptionally beautiful legs, you might wear them, but the average woman doesn't. Colored stockings only succeed in making you look even shorter than you are.

Your furs—ON THE STREET—Choose only the flat furs, such as kidskin, Persian lamb, sheared beaver, and broadtail. Furs which are fluffy (those with thick pile) will make you look tubby, even though you have a slender figure. If you buy a fur coat, be certain that it is made very simply, without too much detail. You should avoid large collars, unusually wide or fancy sleeves, big pockets, and contrasting fur trim. If you buy a fur scarf, cape, hat, stole, or muff, make sure that it is in proportion to your figure. You must give up that ambition for a pair of trailing white foxes. They are too large for you. On the other hand, you are just the right size to wear a scarf made of the smaller skins, such as three skins of mink, marten, or some other small fur of the same family.

FORMAL—Over a long evening dress girls usually prefer a short white fur cape or jacket made of sheared rabbit or bleached squirrel, or a full taffeta coat in a bright, jewel-tone color. Women often choose a loose velvet or heavy silk coat with a fur collar, a stole or jacket of mink or other good quality fur, or a cashmere cardigan sweater with a luxury fur collar. And both girls and women frequently wear the same fur coat for evening that they wear with their other clothes.

Your handbags—ON THE STREET—Keep your bags fairly small and quite simple in line. Plain envelope bags are fine for you and they look well with tailored clothes. Choose a bag with gussets at the sides, so that the bag will spread a little without losing its shape. You can also carry the frameless drawstring pouch bag if you buy a small one. A tiny tailored satchel will be ideal for you if you are fussy about details and always wear hat, bag, gloves, and shoes with medium heels, but no satchel for you if you wear casual sports clothes. Shoulder bags are fine for the young girl who wears casual clothes. Leather bags cost more than fabric bags but they last longer. If you cannot afford a leather bag, buy a good fabric bag rather than a cheap leather one. If you need a special bag in white or other light color for summer, buy a washable bag in plastic.

SUNDAY BEST—The small pouch bag with a handle always looks rather dressed up, but unless it is quite small, it does not look young. Many women prefer clutch bags for all occasions. Keep your bag small no matter what style you select. Beaded or heavy crocheted bags wear well. They are suitable for most occasions and can be worn with anything except formal evening clothes and strictly sports outfits. Silk or rayon fabric, suède leather, or broadcloth (which looks like and is frequently more practical than suède) are all dress-up bags. They are designed to be decorative, not to withstand hard usage, and suède in particular is inclined to "shed" its color.

FORMAL—You might like a small satin envelope with slip covers which you can make up in different colors to match your party dresses. Pin a flower to your plain satin envelope, or add a sparkling clip. Or you may want a small multi-color beaded bag in pastel shades, which you can wear with any evening dress you own. You may have a mesh bag from thirty years ago. If it is in good condition, polish it up, reline it with a piece of crepe or satin, and you'll have a new-old-fashioned type of evening bag.

Your gloves—ON THE STREET—Shorties (those gloves which come just above the wrist) are just right for you. They can be either slip-ons or the one-button style. Gloves can either match or contrast with your outfit, but remember that colored gloves can also make an outfit look "spotty," especially if your hat or bag is also colored. Contrasting colored gloves are best worn as the only or as one of two contrasting notes in your outfit. For everyday wear it is best to buy washable fabric gloves. If you prefer leather for your everyday

gloves, you will find that pigskin is very durable and attractive.

SUNDAY BEST—The least expensive glove for you, for dress-up purposes, is the white shortie or the slip-on in heavy cotton fabric. Do not buy fabric gloves which have a silky look, or gloves made of very thin material. If you want a leather glove for Sunday-best wear, buy the beige shade that goes with every material and every color of your costume. But bear in mind that many suèdes are not washable and must be cleaned. Gloves of black and brown suède are also suitable; but these, too, will probably require cleaning. Never buy a glove which has a big cuff or a fancy decoration.

FORMAL—You can wear long white kid gloves or those which exactly match the color of your dress. Or, if you are still in your teens, you will look especially sweet if you wear the little short one-buttoned white kid gloves to accompany your evening dress.

Your jewelry—The most suitable type of jewelry is not dictated so much by the occasion as it is by your age, your income, and the kind of clothes you prefer to wear. A watch for general use should be a fairly small one on a metal band or ribbon rather than a leather-banded sports watch. The very young girl might wear a small pearl necklace or gold chain around the neck, a single simple bracelet, a little silver lapel ornament, a silver barrette, and a child's ring. But she should not wear all of these at once. Teen-agers sometimes want to wear everything at the same time. But they are at their best with one or two unusual and dashing pieces of costume jewelry to set off their tweed suits or skirts and sweaters. Teen-agers should wear earrings only for dress up, because they are out of place with the clothes they like for school or every day.

Any "wee bit," no matter her age, must be careful to avoid chunky metal ornaments in pins or clips. No great, heavy, swinging gold hoops or earrings for her. No huge metal belts, no big cut-steel shoe buckles. What she can wear are the dainty little flower pins in porcelain which look silly on a larger girl, and the small, fragile-looking earrings which were just made for her. Even diamonds come in her size. So keep your jewelry in scale and wear only two or three pieces at a time.

IF YOU ARE A TALL ONE—

Your hats—ON THE STREET—Wear the dashing felt hats which swoop down over one eye. If any woman can get away with exaggerated hats, you can. But don't go so far as to make yourself ridiculous! Choose hats in colors which contrast with your clothes. Most of your hats should have some brim, to balance the width of your shoulders, and you should avoid tall ornaments on your hats.

SUNDAY BEST—Wear a picture hat, unless you are the casual type and dislike dressy clothes. A picture hat can be of velvet, lace, straw, or felt, with a wide brim, usually trimmed with ribbon, feathers, or flowers. It is very much the "lady" hat. If you like simple clothes, even for best, a large crushed or draped beret or a wide-brimmed soft felt or straw with a beautiful band is also good.

FORMAL—If your dress is not fussy, wear an ornament in your hair. It can be a flower, a puff of feathers, a lovely comb. Place it on the side or back of your head, not on top.

Your shoes—ON THE STREET—Flat shoes or ones with low or medium heels are your type. Flat-heeled street shoes of calf or suède are popular with tall girls, but they look best with tailored or casual clothes. If your feet are of average size, you can wear shoes in colors to contrast with your dress or coat. If you want your feet to appear smaller, buy plain shoes in a color to go with your other clothes.

SUNDAY BEST—Low-heeled or medium-heeled shoes can be made to look dressy by choosing the right leather and stitching and by adding a simple buckle or flat bow. (No reason why you shouldn't wear high heels if you happen to like them!) Same suggestions as above for color. Remember that brown, black, or blue are colors which never look gaudy or out of place.

FORMAL—There are beautiful formal "flats" in gold or silver kid, or in white satin to be dyed to match your dress, or in patterned materials, such as brocade. Wear high heels if you prefer them and if they will not make you taller than your dancing partner.

Your stockings—SOCKS—Worn at the right time (for walks, for sports) they are fine for you. In fact, they make you look a bit shorter. If your legs are of average size, you might wear dark red socks with those flat brown moccasins for the next autumn hike and picnic.

STOCKINGS—Choose flesh tones, bronze, and copper tints if your legs are slender. If you wish to divert attention from your legs, wear neutral tones in beige.

COLORED STOCKINGS—If your legs are slender, and if colored stockings are popular, by all means wear them. Bright colors in strictly sports stockings are also suitable for you.

If You Are a Tall One

Right   Wrong

Your gloves—ON THE STREET—
Fabric or leather gloves in slip-on or

gauntlet (wide-flared top) style are best
for you. If you like sports clothes, tweed

If You Are a Tall One

Right

Wrong

suits, and loose-swinging topcoats, you
may wear your gloves a half size larger

than your wee bit sister. If you like your
gloves, bags, and other accessories a

bit large, why not wear them that way? They will give you a casual and comfortable air.

SUNDAY BEST—Bulky washable cotton slip-ons in white or beige are good. Always remember that a good cotton glove is a better investment than a cheap leather glove. Also suède in brown, black, beige, or white. Your dress-up gauntlet can have a scalloped cuff or a bit of fine stitching by way of trimming. If your hands are average or small in proportion to the rest of your body, you might like a pair of colored gloves to wear with a special outfit. But colored gloves are limited in use and tend to attract attention to the hands.

FORMAL—If you like gloves with evening dress, wear long white or black suède, or a suède to match the color of your dress.

Your furs—Because you are tall, you can wear the bushy, fluffy, and thick furs which overpower the wee bit and are too bulky for the prettily rounded. But even you should avoid fur coats cut with so much fullness that they envelop you and make you look unfeminine. You can wear short jackets or coats in three-quarter length. Some of the furs which you can wear well are raccoon, muskrat, and lynx. These are usually considered sports furs and are most becoming for the college or young business girl. Muskrat (when it is worked like mink), beaver, and otter are thick, soft furs which any tall woman of average weight can wear successfully. Hudson seal and Alaska seal are rich-looking furs and are usually worn by the mature woman. Seal is most often seen in black. Brown seal is an interesting possibility as a coat for a tall young woman.

FORMAL—You can wear all the furs listed for the wee bit. You can also wear two furs in combination, or an entire cape or coat of white fox, or a stole of white or black fox, or a luxury fur like mink. That is, you can if the rest of your appearance will bear out the motion-picture-star-beauty look to live up to all that glamor.

Your handbags—ON THE STREET —You're the girl who can carry a bag as large as a young suitcase and look smart doing it. You can have bags in bright colors to add the one touch of dash to an otherwise conservative outfit. Your best bet is the large brief-case envelope in good calf, or the English-type kit bag with a neat handle, in black, brown, saddle tan, or bright red leather. These bags are perfect for street wear for all tall girls of all ages and all degrees of tailoredness. If you are a dashing person, and can get away with it, you might be the one to wear a plain black or brown coat with no fur, but wear a wide spotted calfskin or leopard fur belt and carry a bag to match. Plain hat, gloves, and shoes with all this, of course. You can wear shoulder bags well if you like sports clothes. You can also carry large pouch bags of leather, felt, or fabric. You might try to make a bag of a material to match your coat or suit. Have it big and soft and squashy.

SUNDAY BEST—Anything you like in leather or fabric—if it is suitable for the rest of your outfit and if it is not too small in size. Since a fine leather bag in a generous size is quite expensive, you will do well to learn how to make yourself a black or brown bag in a heavy faille.

FORMAL—Avoid those dainty, clear, square plastic or lucite boxes. Make a large-sized evening bag of brocade or velvet.

Your jewelry—You can wear almost any jewel if you observe a few precautions:

Don't buy any ornament so small that it looks lost on you.

Don't buy any jewelry which is so big and chunky that it overpowers you. Except for those two cautions and your good taste, you are on your own. Buy nice big flapjack compacts with your initials six inches high on the top. Of course you won't wear fancy drop earrings when you are carrying a shoulder bag and wearing your flattest flat heels. But you might be surprised at the result (if you have the use and the figure for them) if you made a pair of stunning lounging pajamas and wore the dangling earrings with them! If you have a huge old watch chain take all the ornaments off and wear them as a clanking bracelet. Buy a big gold safety pin and use it to fasten your scarves, to hold flowers to your suit lapel, or just to accent the front of your plain dark felt beret. A single ring with a large setting—that's for you. And there are many handsome, inexpensive stones for it. Hunt around in old jewelry stores for rings set with amethysts, opals, turquoises, topazes, or made of just plain silver.

IF YOU ARE PRETTILY ROUNDED

Your hats—ON THE STREET—Hats in the same color as your dress or coat are fine for you. A single color scheme makes you look well put together and does not detract attention from your face, which may be one of your best features. Your hats should be fairly small, with small or medium-sized brims. Be careful not to get a hat that is too small, however, for it will increase the apparent size of your face. Never wear hatbrims which curve down or turn down all the way—they will give your figure a heavy squat look. The most becoming type of hat for you is one with some height to the crown, and a brim which is turned up in an irregular line.

SUNDAY BEST—Wear a draped turban if you allow your hair to show. You can also successfully wear a soft crushed beret in felt or dressy fabric such as velvet, especially if the hat tilts to give a slanted line of height to the head. If you are in your teens or early twenties, wear a poke bonnet in spring —if it goes with your other clothes. In summer you will look your best in hats with a medium brim worn back or tilted.

FORMAL—Your evening dress will do the most for you if it is in a plain material in a pastel or dark color and in a soft material. With it you might like to wear a jewelled comb or a small bunch of flowers becomingly arranged on your head.

Your shoes—ON THE STREET— Wear shoes with medium heels. Pumps are fine if they have a heel of spectator pump size and if they do not have short vamps, which make the foot look shorter and heavier. Your best color in shoes is one which matches your coat or dress.

SUNDAY BEST—A beautiful pump with a medium or medium-high heel is an excellent choice for you. A high heel may add slightly to your height, but it will also make you look unbalanced. If you have prettily plump feet, the kind which look so well in a simple V-throated pump, always wear that pump for dress. Never buy the d'orsay-type pump that is cut low at the sides.

FORMAL—Choose medium-high or high heels—your height should guide your choice. Gold, silver, or a color which harmonizes with the material of your dress will be a better choice for you than a contrast. For instance, if your dress is blue, silver slippers, or slippers of a material combining blue and silver, will be more becoming to you than red slippers.

Right

Wrong

Your stockings—SOCKS—Wear white socks, if you like them, for active sports. Colored socks are less becoming than white ones for you, because they cut your apparent height. You may prefer to wear stockings or go in bare legs rather than wear socks for sports.

STOCKINGS—Neutral beige tones are best for you. You might wear navy, brown, or rust stockings with shoes of the same color if they happen to be the fashion of the moment. Otherwise, stick to the neutrals.

Your gloves—ON THE STREET—Washable cotton slip-ons are most suitable for you. By this we mean the heavy, double-woven material which looks like suède. The same type of glove can be worn in a sturdy leather, such as pigskin.

SUNDAY BEST—Simple, slightly flared slip-ons, or gloves long enough to come between the wrist and the elbow, with one or two buttons. These gloves are most attractive when pushed down or wrinkled toward the wrist. Colors? White with navy coat, suit, or dress. White or black with black coat, suit, or dress. Beige gloves with almost any color outfit. Colored gloves only if they repeat one of the colors in your dress. Do not give yourself a spotted appearance by wearing a red hat, red gloves, and red bag with a navy dress. Your gloves may be of cotton or suède or doeskin.

FORMAL—Long white or colored gloves to match your dress. Gloves are no longer considered an absolute necessity with an evening dress, and you are the type who may do without them if you wish.

Your furs—ON THE STREET—Follow the advice given to the wee bit and buy a flat fur, simply made, without contrasting fur trim. Do not wear thick or shiny furs. You can wear a fur coat if it is beautifully fitted to your figure, and you will be better satisfied if it is made to your measurements. One of your best furs for all purposes is tightly curled brown or black Persian lamb or a sheared beaver. Broadtail is an extravagantly beautiful fur with a flat surface and watery swirled markings like those on moiré ribbon. It has some sheen but can be worn by the prettily rounded. Alaskan seal and mink are also good for you. Personally, we think the prettily rounded figure shows off well in a perfectly fitted plain cloth coat with a fur piece which can also be worn over suits and dresses. Figures of this type should avoid capes. However, follow the advice given to the wee bit.

FORMAL—A coat is best; but you would also look good in a medium-sized stole of a flat fur.

Your handbags—ON THE STREET —If you are inclined to stuff your bags, buy a little satchel. It won't look stuffed, even when it is! If you are the careful type who never has more than fourteen separate items in a pocketbook, then the envelope purse was made for you. Keep the color of your bag keyed to the color of your outfits. If you wear more brown or black than any other color, buy either a brown or a black bag. Colored bags may make you look wider through the waistline and hips, for a spot of bright color there will attract the attention of the observer, who might otherwise see only your most attractive features.

SUNDAY BEST—A little pouch bag on a handle, or a small clutch bag in any leather or fabric to go with your costume. Leathers and fabrics suitable for these dress-up bags are listed among the suggestions for the wee bit.

FORMAL—Wear a simple bag without glitter. It may be the envelope type, or a bag on a frame. Keep the size medium or small.

Your jewelry—Try to wear jewelry with lo-o-ong lines. For example, we'll say your hands are pretty and short. Then have your rings set with oval stones, or with oblong stones, but avoid heavy settings. A single stone set alone will be more flattering to your hand than a group of stones. If you like bracelets, select a single beautiful one. Wear necklaces to give added length to your neck. Pearls are the most becoming and flattering necklace; avoid the choker type that consists of many chains or strands of beads worn together. By all means wear earrings if you like them. Brush your hair softly up from your ears to give a line of height, and select small, close-fitting earrings which follow the curve of the ear. Don't wear dangling earrings. Choose long pins and clips rather than chunky ones.

CHAPTER 14

Taking Care of Your Clothes

YOU may make or buy the most beautiful clothes in town, but if you treat them carelessly, you still won't look your best wearing them. For that reason it is important to make the care of your clothes a regular part of your routine.

You have seen article after article in newspapers or magazines advising you to mend every little rip, check every little snap, wash separate collars and cuffs—all the very instant after you remove your dress. Of course if you change your dress at four o'clock in the afternoon and have nothing else to do before you eat your dinner or supper, you might be able to follow those directions. But you can't if you are either busy at home with your house and children or if you rush in from work and make a quick change from your everyday clothes into your dress-up clothes before you go out for the evening. That "fix every snap every day" advice was geared to a more tranquil life. Our advice is to devote one night a week getting all your clothes and accessories in order. This might be the same night that you put aside for shampooing and other grooming routines. If you are going to be well dressed, your clothes must be in order.

The following are good habits to form:

Hang your dress, coat, or suit on a hanger as soon as you remove it. If possible avoid using thin wire hangers (the kind that come with your clothes from the dry cleaner) as they may leave "stretch" marks in the shoulders or sleeves of your garments. It is best to use a wooden or plastic hanger which is fairly wide, and if there are no shoulder pads sewn into your dress or coat, it is a good idea to sew a pair of pads to the ends of the hanger. This "fills out" the shoulder line of your garment and prevents the hanger from leaving marks. For a garment made of a delicate fabric like lace or chiffon, it is well to use a hanger that is completely padded (not just at each end). Such hangers may be bought already padded with cotton or foam rubber, covered with velvet or some other fabric. You can easily make your own padded hangers if you desire.

Do not hang up sweaters or other knitted garments. Fold them and keep in a drawer or in a box on a shelf in your closet.

If your wardrobe includes stoles made of materials that might crease if folded and laid away for a long time, you can hang them on the cross-rods of the wire hangers which were mentioned before. But first, pad the cross-rods by winding ribbon or strips of material over the rods. In that way your stoles will not show the marks of the metal and they will not slide off the rod. This idea is also good for hanging scarves if you don't want to fold them.

Keep the door of your clothes closet

open at night so that your clothes will have a chance to air.

Wash stockings daily. Fibers are weakened if stockings are allowed to accumulate for the family wash.

Air your sweaters and knitted clothes, then store them flat in a drawer or chest. Do not hang them up.

Use shoe "toes" which you can buy or make of velvet or other fabric stuffed tightly with cotton. Or you can always stuff the toes of your shoes with paper. Air the shoes worn during the day before putting them away. Cover all shoes not in everyday use.

Have run-over heels repaired at once. If your feet perspire, you may need to have the sole lining changed every few months.

Brush your hat if it is to be worn next day; if it is not to be worn for a while, brush it and put it in a box lined with tissue paper. Hat trees look nice in your closet, but a hat tree may cause the hat to lose its shape.

Smooth leather gloves out flat and put them in a flat box.

PRESSING—Pressing is an important step both in making your clothes and in caring for them. Pressing the seams while the dress, coat, or suit is under construction will help to give the finished garment a professionally made look. Pressing all your clothes regularly will help you to look well dressed.

Pressing should never be a last resort. There are men and women who wear clothes day in, day out, and then when an article of clothing (usually a woolen coat or suit) is hopelessly baggy and stretched at the elbows, knees, and seat, they rush it off to the tailor. And the tailor is blamed if the garment does not look like new when it is returned.

Because different textile fibers require different treatment in pressing, you will find them listed separately here.

If you do not know the kind of material the garment is made of or whether it is safe to press it, try pressing a small sample of the material in a seam or some other place where it will not show. Save all identifying tags which come with ready-made clothes, or with fabrics bought by the yard, if these tags contain any laundering, dry-cleaning, or pressing directions. There are some synthetic fabrics, for example, which should be dry-cleaned, not washed. This information will be stated on the label.

Pressing equipment—IRON—One with heat control is best. Then you can set the dial at the correct temperature for silk, cotton, linen, wool, or synthetics, and know that your iron will never become too hot for the fabric.

If you plan to do much tailoring or pressing of suits and coats, you might consider buying an electric steam iron. No pressing cloth is needed with this iron.

If you have an iron without heat control, press synthetics, silks, or woolens first, and leave cottons and linens until the last, since these fabrics can endure a greater heat without injury to the fibers.

IRONING BOARD—Have a well-padded folding one. In an emergency you can use an old table top covered with many thicknesses of clean white material. But a sturdy ironing board makes ironing much less of a task than makeshift equipment.

SLEEVE BOARD—This is such an inexpensive luxury that you should have one. It comes all padded and is obtainable at any mail-order house or department store.

Did you know that no well-pressed sleeve has a crease? If a suit or coat comes from the cleaner with a crease pressed in the sleeve, it means only that he cannot afford fine hand pressing for the price he charges. So buy a sleeve board and press your clothes correctly.

NEEDLE BOARD—This little pad with hundreds of tiny blunt wires sticking up from the surface is wonderful to use when you press corduroy, velvet, or any pile material which might crush or show seam ridges in pressing. It is not expensive.

PRESSING CLOTHS—Use any clean, washed, lint-free cotton cloth for pressing. A piece of washed muslin is fine. Unwashed material may contain a dressing which will stick to the iron. You may also purchase specially treated pressing cloths. These are excellent for woolen clothes.

PRESSING CUSHION—This can be a pad of washed muslin shaped to fit into a shoulder or other curved place, to make pressing easier.

SPRINKLER—You can use a bottle with a sprinkler top for dampening clothes or pressing cloths, or a sponge. Dampen a pressing cloth by dipping it in a small pan of lukewarm water, or sprinkling water on the cloth with your fingers.

Pressing wool—Wool is extremely resilient. It has a springiness unrivaled by any other textile fiber. A well-made woolen garment will spring back to its original shape, and any minor wrinkles will hang out if the garment is given at least one day of rest between wearings. Too-frequent or careless pressing will shorten the life and injure the appearance of any woolen material just as much as too-infrequent pressing.

Press wool with a warm (not hot) iron, using a dampened pressing cloth. You may decide to use two pressing cloths—a dry one on top of a damp one—if you want to steam the fabric thoroughly, although one cloth is ordinarily sufficient. Keep the iron moving. If the iron is held for any length of time in one spot, its shape may be marked

through the pressing cloth and onto the fabric.

Wool is usually pressed on the wrong side. Pockets, lapels, and other places may need to be touched up on the right side. Always do this with a pressing cloth between the iron and the garment.

Pressing silk—Silk is pressed on the wrong side, with a warm (not hot) iron. Use a dry pressing cloth. When this method is used, silk may be ironed even when slightly damp.

Pressing rayon—Different types of rayon require different pressing methods. You are always safe if you use a slightly warm iron and a dry pressing cloth between the iron and the wrong side of the fabric.

Most rayons are easiest to iron when they are slightly and evenly damp, and many weaves can safely be ironed without a pressing cloth, unless the ironing directions on the fabric label advise otherwise.

Iron rayon dresses on the straight up-and-down grain of the cloth. This applies to hems as well as to skirts, sleeves, and dress tops. Rayon may stretch and ripple if it is ironed on the crosswise grain.

Pressing nylon—Nylon seldom needs pressing. It can be pressed with a dry pressing cloth between a warm iron and the fabric. Iron nylon while damp—almost immediately after washing.

Pressing plastics—Don't. Most plastics are not pressable. The wrinkles will hang out.

Pressing linen—Press linen on the wrong side with a hot iron to get the correct dull finish. Linen clothes should not be shiny on the right side. No pressing cloth is needed ordinarily, but a damp cloth may be helpful in pressing out stubborn wrinkles. Always use a pressing cloth if you must "touch up" a pocket on the right side of a linen dress or suit. Iron linen while it is slightly and evenly damp.

Pressing cotton—Iron cotton without a pressing cloth and with a hot iron. A linen-finish cotton should always be pressed on the wrong side. Ironing on the wrong side gives a finer appearance, though there are many times when you will find it quicker and more convenient to iron men's shirts and everyday cotton dresses on the right side. Cottons are ironed when damp.

Pressing velvet and corduroy— You can use the needle board mentioned on the preceding page, or the steam method. To steam a garment hang it on a clothes hanger over a bathtub. Allow the hot water to run into the tub until the room is filled with steam. After an hour or so, remove the garment and hang it in another room, making sure it does not touch anything until it is thoroughly dry.

MENDING, DARNING, AND PATCHING—Keeping your clothes and accessories as well as the clothes of the family in good repair is just as necessary as laundering, cleaning, and pressing them. You will find directions for wardrobe mending, darning, and patching in Chapter 19.

REMOVING STAINS—Stains on garments are always a problem. To remove them at home sometimes requires a little knowledge of chemistry, at least enough to know what type of cleaning agent and what cleaning method are most effective for the various types of stains. With the aid of a cleaning pad of some absorbent material and plenty of clean cloths, preferably of the same fabric as the garment to be cleaned, you will be able to remove many of the common stains yourself. Others are better left to a professional cleaner.

General directions for stain removal—Treat all stains as soon as possible after they occur. When a stain is allowed to remain on the piece of material, it may penetrate the fibers of the cloth and become much more difficult to remove.

Always test the cleaning agent on a small piece of the material before attempting to remove the spot. This small piece may be a little of the material clipped from an inside seam. It is important to do this, because some cleaning agents will leave a ring or mark.

Always treat stains before laundering. All stained articles should be set aside and the stains removed before they are put in the wash. One reason for doing this is that the hot water used for laundering will "set" the stains.

If you do not know what the stain is, or if you feel that you cannot remove it yourself, send the article to a good cleaner. You can help the cleaner do his job well if you will tell him the nature of the stain if you know it—that is, grease, tar, et cetera—and make no attempt to remove the stain yourself before taking the article to him. If you do something to "set" the stain, even the best cleaner may not be able to remove it without injury to the cloth or dye.

WARNING! When using any cleaning fluid inside the house, open the window to get enough air to counteract any fumes from the cleaning agent. Be sure there is no lighted gas range flame or lighted cigarette in the room. Use great caution regardless of the mildness of the cleaning fluid and the "safety" assurance on its label.

Specific instructions for stain removal—Below are given the most common causes of stains and the most satisfactory ways to remove them:

CHEWING GUM—Scrape off as much as possible. Dampen a clean white cloth with carbon tetrachloride and apply with a circular rubbing motion. If directions are included on the bottle, follow those.

COFFEE—Use cool water. Soak the stain immediately, wash in mild soapsuds, and rinse thoroughly. If the garment is not washable, sponge the spot with cool water, allow it to dry, then sponge with cleaning fluid.

EGG—Try clean cold water first. If that does not remove the stain, try soap and cool water. Hot water hardens egg and may set the stain. The same treatment applies to meat, fish, and cheese, except cream cheese.

FAT—See Oil. Same treatment. Fats include cream cheese, butter, cream, mayonnaise.

FRUIT—Use cold water. The trick here, as in treating most stains, is to act at once. A stain which has a chance to dry is much harder to remove than a fresh stain. If the fabric is washable, soak the stain in cool water; then apply a household bleach, such as hydrogen peroxide. If the garment must be dry cleaned, sponge the stain with cool water, apply a soapless shampoo, and allow it to stand for several hours. Then apply a few drops of white vinegar.

GRASS—On white cotton or linen wash and hang in the sun to bleach. Washing is usually sufficient. Do not expose colored materials to the sun, for they may not be fade-proof. For garments which are not washable use cleaning fluid, follow with a sponging of denatured alcohol, then a second sponging with cool water.

GREASE—See Oil. Same treatment.

INK—Permanent ink is difficult to remove. You are wise if you use only washable ink at your house. This type of stain can be removed by soaking the stained portion of cloth in cold water or milk for fifteen minutes before washing in a mild suds and rinsing. Javelle water or one of the chlorine compounds may be used safely only on white material, for it will remove the color from the fabric at the same time it removes the ink. These compounds have a tendency to weaken fibers of material, so the stained spot should never be soaked in one of the bleaching agents for more than ten minutes. If the material is colored and is not washable, you may try a solution of denatured alcohol and water, but you would probably be wiser to take the stained garment to a cleaner.

LIPSTICK—Always treat a lipstick stain before washing the article. If lipstick remains after ordinary washing it will almost always be a permanent stain. To remove such stains buy a commercial cleaner especially for lipstick removal at the drugstore. For emergency removal of a small stain, try a little nail-polish remover, unless the material is rayon. You will be able to prevent many lipstick stains by using cleansing tissues between your lips when putting on your good dresses. Blot your lips on the tissue after applying lipstick and you will not smear it on clothing or napkins.

MILDEW—Mildew is a fungus growth. It is sometimes caused by leaving dampened clothes unironed, but in damp climate it may attack any material not exposed to the air. New or slight stains can sometimes be removed by washing and drying in the sun. Old stains, however, can seldom be taken out entirely.

NAIL POLISH—If the stain is on cotton, polish remover may be applied, but this cleaning agent cannot be used safely on rayon. Send a rayon garment to the cleaner at once.

OIL—Oil or grease stains can sometimes be removed by placing the stained spot between two clean blotters and pressing with a warm iron. For a large spot, try carbon tetrachloride. These treatments are for clear oils, such as sewing-machine oil. A stain from heavy, dark oil should be given to a professional cleaner, unless it is on a washable material. For washables, the treatment is hot water and soapsuds.

PAINT—Ask your druggist for a paint remover, or send the garment to the cleaner.

TAR—Same treatment as for chewing gum. If it is a large stain, or on non-washable material, better send the garment to the cleaner.

RUST—For white cotton or linen, wash and bleach in the sun, or in small amount of chlorine compound in water. (Read label on the bottle for the amount.) There are also satisfactory rust-removing creams which are easily and safely applied to most materials.

WATER SPOTS—If a material is so delicate that it water-spots, the best treatment is to send the garment to the cleaner. Or you can test a small piece of the fabric clipped from a seam to see if it washes without shrinkage or loss of color. If washing seems to be safe, put the entire garment in clean, cool water. For velvets, velveteens, and corduroys, water spots can be removed by steaming the garment over the spout of a teakettle filled with hot water, or by hanging the garment in a closed bathroom with the tub filled with steaming hot water.

CHAPTER 15

Remodeling Your Clothes

A WOMAN who is adept at remodeling her clothes will get a great deal of satisfaction out of this type of sewing. Not only is there a saving in actual cash, but there is also a fine sense of accomplishment in having increased the life of a garment. You will certainly find it worth your while to go through your closets to see if there are any clothes which might be recut, re-trimmed, or even combined with others to make a new outfit.

WHAT IS WORTH MAKING OVER?—
To be sure that your time and effort will be used to the best effect, examine the things you want to make over. Hold them up to the light to see whether the material is in good condition. Woolens attract moths and you may discover pin-point holes. Silk, cotton, and clothes made of synthetic fibers may have small tears. If there is still enough sound material, however, clothes with slight damages can always be salvaged. Some materials can be turned and used on the wrong side. In many cases a new pocket or a bit of embroidery can be added to cover up a place which has a tiny hole or tear if the rest of the material is still sturdy enough to give good wear.

SELECTING YOUR PATTERNS—When
you are remodeling a dress it is essential to get a pattern that is neither too complicated nor calls for large pieces of material. For instance, if you are going to remodel a two-piece dress that has a narrow skirt, do not buy a pattern with a princess line or a wide flared skirt. The same principle applies if you are making over a jacket with set-in fitted sleeves—do not buy a pattern with raglan shoulders or wide puffed sleeves. The pattern you buy for your new dress must not include any pieces that are larger than the pieces of your original garment. Of course there may be a place or two where you will have to do a little inconspicuous piecing, or you can add new contrasting material. But do remember, as a general rule, not to buy a pattern where more material is required than you have at hand.

PREPARATION OF MATERIAL—Garments should be washed or dry-cleaned before you start to rip them apart, as it is always more pleasant to work with clean material.

Rip the seams with a one-edged razor blade, or with a small scissors clip the threads at short intervals and pull apart gently. Used material may not be strong enough to stand quick ripping of the seams, so do it carefully.

When the garment is ripped apart, it should be pressed. If the material has a definite right and wrong side, make some mark on the wrong side of each piece to identify it and keep it from getting mixed up later on when you are cutting. Also, before pressing mark the "straight" of the material on the right side with tailor's chalk or long bastings, to aid you in cutting from the new pattern.

PIECING INSUFFICIENT MATERIAL—

If it is necessary to piece material which is not large enough, do this in such inconspicuous places as the top of the back waist at the point where it joins the front seam under the arm. A piece can be inserted to make a skirt wider either by a whole gore the full length of the front or the back or both sides of the skirt. A skirt can also be pieced at the side seams. If you find that a little piece has to be added when you lay the pattern on the material, stitch the piecing together into position and press the seams out flat on the wrong side before you start to cut out the pattern. The piecing will not be noticeable if you make sure that the materials joined together run the same way on the grain, that the designs, if there are any, match, and that the seams are flat and have not been puckered by stretching when they were stitched together.

Sometimes it is better to use contrasting material for remodeling. You can use a garment which has done its original service and is ready to be cut up for remodeling, or you can buy a piece of new material which looks well with the old fabric you are using. A sleeve, vestee, bolero, or bands on a blouse or skirt can be effective in contrasting material if there is not enough of the original garment material for a complete remodeling job.

CUTTING—Now that the material has been cleaned, ripped apart, and pressed, spread it out right side up. Place the pattern pieces over the pieces of fabric, making sure that each is placed on the straight of the goods. Then, before you do any cutting, check again to see if and where you will need to piece. It is better to take the time to do this before you cut than to discover too late a short piece that you overlooked.

SUGGESTIONS FOR MAKE-OVERS— Clothes closets and dresser drawers invariably contain many articles of outmoded or outworn clothes which are still in very good condition and are merely waiting to be rejuvenated. Every sewer has her own specific ideas about what should be done with the usable things that she discovers. These general examples may help you with your own special make-over problems.

Turning a man's shirt into a blouse—Collars and cuffs may be frayed, the buttonholes may be torn, or maybe Dad just doesn't like the color or stripe in his shirt. It will make an attractive tailored blouse for the lady

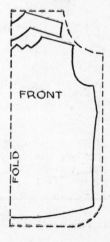

FRONT

FOLD

of the house. Use a basic blouse pattern and lay it on the ripped parts of the cleaned and pressed shirt. As a rule the front of a woman's blouse is cut from the back of a man's shirt and the back of the blouse is made from the front pieces of the shirt.

If you do not want a buttoned-down-the-back blouse, select a pattern which can be seamed down the center back. You can also use the shirt fronts

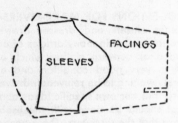

for your blouse front by reversing the buttonholes, and sewing buttons over the buttonholes which were in the man's shirt. (A woman's blouse buttons from right to left.)

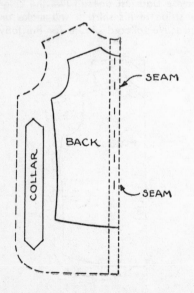

By following the same general directions you can cut down one of your own discarded blouses to make a pretty blouse for your daughter. Buy a pattern for Little Sister and cut out the blouse as described above.

Child's dress—No little girl can have too many dresses, and when you consider how quickly she outgrows them, it may be wise not to invest too much in new clothes. Here is where ingenuity can be used in cutting down Mother's or Big Sister's wardrobe. If there isn't enough of one material, a charming dress can be made by com-

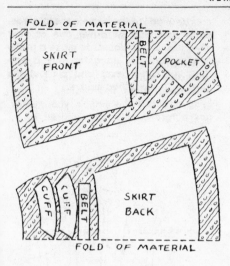

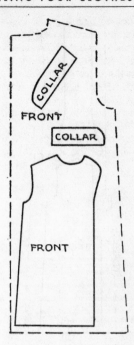

bining two materials. The accompanying illustrations offer a suggestion for
the resourceful sewer.

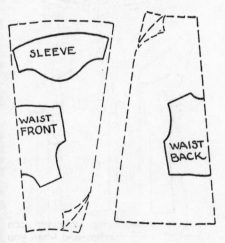

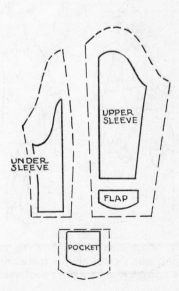

Small child's coat—Your schoolboy
can have a fine coat made from his
father's or older brother's worn or outgrown coat if it doesn't have too large
a check or plaid. Small boys just aren't
the size for those patterns.

can be made over from one which her older sister has outgrown.

Making a man's suit into a woman's suit—This is one of those make-over tricks that women like to brag about. If the man in your family has outgrown a suit or is tired of it,

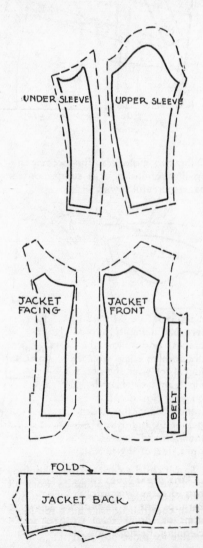

The illustration shows how to cut down a man's coat, but the same principle applies to a little girl's coat which

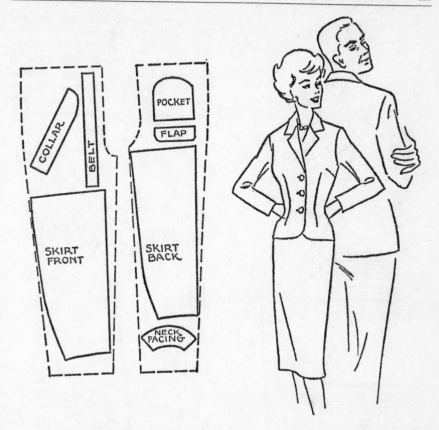

claim it before the moths do. Buy a pattern for a simple tailored suit, cut your pieces, and follow the sewing directions which come with the pattern. The jacket for your suit can be the popular hip length or waist length, depending on your figure and the current fashion trend. Stitch the old buttonholes together by hand and sew buttons over them. Make your buttonholes on the right side of the jacket.

One dress from two—Do you have two dresses which are partly worn? Perhaps one is threadbare under the arms or shrunk from washing or dry cleaning. Perhaps you are just tired of

the other dress and want something new. Here's the place to use your imagination and combine the two dresses. Use a simple pattern with very little trimming, for combining materials can make a dress look "dowdy" unless you consider the same points as you do when choosing material for a new dress. For a slender person, the top of the dress might be of one material, perhaps a print, and the skirt a harmonizing plain color. You might insert sleeves of another material, or make collars or scarves of different fabric.

Evening dress cut shorter—Do you have an evening dress which just hangs

One Dress From Two

in the closet because it no longer looks well on you? If so, you can recapture its value for dress-up occasions by shortening the hem line and maybe altering the length of the sleeves. This remodeling job is simple, quick, and inexpensive, and you'll still have a dress for social functions without its being limited to the strictly full-length formal.

OTHER REMODELING POSSIBILITIES —The scope of remodeling possibilities is so unlimited that nothing in your wardrobe need be wasted. You can transform one of your skirts into one for your young daughter. A pleated skirt can be turned into a slim trim one. A tight skirt can be made more comfortable for walking by slitting one or

Evening Dress Cut Shorter

both sides.

If you have a two-piece suit with a jacket you do not like you can cut down the jacket and make a bolero of it, or remove the sleeves and convert the jacket into a jerkin.

When a dress has sleeves which are too tight or are worn-out, you can remove the sleeves and make a jacket or

bolero of contrasting material to wear over this sleeveless dress. If the dress is of wool, it might be turned into a sleeveless jumper to be worn with a variety of blouses. A third suggestion is to make bishop sleeves of a solid color to fit the cutout armhole.

If you're handy with knitting needles you can replace the worn-out sleeves in a woolen blouse or jacket with knitted woolen sleeves, and they can be so chic!

A bathrobe for Junior or even Little Sister can be made by cutting down Dad's or Mother's bathrobe. For Mother or Daughter a practical bathrobe can be made from a discarded candlewick bedspread.

Men's shirts when they become worn under the arms, on the collars, or the cuffs, needn't be discarded. Use the shirt backs and the two fronts to make aprons for the children and yourself. They can even be made into rompers and sun suits for the baby.

Lingerie can also be made over. A nightgown can be cut down into a slip or a petticoat, a bed jacket, or a little girl's nightgown. A slip with a torn lace yoke or straps, or one that has become too short, can be made into a petticoat

merely by removing the top and stitching an elastic or tape around the waistband. The evening slip which is no longer used need only be shortened and hemmed to make a daytime slip out of it.

The upper and lower parts of pajamas may not always give equal wear. As a rule the trousers wear out first. If this is the case, don't discard the pajama jacket; instead, make another pair of trousers. They don't have to be the exact color or design as the jacket —in fact, a pajama set can be most attractive if the top contrasts with the bottom.

Your clothes closet is probably concealing a variety of clothing which you can use as some clever remodeling— all you need is imagination and patience.

CHAPTER 16

Gathers, Shirrings, Ruffles, and Headings

GATHERS can be used to add fullness or to control fullness. They can be functional or they can be decorative. Functional gathers are those that ease in fullness. Gathers used for decorative purposes include shirrings, ruffles, and headings.

Gathering is done by taking a row of small running stitches and then pulling the thread gently so that the fullness falls into folds or measures the required width. It may be done by hand or by machine.

Gathering by hand—Use a thin needle and a thread that is fine but strong enough not to break when the gathers are pulled into place. Always knot the thread. Take small running stitches across the material to be gathered. If it is a short distance, run the stitches the full width across, then push the material along the thread until the gathering measures the desired length. If you are gathering longer pieces of material, such as ruffling for curtains, pause every few inches and gently push the material back on the

stitches you have just taken. If the gathers need reinforcement, add a second row of running stitches about ⅛ or ¼ of an inch below the first row, or even a third or fourth row if necessary. As each row of gathers is completed, stick a pin at the end of the thread and wind the thread around it; or tack the thread so that the gathers won't loosen and spread out.

Gathers to hold fullness—When fitting a sleeve into an armhole, or matching a curved seam to a straight seam, take small running stitches

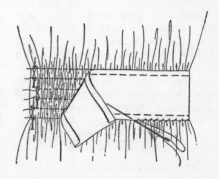

around the curved edge in two rows
⅛ of an inch apart. Pull the gathered
edge until it measures the same as the
straight edge.

GATHERING BY MACHINE—Gathers
on the machine are made by loosening
the tension and using a large stitch.
Leave the threads at each end long
enough to work with. Pull the bobbin
thread carefully, pushing the material
along this thread until you have the
desired fullness. If you want a double
or triple row of stitches, space the
machine stitching about one quarter of
an inch apart, then pull all the bobbin
threads evenly to form the gathers.

SHIRRING BY HAND—Shirring is
made up of rows and rows of gathers,
usually about ⅛ inch apart. Shirring
may be done in as few or as many
rows as desired. It may be used separately in narrow and wide bands for
trimming, in the same way as lace or
embroidery insertion is used, or made
directly on the dress itself in the shape
of a yoke on the blouse or trimming
on the skirt. Shirring is also used at
the tops of dressing-table flounces and
on other household articles. It is best
suited to sheer and lightweight materials.

Using a stay under shirring—
When shirring is made by hand, it will
strengthen the shirred section if a stay
is sewed under the gathers. Cut a strip
of material the width of the shirring,
allowing at least an additional ½
inch for hem allowance at both sides
of the strip. Baste the strip in place
over the shirring on the wrong side,
then turn under the hem and catch
stitch the first and the last rows of
gathers.

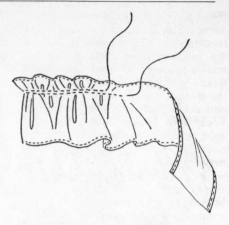

SHIRRING BY MACHINE—This is
done the same way as gathering by
machine. Space the rows of stitches
evenly, from ⅛ to ¼ inch apart.
When all the rows have been stitched,
pull each bobbin thread separately,
to form the shirring.

USING ELASTIC THREAD—An ad-
vantage in using this thread is that,
when pressing the material which is
shirred, you can stretch the stitched
part and thus get a flat surface for
the iron. Elastic shirr-stitching should
shirr in the ratio of 2 inches to 1. From
4 to 6 rows makes a good shirring,
although you can use elastic thread
for only 1 row. This thread is especially good to use for heavy fabrics,
rather than lightweight or sheer ones.
Wind the elastic thread tightly on the
bobbin of the sewing machine until it
is almost full. The tension of the bobbin case should be tight enough so
that the elastic thread pulls out with
considerable stretch. Use your regular
sewing thread on top of the machine
in the same or contrasting color as
the elastic. Use a contrasting color if
you want the stitching to be an extra
trim. Set the machine for a long stitch,
about 7 to the inch. First test stitching
on a scrap of the material to be used,

for about 3 or 4 rows. If the top thread forms loops, it means the top tension is too loose. With the presser foot of the machine down, tighten the top tension enough to give the elastic thread stitching sufficient snap. Fasten the threads securely at the beginning and the end of each row. When you begin the second and subsequent rows, hold the previous rows stretched apart at least the toe width of the presser foot. To give your finished work a neat, tight look, steam the shirred section when you are through. Launder or dry-clean the fabric in the usual way for the material you used. When ironing shirring, set the iron temperature at nylon or rayon.

RUFFLING—To make ruffling you must have a piece of material at least one and a half times the length of the piece to which the ruffle will be attached. In other words, if you want to make ten yards of ruffling you will need a strip of material fifteen yards long. The strips

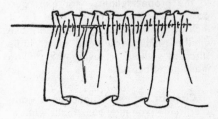

of material to be ruffled are cut on the cross-grain in whatever width is desired for the ruffle, then joined for use on stiff material. Experiment with the seams open and hem the strip on both sides before you start ruffling. As in making gathers, you may make the ruffling by hand or by machine.

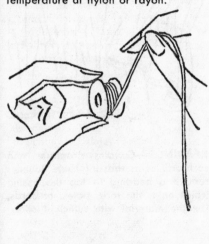

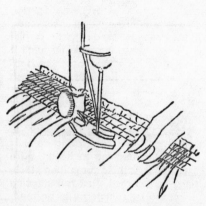

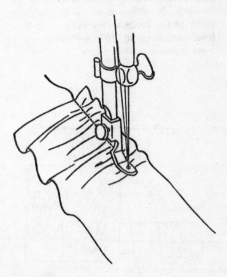

Another way to make ruffling—yards and yards of it at a time—is to use the machine hemmer and to hem the long strip of material with the narrowest machine hem you can make. Next, put the pleating attachment on the machine and work with a sample piece of material until you have adjusted the pleats to the proper fullness—for most purposes, 1½ inches of material for 1 inch of finished ruffling. You can make all the ruffling you need at a single stitching without removing the ruffling machine attachment.

Circular ruffle—Instead of a gathered ruffle, you may sometimes want to make a circular ruffle without fullness at the top where it joins the material. This type of ruffle is often recommended for use on stiff material. Experiment with the circular shape by cutting it in paper first. When you have worked out the shape and length of ruffle you need, cut the material. The circular ruffle may be attached in one of two ways: by basting it directly to the material and seaming it underneath, or by turning under the top edge and basting and stitching it at the top. In either case, snip the top edge of the ruffle every inch or so before attaching it. This will prevent it from pulling.

Double ruffle—Make a continuous strip of material as you would for a single ruffle and hem both ends of the material. Make 2 or 3 rows of running stitches down the center and draw into gathers. To apply a double ruffle, stitch it to the material through the center along the gathers. As an added trimming you may cover the gathers with a contrasting binding or narrow ribbon and stitch it down the center.

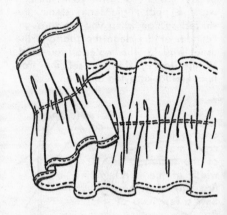

HEADINGS—Curtains, draperies, and such articles as dressing-table flounces require a heading to top the casing which holds the rods, poles, or cords. Cut the material with sufficient allow-

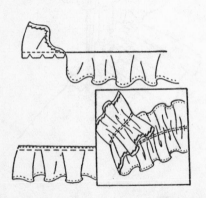

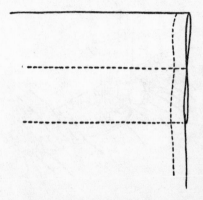

ance to turn over and hem. If you cannot spare material for this, stitch an extra piece to the top and turn that over, making sure that the joining seam does not show on the right side.

Gathered heading—If you want a heading which can be used for a dec-

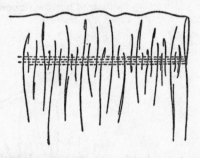

orative finish and not with a rod or cord, make a narrow hem in the top of the material, then turn down the width of the heading and make the first row of gathers through the hem. Sew a few rows of stitches above the first row, spacing them evenly apart and leaving enough material above the top row of stitches to form the heading. Pull the material over the threads to form the gathers.

Corded heading—Turn down sufficient material to allow for a casing for the cord. An attractive heading is made with two or three cords. Measure the amount of material to turn down. Turn under a narrow hem and make the first stitching. Allow enough width between the rows to insert the cords, and stitch across the material. After the cords are pulled through and the gathers are properly adjusted, tack the ends of the cord to the back part of the casing through which it is pulled. Finish the outer ends of the material neatly so that the ends of the cord are not visible.

CHAPTER 17

Lace, Edgings, and Other Trimmings

LACE is truly a luxury material, whether it is used for a whole dress or only for trimming and whether it is made of cotton, rayon, silk, or nylon. It is so adaptable that it can add daintiness to a woman's lingerie as well as to a baby's finest dresses. At the same time it is equally attractive in dresses or in fine household linens. To carry out the feeling of delicacy it is preferable to attach lace by hand. However, despite its dainty appearance, lace is usually strong and may in some instances be stitched on the machine.

Lace edging—There are various widths in which lace edging may be bought and of course a variety of ways to use it. It may be sewed directly to the edge of the fabric on which it is used or it may be set into the material with "beading"—a very narrow lace sold at trimming counters.

Lace bands and gathered lace—Before applying lace edging you must decide whether you want it to be straight or gathered. If you put lace edging on a curved piece of material

such as a flare, or on scallops, it is best to gather the lace slightly, because a straight edging cannot be applied neatly to a curved edge. To gather the lace edging, look for the separate thread which is woven close to the straight edge or selvedge. Take hold of the end of the thread with one hand and with the other hand push the lace gently along this thread; you will find that you can gather the lace as much as necessary by merely pushing it along.

Joining lace to a raw edge—Baste the lace close to the edge on the right side of the material. Turn the material to the wrong side. Then roll the edge of the fabric and catch the lace with each stitch that you take in the hem.

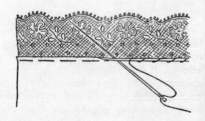

Joining lace to a hemmed edge—
Place the wrong side of the lace along
the wrong side of the material. Hold it
with the lace toward you. Sew the lace
to the material with fine overcast

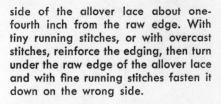

side of the allover lace about one-
fourth inch from the raw edge. With
tiny running stitches, or with overcast
stitches, reinforce the edging, then turn
under the raw edge of the allover lace
and with fine running stitches fasten it
down on the wrong side.

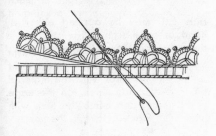

stitches, keeping the stitches loose, so
that when the overcasting is finished,
the lace and the material may be
spread out flat. Use a fine needle and
a fine single thread.

Joining lace with beading—Make
a rolled hem on the material which is
to be edged, catching the beading into
each stitch as you make it. Then roll the
outer hem of the beading, catching the
lace in the stitches as just described.

Lace inserts—Baste both selvedges
of the lace insert over the right side of
the material. Join both edges to the
material with a satin stitch. If the material is to remain under the lace, no
other sewing is necessary. If you want
a cutout lace insertion, snip away the
material under the lace very carefully
with a tiny curved scissors. With a tiny
running stitch hem down each edge of
material flat, catching the edge of the
lace very carefully as you stitch. Cut
away the raw edge of the turned-under
material as close to the lace as possible.

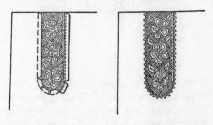

Edging on allover lace—Allover
lace may be edged with the very narrowest or with a wider type of lace
edging. If the edging is to be inconspicuous, you may buy picot lace
edging which is made just for the purpose. Baste the edging on the right

Joining lace inserts with edging—
Hold the edging and the insertion with
the wrong sides of the material together and join them together with very
small overcast stitches, using a fine
needle and fine thread. These stitches
should be loose enough to allow the
edging and the insertion to be spread
open flat after the seam is made.

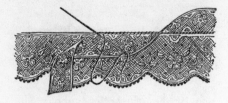

Joining corners in lace—Cut a V in the lace as shown in the illustration but do not cut through the edge. If there is a definite pattern in the lace,

Braiding (passementeries)—Used with discrimination braiding can add smartness to an otherwise plain suit. It comes in a variety of types and mate-

be sure to match it properly before you make the mitered corner. Join the two edges with fine overcast stitches, keeping the two right sides of the lace together. Then spread the lace out flat.

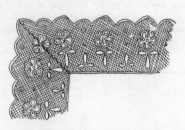

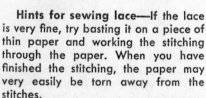

Hints for sewing lace—If the lace is very fine, try basting it on a piece of thin paper and working the stitching through the paper. When you have finished the stitching, the paper may very easily be torn away from the stitches.

Always use paper when stitching lace by machine; place the paper beneath the lace.

Always use a matching thread to sew lace; use cotton thread for cotton lace, silk thread for silk lace, et cetera.

rials and may be applied either by hand or by machine. The stitching is done through the middle of the braid

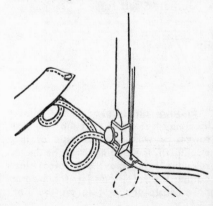

and again on the inner side if it seems desirable. Silk ribbon braid is used as a plain edging or for looped designs such as the "frog" closing.

Embroidered edgings—These can be bought by the yard, either gathered or ungathered. The latter is usually cheaper. If you decide to gather the edging yourself, buy one and a half times the distance to be trimmed. Gather the edging and finish the raw edge with a bias binding of the same color. If you buy the edging already gathered, buy only the amount needed, since it is measured by the length of the binding.

Embroidered edging can be sewed flat to the edge of collars, cuffs, or hems without being gathered.

Other types of edgings—These range from the gay colored rickrack used so effectively on aprons and cotton dresses to pleated ruffling, eyelet, gathered lace or net, and bias cord.

Rickrack

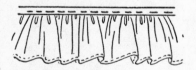

Gathered self ruffle

Pleated self ruffle

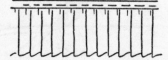

Eyelet or other purchased edging in various widths

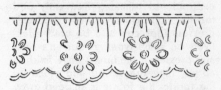

Narrow lace (gathered)

Lace, not gathered, or net footing (for lingerie)

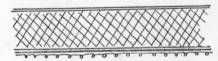

Self bias cord made into loops

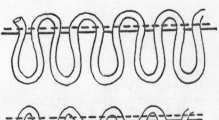

TRIMMINGS

Embroidered inserts—Inserts of embroidered trimming frequently add to the attractiveness of children's dresses. They can also be used effectively on some types of women's summer dresses. If the inserts have finished edges, they are sewed into place on the fabric, the fabric is snipped away beneath the insert, and the raw edges turned under and catch stitched. If the insert edges are raw, they, too, must be turned under and caught down.

Allover embroidery—Sheer material embroidered in an allover design of the same shade can be bought by the yard. It also comes in heavier fabric embroidered in brilliant colors. It is generally used as trimming on collars, cuffs, pockets, and vestees. It may be made up as part of a dress in the form of a short jacket.

CHAPTER 18

Decorative Stitches

SIMPLE DECORATIVE STITCHES—A touch of simple embroidery or other decorative stitching is often enough to transform a plain little dress into something very special. In the same way a bit of fine handwork can turn an inexpensive bridge cloth into something fit for a tea party. Much of this work which looks so difficult and commands such fabulous prices when done on fine blouses, lingerie, children's clothes, or table linen is truly easy to duplicate at home. Often the designs used are merely combinations of the elementary stitches shown in this chapter. Try a few on some scraps of material. Then, when your needle knows its way around, put it to work to add new touches of beauty to your wardrobe and household. The one principle to keep in mind in using decorative stitches is that a few are much more likely to be effective than too many.

Decorative stitches show to best advantage on plain materials, such as cotton, silk, rayon, or wool.

The yarns or threads used for decorative stitching range from the spool of mercerized colored cotton thread ordinarily used for hand or machine sewing to woolen yarns. Rows of machine stitching can sometimes be used effectively for decoration. Woolen yarn is generally used for decorating woolen materials. The usual six-strand embroidery thread sold in skeins and the single-strand heavier pearl cotton sold by the ball can both be used on most materials. All threads used to trim washables must be color fast. Silk floss and rayon floss are, however, better to use on rayon, silk, and woolen materials.

You will enjoy planning color combinations for your fancy stitches. Always take a sample of your material with you when you buy your trimming thread or yarn. If you use a transfer pattern which combines some of the simple stitches shown here, you will find the design printed in color on the transfer-pattern envelope. These colors are a good guide to use when buying your thread. The areas of color, as well as the colors themselves, will determine the attractiveness of your completed design. If you want to work out your own ideas, do it on a sample piece, then pick the best.

Machine stitching for decoration—Plain colored cottons, spun rayons, or linens can be beautifully trimmed with rows of colored machine stitching in colors which go well together. For a curved design, place tissue paper on which the design has been traced over the material and stitch through. Tear paper away from the stitching after it is completed. For straight lines, make the first row of stitching close to an edge which will serve for a guide. Stitch every additional row an even distance from the first row, using the width of the machine presser foot as a guide.

More intricate forms of stitching can also be done by machine with the zig-zag attachments. Directions and suggestions are given in the booklets supplied by the manufacturer of your machine.

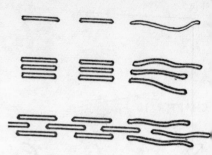

Couching stitch is an overcasting stitch made with a lightweight thread, to hold one or two strands of heavier thread in place. Mercerized sewing thread can be used to hold woolen yarn or pearl cotton in place. Couching

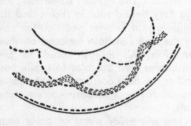

Saddle stitch or cobble stitch is a row of straight stitching taken by hand, with the upper stitch slightly longer than the one on the underside of the material. Saddle stitching is almost like uneven basting. The size of the stitch is

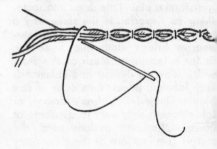

stitch is usually made in a thread which matches the heavier thread, though two colors can be used effectively if the stitches are kept very regular and even. Rows of it make a stunning border for neck, sleeves, or around the bottom of a dress. If the dress has a hem, make the stitches above the hem line, so that the hem can be lowered without destroying the effect of the decorative stitching.

determined by the size of the thread and the space to be stitched. Try two long stitches and one short stitch to an inch. If that doesn't look well, change the size of the stitch. Rows can be used in combination, as shown. Pearl cotton is fine for saddle stitching.

Seed stitch is a very small running stitch done with a twisted thread and used in a group to fill in an outline. It is often used to work the centers of flowers.

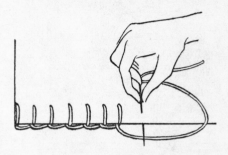

whatever design it is used, the space between the groups should be even, for the beauty of a blanket stitch lies in its spacing. It is one of the easiest stitches, and you can work out many delightful variations to suit your needs.

Outline stitch is a solid row of stitching made by taking a stitch about ¼ inch long on the right side of the material, then a short backstitch which comes up very close to the first stitch. When the backstitches are close to the

long stitches, the outline stitch gives the appearance of one continuous line of thread. Outline stitch can be used for a border, for leaves and stems in flower designs, and many other places where a bold, solid line is needed.

Blanket stitch may be evenly spaced with one stitch exactly like the stitch next to it, or spaced irregularly, with three stitches together, then a space, then three more stitches grouped together. The center stitch in these groups of three stitches may be longer than the other two (if desired) but in

To make the blanket stitch, insert the needle at right angles to the edge of the piece and bring it out at the edge. Repeat, each time passing the needle over the thread, as shown in the illustration.

The blanket stitch can be used to edge felt hats or belts (use wool yarn for this), to edge flannelette baby sacques or wrappers, and on peasant blouses. The stitch can also be used to finish an edge of material or as part of a design for which the blanket stitch makes the border.

Satin stitches are even, flat, smooth stitches placed closely side by side. This decorative touch is used for solid work; that is, for leaves, flowers, and other similar designs. The satin stitch is easy to make, though it takes a little practice to produce the smooth even effect. The space which is to be satin stitched is first padded with small even running stitches. This "raises" the finished design. Then the padding stitches are covered with close, even overcast stitches which follow the outline of the design.

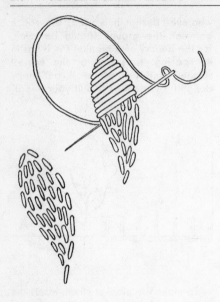

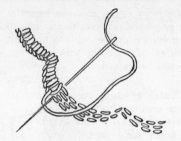

Cross-stitch is actually two stitches taken one across and at right angles to the other. Make a row of even stitches slanting in one direction. Then cross each stitch at the mid-point with another row of stitches slanting in the opposite direction. Cross-stitching, care-

Scallops can be made with the blanket stitch. The exact space for the scallops should be marked along the edge of the material, preferably by being pressed on from a transfer pattern. Pad the section where the scallops are to be worked with a series of small running stitches. Make the blanket stitches even and close together. Do not cut the edge of the material along the curved outer edge until the scallops are completely worked. Two strands of a six-strand cotton embroidery thread are often used for scalloping on dress-weight cottons and linens and for table linens and bedding. Scalloping is popular for edging necklines, sleeves, and for sheets and pillowcases. Practice a little to insure smooth, even scallops. Some women prefer to place their material between embroidery hoops when making scallops. This does hold the material firmly, but hoops are not actually necessary for this stitch or for any of the others described in this chapter.

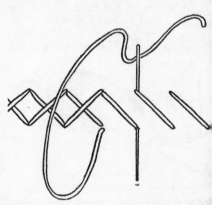

fully done, can be used effectively for many decorative purposes. Rows of cross-stitching can be used to form de-

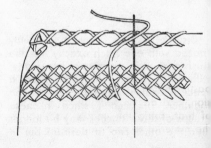

signs or a single row can be used as an edging. Cross-stitching is especially popular for use on table linens and on articles of clothing such as blouses, aprons, et cetera.

Catch stitch is similar to the cross-stitch and can be used for many of the same purposes. It is especially good as a finish for women's coats or suit linings, and to make a flat finish on a hem or a seam edge. Work from left to right. Bring the needle through the hem or seam binding, carry it diagonally up and back, and take a small stitch above and parallel to the hem. Carry the thread down and take another small stitch in the hem. Continue in the same manner as a cross-stitch, making the stitches as long or as close together as you desire. Generally speaking, the finer the fabric, the smaller the stitch.

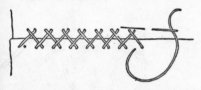

Feather stitch is a variety of outline stitch. It is used for trimming on babies' and children's clothes, underwear, and other articles where decorative stitching is used as a fine touch. First run a

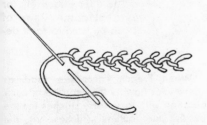

basting stitch as a guide for your design, and do the feather stitch on top of that. Bring the needle up through the material to one side of the guide line. Hold the embroidery thread down over the basting line with the thumb of one hand. With the needle in the other hand, take a short, slanting stitch on the opposite side of the basting line. Continue down the line until the design is finished. The feather stitch may be spaced as wide apart or as close as seems desirable; it may run along straight, curved, or scalloped lines.

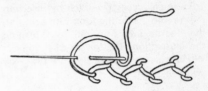

Lazy-daisy stitch is a loop stitch used chiefly in working flower designs. Insert the needle on the wrong side of the fabric and bring it through to the right side. Insert the needle on the right side of the fabric close to the place through which it was drawn. Take a stitch, bringing the needle out at the point of the petal, and looping the thread under the needle point, as shown in the illustration. Pull the needle through and catch the petal loop with a tiny stitch, bringing the needle into the position for the next stitch. If you are not using a stamped design, it is a good idea to draw the design on your fabric first, as a guide. Combinations of lazy-daisy stitches with a few French knots for a center can be worked into interesting flower designs.

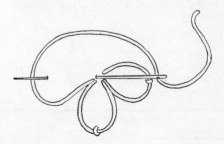

Chain stitch is another outline stitch. Insert the needle on the wrong side of the fabric and bring it through to the right side. Hold the thread with the thumb of one hand and insert the needle very close to the place where the thread came up.

Take a short stitch through the material, keeping the thread under the needle so that it forms a loop. Be careful not to pull the thread too tight. Take each successive stitch by inserting the needle inside the loop and bringing the needle into position, as shown in the illustration. The length of the chain stitch will vary according to the way you are using it.

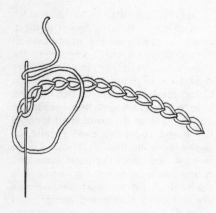

French knots are small, tight knots which can be worked out in intricate designs. Insert the needle on the wrong side of the fabric and bring it through to the right side. Place the point of the

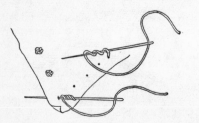

needle very close to the place where the thread was pushed through the fabric but do not insert it into the fabric. With the thread held taut in the other hand, wind it three or four times around the point of the needle. Continue to hold the thread tight while you push the needle through carefully, pulling the thread through the loop until it is knotted. Repeat the process again, as close or as far apart from the French knot as the design indicates. The heavier the thread and the more loops around the needle the larger the French knot will be. For dainty designs use only two threads of a six-strand floss. The French knot is most often used in combination with other stitches, since it is rather a thin decoration when used alone. For example, a border might be made of a row of saddle stitching with a French knot in a different color between every saddle stitch.

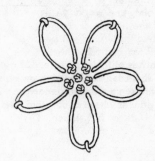

When French knots are used as centers for flowers they can be in combination with lazy-daisy stitches for the petals and outline stitches for the leaves and stems.

Bullion stitch is made in the same way as the French knot but the threads

stitch of the hem from the back at the point where the needle was first inserted. Draw this group of threads to-

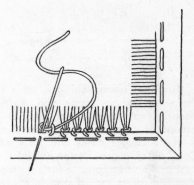

are not wound so tightly and the needle is pushed down through the material somewhat farther from the point at which it was picked up. The twisted threads will then lie flat, as shown in the illustration.

Hemstitching or drawn work must be done on the straight grain of the material. It makes a fine finish just above a hem. Turn up the hem and crease it, so you know just where the top of the hem will come. Starting from that point, and working away from the top of the hem, pull cross-threads until you have the width you desire to hemstitch. Then baste the hem in place. To do the hemstitching, pick up three or more threads with your needle and then draw the thread through. Bring

gether. Pull your sewing thread tight and go on to the next group of threads. Continue until the row of hemstitching is completed, making each group of threads uniform. This is known as single hemstitching, and is shown in the accompanying illustrations.

Not all hemstitching is done on top of a hem. Sometimes it is used as a trimming in the center of a dress or blouse, or on table linen. In that case you will not turn up a hem, nor will you catch the top of the hem with the needle. Instead, mark a light pencil line at the point where you are to start pulling the threads, and take up each tiny stitch with the needle touching the line. If this is the case, work carefully, as you have only the one thickness of material without the added strength of the thickness of the top of a hem.

For double hemstitching, the threads are caught down and fastened on each side. These groups of caught threads resemble spokes.

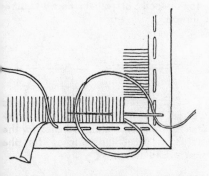

he thread around over the small group of cross-threads and pick up a small

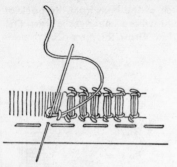

Diagonal hemstitching is done in the same way as single and double hemstitching except that the little groups of threads are separated as they are caught down and fastened. One half of a group joins half of the next group of threads, to form a diagonal line rather than a straight spoke.

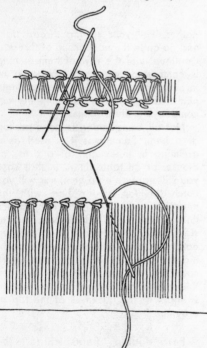

Plain fringe is made by pulling cross-threads at the edge of the ma-

terial to the width desired and combing the loose threads to straighten an tangles.

Raveled fringe is made on a bia edge of stiff material such as taffeta This type of fringe is made by firs fraying the edge of the material for depth of not more than 1 inch. The

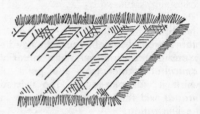

edge is then pulled between the thum and the finger to "pinch" it and pro duce an interesting effect. Be sure the material is a true bias.

Knotted fringe is made after rolled hem has been hand stitched o a narrow hem stitched by machine Groups of threads are pulled throug the hem to form the fringe. Knot eac group of threads close to the hem When all the threads are knotted measure them, and cut the ends so tha the fringe will be even. Use pearl cot ton, wool, or other heavy-texture thread.

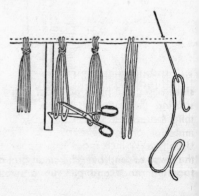

You can also make knotted fringe without turning up a hem by drawing threads on the straight of the material to the width desired, then tying off even groups of these threads with a needle and thread, as shown in the illustration. This type of fringe is often made on guest towels.

Fagoting is a decorative method of joining seams. It is also used to make shaped yokes or strips. There are two methods of fagoting, the crisscross and the bar (or spoke), each of which is described separately. The material is prepared the same way for each method. The two edges of the fabric are turned down ¼ inch on the wrong

allow less or more space as needed. Pearl cotton or buttonhole twist is a good thread to use for fagoting.

Crisscross fagoting is another fagoting stitch. Start on the wrong side and bring the thread through close to one edge. Slant the needle downward and take a stitch about ¼ inch lower on the opposite edge of the fabric. Pass

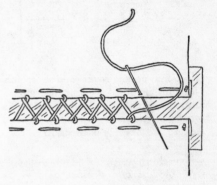

the needle over the thread, as shown in the illustration, and pull the thread through. Then take the next downward stitch on the opposite side, continuing in the same manner for the length of the space to be fagoted.

side. Baste and press both sides before starting the fagoting. If the fabric is thin, baste the folded edges of the material on a piece of stiff paper. Usually a ¼-inch space is left between the two edges; but if you want the fagoting to be narrower or wider,

Bar fagoting or spoke fagoting is made by bringing the needle through from the wrong side, close to the edge, and tacking the thread by going through once more. Directly opposite, on the other edge, take a small stitch and again fasten it by tacking. Then

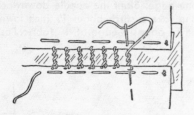

bring the needle over and over this "foundation bar," winding the thread around it until the other edge is reached. Fasten by tacking. Repeat, making the bars ⅛ inch apart.

Smocking is popular for peasant-style blouses and dresses as well as smocks and other casual types of clothes. Mothers like smocking on the best dresses of their little girls. Smocking should be confined to material of solid color or a tiny print. It calls for extra width in the dress or blouse, which will be taken up when the smocking is completed. Embroidery floss is best for smocking, used single or double for thin material or in many strands for heavier material. It is recommended that you buy a smocking pattern, which you can transfer to the material before the garment is completed. Follow the pattern directions for the particular design.

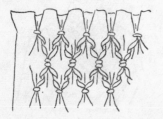

If you do not use a pattern, mark even rows of dots on the fabric to be

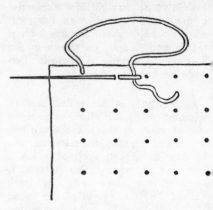

smocked. Knot the thread, pull the needle through from the wrong side, make a backstitch to the next dot, and then pull both dots together. Take another stitch over the first backstitch and push the needle through the fold at a point midway to the dot below.

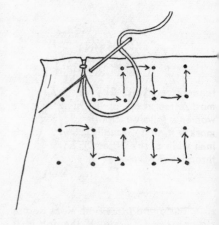

Take a small backstitch over the fold and insert the needle in the next pair of dots, drawing them together as you did the pair above. The stitches will

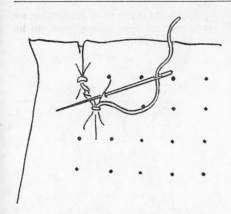

within the triangle, bringing the thread out at the corner.

Take a small horizontal stitch at the point of the triangle. Then take a horizontal stitch beneath the triangle from one corner of the base to the corner where the stitch began.

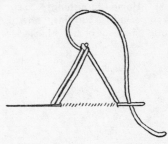

form a diagonal line. Continue to work back and forth between the two rows of dots, taking a stitch through the fold each time.

Repeat the stitch to the point and from the point to the base, until the triangle is filled with smooth rows of stitches. Finish with 3 or 4 stitches on the underside.

Decorative arrowhead—Sometimes made at the end of a row of saddle stitching or at the top of a pleat at the point where fullness is released. It can also be used at the corners of

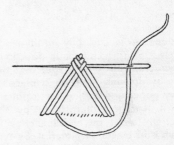

tailored pockets. The arrowhead is most often used as a fine finish on women's tailored clothes. To make it, mark a triangle, usually from ¼ to ½ inch wide at the base. Do not knot the thread but take 3 or 4 small stitches

Appliqué—A piece of material cut in the shape of a design or a band and

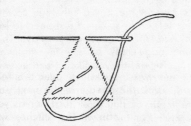

sewed to a contrasting material is called appliqué. It may be of any material—cotton, rayon, lace, velvet, or even leather.

This can be used effectively as trimming on blouses, dresses, aprons, hats, sweaters, belts, bags, or children's clothes. Home furnishings, such as luncheon cloths, curtains, and bedspreads, may also be trimmed with

appliqué. You can buy ready-made patterns for it which include directions, but you can also create your own designs by drawing them on a piece of heavy paper and cutting out a pattern from it. Use the pattern to cut out the material. This is an excellent way to use up odd pieces of material. Be sure to allow enough material for turning under all edges at least ¼ inch. Felt and leather pieces are the exception since the edges of these materials need not be turned under.

If the edges are to be turned under, baste a narrow hem all around. Then pin the pieces to the article which is being appliquéd, and when you are sure each piece is in the right place, stitch it on. Any one of a number of stitches from slip stitch to blanket stitch can be used. Use fine, self-color thread if you want the stitching to be inconspicuous—heavier thread in a con-

trasting color if you want the stitches to stand out in relief against the background of appliqué.

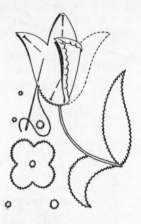

For a very flat finish you can machine stitch the pieces after you have basted them in place. Make a row of stitching as close to the edge of the appliqué piece as possible. If it is a large piece, you might want to run a second row of stitching inside the outer row, closely spacing the two rows together. For pieces which do not have turned-under edges there is a zigzag attachment for the sewing machine which you can use.

Lace appliqué is used on dressy afternoon clothes, for evening dresses, and for delicate lingerie. Designs may be appliquéd in lace to give that expensive and professional appearance. If lace bands are to be used as the edge of the garment, make sure that the outer edge has a selvedge of the lace left on it, so it will not need to be finished off in any other way. The inner edge may be cut in whatever shape or design you like. Whether you cut out from narrow or allover wide lace, plan designs so that they follow the motif of the lace itself. Cut very carefully, or the tip of the scissors will snip the wrong threads. Curved manicure or pedicure scissors are good for this type of cutting.

When you have cut out the lace design, pin it on the material where it is to be appliquéd and baste it in place.

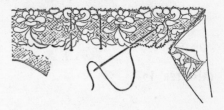

Do not pull the lace tight, but work it in lightly and carefully. With a thin needle and a single strand of matching mercerized thread fasten the lace with tiny overcast stitches. If your stitches are close and small, it is not necessary to turn under the lace, as it will not ravel. When the lace has been sewed on, cut away the fabric beneath it so that the lace appliqué becomes an open design. Again be careful in cutting. Cut close enough to leave a narrow edge of material underneath the lace yet not so close that the material will pull away from the lace. You do not need to cut away the material under the lace appliqué if you do not wish to have the lace parts transparent.

Lace can also be appliquéd by machine. Use the zigzag sewing-machine attachment and work carefully. It makes a stitch longer than the standard machine stitch.

This zigzag attachment is also good for joining lace to lace, or for adding a narrow lace edging to a larger piece of allover lace which does not have a finished edge. When sewing lace to lace, however, it is a good idea to put a piece of tissue or other thin paper under the material and stitch through the paper. When you have finished stitching, the paper can be pulled away quickly and easily.

As a final word, whenever possible the lace appliqués should be sewed on the material before the article is put together, since it is easier to work on flat pieces than on a finished garment.

CHAPTER 19

Sewing and Mending for the Family

MANY a girl starts married life with only one thought about sewing for the family. She will turn the worn collars and cuffs of her husband's shirts! This is certainly a worthy ambition—and one guaranteed to impress a new husband with his bride's capability! But as time goes on this young homemaker will find more and more ways in which her ability to sew will help her to keep her family well dressed. Sewing for the family can be divided into three classes:

1. **New clothes.** Decide what clothes you should make for yourself, your husband, and children, and what clothes it would be wiser to buy.

2. **Remodeled clothes.** Decide which clothes are good enough to make over. There is no point in spending time and energy in sewing on material which is too worn to be worth the work involved. See Chapter 15 for more information and instructions on made-overs.

3. **Clothes to repair.** See that buttons and hooks are fastened on clothes, socks are mended, torn spots are patched or rewoven.

If you are a practical mother, you will encourage your little girl to share the responsibilities of the family sewing and mending. A little girl of six or eight usually enjoys doing what Mother does, and this is as good a time as any to begin teaching her to sew. She can learn to make clothes for her doll as well as little aprons for herself. And she can even learn to darn.

As her teacher, you will have to be patient with her, for you cannot expect her to be quick or perfect in her work. Nor can you expect her to sit still for more than fifteen or twenty minutes at a time. She will do better work if she is allowed to stop sewing when she begins to tire of it, and you will find that as her interest grows she will spend longer periods at her task. One last word: Don't forget to praise your little girl's work. Judge it by her age and ability, not by your own, for nothing will do so much to encourage her interest in sewing as the feeling that she has earned your praise and recognition by her effort.

CLOTHES TO MAKE FOR CHILDREN
—By all means make your children's clothes. Prices asked for ready-made

children's clothes are often very high. Of course there's no denying that many a woman has almost stitched herself blind making baby clothes when she would be doing herself and the baby more good by taking a walk outdoors. But the average mother will make some baby clothes for sentiment's sake and

will make most of her small children's dresses, rompers, play suits, and sun suits if she wants attractive clothes at a budget price.

The finest children's clothes are made in cotton, linen, lightweight woolens, and drip-dry fabrics. Only for very special occasions should a child's dress be made of silk, rayon, or nylon crepe, and these are not recommended for general wear. A child is dressed in good taste for summer best in white or pastel linen, voile, or organdie; and for winter best in a velveteen dress with gathered skirt, or a dark velveteen jumper with a sheer white guimpe or blouse.

The velveteen might be a princess dress, with short sleeves. A velveteen dress with no other trimming can have a small collar of Irish crochet lace. A more delicate lace can be used to trim an infant's very best dress.

Keep her hats simple—a cloche or Breton sailor in felt or straw, with a ribbon band and streamers down the back. Little berets and Scotch caps are good too. Keep her clothes short—

above the knee until she is ten or twelve. Children—both boys and girls —usually wear clothes halfway up the thigh until they are five or six years old.

Make corduroy or denim overalls for hard, rough play. These sturdy cottons wash and wear like iron.

Another increasingly popular trend is to match your daughter's outfit to

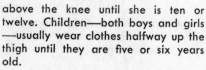

yours. Mother-and-daughter outfits are charming and easy to make. Select a pattern which is becoming to you yet simple enough so it will look well on a tiny figure. A pinafore style is good,

and so are mother-and-daughter aprons. Your daughter will love to wear her matching apron when she is helping you around the house.

Don't forget the rightness of the buttoned-down-the-front princess coat for any little girl. Then there is the straight coat so often made in navy or gray chinchilla cloth or melton for winter. This may be worn by either boys or girls. The girl's coat is buttoned from right to left and the boy's from left to right.

CLOTHES TO MAKE FOR GROWN-UPS—Whether you are the mother of a family or the daughter who sews, in the section which follows you will find suggestions for making things for the members of your family.

Home dresses—Somehow the name "home dresses" makes them sound prettier than just plain house dresses. At any rate, every woman—even a business girl—finds she has use for several. They can be bought ready-made, but most of them—at least those within reach of the average budget—are poorly finished and are of an inferior material. It is much more satisfactory in every way to make your own dresses. After you have made a few, you will have a pretty good idea of about how much material such a dress takes and will be able to take advantage of a yard-goods sale, buying up several remnants at a time. This practice is not recommended for any other type of garment, but for home dresses it is seldom wasteful, since you will probably want several dresses in the same pattern and since the scraps can be utilized for quilts, pot holders, aprons, and other utilitarian articles.

Another advantage of having a piece of material on hand is that it offers the perfect outlet for that rainy-day urge to sew.

Aprons—There are aprons and aprons. They can be strictly utilitarian for housecleaning and gardening or gaily elaborate for serving when you're a hostess at a tea or a cocktail party. You can use remnants or leftovers from your other sewing, or even that old standby—a man's shirt that is no longer serviceable. Aprons have no age limit—from tots to grandmothers—and you will enjoy making them for gifts as well as for your own use.

You can buy patterns with directions for cutting and sewing. But you may also devise your own patterns and may combine two different materials if you are using short lengths. Aprons can be finished with contrasting bands and pockets, ruffles, appliquéd designs, rickrack braid, bias bindings or lace.

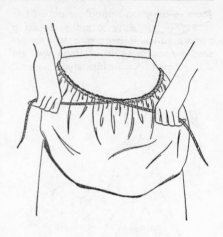

The apron shown in the illustration is usually called a "basket apron" because of its carrying capacity. It is useful in the house or back yard, for small working tools or clothespins. Use a strong cotton fabric. Make a one-inch hem, turn it over and stitch on the right side of the apron. Using a buttonhole stitch, make two eyelets an inch apart in the center of the turned-up hem. Through each eyelet draw a cord or a shoelace to serve as a drawstring. Pull each string through at the open top. Cut a belt of double thickness of material. Baste the belt to the top of the apron, including the two ends of the pulled-through drawstrings. Stitch the belt at the top and the bottom. Untie the strings and flatten the apron when laundering.

A bib apron with a strap to go around the neck is easy to cut and sew. Use a heavy cotton fabric, with wide tape or a double thickness of self fabric to be sewed on for the neckband and the two side belt pieces. A pair of pockets can be added in contrasting material if desired. This apron can also

Here is an ideal apron for the home sewer or the knitting and crocheting enthusiast. It has handy pockets for her spools of thread, thimble, needles, and eyeglasses. Cut it from a straight

piece of material, allowing six to eight inches additional length at the bottom if the material can be used on either side. Make a hem, turn up and stitch on the right side. Now turn up the extra length which you allowed. Stitch it down the center to form two pockets— or, if it's a wide apron, make two stitchings, several inches apart, to form three pockets. Hem the sides of the apron. Gather the top into a straight band made from two thicknesses of material. Stitch down. This band, of course, should have enough length at each side to allow for tying in the back. If the material is not reversible, cut an

be made of plastic material, or of heavy canvas or oilcloth for the man of the house to wear when puttering around the garage or for other household chores or hobbies. It also makes an ideal apron for the backyard barbecue.

extra piece of material to be seamed together at the bottom before turning up for pockets. You may, of course,

prefer to use contrasting material for the pockets and for the band too.

Little girls especially will love aprons

made from colorful scarves and large handkerchiefs; they are attractive for the woman of the house as well. You can make an apron from a single scarf, or you can work out colorful designs by stitching two or more together or by arranging handkerchiefs on solid-color material and using a scarf or handkerchief as a bib.

To please the eyes of your family or guests you may indulge in aprons made in gay or pastel colors, of delicate patterns and materials, such as organdie or dotted swiss. You can even make aprons of silk or rayon taffetas or moirés to wear when you are entertaining at home. The latter, however, may not be washable, so take that into consideration before you spend too much money and effort in making one. Gift aprons, as a rule, fall into this dressy class.

Plastic material, which can be bought by the yard, is also used for aprons. Since plastic does not fray, it is not necessary to turn under a hem: the edge can be left straight or cut with a pinking shears for that little saw-tooth edge trimming. Do not sew by hand. Stitch by machine. Place a piece of tissue paper beneath the plastic on the side next to the machine. Use a fairly long stitch (try 10 or 12 to the inch). Of course you know you don't launder plastic material—you wipe off the surface with a damp cloth to clean it. And don't put large pockets on the apron—the plastic might not be strong enough to hold the weight if you are inclined to fill the pockets heavily.

Turkish Towel Wrap—This brief wrap may be made as a mother-and-daughter outfit for use after a shower or swim, or for playing or sunning in the backyard. You can use a big bath or beach towel, or you can buy terry cloth by the yard. Hold the material or the towel around you. Measure and mark how high up and how long you want it, allowing 2 inches for turning under at top and bottom, plus 2 inches in the width for making the seam. Mark where your waistline comes, and run a basting stitch around the waistline as a guide for stitching on the machine.

First stitch with elastic thread on the wrong side of the material through the basting that marks the waistline. (See page 228 regarding shirring with elastic thread.) Then stitch 2 rows of elastic thread 1 inch apart above the waistline, and 2 rows below, which makes a total of 5 rows of elastic shirring. Now stitch the seam, try on the wrap, and turn under at the top and bottom to the desired length. Finish off with a cotton fringe top and bottom. You may want to make more or fewer rows of elastic thread stitching, depending on the height and proportion of the wearer of the wrap.

LINGERIE FOR THE TROUSSEAU— Whether it is for your own hope chest or for some member of your family who is happily planning a trousseau, intimate apparel made at home has a sentimental value which no ready-made things ever have. What can or should go into a trousseau is a matter

Lingerie—Handmade lingerie adds luxury to any feminine wardrobe, but few women can afford to buy it. If you have always wished you could wear the dainty handmade underthings you will find they are easy to make and inexpensive as well.

TAILORED SLIPS, NIGHTGOWNS, PANTIES, PAJAMAS, BED JACKET of nylon, silk, rayon, cotton, and drip-dry materials.

LACE-TRIMMED OR EMBROIDERED SLIPS, NIGHTGOWNS, PANTIES, BED JACKET of rayon, nylon, silk, or sheer cotton.

EVENING SLIP, full length, of nylon, rayon, or silk.

TAILORED HOSTESS GOWN AND HOUSE COAT of cotton, quilted cotton, wool, or corduroy. The shortie brunch coat or duster comes in this category, since it is really a house coat cut short.

DRESS-UP HOSTESS GOWN, HOUSE COAT, NEGLIGEE of silk, rayon, velvet, or sheer wool, trimmed with lace or other types of trimming or with self fabric.

LOUNGING PAJAMAS—If you're the type who looks glamorous in them make them of the same materials as above.

BATHROBE—One made of terry cloth for mild weather; a corduroy or woolen one for colder weather.

BRASSIERES—Made of cotton, rayon, nylon, net, or lace. If your figure is large enough to require a bra with substantial reinforcement, you will probably be wise to buy ready-made brassières.

STYLES OF LINGERIE—Whether your lingerie is simply tailored or trimmed with lace and ribbons depends entirely on your own taste and the kind of clothes you customarily wear.

It is best to stick to the classic styles when choosing a house coat or hostess gown because their styles tend to follow the changing modes in fashion and you don't want yours to be outdated before you have enjoyed wearing it for any length of time. If you avoid extremes of cut, such as pinched-in waistlines or dipping hem lines, and designs and colors which shriek and will make you (and the groom) very tired of look-

to be decided by the woman who is assembling it. To a great extent it depends upon her taste, her pocketbook, and her own needs. Obviously it is quite impossible to say that any specific item must be included. Generally speaking, however, a trousseau usually includes the following:

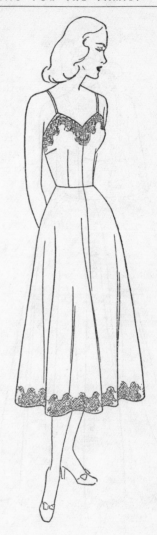

ing at them, then there is no reason why these garments can't always be fashionable without being faddish. It is poor economy, in a trousseau, to make anything from a temporary high-style pattern.

Slips, too, should follow simple lines, even though you may trim them elaborately. You will be thankful for their simplicity should it be necessary to make alterations later—widening or narrowing them, turning up the hem, or adding a longer hem line of matching material or lace to meet dress-length requirements.

An evening slip will last for years if it is made correctly. It should be cut along simple lines, tailored, and long enough to reach to about 1 inch above the hem line of a long evening gown. It should also be cut as low as possible in the back to permit you to wear the lowest-cut dress.

Bed jackets have no particular style to them—whatever you prefer in the matter of style is all right at any time. When you're on a vacation or a visit, the prettier the bed jacket the better. Indulge your whim for all the fluff and

Nightgowns and pajamas, as a rule, should be very long, for they are ungraceful when they are that awkward length somewhere between the knee and the ankle. The shortie nightgown, and the "baby-doll" nightgown with matching panties are, of course, exceptions to this rule.

MATERIALS FOR LINGERIE—If only for sentimental reasons, you will want your trousseau to last a long time so that you can enjoy wearing the things you made. Therefore, do not practice false economy in buying materials. Look for remnants, yes, but not for cheaper quality. These are the best choices you can make in materials:

Cotton—batiste, crepe, nainsook, lawn, voile, fine broadcloth, and cotton and dacron broadcloth.

Silk and synthetic mixtures—crepe, crepe de Chine, jersey knit, crepe-back satin, chiffon, georgette, dacron crepe, arnel, and nylon tricot.

Wool—Sheer crepe, fine challis.

For a house coat or hostess gown use flannel, jersey, or any lightweight woolen dress material. Velvet, velveteen, corduroy, and polished cotton are also suitable.

Self trim, applied in bands and stitched down flat, is always good, because it eliminates the laundering problems which arise when two different types of material are used in one garment. An effective lingerie trimming is satin bands on crepe, or vice versa. Whatever your choice, make sure you use the same type of fabric; that is, rayon satin and rayon crepe, or silk satin and silk crepe. Remember this even when buying ribbon for trimming. Lace trimming, applied in bands, edging, or appliquéd, should be carefully selected; a good cotton lace is preferable to rayon lace. It will withstand laundering better and retains its strength longer. NOTE: If you use a lace trim on rayon, nylon, or jersey knit lingerie which does not require much ironing, the lace will look quite well without ironing after the garment is washed.

When you've decided on the materials and the trimmings you want to use, make certain they will not fade or shrink and are not of an inferior grade

lace trimmings you like. If you're an avid reader in bed and use a bed jacket constantly at home, keep it simple so there will be little or no trimming to get easily soiled or wrinkled and require too frequent launderings. A serviceable tailored bed jacket can be made from the pattern for a pajama top or a coolie jacket.

which will come apart after a few launderings. Those materials which you will have dry cleaned, such as the velvet or wool house coat, should also be the best quality you can get for your money, because you want them to be attractive for a long, long time.

SEWING HINTS FOR LINGERIE—If you are not an experienced sewer, start by making lingerie that is cut on the straight grain of the material; later on you can make the bias-cut slips and nightgowns which require more intricate cutting and sewing. Bear in mind that when you wear bias-cut lingerie it is apt to get much shorter as you move in it, for slips have a habit of "riding up" when you sit down. For this reason it is best not to wear a bias-cut slip under a sheer dress.

The same holds true for the evening slip, and if you plan to wear it under a lace dress, you won't want it to slip up to your knees when you sit down or creep up when you dance. While we are on the subject of evening slips, if you have a strapless evening gown, you can make detachable shoulder straps to be snapped on and off the slip, and if you're afraid the slip won't stay up, use a few stays from an old girdle and sew one under each side of the seam of the slip, from the waistline up to the top of the slip. These should hold it up.

Lingerie which gets frequent laundering must have strong, flat seams and no exposed edges to fray. (See Chapter 6 on seams.) The hems, especially on bias-cut garments, should be very narrow, and preferably rolled. (See Chapter 7 on hems.) Lace edgings, appliqués, and all other trimmings and decorative stitching must be put on as flat and as securely as possible. (See Chapter 17 on appliqué and decorative stitching.)

In making the more delicate lacy outer garments, such as hostess gowns or negligees, use the same care as in making underwear. However, for the less intimate outer garments, such as the hostess gown and the house coat of velvet, wool, or other heavier material, you can use the same cutting, fitting, and sewing methods as you use in sewing your dresses.

CLOTHES TO MAKE FOR THE MENFOLK

—Small boys' suits can very well be made at home if you wish to save money. They are simple to sew and require little tailoring skill. You can also make the short trousers worn by the older boy of six or seven. And even though you may think it is easier to sew for a girl, you can also make the chinchilla box coat which is standard equipment for little boys. Mothers can sew sports shirts for the boys and men of the family. Pajamas for men and boys are almost like tailored pajamas worn by girls and are no harder to make. Men's lounging robes and smoking jackets also can be made at home.

Many women sew for men as a labor of love—making something very special and monogramming it for a gift. A hand-hemstitched handkerchief in fine linen and a scarf in heavy white rayon or pure silk are typical gifts. However, they must be simple and made to perfection for the man to like them.

MENDING

—The mending, darning, and sewing-buttons-tighter-before-they-pop-off, can be greatly simplified by looking over all clothes before they are washed or sent to the cleaner. If worn spots are reinforced before they go through the washing machine, the hole that is about to appear is usually warded off for another few washings.

For directions for sewing on buttons, snaps, hooks and eyes, see Chapter 10.

HOW TO AVOID SLIDE FASTENER TROUBLE—Close all slide fasteners in washable clothes before putting them in the water in order to keep the slide fastener from spreading and to keep the garment in shape. The other two chief causes of slide-fastener grief are: (1) pocketbooks filled to the top, with a handkerchief just waiting to be caught in the fastener; and (2) edges of material which catch in a dress slide fastener. When a slide fastener has jammed, patience and a hairpin are helpful. But if the teeth of the slide fastener are bent, you may have to replace it. Directions for inserting come with all slide fasteners.

GIRDLE REPAIRS—Save good elastic garters from your discarded girdles, so that you will have a supply of garters on hand to replace those which wear out. Notice how the old garters were stitched to your girdle. Usually the end of the elastic is stitched between two thicknesses of material, or between the girdle and a piece of tape. Rip off the old garter, slip the new one into the same position, and restitch by hand or by machine.

Never tighten an old girdle by taking a seam in an elastic panel, because the elastic threads will be cut by the machine needle. Stitch on the fabric. When you find a loose end of an elastic thread in the girdle, fasten it securely by wrapping the end with sewing thread. Knot the sewing thread to the elastic. Thread a needle with the sewing thread and reweave the elastic thread in and out of the section from which it was torn. Then fasten the end of the elastic in place by stitching it down with the sewing thread.

MENDING RIPS AND TEARS—Mend a rip by stitching it on the wrong side —by machine, if possible; otherwise with small hand stitches. Stitch beyond the place where the rip began and fasten the threads firmly. If the stitching is done by machine, pull the bobbin thread through and tie it to the thread passing through the needle. If the stitching is done by hand, take three small stitches, one on top of the other, to fasten.

Mend a tear by stitching a narrow dart on the wrong side of the material. The widest part of the dart should be at the outer edge of the cloth, where the tear began. The dart should extend 1 inch beyond the place where the tear ends. Make the point of the dart very narrow and sharp. When the dart is pressed, the mending will often be scarcely noticeable.

USE OF MENDING TAPE—For quick and satisfactory results in mending a tear on any except sheer material, buy several inexpensive kits of mending tape in different colors. This tape is applied to the wrong side of the tear and is permanently pressed on with a warm iron. The tape stays in place through washing and dry cleaning. Directions for applying come with the tape.

REWEAVING PROBLEMS—Professional reweavers make a specialty of repairing tears, moth holes, or cigarette burns in an otherwise good garment or piece of fine household linen. Their method is to pull out threads from a hem or some other place where they will not be missed and then knot these threads to the ends of the threads around the hole or tear. The ends of the thread around the hole are raveled, in order to fasten the new threads firmly in place. The replaced threads are woven into place until the hole or tear no longer exists. This work can be done at home if you have great patience. However, repairs of this sort require skill and practice. Most reweaving shops have a mail-order repair service which you can use if you live at a distance.

DARNING—You will find a darning egg extremely useful in any kind of darning. If you don't have one, use a small cold cream jar or any rounded, smooth object which fits easily into the stocking and can be placed beneath the hole to be darned. Have the stocking right side out. Clip off any loose threads around the hole. Use matching wool for wool socks, cotton darning thread for cottons, and nylon thread for nylon hose. Do not knot the thread, for a knot will be uncomfortable when the stocking is worn. Instead, start your

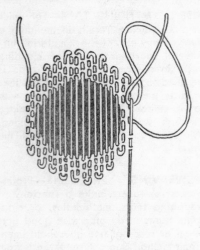

darning by taking several small stitches in the material, about ½ inch from the hole. Turn the stocking and take another row of stitches beside the first one. Cover the hole with lengthwise threads in this manner, each row ending in six or eight small stitches which cover at least ½ inch of the weakened area around the hole. Cut the end of the thread after the hole has been covered. Crosswise threads are woven in and out, over and under the

lengthwise threads. Crosswise threads should extend ½ inch beyond the worn edges of the hole, with small stitches in even rows.

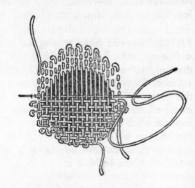

Some sewers mend runs in stockings by machine. Turn the stocking wrong side out and fold along the run. Stretch the stocking. Pin it to a sheet of paper. Stitch just inside the run with matching thread. Remove the paper and fasten the threads.

REINFORCING—This is a form of darning used to give strength to a weakened spot before a hole appears. Reinforcing is done from the right side, to keep the stitches as inconspicuous as possible, using darning cotton or wool. Long stitches on the underside of the material are anchored by tiny, almost invisible stitches which are taken on the right side. The long stitches on the wrong side relieve the material of a portion of the strain and may delay the appearance of the hole for some

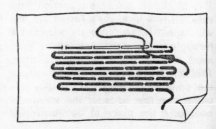

time. Darned reinforcements are most often used under the arms, at the elbows of woolen dresses or jackets, and in the knees of slacks. This type of reinforcement, however, is not suitable for thin cottons, rayon, or silk.

PATCHING—To make a neat patch on a fine material first trim the edges of the hole to make it a small oblong or square. Clip the opening 1/8 inch at the corners, so that the edges will turn and lie flat. Then cut a piece of matching material about 1 inch larger than the hole on all sides. (If you are patching a printed material, try to match the print, so there will be no break in the design.) Pin the patch to the underside of the hole, working from the right

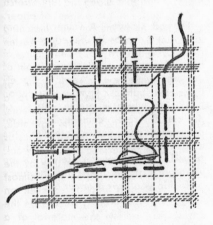

side. Baste it in place if you think pins will not hold it. Bring the needle through to the right side of the garment at one corner of the opening. This will leave the knot of thread on the underside. Using the needle, turn under one raw edge of the square or oblong. If the place to be patched is

small, turn under an entire edge from corner to corner, pressing it flat between thumb and forefinger. With the needle pointing toward you, take a small stitch in the patch and then slide the point of the needle into the folded edge of the hole, to make another stitch which will be invisible. The third stitch is another small one taken in the patch. These stitches (called slip stitches) are used to fasten patches to the material. The thread is fastened with three or four tiny stitches, taken one on top of the other, after the patching is completed.

MEN'S CLOTHES REPAIRS—You can use the methods discussed above in mending, darning, reweaving, and patching the clothes of the men and boys in your home. In addition to these, there are some repairs which are specifically used on masculine apparel.

Sturdy patches—On work clothes and play clothes apply patches with short hemming stitches taken close to-

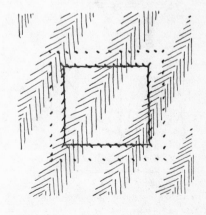

gether. For extra strength also turn down the raw edges of the patch (which is, of course, on the underside of the garment) and hem these raw edges to the garment. This patch will not be dainty, but it will be strong.

Elbow patches—Suède leather patches can be sewn on the elbows of play clothes worn by schoolboys, or on men's sports jackets. These patches are put on with small overhand stitches close together.

But a good jacket or coat which has a spot wearing thin on the elbow needs closer attention. Turn the sleeve inside out, rip the lining at the bottom of the sleeve and roll it up into the sleeve so it will be out of the way when you make the repair. Cut a piece of thin woolen material or rayon lining a little larger than the thin spot. Baste over and around the spot on the wrong side of the sleeve. Making your stitches parallel to the lengthwise grain of the cloth, tack with rows of tailor's basting, using loose stitches spaced about a half inch apart. If the cloth is worn very thin, make these lines of stitches closer to each other.

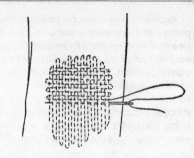

darker than the material darn over the thin spot. Catch the stitches to the patch underneath. Your vertical and horizontal darning stitches should be kept in line with the yarns in the sleeve.

Trouser knee patch—If a spot is worn thin on the knee, it can be patched by the same method as given above for the thin spot at the elbow.

Frayed sleeve—A vulnerable spot in a suit or coat is the edge of the sleeve. If it has frayed, rip the lining at the cuff and turn it up to keep it out of the way while you're sewing. Rip off the sleeve buttons. Remove the cotton interlining which is usually placed at the cuff for reinforcement. Turn down the sleeve hem and cut through the crease precisely on the line where it is frayed. Trim off very closely both the worn parts of the sleeve and the piece of facing you have just cut off.

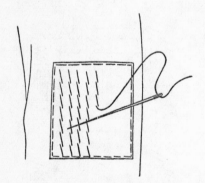

Turn the sleeve to the right side and with thread of the same color or slightly

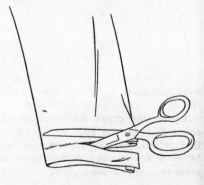

Replace this piece, matching the pieces at the seams, and pin it to the sleeve (right sides of material facing each other). Baste a very narrow seam, about ⅛ inch. Stitch on the machine.

Press out the seam in the sleeve and facing as well as the new seam you just stitched. Turn the facing down and machine stitch the new seam on the facing very close to the joining to prevent this narrow seam from rolling up. Then turn the facing up into the sleeve again and baste it just inside the sleeve. Fold over and finish the corners of the cuffs as they were originally. Turn in the raw edges. Then tack the facing back into the sleeve with a loose stitch. Slip stitch the lining back into place at the bottom of the sleeve. Press. Resew the buttons.

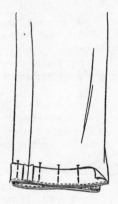 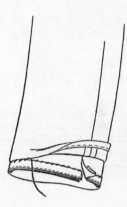

Worn coat collar—Baste with a contrasting thread on the roll line where the collar is worn.

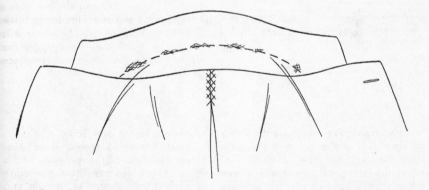

Rip the lining and the collar apart at the neckline. Turn up the inside of the collar and make a fold on the line of basting. Baste about ⅛ inch from this fold on the inside of the collar, tapering the stitches at each end of the collar. Stitch on the machine. With sharp-pointed scissors, snip through the fold. Then press this narrow seam open.

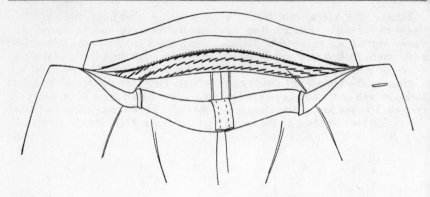

Turn the collar back, baste to the lining over the newly stitched seam to avoid

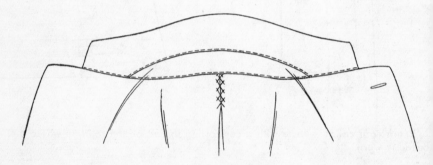

stretching or puckering, then baste to the neckline and slip stitch the lining back into place. Press all seams carefully.

Relining sleeve—Remove the lining by ripping it at the cuff and the armhole. Rip open the seams of the lining, press the pieces flat (a man's sleeve lining usually has two pieces), and use them as a pattern to cut the new lining. Use pre-shrunk lining material. Make sure the old lining hasn't shrunk so that it is now too small for the coat sleeve. If it has, be sure to make this allowance in the new lining.

Stitch the lining seams. Press. Machine stitch around the top edge of the lining about ½ inch from the edge to keep it from stretching. Turn in and baste the hem at the top of the sleeve lining.

Pull the lining over the sleeve, wrong sides facing. Turn up the lining at the cuff line. Pin to the cuff and baste. Pull

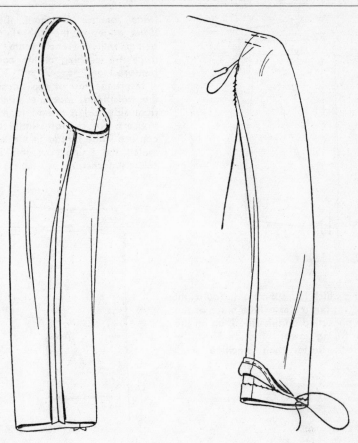

the lining up to the armhole. Pin to the armhole for a good fit. Baste. Finish with slip stitching at both cuff and arm-hole.

Replacing a trouser pocket—Rip the stitches from the waistband where the pocket is attached. Cut a paper pattern for the pocket. Mark the side to be laid on the folded material when you cut the new pocket. Make allow-ance for a ⅜-inch seam. Cut the old pocket away from the two facings in-side the pocket mouth. Leave some of

the old pocketing, which is stitched back of the facing. This will make it easier to replace the new pocket.

Turn under the seam allowance of one edge of the new pocket piece. Pin it to the remaining piece of the old pocket facing, which is on the side of the trousers facing toward the back. Baste, then machine stitch twice for reinforcement.

Turn under the seam allowance on the other edge of the new pocket piece. Pin it in place on the old pocket

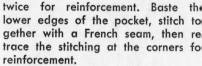

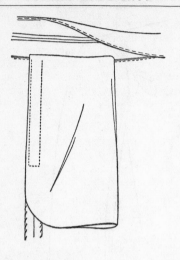

twice for reinforcement. Baste the lower edges of the pocket, stitch together with a French seam, then retrace the stitching at the corners for reinforcement.

Insert the top of the pocket under the waistband. Machine stitch on the right side, using thread to match the trousers. For a professional look you can use white thread in the bobbin to match the lining, but this isn't absolutely necessary.

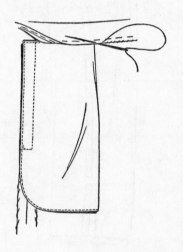

facing which faces the front. You might have to turn under a little more of the new pocketing on this side than on the side facing toward the back of the trousers. Baste; then machine stitch

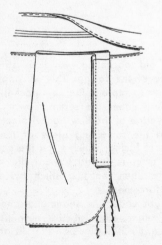

Repairing a trouser pocket—A small hole may wear through the corner of a pocket. When this happens, machine stitch rows along the old stitching a fraction of an inch above the little hole. Do not cut off any material below the stitching.

If the hole is too big for this simple repair, or if the lower part of the pocket is badly worn, you can still repair the bottom half without having to take out and replace the entire pocket. Cut off the torn lower part of the pocket.

Use it as a pattern to cut a new

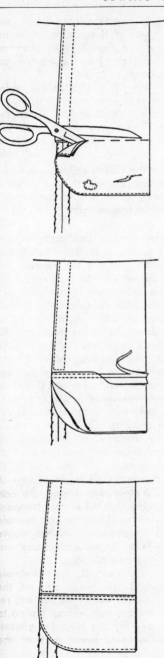

piece, allowing ⅜ inch at the bottom for seaming and twice this allowance on the top. Stitch the new piece to the upper half of the pocket, so that the seam edges will be on the outside of the pocket. Press the edge of the seam toward the top of the pocket. Turn under the raw edge and finish with a flat fell seam.

Then turn the pocket inside out. Baste a ⅛-inch seam around the bottom and side. Stitch on the machine. Turn the pocket back into the trousers and finish with a French seam, stitching ¼ inch from the edge.

Replacing torn-off buttons—If the man of the house has pulled off a button, and with it some of the cloth from his coat, vest, or trousers, it's not beyond repair. If the torn spot is smaller than the button itself, slip a piece of material under the hole as reinforcement. With matching thread, darn over the spot and through the extra piece of material for strength. Then sew the button back in place.

If the cloth is torn so that the hole extends beyond the button, you will have to match the material. You may be able to do this by snipping a piece from the inside facing of the coat or vest. Make as neat a patch as possible, matching the weave of the material. Resew the button over it, but to make sure it doesn't pull directly on the patch, sew the button on with a shank. See Chapter 10 on sewing buttons.

Underarm patch—Cut away the worn portion of the sleeve and underarm in the shape of a square. Each corner of the square should be at a seam line. (There are four seams meeting at the underarm.) Rip the seams back ½ inch, to allow for turning under the raw edge.

Cut the patch ½ inch larger all around than the opening it is to cover.

There are two ways of finishing this patch. It can be pinned into place, basted from the right side, and overcast by hand. This finish is used for an everyday work shirt whenever there is no machine available.

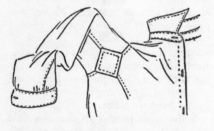

A better-looking finish is obtained by pinning the patch in place on the wrong side of the garment, with the right side of the patch face down. Baste the raw edges of the patch to the edges of the square opening.

Stitch by machine with four separate seams, running each seam off the edge of the patch at the corners. Be certain that the seam comes exactly to the

corner of the square opening. This corner stitching is a bit tricky. Practice it on an old garment first, so that you will not run into trouble later.

Turning collar and cuffs—Carefully rip the collar from the neckband. (The double collar is set between the double thickness of the neckband.) Reverse the collar; that is, turn the worn side to the back. Fold the collar in half, matching the points and making a crease down the center back. Pin the center back collar into the center back neckline, matching the creases. Pin the collar into the neckband from the center to the two ends. Do not stretch or pull. Baste the collar in place, providing the same seam allowance as in the original stitching. Stitch the collar in place by machine, on inside of the neckband, using the same size stitch as originally used on the shirt.

You can turn cuffs in the same way you turn a collar, but, since cuffs wear at the edges, it is not always practical to turn them unless they are double French cuffs which fold back and fasten with links.

CHAPTER 20

Sewing for the Home

SEWING is a pleasant occupation that can be put to many uses. In addition to articles of wearing apparel and gifts there are many household articles that can be made inexpensively at home.

The best way to plan household sewing is to spread it through the year, so that there will be no great rush to complete a big piece of work such as new slip covers for the living room when you should be finishing up your child's spring coat.

When you are a very beginning sewer (once you have completed a dress you are past this stage) two of the easiest and most pleasant kinds of household sewing you can do are tea towels and luncheon sets. The tea towels are practical and can be finished up so quickly that in an hour of one afternoon you can prepare a year's supply for stitching and then do the stitching in an hour the next morning.

TEA TOWELS—Toweling is least expensive when bought in 10-yard bolts. Pure linen is the most absorbent and best toweling. It dries quickly and does not leave small particles of fiber or lint on dishes and glassware. You can also make tea towels from sugar bags. Many good housekeepers have never

used anything else. Make your tea towels at least 30 inches long. If this length is used, you will be able to make a dozen towels from ten yards of material.

Straighten the two ends of the toweling before cutting it into lengths by pulling a thread straight across, from selvedge to selvedge. You must pull a thread, because toweling does not tear well. Cut across the toweling on this line.

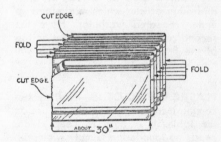

Divide the material evenly. You do not need to measure accurately with a yardstick. Merely fold your toweling into as many towels of the length you want.

Crease the toweling at each fold. Make a tiny cut across the fold and pull a cross-thread to use as a guide line for straight cutting.

The hem on a tea towel should be about ¼ inch wide, though it may be slightly wider. For a ¼-inch hem, first turn the straight-cut edge of the material down ⅛ inch from selvedge to selvedge. Crease the fold sharply between your thumb and fingers. Turn again to conceal the raw edge. The second turn should be about ¼ inch wide, which is the width of the finished hem. Pin or baste the hem for stitching, keeping the selvedges even.

When you hem a tea towel by machine, start your stitching 1 inch from a selvedge end of the hem. Edge stitch to the selvedge, and then, with the machine needle in the material and the presser foot of the machine raised, turn the towel completely around. Lower the presser foot and edge stitch the entire hem. When you come to the other end of the hem, turn the material and stitch back for 1 inch before cutting and tying the threads. This double stitching at the ends gives added strength to the hems so they can withstand constant use and many washings. The same method for finishing hems is used for sheets, curtains, and other articles which must stand up under repeated washings. Have the second row of stitching directly on top of the first, so that the two rows will look like one.

PLASTIC TABLECLOTHS—Plastic is becoming increasingly popular for use on the table. It is easy to keep clean, needs no laundering (simply wipe with a damp cloth), and can be used in many effective ways. If you have a solid-color linen or cotton luncheon cloth, cover it with one of the white plastic allover designs. You will find that this not only makes an attractive luncheon table but a practical one as well. Or, if you want the full effect of a gay-colored pattern, choose a plastic material in one of the many motifs available and use it directly on the table. Plastic materials can be bought by the yard in a variety of colors and designs. Buy plastic material as you would oilcloth in a size to fit your table. Finish the edges by cutting with pinking shears, or, if you prefer more trimming, add an edge of plastic ruffling in a plain color to match the design of the cloth.

LUNCHEON SETS—The simplest set to make is a fringed one. You will need one oblong place mat to go under each plate, one square napkin for each person, and—if your table is large enough for it—a single long runner for the middle.

Choose a plain material if your dishes have a flowered pattern or some other colorful design. Make your luncheon set in one solid color or a combination of solid colors. For example, the place mats might be coral or yellow and the napkins and centerpiece blue.

The material used can be any rather heavy cotton, rayon, or mixture which will fringe easily and withstand frequent washings. Linen can also be used, but it is rather expensive if this is your first experiment. An effective set can be made from the heavy bleached cotton flour or feed bags which are often available from mail-order houses and from bakers. Heavy unbleached muslin is another possibility. These white bags or muslin can later be dyed any color you wish.

You will need about 1⅓ yards of material, approximately 36 inches wide, to make a luncheon set for four. If you have an odd piece of material at hand, don't worry if it is a few inches short of this amount. Just change the size of the pieces. Some of the most attractive sets are made in two colors. If you want your set in two colors and are buying material, buy

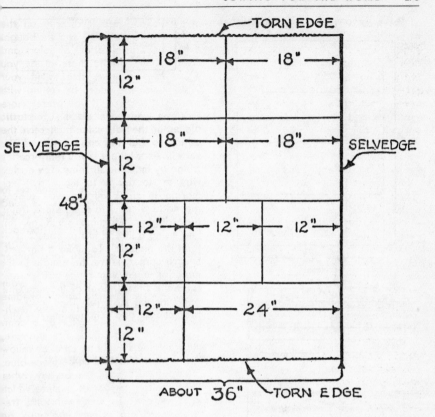

²⁄₃ yard for the place mats and ²⁄₃ yard in a second color for the napkins and the center runner.

If the material has a cut edge and not a torn edge, you will need to pull a thread to get a straight line, as you do for straightening the edge of toweling.

The accompanying illustration shows how to plan your luncheon set from 1 ⅓ yards of material approximately 36 inches wide.

Tear all the material for your set into four strips, each 12 inches wide, running across the material from selvedge to selvedge.

Make the place mats by cutting two 12-inch strips in half.

Make three napkins by folding one

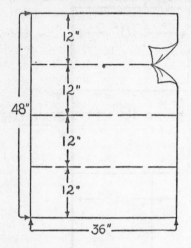

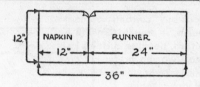

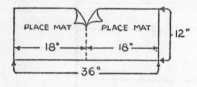

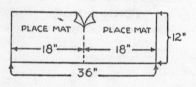

When you have all the necessary pieces in the set, cut off all selvedge edges, so that they can be fringed. The set will wear longer if you reinforce the fringe by machine stitching. The easiest way to do this is to make a 1-inch margin in chalk all the way around the edge of each piece before doing the fringing. Machine stitch on this line, using a thread just a shade darker than the material. To make a perfectly square corner, leave the needle in the material when you reach the corner, raise the presser foot of the machine and turn the material. Then lower the presser foot and continue the stitching.

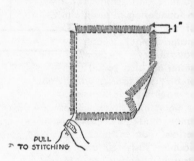

12-inch strip in thirds and cutting. The fourth napkin is made by folding down one third of the last 12-inch strip. Crease along the fold and cut.

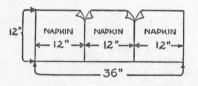

The remaining piece of material (two thirds of the final 12-inch strip) will be the center runner.

If you decide to reinforce the edge with hand hemstitching, complete the fringing first. See directions for single hemstitching in Chapter 18. The fringing itself is easy. All you need to do is to pull cross-threads. Make the fringe one inch deep on all four sides of each place mat, napkin, and runner. Comb out the fringe with an ordinary comb if you want it to look especially nice.

CURTAINS—Good ready-made curtains are usually expensive. Whether ou buy curtains or make them at ome, it pays to get the best you can ifford, because curtains get hard wear. Most women prefer curtains of washa-ble material, because of the high cost of dry cleaning.

Curtains for informal rooms, such as he kitchen, children's room, breakfast ook, bedroom, or playroom, should always be made of washable materials and may be the straight tieback or uffled style, or they can be single sash curtains, double sash curtains, café curtains, or cottage curtains. Furnish-ings in the room will, in most instances, jovern your choice of fabric and style. or the informal curtains you can use white, cream, or ecru sheer cotton ma-erial, such as marquisette, scrim, lawn, voile, and organdie. Lawn and or-jandie can be bought with a per-manently crisp finish which does not equire starch with every washing. Mar-quisette and scrim need a little starch n laundering to maintain the crispness of the material. Voile is a very soft naterial, but it can be starched if you think it necessary. Fine curtain naterials also come in drip-dry cotton or blended fabrics which require little or no ironing after washing.

Very effective curtains are some-times made by combining two ma-erials. For instance, you can make double sash curtains or even the traight tieback or straight-hanging curtains of one of the materials listed above and add a flat border of a figured cotton material. If you are making tieback curtains, the ruffles and tieback can be a contrasting figured cotton material with the curtain tself in a solid color. Although white and ecru are the standard colors, you can use any pastel or bright color you ike so long as the room in which the curtains are to be hung is informal enough to warrant it.

Cottage curtains can be of two dif-ferent materials also. Those on the bot-tom of the window can be made in a solid color with the top curtains of a matching figured material.

If you plan to use two materials in sewing your curtains, it is wise to laun-der them before you cut and stitch, be-cause they may shrink a little, and it is just possible that the two materials may shrink in different amounts and pull your curtain out of shape.

Although it is usually wise economy to use durable material for curtaining, it is sometimes necessary or desirable to curtain a few windows at a minimum cost. One very inexpensive way is to use cheesecloth. The curtains will not look the same nor wear so long as those made from better materials, but when they are washed and starched frequently they make the room bright and inviting. Novelty curtain materials, such as dyed or printed cotton feed bags, sheer dress materials, and tea toweling can also be used. They can be made up quite effectively for a gay kitchen.

For a child's room there are ging-hams, cottons, drip-dry materials, and novelty prints with toy and animal figures printed on or woven into them. In choosing the pattern you should con-sider the age of the child and whether the curtains are for a girl's or a boy's room. For the teen-agers plaids and stripes are generally more acceptable than figures or floral designs.

Bathroom curtains, which are usually sash or cottage style, are often made of plastic material to match the shower curtain. You can sew curtains for both the window and the shower. The win-dow curtains may be ruffled and the edges of the ruffle will not need to be hemmed, since plastic does not fray; pinking shears will make a good edge on the ruffles, or you can finish them with a narrow hem or a bias-binding tape. The shower curtain, however, should have a hem at the bottom wide enough to hold weights. These can be bought by the yard in a continuous tape.

Plastic material can easily be stitched on the machine merely by loosening the tension and making the stitches longer. Ruffling is now sold by the yard in many attractive colors and designs.

Curtains for formal rooms, such as the living room, dining room, library, or even a bedroom done in a formal style, should be made of the more expensive fabrics. Ninon, a sheer rayon material, makes beautiful curtains. Many ninon materials are not washable, so be sure to read the label on the curtain or yard goods before you buy ninon for curtains. If you live in a section which is smoky and dirty, dry cleaning curtains can be expensive. And don't accept the salesclerk's word that the material is washable. If it is, the label will say so.

The heavy lace curtains so popular in the 1920s are now rarely used in formal rooms. However, there are many houses which still retain the furniture and decorations of the Victorian era, and for these heavy lace curtains are quite appropriate. As a rule curtains such as these are bought ready made, although some shops do carry the lace-designed curtain material by the yard. They look best, of course, when they are hung straight and reach all the way to the floor.

These same curtains can occasionally be used in houses furnished in the modern manner. However, they are not recommended indiscriminately, and in most modern homes it is best to use curtain materials which are simple in design and of the more modern weaves. As a matter of fact, the more modern the furnishings, the more the tendency is to eliminate glass curtains and substitute for them Venetian blinds with side draperies of heavier materials.

Washable cottons can be used in formal rooms if they are chosen with discrimination. Figured cottons, of course, are not adaptable to formal rooms, but cotton lace material and the sheerest voile and marquisette are frequently suitable, as well as fine sheer weaves in quick-drying nylon, or materials which are drip-dry such as dacron or Fiberglas.

The picture window has recently become quite popular, not only in the living room but in many other rooms of the house. Picture windows cannot be curtained in the same way as the ordinary smaller double-hung or casement windows. In most cases curtains are dispensed with so that the lovely outdoor view can be treated as a picture framed by the large window. Although a Venetian blind and draperies are the usual treatment for these windows, simple curtains made of fine voile, marquisette, or ninon can be hung on pull devices attached to a rod so that they can be drawn across the window at night.

Making curtains—TAILORED CURTAINS—The most popular way to curtain a window is with a pair of tailored curtains. It is a style suitable for any type of material and very easy to make. Each curtain is made the full width of the material, which is usually 36 inches. The length is a matter of taste: the curtain may reach to the window sill, the baseboard, or all the way to the floor. Whatever length you choose, take the curtain measurements with the rod in place.

Straighten the end of the curtain material and measure off the curtains, adding about 8 inches to each one for a hem and a heading allowance. Pull cross-threads so that you will have a cutting line.

If the material is not already side hemmed, make the side hems first.

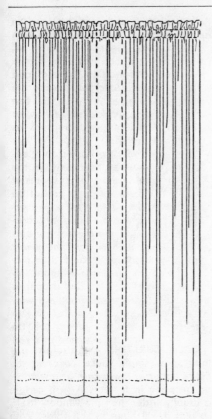

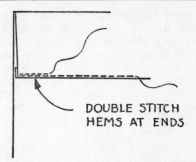

DOUBLE STITCH
HEMS AT ENDS

the heading to begin. Finish the ends of each row of stitching as you did the bottom hem.

Slip the curtain rod through the lower part of the divided hem and adjust the gathers evenly with the side hems marking the center of the window.

Putting a piece of paper over the end of the rod makes it easier to slip the rod into the curtain without snagging the material.

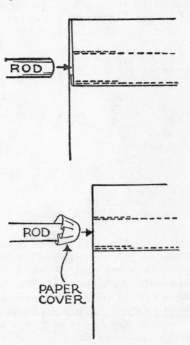

These are usually 1 or 1½ inches in width and may be made on both sides of each curtain or only on the sides which will face each other when the curtain is hung. Stitch.

Turn up the bottom hem. In sheer materials this is usually from 2½ to 3 inches in width; in heavier materials, the hem may be as deep as 8 inches. Stitch. At each end of the hem turn the curtain around and stitch back 1 inch or so over the first stitching to strengthen the hem.

Next turn down the top of the curtain. Decide how deep a heading you want—1 or 2 inches—allow an additional 2 inches, and stitch the top hem of the curtain. Make a second stitching at the point where you want

RUFFLED CURTAINS are much wider than tailored curtains, each curtain consisting of two or more widths of material seamed together with a ⅛-inch

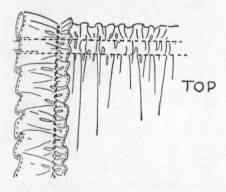

TOP

allowance. The bottom and side edges of the curtain are turned under ¼ inch and hemmed before the ruffling is attached. (In measuring length be sure to allow for the depth of the ruffle.) The top hem is a narrow one of about 2 inches. The ruffled heading may be

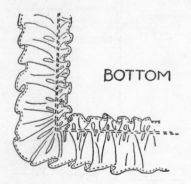

BOTTOM

made separately, then stitched to the curtain so that the top hem of the curtain forms the back of the casing which holds the curtain rod. The ruffling along the sides and the bottom should be stitched before the heading is attached. Ruffling can be bought by the yard or made at home. You will find instructions on how to make ruffles ad headings in Chapter 16.

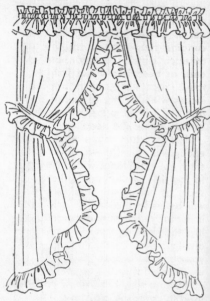

SASH CURTAINS are straight curtains in a single piece covering the entire upper or lower sash of a window or the pane in a door. A sash curtain is usually wider than the window itself, so that it will hang in soft folds. With the rod in place, measure the distance from the top of the rod to the window sill. Add 5½ inches for hem allowance to get the length of each curtain.

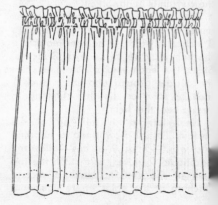

Straighten the end of the curtain material by pulling a cross-thread and cutting along the line. Measure off the curtain lengths, pull cross-threads to act as guides for cutting, and cut the curtains. Hem the top and the bottom of each curtain, double stitching the ends as described under Tailored Curtains. Each hem should be about 2 inches wide. A second row of stitching about 1 inch from the top edge of the curtain makes the heading.

If the curtain material is not wide enough to give the desired fullness, stitch an additional width of material to the side of the curtain, keeping the seam as narrow as possible so that it will be inconspicuous. If your material is not long enough to allow for a heading, the heading can often be made in another, even contrasting, material; or you can add a band of colored or figured material at the bottom.

When a single curtain of this type is used to cover the glass in a door there will be a rod at both the top and the bottom of the curtain. The ruffled heading for a door curtain is made narrower than for a window curtain. Make one at the top and one at the bottom of the curtain by running a second row of machine stitching a half inch from the fold at the top and the bottom hems. The curtain is then stretched tightly between the two rods.

COTTAGE CURTAINS consist of two separate sets of curtains, one for the upper and one for the lower sash. The total width of the curtains should be about one and a half times the width of the window. This allows for generous fullness. If the curtain material is too wide for a single curtain, it can be split. Since a tightly woven selvedge may shrink more than the rest of the material, it is sometimes a good idea to cut off the selvedge at both sides. Make 1-inch side hems for the middle of the window and narrow hems at the outside edges.

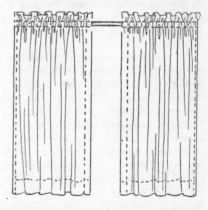

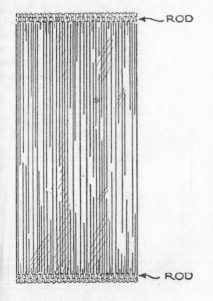

CAFE CURTAINS are both decorative and practical. They may be used in a room which has an Early American, traditional, or modern decorating theme. The materials used for café curtains should not be flimsy or transparent. They may be made from material of a solid color, with or without contrasting trim, or from a figured material.

A variety of lengths can be used depending upon your decorating purpose. You can have just one curtain at the bottom half of the window, or a double tier of curtains (one at the top half of the window and one at the bottom). In some cases, where you have a very long window, or a French door which you want to treat as a window, you can make three tiers. When you have two or three tiers of curtains, you do not need a window shade. Just adjust the café curtains to provide whatever degree of light you wish in the room.

Café curtains are hung from rings that are sewn to the heading of the material. These rings may be brass, wood, or hand-sewn "rings" of the same or contrasting fabric as used for the curtain. The rods are usually made of wood or of the same type of brass used for all other curtains. However, as the wooden rod shows, it should be painted or finished off in some manner so as not to detract from its decorative quality.

To make the curtain, first measure the length you desire and then add 6 inches for heading and hemming. Measure across the width of the window, allowing enough material (perhaps twice the width) to give the curtain a graceful fullness and "hang." If you want to use a contrasting heading and band at the bottom of the curtain, you need allow only 2 inches for heading and hemming. Cut the contrasting material from 4 to 5 inches wide to allow for turning in. Before you cut the material, cut a scallop pattern from a piece of heavy paper. Make the scallops shallow with the points about 3 inches apart. The illustration shows the way to sew the curtain when using contrasting material at top and bottom. If you just use the one fabric, instead of turning the bands at top and bottom to the right side of

the curtain material, turn them to the wrong (i.e., the under) side of the curtain.

You may prefer to use ball fringe, other fringe, rickrack, or flat braid as a trimming around the sides and bottom of the curtain. This trim should be stitched on after the curtain is completed.

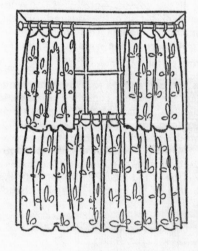

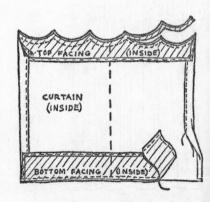

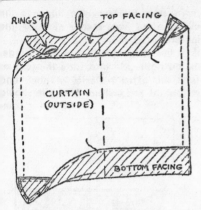

DOUBLE SASH CURTAINS are separate curtains for the top and the bottom sashes of a window. These are made in the same way as the single sash curtain and are most often used where a completely curtained window seems desirable.

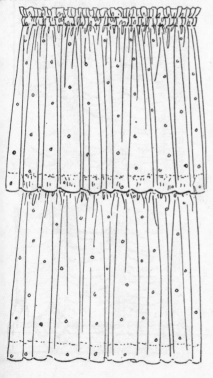

Remodeling curtains—When you move to a different house or apartment, or when you want to transfer curtains from one room to another, you may discover that they do not fit the new windows. This does not necessarily mean that you must buy or make new curtains. Many curtains can be remodeled to meet the new requirement.

If the curtains are too short, add straight cotton or rayon fringe in white or ecru. Informal curtains, such as tiebacks, cottage curtains, café curtains and sash curtains can be lengthened by adding ball fringe. If the curtain is a figured material, a deep border of a solid color may be added at the bottom or used as a deep contrasting heading on the top of the curtain. If the curtain is of a solid color, add the necessary length in a figured material. Before adding new material, wash and iron it to make sure it does not fade or shrink after the curtain is remodeled.

Long curtains which are no longer in use can always be cut down for a shorter window. Even if one curtain in a pair of long curtains has worn out or been damaged in some way, the remaining curtain may still be long enough to make a pair of shorter sash curtains.

AUSTRIAN SHADES—These shirred shades with fringed, scalloped bottoms are enjoying a revival. They are made either in luxurious fabrics for formal rooms or in simple materials for informal interiors. The shade may be used by itself as the complete window decoration, or in conjunction with draperies and valance. If you use draperies, they should hang straight at each side of the window and be made in a fabric of a very simple design. The valance or cornice should match the drapery. If you use the valance alone, that too should be of simple material and design. The Austrian shade in itself has an importance that should not be diminished by the addition of a fancy style of drapery or valance.

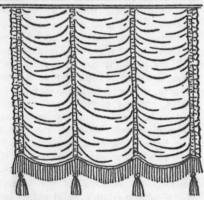

Before you buy the material for the shade, measure the window from top to sill. Allow two to three times that length for your fabric, depending on whether you want full or scant shirring when the shade is let down to the window sill. Measure the width of the window from side to side, and allow 3 inches extra for the two side hems, plus 2 to 4 inches extra for the scalloped area. The more material you allow for this area, the deeper your scallops will be.

When you purchase the material, get the special shirring tape which has cords woven in and rings sewed on to it. You will need a tape at each side of the shade, plus 2 or 3 lengths of tape for the scallops. If you have a very wide window and want more scallops, get more lengths of tape. Also buy traverse cord for pulling the shade up and down, fringe to match the color of the shade or to harmonize with it, and tassels to put at the bottom end of each shirring tape. The tassels may be omitted. Your final purchase should be a round ⅜-inch rod of metal or wood to weight the shade at the bottom.

To sew: first make a tubing to fit over the rod from a strip of the shade material. Cut the strip 2 inches longer than the rod, seam it, then turn it over to the right side and slide the rod in. Tack the extra material at each end so that the rod will not slide out.

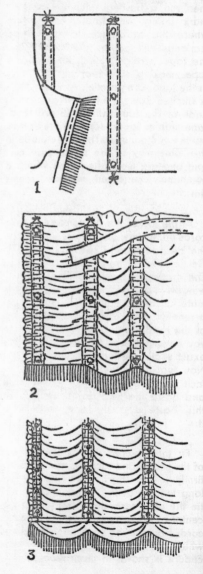

1

2

3

At both sides of the shade, turn in 1½ inches of the material and baste. On these two turned-in sides, one inch from the edge, stitch the shirring tape as shown in illustration 1. Measure the width you desire each scallop to be (generally this is from 10 to 12 inches), then run a basting stitch through, or mark lightly with chalk, the places where the tapes are to go. These markings will act as guides to keep the tapes straight. Stitch the strips of tape, making sure that all the rings in the tapes are parallel. After the tape is stitched down, tie the woven-in cord ends at the top and bottom of each tape with a temporary bow. Now turn up the bottom edge of the shade ⅜ inch on the right side of the material, and baste it. Baste the fringe over the hem and then machine-stitch it down flat.

At the top of the shade pull the tape cords up, evenly, until the shades reach the desired length: see illustration 2. Tie and knot the cord ends tightly. The shade will then be wider than the window because you allowed extra material for the scallops. By hand, sew a running stitch ½ inch below the top of the shade, and pull the thread until you have gathered the material to the exact width needed to fit the window. Now turn down the gathered edge ½ inch from the top, on the wrong side, and baste the hem down. On top of this, baste a sturdy tape, then stitch it.

Fit the covered rod at the bottom of the shade and tack the rod-covering firmly to the strips of tape. Now cut long lengths of the traverse cord and tie the ends securely to the rod at the center of each tape. Slide the traverse cords from the rod up through the rings, which are part of the tape. This procedure is shown in illustration 3.

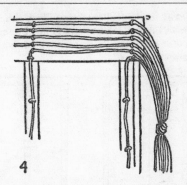

4

To hang the shade you need to attach a flat board (1 inch thick) to the top of the window frame. Before attaching this board, insert small eye screws in its back. Attach the shade to the top of the board, either by inconspicuous tacks hammered through the tape which is sewed under the hemmed top of the shade, or by snaps. If you prefer snaps, instead of sewing an ordinary sturdy tape to the top of the shade, sew one part of a "snap tape" which is made especially for upholstery use. Nail the companion part of the "snap tape" to the top of the board. Then snap the shade to the board. The advantage of this method is that the shade can easily be removed for cleaning.

When the board is fixed to the window, and the shade is attached to the board, draw the traverse cords through the screws to one side, as seen in illustration 4. Adjust these cords until you can raise and lower the shade evenly. Then knot the cords together, and finish with a tassel at the end of each cord.

SKYLINE SHADE—This modernized version of the Austrian shade, without the scallops, is an interesting way to dress the windows of an informal home or a studio. The fabric which works out most effectively for this shade is of a solid color, smooth texture, and medium weight. Contrasting braid makes an excellent trim. The shade shows up best when there is no drapery to detract from its decorative or functional quality.

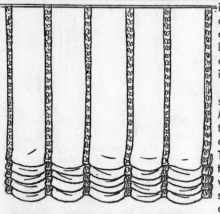

Measure the length of the window from top to sill, allowing 5 to 6 inches for hemming at the bottom and top of the shade. Allow 3 inches across the

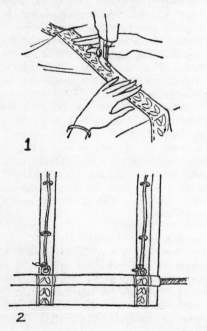

1

2

width of the window, for hemming both sides of the shade. When buying your material, get the necessary length of shirring tape and traverse cord (as described for Austrian shade), the ⅜-inch rod for the bottom of the shade, and the flat 1-inch board for the top of the window. In addition, buy the flat braid to go on the shade as a trim, either in a design or a solid contrasting color.

To make the shade: turn under and stitch hems at both sides of the shade. Measure the widths at which you want to place the cord tapes, and sew them as explained for the Austrian shade. Then on the right side stitch the trimming braid directly over the area where the cord tapes are on the wrong side. This covers the machine-stitching of the cord tapes: see illustration 1.

Turn up and stitch the hem at the bottom of the shade, making an extra stitching to provide a tubing through which the rod can be inserted: see illustration 2. Bring hem up as close to the rings on the cord tape as possible, so that there will not be an empty gap between the bottom rings and the bottom of the shade. (Before inserting the rod, if you want to add a short fringe at the bottom of the shade, machine-stitch it on the right side ½ inch above the folded edge of the material.) Cut long lengths of the traverse cord, and tie the ends to the bottom rings of the cord tape. Then draw the cords through the rings. If you want narrower folds (when shade is drawn up) than the cord tape allows, sew extra rings on the tape and space them half-way between the existing rings.

On top of the shade turn down ½ inch of the material to the wrong side, and to this sew the plain tape or the "snap tape." Attach the shade to the board in the same way as directed for the Austrian shade. Also follow the same directions for pulling the traverse cords through the board screws and for attaching tassels.

DRAPERIES

DRAPERIES—Draperies can be used over straight glass curtains, ruffled tie-

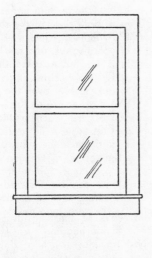

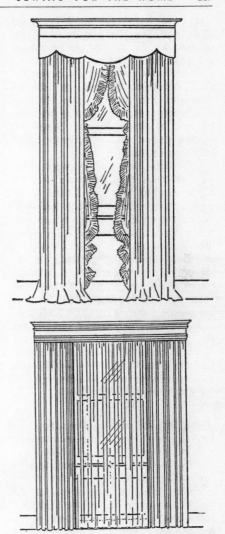

backs, or on windows which are not curtained but are fitted with Venetian blinds. They are appropriate for almost any room in the house except the kitchen or bath.

In addition to their decorative value they can do much to solve many common window problems by being so designed that windows appear wider or taller than they actually are.

Draperies are usually made of firmly woven material, such as linen, chintz or cretonne, heavy rayon or silk brocade, heavy cotton weaves, fabrics with metallic threads, and even velvet. Choose your drapery materials to go with the other furnishings of the room. You will probably want to use solid-color material in a room with figured wallpaper. But if the walls are solid color and the rug has a small, inconspicuous design, you will be able to use color and design in the draperies and can have matching slip covers for your furniture. Figured or printed draperies are usually more effective than plain ones, but you must be careful not to have figured draperies, figured paper, and a figured rug all in the same room!

Be careful, too, not to select material which is too elaborate for the place in which you live. Chintz, linen, and cretonne draperies can look well in any setting if the design is suitable. But velveteen or satin-striped draperies will look out of place in the country or in an informal living room. For the recreation room and other informal rooms plastic materials are sometimes used. You will find instructions for sewing plastic material on page 256.

Estimate the amount of material for the draperies carefully. A generous width of material (at least one and a half times the width of the windows) is as necessary for attractive draperies as for glass curtains and tiebacks.

Making draperies—Draperies can be lined or unlined. Those of medium-weight material, such as chintz, are usually lined. Sateen in matching or contrasting color is a suitable lining material. To make lined draperies, cut the drapery material and the lining the same length, allowing for hems at the top and the bottom. Put the right sides of the drapery material and the lining material together and stitch the top and the two sides, leaving the bottom edges open. Turn to the right side and press. Turn the bottom edges in, so that the raw ends of the bottom hem are between the drapery and the lining. Slip stitch this bottom hem by hand.

Unlined draperies should have hems at least 1 inch wide on both sides,

so they will not look skimpy when finished. These side hems can be finished by hand with a slip stitch or by machine.

There are many ways to finish the top of the draperies. They may be hung under a valance board—we shall discuss various types of valances a little later—or they may have a small connecting valance of the drapery material.

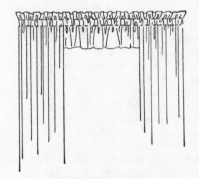

Other ways of finishing draperies include a simple heading such as that described for glass curtains, rings of wood or plastic evenly spaced and

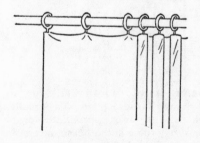

stitched to the top hem, pinch pleats, and box pleats. The pleats give draperies a professional finish, and they are easy to make.

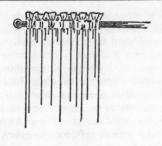

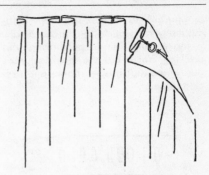

To make pinch pleats allow approximately 1 inch for each pleat, depending upon the thickness of the material. Group the pleats in sets of two or three, as shown, and space the groups about 3 inches apart across the top of the draperies. There should be at least three or four sets of pinch pleats in each half of a pair of draperies. The pleats are made from the extra fullness in the drapery. It is important to keep them even. Pin the pleats in place about 2 inches from the top edge of the finished drapery, and then catch them in place with a needle and thread.

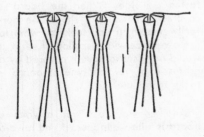

Box pleats are folded, as shown in the illustration. They are evenly spaced and large enough to take up all the extra fullness in the drapery.

To give the proper professional appearance to your pleated hangings they must be put up on rods with curtain rings. The curtain ring can be of brass or plastic—the important thing is to find a ring or slide to fit the curtain rod. Rods are usually round so that the rings will slide over them easily. Rings for a plain drawn drapery can be stitched to the top, but on a drapery with pinch pleats the rings should be stitched to the wrong side of the drapery at the points where the pleats are caught—usually from one to two inches from the top. This allows a heading to extend above the curtain rod. A small section of the ring is sewed to the drapery by hand, and it should be sewed very securely.

Self-pleating bands made of canvas or Pellon can be bought by the yard at upholsterers or department stores. This backing comes in various widths and has groups of slot openings cut into it as shown in the illustration. These groups of 1–2–2–1 slots are spaced about 3 or 4 inches apart to allow for spacing between the "pinch" pleats. No rings or hooks are required.

At the top of the drapery or curtain, on the wrong side of the material, sew the backing with 4 rows of machine stitching. It is not necessary to turn in the edges of the backing as they are smooth and will not fray. Insert the rod through the slots and push the drapery

or curtain together. You will automatically form perfectly spaced pleats.

Make sure when purchasing this
backing that it has the manufacturer's
guarantee that it is washable and dry-
cleanable.

Valances offer a wide range of
possibilities. They can be painted to
match the room or they can be made
in any of the ways described below.

A valance cut from wood or com-
position board can be covered with the
material used for the draperies, but a
contrasting material is often more effective. For instance, if you have a
solid-color drapery and plain wall, you
might want to cover the valance with a
figured material which harmonizes
with the solid color. If you have a
papered wall or a figured drapery, the
valance board can be covered with a
plain-colored material.

If you feel the material you are
using to cover the valance doesn't
have a sufficiently heavy texture, use a
lining between it and the board. After
your valance has been cut, measure the
covering material at least 2 inches
wider and longer all around the four
sides of the valance (that is, the top,
the front, and the two sides). Lay the
material (and the lining if you are using
one) on a flat surface with the right
side of the material down. Place the
valance board on it; then fold the material over the top of the board and
fasten it with thumbtacks or with carpet
tacks, spacing them about 2 inches
apart. Pull the material taut over the
front of the board and fasten it in the
same way. When this has been done,
fasten the sides. When the board is
covered, the material should be perfectly smooth. If you feel you want to
use a valance with a scalloped edge, it
would be wiser to have it covered by a
professional, for this type of board is
tricky to handle.

Another way to cover a valance
board is with wallpaper. If you have a
solid-colored drapery and a plain wall,
you might like the extra color accent
of a striped wallpaper or some other
suitable design on the valance. If the
drapery is plain and your wall is
papered, you could use the same wallpaper on the valance board.

A substantial valance can be made by using a buckram frame covered with drapery material. When it is finished, the valance can be nailed directly onto the window frame if the valance projects far enough out from the window; or you can nail it on a narrow shelflike board attached to the window frame with angle irons. To make this buckram frame, first cut a paper pattern long enough so that the ends can be bent to form the sides of the valance. If you are striving for simplicity in design and work, cut the pattern straight across, but if you are willing to spend some extra time and care in sewing, you can cut the bottom of the valance in scallops.

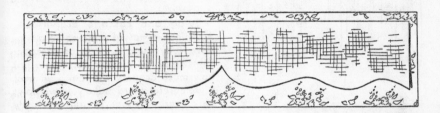

When you are sure the paper pattern is the right size, cut the buckram. Then cut a piece of muslin or flannel for "body," making it 1 inch larger all around to allow for turning under. Cut the covering material and the lining. These should also be at least 1 inch larger all around. If your material has a definite design in it, be sure the design is centered before you begin to cut.

The next step is to sew the material over the buckram frame. Lay the material, right side down, on the table. Over it place the muslin or flannel, then the buckram. Turn the edges of the two layers of material over the buckram, pinning them carefully; if the valance has a scalloped edge, snip the material edges as you turn them. Miter the corners to get a smooth fit. Baste into place, using a large needle and heavy thread. Catch stitch to the buckram, then place the lining over it, turn in the edges, pin down, and slip stitch in place.

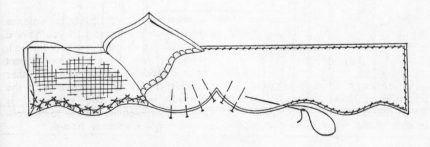

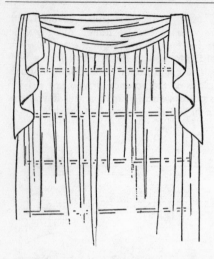

Moss fringe of the same or contrasting color may be added to the bottom

of this valance if you desire a special decorative effect.

To finish the job, sew a strong tape—twill tape, or a couple of thicknesses of the material—to the top of the valance. This tape is for the purpose of turning over the window frame or a board, and the nails are driven through the tape to make the valance secure.

Swag and cascade draperies— A distinctive way of dressing up a window is by using a swag or cascade. The size of the window determines just how much drapery will look well over it. Be careful not to make your windows look overburdened. To fall gracefully the swag or cascade must be made of a material which is not too bulky in

texture. You can line the swag or just turn under a hem with a slip stitch. It is not advisable to use a thick fringe or other type of heavy edging on it, as it detracts from the soft draped effect.

The swag or cascade need not be of the same material as the curtains, but be sure that it is similar in texture and harmonious in color.

For a simple swag over a curtain pole or through loops, all you need is a length of material cut to whatever width you feel will drape well. After you have looped the swag over the pole or through the loops, cut the ends on a diagonal line.

You can cut them in even lengths, or if you have two windows next to each other you might prefer to cut the center pieces of material somewhat shorter.

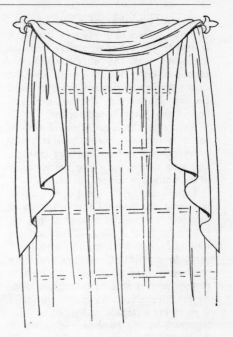

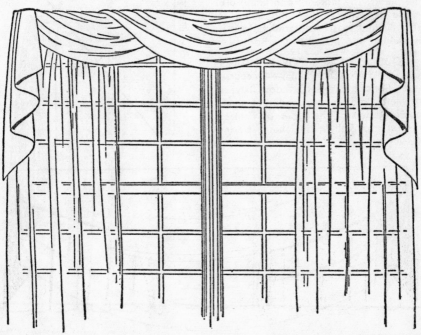

If you use the more complicated cascade nailed to a valance board, it is best to cut a paper pattern first. Do the same with the jabots which are placed at each side. The width and the depth of a cascade and jabot depend on the size of the window, and you must keep them in proportion.

As a rule, the most effective way to use a cascade or swag over a group of windows is to treat them as a single unit and drape the swag across them in a continuous piece.

Experiment with your paper pattern until you are sure of the proportions, then cut your material and lining, allowing at least 1 inch all around for turning in. It is best to use lining for a cascade and jabot, as they are more stationary than the swag, which is thrown over a pole or through a loop. As the illustration shows, the graceful lines of the cascade and jabot are determined by the number and width of the pleats. The material and lining are made separately, then the lining is slip stitched to the material before it is pleated and nailed to the board.

RODS AND AIDS FOR HANGING CURTAINS AND DRAPERIES—Of course you will not be sewing window fixtures of metal, plastic, or wood, but some consideration of the types of fixtures available and their uses should be in-

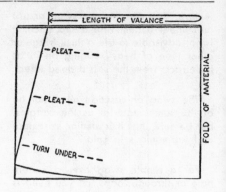

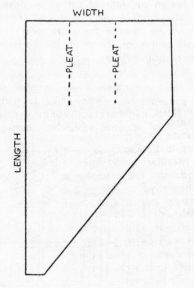

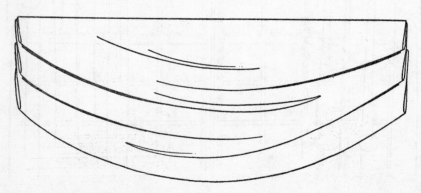

Holdbacks of metal or plastic can be used instead of curtain or drapery tiebacks. These can also be used for a swag valance which is thrown over them. Loops, too, can be used for swags.

cluded in a discussion of curtains and draperies. Choosing the right type of fixture is important if your draperies are to be shown at their best.

Besides being useful and sturdy, rods and cranes and loops should be decorative as well, so that they enhance rather than detract from the finished product of your sewing. Department and housefurnishings stores as well as mail-order catalogues can give you a wide selection of quality, price, and style. Here are some of the basic fixtures:

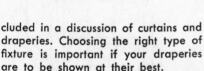

The simplest and usually the least expensive way to hang curtains is to buy a metal extension rod which can

be fitted over a narrow window or extended to fit a wider one. Metal extension rods fit flush against the window sash and are used with sash curtains, cottage curtains, and lightweight tiebacks.

If you want the curtains to extend beyond the window frame, you can get extension rods which are curved at both ends. They come in sets of 1, 2, and 3. If you use one of these multiple rods, you can hang the glass curtain on the rod nearest the window, then the draperies, then the valance, if it is not attached to a frame. Rods of this type are very convenient: you simply slide the curtain, the drapery, and the valance on the proper rods and then hang them all up in one operation.

Optical illusions can frequently be created with curtain rods—especially on oddly shaped windows, such as bay windows, or the curved fanlight window over a hallway door. For the latter there is a special curved rod available. The same curved rod which is used over

the fanlight can also be attached to a wall over a small window set low on the wall of a high-ceilinged room. Hanging the curtains or draperies from such a rod makes the window appear much larger.

Another optical illusion can be created with curtains if you have two windows of different size on one wall —or if the windows in a room are altogether too narrow. When this is the case, extend the rods beyond the width of the windows and fasten them to the wall. Hang your curtains the full width

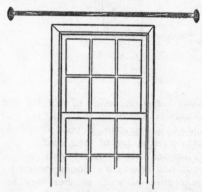

of the rods, and you will be surprised at how much wider the windows will look.

If you do not want a valance across a window or if you would like to hang the draperies in an open doorway on some movable fixture, use swinging cranes which can be attached to the frame of the window or the door with a bracket. These cranes can be of either wood or metal, and you can leave them in the natural state or paint them to match your woodwork. When buying the cranes, be sure that the rings supplied to fit over the rod are of the proper size.

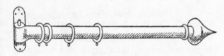

Curtain or drapery poles of metal or wood also come in various colors, styles, and sizes. They are held up by brackets which are screwed into the window or doorframe. Here, too, you must be sure to get rings which slide easily over the pole. In some cases rings are not used, the pole being slipped into the heading of the drapery like a curtain rod. Such a pole can also be used for holding a swag valance.

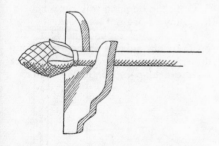

The woman who takes pride in the appearance of her windows is always looking for new ideas in window treatment. You will find there is no limit to the possibilities which can be worked out. Just as a starter: Do you have a group of two or three narrow windows

in a low-ceilinged room? Treat each window as a separate unit with the curtains and draperies extending to the floor. Are these windows in a narrow room? Treat them as a single unit with a continuous swag or valance across the top. Do you have two windows with a small section of wall space between? Fit the wall space with a mirror. It will appear to be a third window and you can treat the windows as a group of three, curtaining the mirror as you would a window. These are only a few suggestions. You will develop your own ideas as you go along.

DRESSING-TABLE SKIRTS—These can be made at home in much the same way you make the glass curtains for your windows. The material which you select for the skirt of the dressing table can be the same as the draperies or bedspread, or it can be of a thin material such as that used for the window curtains. If the material is very sheer, however, it is best to use two or three thicknesses.

Gathered skirt—The skirt is cut long enough to allow for a 2-inch hem at the top and the bottom. Make a heading at the top about 1 inch wide. The easiest way to adjust the fullness in the top of the skirt is to make a casing by running a second row of stitching through the middle of the top hem. Pull a drawstring through the casing. If the dressing table has a front section which opens outward, you will have to make the skirt in two sections and use two drawstrings, one for each half of the skirt. Fasten one end of the string to the side back of the table. Pull the string tight, fastening the other end at the center front or at the oposite side. Adjust the gathers in the skirt evenly and fasten the skirt to the table with tacks or thumbtacks.

DRAWSTRING
THUMBTACKS

For a dainty feminine finish, and also to conceal the tacks which hold the skirt in place, fasten wide ribbon at the sides of the dressing-table skirt just below the gathered heading. Bring the ends of the ribbon together in front and tie them in a bow.

Pleated skirt—Pleats require more time to make than the gathered top, because they must all be exactly the same size and evenly spaced. Stitch the pleats to a plain band of material which is long enough to go around the dressing table. Then tack the band to the table.

THUMBTACKS

Cover the tacks with a band of rib-

bon, as shown in the illustration, or finish the top of the skirt with a double-thickness band of self or contrasting material.

The bench or stool can be covered to match the dressing-table skirt. Cut 3 or 4 layers of heavy material to fit the top of the seat. An old blanket or mattress pad is fine to use for this purpose. Or a foam rubber pillow or cushion could be cut to size and used as a filler for the pad. Cut two pieces of the skirt material ½ inch larger all around than the top of the seat. Put all the layers together. Lay the right sides of the two pieces of skirt material together and machine stitch ½ inch from the edge, leaving one end open. Turn to the right side. Trim the padding to fit and insert smoothly into the finished seat cover in the same way you put a pillow into a pillowcase.

Close the opening with slip stitching. If the layers are not too thick, the pad can be stitched around the four sides on the right side of the material and the raw edges covered with bias tape in a matching or contrasting color.

A gathered skirt for a bench or stool can be made by allowing enough material to go one and a half times around the stool or bench. The skirt

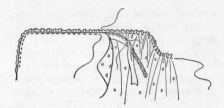

should be long enough for a seam at the top and a hem at bottom. Stitch the two ends together to make the skirt one continuous piece. Gather as for a dressing-table skirt, adjust gathers evenly, and baste the top of the skirt to the underside of the seat cover. Stitch by machine or by hand. If you did not use a bias tape on the seat cushion, a covered cord or a piping stitched between the skirt and the top makes a professional-looking finish for the joining.

CLOSET ACCESSORIES—Matching closet accessories will add much to the appearance of your bedroom, and most of them can be made at home.

Shoe pockets—For a set of shoe pockets use sturdy material, such as heavy unbleached muslin, cotton drill, or cretonne. Make as many pockets as you have space or shoes.

The foundation piece of material to which a double row of shoe pockets (enough for four pairs of shoes) is

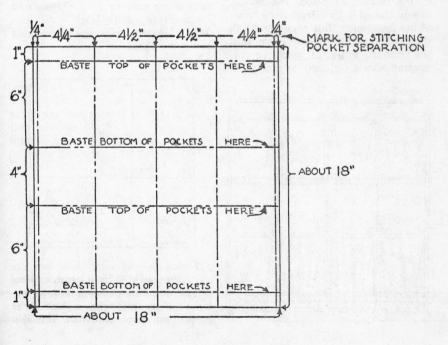

stitched should be about eighteen inches square. If your closet door is larger, you can make 3 rows of pockets rather than the 2 rows shown here. Each of the two pocket pieces is 26 inches long by 6 inches deep. Both strips are bound along the upper

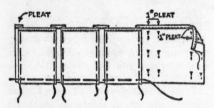

edge before being pleated. Each strip makes four shoe pockets and each pocket is 4 inches across, with an additional 2 inches allowance for pleats.

After the pleats have been basted in place, the two rows of pockets are stitched to the foundation piece. The top row is placed 1 inch from the top of the foundation piece. The bottom row is placed 1 inch from the bottom of the foundation. This allows a 4-inch space between the two rows of pockets. The bottom edge of each row is covered with a flat strip of bias tape,

edge stitched on both sides, and the pockets are separated by a double row of machine stitching. The side edges of the rows of pockets are basted to the sides of the foundation and caught in a bias-tape binding that is stitched all the way around the foundation piece. Four loops of folded bias tape fastened at the four corners of the shoe bag will provide a way to attach the bag to the closet door.

Laundry bag—A laundry bag to match your shoe pockets and other closet accessories can be made from ½ yard of the same material. The fabric must be color-fast so that it will not come off if a damp article is placed in the bag. Be certain that the material is torn on the straight of the goods at the top and the bottom. Straighten it by tearing it from selvedge to selvedge—unless this was done when you bought it. Bring the two selvedges together with the right sides of the material on the inside and pin them together. Stitch a ½-inch seam along the selvedge edges and across the bottom of the bag.

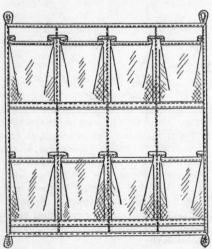

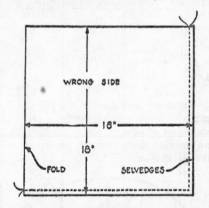

Fasten the threads; then turn the top edge down ¼ inch on the wrong side. Press. Make a second fold 1¼ inches wide. Pin or baste this hem in place and edge stitch by machine.

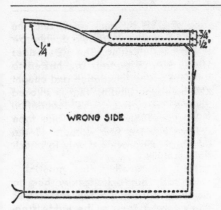

WRONG SIDE

the center top of the front piece for the hanger hook to go through.

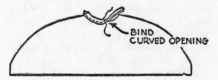

BIND
CURVED OPENING

Make a second row of stitching ½ inch above the first row of stitching. The space between the rows of stitching will form a casing for the drawstrings. The ¾-inch space at the top makes a ruffled heading to finish the bag.

Turn the bag to the right side. Make small slits in the casing at the wide seam and at the fold. Finish the openings with a buttonhole stitch to keep the edges from fraying and insert two drawstrings of ribbon or cord. Tie the ends in bows if you use ribbon, or knot and fray to make a tassel if you use cord.

Pin the two pieces together, then stitch the curved sections together by binding them on the right side with matching or contrasting bias tape. Finish by binding the bottom edge. Turn the first binding to the side, so it will lie flat at the point where the two bound edges meet. Turn under the raw edge where the two ends of the bottom binding are joined. If you measure the amount of binding you need to go around the bottom, you can seam the bias tape before you apply it to the cover. For instructions on how to join bias tape, see Chapter 8.

Garment covers—Cut two pieces of material large enough to slip over the shoulders of your clothes when they are on wooden dress hangers, as shown in the illustration.

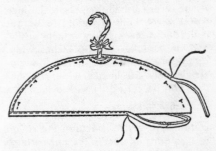

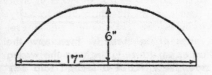

6"

17"

Bind a 2-inch curved opening at

SLIP COVERS—Slip covers bring new life to a hard-used room. They make pieces of furniture compatible which ordinarily would not look well together. They make a room appear cooler for the summer season. They serve as temporary covers for the fine furniture pieces which you buy "in the muslin" at a lower cost and plan to have upholstered later in your choice of material. When you are redecorating your home, slip covers are among your best allies.

Suitable materials—Slip covers should be strong enough to withstand constant wear, dry cleaning, and perhaps home laundering. The material used should not be one which clings or sticks to the clothing. A fairly smooth-surfaced material is a good selection. A glazed finish, such as chintz, is an even better choice, as it will help to resist soil. Besides chintz, the most popular choices for slip covers are cretonne, crash, and a heavy linen made especially for slip covers. Cotton is coming more to the fore, however, because it is easier to launder and is usually lower in price. Other serviceable slip-cover materials include rep (a heavier ribbed cotton), plain or striped denim, galatea, French ticking, damask, and drapery sateen. Of these the rep is the most difficult to handle, since it is a little bulky. There are a few lighter materials, such as gingham and percale, which some people like to use because of their laundering qualities, but they are usually impractical, since they are too light in weight for larger upholstered pieces, they wrinkle easily, and are usually only 36 inches wide. Upholstery materials should be approximately 50 inches wide, so that they can be cut easily with a minimum of wastage.

Monk's cloth, a very loosely woven cotton, is effective, because the rough texture adds interest to the appearance of the finished slip cover. It is apt to pull and ravel, however, and you will be wise to use monk's cloth only after you are past the experimental stage of making slip covers. Plastic material is now being used for slip covers, too, where protection and not decoration is the most important consideration.

Slip covers made at home are less expensive than those which are custom made by a commercial upholsterer, but they are still a good-sized investment. One reason is the yardage required, which in most cases is considerable.

Another reason is that an inferior quality of material will prove more expensive in the long run. After all, slip covers are made with the expectation that they will last for a number of years, through many dry cleanings or launderings. This does not necessarily mean that you must buy the most expensive material available, but it does mean that you should select your material carefully.

Find out whether the material is color fast, not only for washing or cleaning, but against sunlight as well. Many fabrics fade in the light. If you plan to launder your slip covers, find out if the material is pre-shrunk or what percentage of shrinkage you must allow for. If you buy contrasting material or trimming to be used in the slip cover, make sure that this is also of the same color-fast and shrink-proof quality, so that a perfectly good slip cover will not be ruined by the fading or shrinking of its trimming.

Also investigate the cottons which have special crease-resistant and water-repellent treatments which improve the natural quality of the cotton fiber. And when you buy chintz, inquire if it has the so-called permanent-glaze finish.

Occasionally slip covers are made of rayon moiré, taffeta, or similar materials, for bedroom use. These are for formal rooms only, and are not recommended for practical use to take the place of cotton or linen.

When making your purchases, do not rely on the salesclerk's information alone, but ask to see the label which accompanies the bolt of material or the trimmings if the shrinkage and dye features are not printed on the selvedge of the material. Remember that a haphazard selection of materials can spoil the effect of your slip covers after you have gone to all the trouble and expense of making them.

Suitable color and design—A piece of furniture should be slip-covered as you would dress a woman —to bring out the good points and to conceal those not so good. If a chair is too large in a small room, the slip cover should be a plain material or one with an inconspicuous design done in a quiet and subdued color. If the room is large, with plenty of space for all the furniture, then you can use the lush, sprawling bouquets of roses large enough to cover an entire chair back —provided, of course, that you have enough quiet areas in rugs, walls, or other pieces of furniture to keep the atmosphere of the room restful.

In a small room the sofa might have a plain cover, since it is the largest piece. One chair might also be covered in a plain material and the second chair in a figured or flowered material. Make draperies to match either the plain or the figured material. In a large room the sofa and one chair might have gaily-printed slip covers, with only the second chair covered in a solid color repeated in the print. In this case the draperies might well be printed, with tiebacks and facings of the solid color which was used for the second chair.

Amount of material required— Describe your chair or take a picture of a chair like yours when you go to buy slip-cover material. The usual medium-size wing chair without ruffles or pleats at the bottom takes about 7 yards of plain material 39 to 45 inches wide. If you use a material with a small design that does not require matching, you can buy the same amount of material, but if the material has a large bouquet or other design which must be centered on the chair back and on the seat cover, allow an extra yard.

In addition to the picture, take the measurements of the furniture with you when you go to the store. These meas-urements are taken in inches, as shown in the sketches:

1. Center back of chair (or sofa) from top to legs.

2. Center front of chair from top to seat.

3. Center front of chair seat (cushion removed) to legs.

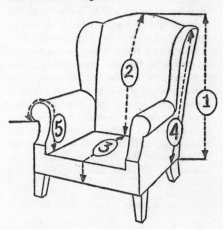

4. Twice (because there are two wings) the distance from the top of the wing to the legs.

5. Twice the distance over the curve of the arm to the seat.

6. For the seat cover, twice the distance from the back to the front, plus

7. Four times the thickness of the seat.

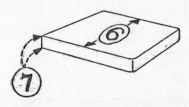

For pleats or ruffles at the bottom, measure the distance around the bottom of the chair or sofa where the legs and the upholstery join. Double this measurement to allow for pleats. This will be the length of the material needed for the pleats. The distance

from the top of the leg to the floor (as shown) is the depth of the material needed. Suppose you need 216 inches of material to pleat around the bottom of a chair, and suppose the pleats must be 6 inches deep. You would need 1 yard of material to make the pleats— enough to make six strips 36 inches long by 6 inches wide. These strips are pieced into a single strip 216 inches long plus ½ yard for seams and hems.

There are three ways to economize on material for slip covers. (1) Cover the section of the chair under the cushion with any piece of sturdy material you happen to have. (2) If the chair will look well without them, omit the pleats or ruffle which cover the chair legs, and finish off the slip cover at the top of the chair legs. (3) Run the slip cover straight down to the floor, with only an inverted box pleat at each of the four corners.

In the section which follows we are going to show you how to lay out the material for cutting your slip covers. Before you go out to buy your slip-cover material, we suggest that you make a paper pattern and lay it out on the floor, using a layout similar to the one which is drawn here. That will give you a close approximation of just how much you should buy and help you to save material when cutting.

And while we're on the subject of shopping for material, here is a suggestion which will give your slip covers a professional finish. Covered cording or heavy cotton fringe for the seam joinings is inexpensive. You will need 10 to 12 yards of cording or fringe for the average chair.

Cutting cover—There are two ways of doing this. You can work with the paper pattern you make for estimating your material if you find it easier to work that way, or you can save time and get good results by pinning your material wrong side up on the chair or sofa, as shown in the illustrations which follow. Cut the material with a 1-inch seam allowance on all edges, with the exception of any piece of the cover which fits into the seat of the chair. On these pieces cut a 4-inch seam allowance.

1. Start with the inside of the chair back; that is, the part you lean against.

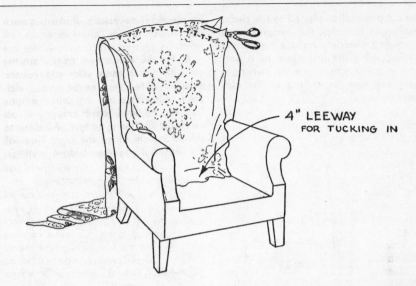

4" LEEWAY
FOR TUCKING IN

Place your material wrong side up, centering any large design. Pin. Cut, allowing for seams and tuck-in at seat.

2. Pin the outside back, also wrong side up, to the chair. Center the design, if there is one in the material. Cut with seam allowance.

3. If the chair has wings and there is a definite design in the slip-cover material, be sure that the wings are covered alike. It is best to cut out the material for the front and the back of the wings in two separate pieces, then to pin all these sections of the slip cover together.

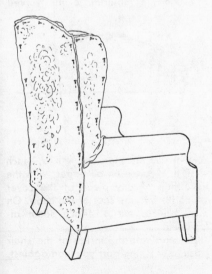

4. Pin the side pieces beneath the arms into place. Be sure to have the design similar for both sections. Cut. For this piece and for the wings you

can cut one section pinned to the chair, then unpin it, match the design on the remaining material, and cut the second section, using the first piece as a pattern to guide you. Place the two right sides together for cutting of the material.

be pieced if necessary. Make a generous 4-inch seam allowance on all sides.

6. Pin the arm covers next. Pin one, cut with 4-inch seam allowance where it will join the seat cover and 1-inch seam allowance on all other edges. The second arm cover may be cut, using the first as a pattern. All designs should match. Place the right sides of the material together before cutting.

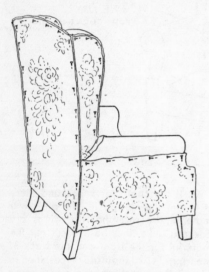

5. Pin the seat cover to the inside back. Since this will not show, it can

7. Pin the material to the curved

front section which joins the arm cover to the side piece. Cut with 1-inch seam allowance. Remove, place right side down on the remaining material, matching designs, and cut the second section for the opposite side of the chair. Pin sections in place, joining them to other sections of the cover. You may need to make small darts at the place where the arm cover joins this small curved section. If you do, baste them in when the slip cover is pinned together on the chair wrong side up.

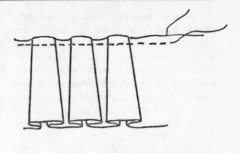

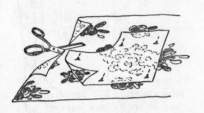

8. Pin with design centered, and cut the front section called the apron, which serves to join the seat cover and the side sections.

9. If you are having a pleated skirt at the bottom of the slip cover, cut strips to be pleated and seam together. Hem by machine. Crease and press to form pleats. Stitch by machine across pleats at the unfinished top edge, to hold the pleats in place until they are stitched to the slip cover.

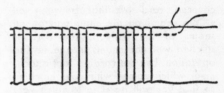

10. Center material wrong side up on the cushion top. Pin. Cut with 1-inch seam allowance. Repeat for the cushion bottom. The design must also be centered on the bottom, since the cushion should be reversed periodically to equalize wear.

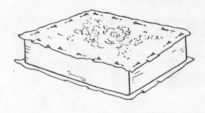

11. Pin the cushion side pieces or "boxing" to join the top and the bottom. Cut with 1-inch seam allowance.

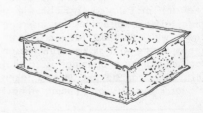

Remove the carefully pinned slip cover from the chair or sofa. The pinned line in all cases will mark the exact seam line. Take a piece of tailor's chalk and mark this line on every piece of the pinned-together slip cover. Then if a pin drops out you still have the line to use as a stitching guide. Baste at the curves of the arms or in any other tricky spot.

For a professional finish, insert covered cord (welting) between all visible seams on the chair and on all seams of the cushion. The cord is stitched with the seams in one sewing operation. Use the cording foot attachment which comes with your machine so that you will be able to stitch very close to the ridge of the cording. If there is not a cording foot in your box of machine attachments, and you cannot obtain one, stitch the seam with your regular machine presser foot. When you turn the slip cover right side out, you will see that the cording lies between the seams in the same manner that piping does.

Try the slip covers on the chair and the seat cushion. This last trying-on is the time to make any needed adjustments. The final step is stitching the pleating or ruffle to the bottom.

Press the slip cover when it is completed before putting it on your chair or sofa.

Plastic slip covers—A simpler, less expensive slip cover for a chair, couch, or any other piece of furniture you want to protect temporarily is one made of plastic material. It will not wear so long as covers made of cotton or linen, and you should not expect it to. However, you may find a plastic cover convenient as a temporary measure if there are small children in the house, for covering the furniture at your summer house, or for protecting the furniture during an absence. As far as appearance is concerned, however, the plastic cover remains primarily a useful one rather than a decorative one. You can buy plastic in the natural neutral color and use bias seam and hem binding of white or of contrasting color for trimming. Or you may prefer

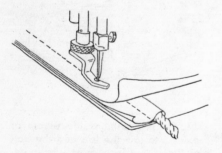

Leave one back seam of the seat cover open, also one back seam of the chair (or sofa) slip cover. Finish with a slide fastener (directions for inserting come with all slide fasteners), with snaps, or tie with strings. The reason for making these openings is so that the covers can be put on and taken off for laundering or cleaning without difficulty.

to buy one of the new colored designs and match them to draperies if you are planning the covers for a cottage.

The illustration shows how the cover is usually made: the back, seat, and front can be cut in one piece. When sewing a plastic slip cover, do not make separate boxed covers for the cushions. A single piece can be cut, starting from the side of the seat, and extending over the arm down the side to the floor. Use one piece for the outside back of the chair. If the legs are wide, of course a separate piece can be put in, as shown in the illustration.

First stitch the seams of the slip cover right side up. Cut edges closely, then stitch the bias binding over them on the right side. Cut the bottom even all around and finish with bias binding. If you do not use binding, simply stitch the seams on the wrong side, for plastic will not ravel. If you want to make a firmer finish, sew the slip covers with French seams. Turn up the hem and stitch. When sewing plastic, use a large machine stitch. Place a piece of tissue or thin newspaper under the material. After the stitching has been done, you can tear off the paper easily. Do not press plastic. Do not launder it—wipe any soil off the surface with a damp cloth.

Slip cover for studio couch—The studio couch or day bed has become a standard piece of furniture that is both useful and decorative. Today it is used in the living room as well as in bedrooms, recreation rooms, and sleeping porches. Obviously the slip-cover material you select for the studio couch must be chosen according to the type of room in which the piece is being used.

Be sure to buy sturdy material, for the studio couch seems to invite people to put their feet up and relax, and it usually gets more hard wear than any other piece of furniture in the room. Be on the lookout for material with crease-resistant features also.

Take all measurements and cut a paper pattern, as explained previously. Make all neccessary seam allowances; then buy your material, cut, fit, and sew in the same way as you would other slip covers.

Attach the "boxing" to the top and the ruffle with plain, French, or corded seams. The ruffle around the bottom may be box pleated or gathered, or it may be plain with inverted pleats at the corners only. If you don't have much material, pleat or gather around the front and the two sides only and leave the back, which rests against the wall, plain. If you run short of material, you can even use a different piece of material for the back. The wise sewer, however, estimates the material so there will be pleats or gathers on all four sides. The cover can then be turned occasionally to prevent its becoming worn too much along one side.

As a rule the studio couch has three oblong cushions with boxed edges along the wall. These are sewed with the same type of seam as you use on the cover. If the pillows inside these tops are used for sleeping, sew a slide fastener or hooks and eyes along the lower edge of the cushion top, so it

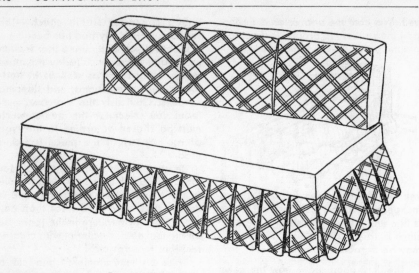

can easily be removed and put back again. The material used to cover the cushions can be matching or contrasting.

Slip covers for bedframes—You can modernize an old iron or wooden bed, or that cherished brass bed, by making a slip cover for the headboard and the footboard. An unattractive wooden bed can be brought up to date by cutting the headboard and lowering it and by removing the footboard entirely. The lower headboard can then be slip covered in a material which matches the bedcover and harmonizes with the draperies. Always have a removable slip cover

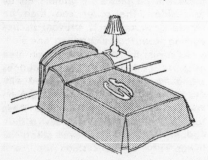

for the headboard, as it will require washing or dry cleaning just as the bedcover itself.

While you can cut a slip cover for a chair or a sofa directly on the furniture itself, the headboard of a bed offers nothing in which to stick the pins while cutting. The best way, therefore, is to cut a paper pattern for the headboard slip cover. Press the paper smoothly over the headboard—it helps to have another person working with you on this if possible—then crease the paper to follow the shape of the headboard at the top.

Cut your material from this paper pattern, allowing a 1-inch seam all around. You will need two pieces for a headboard, one for the front and one for the back. You will also need a straight strip of the material about 2 inches wide for a boxing to join the front and the back pieces. If you have a two-color decorating scheme, you can use a different color for the boxing.

The slip cover should be lined with a material that is fairly heavy, so that it will not shift about when the bed is being made, and so that it will hang

well. You can use a layer of old blan-

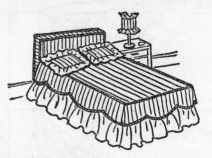

kets which have been washed, or an inexpensive cotton mattress pad which is firm and quilted and stays where you stitch it. (If you are using a new pad, it may be a good idea to launder it first, so that there will be no risk later of having the lining shrink while the top cover does not.)

Cut the padding from the same paper pattern which you used for the slip-cover material. Pin the padding to the wrong side of the slip-cover pieces. Pin the 2-inch wide strip of boxing (which must also be padded) between the front and the back of the slip cover. These pieces should be pinned with their right sides together, so that the seams will all be on the wrong side. Baste the pieces together before stitching. Covered cording can be stitched between the seams of the headboard cover just as in other slip covers. (See directions for cording which are given in this chapter for the chair slip cover.) Bind or hem the headboard slip cover at the bottom and press before slipping it over the headboard.

Miscellaneous covers—There may be a number of odds and ends of furniture in your house which you want to rejuvenate with slip covers. If you have a small table which is the worse for wear, you can make it useful and attractive by sewing a special cover for it and edging it with a fringe or some other type of trimming. This new cover can hang almost to the floor if you like.

Or perhaps you have a treadle drophead sewing machine in your bedroom. By making an attractive cover you can convert it into a charming dressing table. If it's kept in a hall or some other room, it may be wiser to make a tailored box-pleated cover of plain or figured cotton for it.

In a smaller house, where there is no guest room, a folding bed will be less conspicuous if it is covered with an appropriate slip cover when not in use.

Even the ordinary kitchen chair can be made gay and attractive by a padded slip cover for the back and the seat. You can even make your own chair pads by cutting the padding to fit the seat and covering it with one of the new plastic materials. An old dining-room chair can also be rejuvenated by covering the faded upholstery on the seat and the back. A cover made to go over an old piano stool, perhaps with a seat of padded material, is also an idea worth considering.

You can make covers for so many things that the list is endless. The sewing procedures are the same for each type of cover. They can be cut from a paper pattern or they can be fitted by pinning the material right on the article which you want to cover.

BEDSPREADS—A bedspread can be as tailored or as frilly as you choose as long as it is kept in harmony with the type of furniture and the decorating scheme in your bedroom.

Before you buy your material you must realize that if you are going to use cotton bought in the dress-goods department it will run only 36 to 39 inches wide; thus one width of material will be needed for the top of a single bed and additional widths to hang down at the sides. If your bed is not

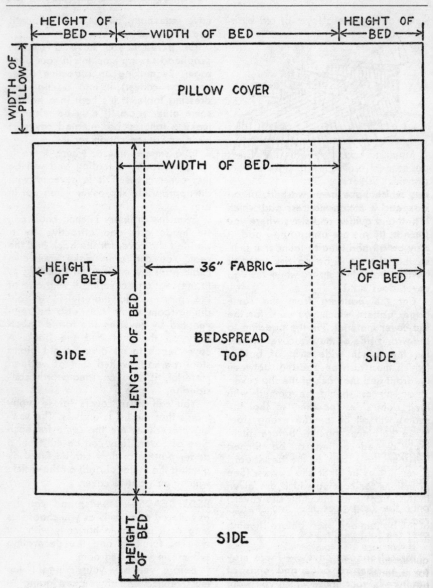

too high off the floor, one width split down the middle could be used for the side ruffles. For gathered or pleated sides you must allow at least one and a half times the length of the bed or the sides will look skimpy.

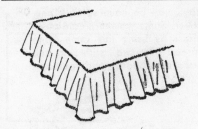

your basic measurements: if you plan to use pleats and ruffles of the same material, figure the amount needed separately and add this amount to the basic yardage requirements.

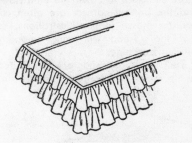

Material bought in the upholstery department usually comes in the more practical 50-inch width. If you have a narrow bed, you may be able to make a spread from a single width by allowing the material to extend over the bed on both sides and adding a trimming edge to the bottom.

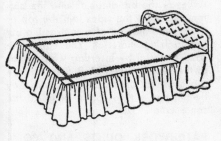

When measuring your bed, make allowance for the extra length needed at the head of the bed for turning the bedspread over and under the pillow or bolster. If you lay the bedspread flat and use a separate cover for pillows or bolster, you will need to measure only the length of the bed with a reasonable allowance for dropping over the foot of the bed.

If you are not too sure of your requirement in yardage before you shop for material, cut a paper pattern of the top of the bed and the sides. Make seam allowances all around. Spread them out on the floor, confining your area first to 36 inches, then 50 and 54—the standard widths of material. In that way you estimate the yardage needed for each width. These will be

No matter how modern the other furnishings of a home are, most women still love the traditional bedspread with the gathered skirt around the sides, made with either one wide ruffle or in two narrow tiers or a circular ruffle. For this type of covering usually dainty materials are used, such as organdie spread over a pastel-colored sateen, or a quaintly sprigged cotton print bound at the edges with matching or harmonizing plain cotton material. In the more formally decorated bedrooms rayon taffetas and moirés are often used. These materials are cut and sewed in the same way as the sheer cottons; but of course they are not so

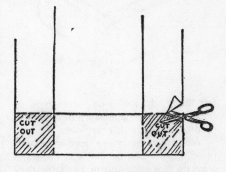

long wearing and generally have to be dry-cleaned rather than laundered.

If the bedroom furniture is of the modern, streamlined design, the bedspread should also follow that trend. In most cases the gathered flounce is left off. The material is bought in a width sufficient to cover the entire bed and the bottom corners are often cut out, as shown in the illustrations, so that the spread will hang smoothly without bunching.

Tailored bedspreads are not limited just to the dainty cottons. Suitable ma-

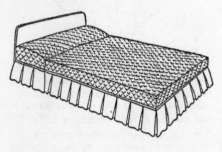

terials are also available in darker colors and heavier-textured weaves. The seams are often corded, and the side pieces are joined in the boxed manner used on upholstery slip covers.

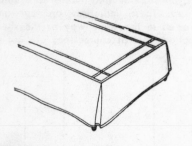

For those who still want some type of flounce, even on a modern bed, a box-pleated finish is appropriate.

When day beds are used in a bedroom, covers can be made in the same way as those for larger beds, or they can be treated like studio couches. Two day beds, pushed together during the day, may be covered with one large cover. Some women create an original effect by using this same "one bedspread over two" with twin beds that have headboards and footboards.

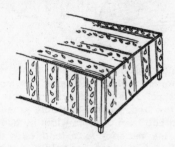

It is sometimes effective to use two materials in a bedspread. The side ruffles or the bandings around the bottom or where the sides join the top of the spread may be of a contrasting but harmonizing material. You can often save material by inserting wide bands of the second material. Ruffles that are too short to turn under and hem may be finished with a cotton fringe of the same color.

PATCHWORK QUILTS AND COMFORTERS—Those leftover scraps of material—the figured and plain cottons, even silks or rayons or velvets if you want to be luxurious, or the ties of the men in your family—can be the beginning of a pleasant sewing hobby. There is nothing like a charming patchwork quilt or bedspread to give you the dignified feeling of owning an "heirloom piece."

Choose or design the pattern you want to use. Then sort out your pieces of material, using the same weight (such as all gingham or percale, or all silk or satin). You can buy patchwork patterns which give you full directions, or you can cut out your own patterns from pieces of cardboard. Lay these cardboards on the material and mark with a pencil or tailor's chalk, then cut

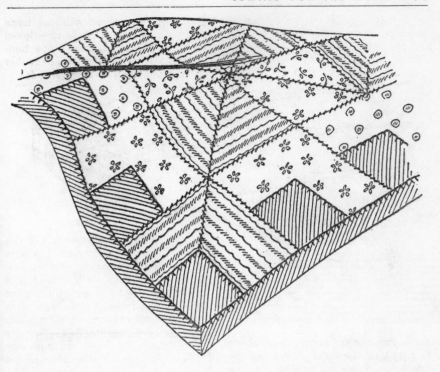

out the patches. In cutting be sure you have made allowance for sewing together.

The patchwork pattern is made by pinning the patches together and basting in small groups, to form the design. If desired, finish the joinings with some decorative stitch (see Chapter 18 for suggestions), using mercerized or heavy silk thread, such as buttonhole twist. Join the small groups of patches together to make the entire quilt. Finish the edge with a binding applied with the same type of decorative stitch used for the small patches.

There are two methods of quilting. The traditional way is to have the piece of material which will be the underside cut to the desired maximum size. You can use figured material, or un-

bleached muslin, or even a discarded thin bedspread or sheet for this purpose. Over it lay an interlining or padding—you can buy special material for this—or use a discarded blanket. Cut the interlining 1 inch shorter on all sides, so that you can fold the outer material over for hemming. The finished patchwork is laid on top of this and fastened or quilted by tacking at evenly spaced intervals. For really satisfactory results you need a quilting frame to keep the layers even and allow you to work on both sides of the quilt. Make sure that all material used for the underside and the interlining is color-fast and non-shrinking, so that there will be no difficulty in laundering the quilt.

Modern quilting is done on the ma-

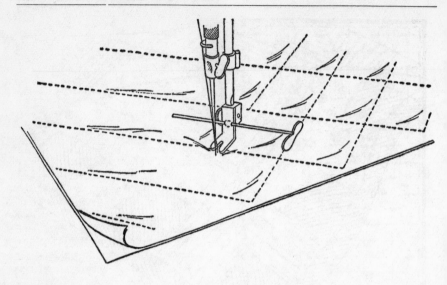

chine. Proceed the same way as above in preparing the outer covers and the interlining. Baste all around the four sides. Trace a design on the top cover —diamond shapes, or squares, or whatever pattern you prefer. Attach the quilting foot to the sewing machine, then set the quilter bar to follow the preceding row of machine stitching as you do the work. This spaces the rows evenly.

MAKE-OVER QUILT AND BLANKET —Two clean, worn blankets can easily be converted into a quilt or comforter. Pin the blankets together, cut them to even size, and baste around the four sides. Cover the top and the bottom with flowered or bright-colored chintz or some other tightly woven cotton material. Fasten the blanket and covers together with a design made of rows of running stitches, or with double loops of bright woolen yarn threaded in a needle and drawn through blan-

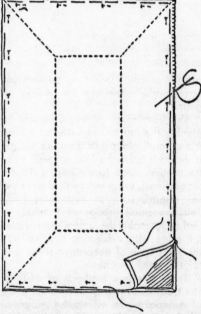

kets and coverings. The ends of the thread are tied in square knots, as

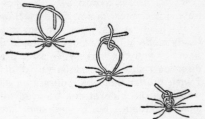

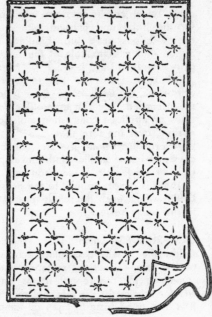

MAKE-OVER SHEETS—Torn sheets can be cut down to be made into pillowcases. Sheets worn thin in the middle will give additional months of service if they are split lengthwise down the center, the split edges narrowly hemmed by machine and the selvedges stitched together to make a center seam. Large sheets which are worn can also be cut down to fit a crib or baby carriage.

MATTRESS COVERS AND PADS— Here is another way to use sheets and blankets which have become worn. Some housekeepers like to keep their mattresses covered. A strong cotton material is needed for the purpose. If you do not have old sheets you want to use up, you can buy unbleached muslin or some similar type of fabric.

Pin a sheet or a length of fabric on the top of the mattress. Allow for seams all around and cut it to size. Remove it and cut the second sheet or piece of fabric the same size. Next, measure the height of the mattress, and cut the material that height plus seam allowances. You may have to piece this material for the "box." In fact, it won't matter if you piece the top and the bottom coverings, either, so long as the seams are so placed that they will not be uncomfortable to sleep on. Baste, then stitch the top and the bottom to the side piece all around. Leave open at the foot of the bed, so the cover can be put on and taken off (like a pillowcase) for laundering.

shown. The four sides of this make-over quilt can be seamed, bound with contrasting material, or finished with blanket stitching.

If a large blanket has worn spots through it and cannot be salvaged as a covering for the large bed, it can be cut down to fit Junior's bed or Baby's crib and the edges rebound with tape.

A square knot is made by crossing the left thread over the right, then the right over the left.

If you prefer a pad over the mattress, for comfort or for the protection of the mattress itself, you can buy one ready made in any number of standard sizes, or you can make your own. Use discarded sheets or muslin cut about 1 inch shorter than the mattress on all sides. An old blanket can be used for inner padding. Baste and machine stitch as explained above, spacing quilting stitches more closely together, about 1½ inches apart, horizontally and vertically.

POT HOLDERS—These, too, can be made of remnants of new material or of your sewing leftovers. Scraps of a worn blanket can be salvaged for padding the inside of the pot holders, or you can use two or three thicknesses of wool fabric. For the outside, use gingham or printed percale, or some similar firmly woven cotton material. Cut the two outside pieces and the padding all the same size in whatever shape you like. Make the pot holder large enough to fit around the handles comfortably. Baste all the pieces together ¼ inch from the edge and finish the edges by basting a bias binding of contrasting color and machine stitching in place. It is important to quilt a pot holder so it will retain its shape and be more useful. By hand or machine run a quilting stitch back and forth across the pot holder or in round rows.

Sew a small metal ring (not plastic, as that might burn if it came in close contact with the flame of the stove) by which to hang up the holder. You can also crochet a loop or sew one from the same bias tape which trims the holder.

MORE HOUSEHOLD MAKE-OVER HINTS—Worn face towels can be cut down into smaller guest-size towels.

Worn Turkish towels can also be cut down into dishcloths or face cloths with a crocheted edge in a contrasting color. Towels can be cut down into bibs for the baby and finished with crocheted edges or a bias binding, a button and a buttonhole at the back, or two ends to tie a bow.

Breakfast cloths or bridge cloths with tears or small holes should not be discarded. You can embroider designs or appliqué contrasting material designs over the torn spots.

A large tablecloth, if worn, can be cut down into a smaller cloth and napkins, or made into a luncheon set.

There is almost no limit to the possibilities which each household presents to the home sewer.

LAMPSHADES—Lampshades should follow the interior-decorating scheme of the room—luxurious materials and trimmings for the formal rooms and simpler fabrics for the informal rooms. It is also good taste to keep all lamp-

shades in one room related to one another and not have too many different colors or styles.

Basically all lampshades, whether simple or elaborate, are made in the same way. For informal rooms, such as a bedroom, dinette, recreation room, baby's or teen-ager's room, make lampshades of chintz or other figured cotton materials in pleated, gathered, or plain style. A frilly shade such as that on a boudoir lamp doesn't need a lining; it can have just a pretty gathered skirt tied with a ribbon. This may be of lace or some thin material, such as plain-colored voile or dotted swiss banded with figured material, ribbons and bows, or embroidered ruffling.

The formal lampshade, however, should be lined with a soft material—rayon, nylon, or silk—in white or an off-white color, which gives a good glow. The tape used to wind the metal frame should be matched as closely as possible to the color of the material.

Silk, rayon, or nylon fabric is suitable for the outside cover of the shade. It is often left smooth, but you may pleat or gather the top if you prefer. Chinese silk shantung makes a nice lampshade for a fine porcelain base. Trimming to finish off the top and the bottom of the shade should be of good quality so that the effect will not be spoiled by inferior trimming.

Incidentally, some women wash their lampshades (frames and all) in lukewarm suds. If you do that, make doubly certain that the material and the trimming are color-fast and shrink-proof, and that the metal frame won't rust!

The procedure for making a lined lampshade, whether the top be plain, pleated, or gathered, is:

Use bias tape of the same color as the material for the shade, or cut bias bands of self material, to wind around the frame. Tack ends tightly.

Pin the lining at top and bottom. Allow for the seam before cutting. Stitch the seam. Sew the lining at the top and bottom. Trim off the material, leaving enough to turn under at the top and bottom.

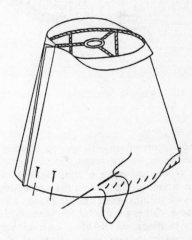

Gather with a running stitch the top and bottom of the outer material. Pin to frame. If you make fine pleats, you will have to pin each pleat separately at the bottom and at the top. They will be deeper at the top. Remember that before you pin you must turn under the edges of the lining at the top and bottom and pin over them. Slip stitch the seam. After the material has been sewed to the top and the bottom of the frame, trim the excess off but allow enough to turn under. Sew the braid or other trimming over the turned edges, making sure that no raw edges of the material show through. For a professional finish, the trimming

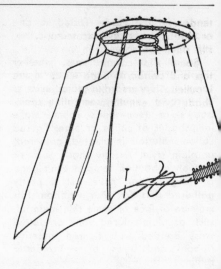

should come flush with the top and bottom wires of the frame.

When you make a lampshade without a lining, proceed in the same way to wind bias tape around the wire frame. Cut the material for your shade in one piece, on the bias, long enough to reach around the bottom of the frame and allow for the seam. Pin the material to the frame at the top and bottom. Sew the material to the frame, then sew the joining seam with a flat fell, making sure it looks as neat and finished on the underside of the shade as on the top, since there is no lining. Trim the edges at top and bottom, turn them down, and cover them with trimming as explained above.

Don't discard a lampshade which is worn or not needed at the moment. Save it; you can use the frame later on and you can rip off the cover and use it as a pattern for cutting the lampshade you may want to make.

Slip covers for lampshades are easy to sew. Use transparent or translucent plastic material if you want your lampshade to show through the cover. Otherwise use figured chintz or any other cotton material. The simplest method is to cut a straight piece 2 inches longer than the shade measures at the widest part and allow an additional 3 to 4 inches on width of material for hemming.

First join the two narrow ends of the material. Make a French seam, as a lampshade cover does not have a lining and you want a neat finish. Turn up a ½ inch and stitch the bottom hem. At the opposite edge of the material turn down 1 inch and stitch a hem, leaving a slit open through which you can pull a string or elastic. Put the cover over the lampshade and see that the bottom of the slip cover hangs about ¼ inch or more below the bottom of the shade. Then pull the ends of the string or elastic together until the gathered top of the slip cover extends over the shade. Tack the string or elastic, cut off the excess ends, and slip stitch the opening in the heading.

Some slip covers have headings top and bottom through which elastic is pulled. They are adjusted to the lampshade and extend over the edge of the shade at both top and bottom.

If you want the slip cover to be more decorative, make it in the form of a pretty skirt, with bias binding or other trimming at the hem and a pretty ribbon pulled through at the top and tied in an attractive bow.

CHAPTER 21

Clothes for the Expectant Mother

MOST mothers-to-be say that the thing they dislike about their months of waiting for a baby is the fact that they feel they do not look their best. If that is the way you feel, it is time for you to change your mind, for you can look well and pretty during the months when you are a lady-in-waiting.

In the first place, for three or four months you can continue to wear the clothes you have. You don't need to huddle in a coat. Doing so only makes you more conspicuous, especially in warm weather. And you don't have to wear dark colors. At the end of three or four months your clothes will be pulling up a little in front and they will be a bit tight, but by this time there is a new fashion season under way and you will be wanting a new dress anyway. So you plan a special, look-pretty-please outfit.

The most important thing to remember when you buy or make maternity clothes is that no matter what your figure was before, or what it will be after the baby arrives, it is going to become pear-shaped. There are maternity foundation garments and brassières which are designed to help you look well and feel comfortable, but even with these you must take certain factors into consideration when you plan your maternity wardrobe.

You are heavy through the waist and the hips, and your clothes must have up-and-down lines to make you look more slender. This is true even for a tall person. The up-and-down effect may be achieved with stripes and by the general design of your clothes. If you choose a skirt with a slight flare, it will help to balance your wider hip line. Straight tight skirts will only emphasize your changing figure. You can also wear your skirts slightly longer than usual if you feel your figure looks too clumsy with your normal hem line, but even an expectant mother should not wear her skirts noticeably longer than those worn by other women. After all, pregnancy is no excuse for a slovenly appearance.

When you make a maternity dress, make the hem 3 or 4 inches wide rather than the usual 2 inches. Then you can lengthen the hem line as it becomes necessary.

from young looking. The reason for their matronly look can usually be traced to the way the waist front and neckline have been treated. In some articles written on maternity dresses, mothers-to-be are told that they should always have softness at the neckline.

When you choose a belt, remember that wide belts are off your list. Narrow belts of the same material as your dress are best for you. You can also wear a belt set into the waistline. Avoid buckles and buttons that are large or shiny; keep them small in size and as inconspicuous as possible.

Sometimes maternity dresses are far

As a result, you will find many maternity dresses in which this softness is in the form of ruffles, jabots, lace collars and surplice closings—styles that are really much more suitable for a sweet grandmother than they are for you! Of course you do need fullness at the front of your dresses, because your breast is changing in size, but you don't need frou-frou! Your problem is similar to that of the adolescent girl who is "filling out." You need clothes that will allow you ease and freedom of movement, but which at the same time do not call attention to your changing body contours.

When you look for a maternity dress pattern, or for a ready-made maternity dress, for that matter, buy one that has gathers on the shoulders. This will allow for fullness across the bust. A becoming neckline can be oval in shape, V shaped, U shaped, or square. Sometimes it is softened with the addition of a narrow ruffle in white or some pastel color.

When you are going to have a baby, a simple dress worn with a pearl necklace will give you a smart, well-groomed appearance for almost any occasion.

All your maternity clothes can look well on you—even house dresses. The idea of wearing a smock over everything is all right, but it can grow deadly monotonous after a few months. Why not save the smocks for the last few weeks, and consider some of the ideas given here?

HOUSE DRESSES—Choose house dresses which wrap around, have plenty of expansion room, nice flaring skirts, pretty necklines, and in your favorite colors. If you wear dark colors in your street clothes when you are expecting a baby, you should wear all the light, gay, becoming colors that you like in the house. Avoid the practical buttoned-down-the-front dress you may once have worn about the house, for this type of dress is not designed for the pregnant woman. If your normal figure is slender, you might like to wear full-skirted dirndls for the first six months, but pack your slipover sweaters and narrow skirts away in moth balls during the entire waiting period.

PLAY CLOTHES—For relaxing indoors or outdoors, you don't need to deprive yourself of the fun of wearing pretty costumes which include long or short pants. An expandable beltline is, of course, an essential in making or buying the shorts or slacks. The top should

be well fitted at the shoulders with a graceful fullness allowed at waist and hipline. You can make several different styles of tops to wear with one pair of shorts or slacks. You can also add variety to your wardrobe by using these tops with your solid-color skirts.

will attract attention to your face, which is at its loveliest now. If you wear printed dresses, keep the prints small with all-over designs. Since you cannot wear extreme fashions in clothes, this is the time to buy yourself one or two beautiful accessories, such as pocketbooks or gloves, to add style to your outfits. They are a good investment, too, for you will still be able to wear them after the baby comes.

EVENING CLOTHES—If you wear formal clothes, you will be able to find both patterns and ready-to-wear evening dresses in maternity styles. Many young women, however, follow the style devised by a famous dress de-

DRESSES FOR "DRESS-UP"—Have them simple, with plenty of fullness in the waist and hips. Pretty necklines

signer for his own wife, a tiny little woman who was a motion-picture star. It consists of long, slightly flared skirts in dark colors, with expandable waistbands, over which are worn mandarin jackets in small-patterned brocades or other stiff materials with enough body to stand away from the figure. Because his wife was so very tiny, the designer made the proportions of the jacket less full than they might have been for a larger woman, but the effect is the same on almost any figure. The long skirt adds height and slenderness to the figure; the stiff jacket conceals the abdomen; and the back flare in the jacket prevents the wearer from looking sway-backed.

If you plan an outfit like this as carefully as you plan any other dress, you can be sure of one thing—you won't look just like any other woman who's going to have a baby!

COATS AND SUITS—No fitted coats for you. Outer clothes should be loose and comfortable. A full-length coat with an easy swing is generally most becoming. Try to avoid exaggerated fullness in the sleeves or in the coat itself and don't buy a coat with raglan sleeves, for they will make you appear wider across the bust.

If you are tall, you might like a suit with a boxy jacket. Wear the jacket slightly longer than you would ordinarily; the finger-tip length will do the nicest things for your waist and hips. If you are short, you may find a suit which looks well on you, but most suits will make you appear heavier.

If you are the dashing type, why not wear a cape? It is a wonderfully concealing garment, but of course it calls for a woman who can wear it with an air.

HATS—Oddly enough you may need to change your style in hats when you are going to have a baby. If you have been wearing tiny berets on the back of your head, or a tiny stovepipe crown sticking up toward the sky to make you look taller, you will find that these hat proportions are too small to balance the size of your changing figure. Put on your tiniest hat, stand before a full-length mirror, and you will understand what we mean.

What to do? Buy a new hat in one of your favorite styles, but buy one

that is trimmed so that the hat appears a little larger than it actually is. This trimming may be a brim, a feather at the side, a bow of ribbon, or flowers. You are not limited in the type of hat you can wear—it can be a sailor, a Breton, a beret, a casual brimmed felt, but it should be a becoming one.

SHOES—You can wear your usual shoes for the first two or three months. Later you will want to buy a pair of good-looking shoes with medium or low heels. These need not look like "comfort shoes," but they should be comfortable and provide good support for your weight. Wear a darker neutral shade of stocking to add as long a line as possible to your figure.

GROOMING—Pay special attention to the care of your hair, skin, and nails, and especially to the neat appearance of your clothes. This will give a lift to your spirits now and later on help to make you the prettiest possible mother.

CHAPTER 22

Accessories and Gifts You Can Make

ACCESSORIES are the "plus" in a woman's wardrobe—they are the signs which point to her originality in planning her clothes. The most beautiful costume can look unfinished if it is not accompanied by something which gives it a smart touch, even if it be only a contrasting pair of gloves, or a striking necklace. The accessories which you make yourself must look as if they were selected with great care to harmonize with the outfit you are wearing; that is, the casual type of clothes need their own kind of accessories made on simple lines, and the more formal clothes call for the chic type of accessories.

To make the right choice of accessories you must first study your own type and see which accessories suit each dress, suit, or coat that you wear. It usually proves more economical to plan some of these accessories so that they are interchangeable and do not have to be limited just to one outfit. The amount of money you spend is not so important as the precise care you exercise when you select the accessory.

Something you make at home, from a piece of material or a button or jewelry that you rescued from an old bureau drawer, can prove ever so much more attractive than the things which you buy and often pay high prices for. And a final word of caution: Do not overload your costume with too many accessories! One well-planned touch is worth more than several which overcrowd your outfit.

SOME HINTS FOR MAKING AC- CESSORIES—Cut out a pattern in wrapping paper for any accessory you plan to make. If you don't like the style just as it is, or if the piece is too large or too small for you, don't be afraid to change it. But make all your mistakes in paper, so that you won't make them later.

Hem narrow rolled edges of accessories such as scarves and bows by hand rather than by machine. This will give them that expensive custom-made look.

When taffeta is used for accessories such as collars and cuffs, you can obtain unusual effects by fringing the edges rather than hemming them. The fringe should be about one inch deep.

Linen and cotton can sometimes be combined effectively with silk and rayon or other synthetic fabrics. You can make linen or cotton accessories for a silk or rayon or nylon dress.

Felt bought by the yard is excellent for making bags, hats, and belts. It is an easy material to work with, since the edges do not require hemming. Felt can be stitched by hand or machine. Pasting or gluing is not suggested, since the pieces may come apart.

Suède leather can be used in the same way as felt, but it is more expensive. Suède is especially attractive when used in soft sashlike belts with a fringe cut along the edges. This leather can be bought in bright and pastel colors from any convenient leather supply house, or it can be ordered by mail. It is usually sold by the skin, half skin, or quarter skin. Although suède may seem disappointingly stiff when first you handle it, if you rub and work it between your fingers it will become butter soft. Chamois leather, the kind sold in a drugstore and used to polish windowpanes, is less expensive. It is not so fine in texture and it comes in only one color, but it is a good accent for brown or black sport clothes. Chamois can be used like suède, but because of the soft texture neither of these materials is suggested for making bags.

Collect all the small, attractive pieces of old jewelry you have to add the finishing touch to accessories— men's watch fobs and seals, that gold fleur-de-lis pin Grandmother wore to fasten her watch to her shirtwaist, the little pansy pin in purple enamel. Don't forget hatpins. There may be one or two old ones with fancy heads which will be perfect to ornament a plain hat.

Never make more than two accessories to match. That is, you can have hat and gloves or a bag and a hat of the same material. But if you want to be well dressed, you will not have hat, bag, gloves, and belt all of the same material.

Your scrap box can be your best ally. Remnant counters are another good source. Flowers, veiling, ribbons —all these will come to life beneath your fingers. Try using an imitation coral necklace to stud your wide grosgrain belt if you have the small waistline for it. Wear the belt on a simple black dress and you'll bring Paris to Main Street.

The ideas in this chapter are just starters. You'll be certain to develop original accessories all your own.

BAGS—When you cut out a bag of felt or leather, place the pattern you have made on the material as you would place a dress pattern. That is, the pieces of the bag must be on the straight up-and-down or straight crosswise grain of the felt or leather. If the bag is cut crooked, then it will not "hang" well when finished. For this reason mark every piece of the pattern with an arrow to indicate the straight up-and-down or the straight crosswise grain of the material. Each bag design has markings for you to copy. Use these arrows as guides for placing the pattern pieces correctly. The arrows with numbers show the measurements of pattern pieces, in inches, from point to point. It is easy to find the straight grain of felt, for felt comes by the yard and has a straight selvedge edge. The straight grain of leather will be an imaginary line drawn in the center of the skin from the neck to the tail. If you buy only a section of a skin, you will have to decide, by looking at the pieces, what part of the entire skin you have. Mark a straight line on the wrong side of the skin, a line which would be parallel to the center back line. Place your pattern pieces on the wrong side, using the line you have made as a guide for correct placement. (Your pattern pieces will also be marked with lines showing how to place them on the straight of the material.) Always test your machine stitching on a double thickness of felt or fabric before sewing the bag. Many leather bags are hand stitched rather than machine stitched to give them a more expensive look.

Easy-to-make envelope—Try this clutch bag in felt for your first bag. It requires about ⅓ yard of 36-inch-wide felt. No lining is needed.

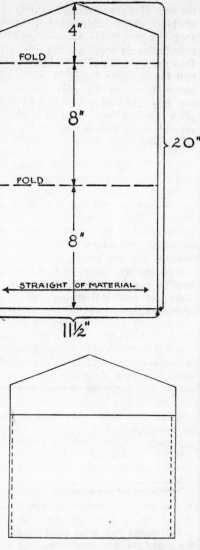

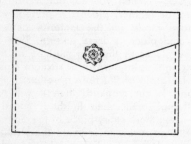

1. The bag and the flap are cut in one piece. Cut the paper pattern first. Then fold as directed, to see if the bag is the right size for you. Make the pattern larger or smaller if you wish.

2. When you have the right size, cut out the material, fold it, and stitch by machine. The stitching is done on the right side ¼ inch from the edge. Fasten the threads firmly, so that the stitching will not pull out. Tie the two thread ends on the underside in a square knot. See page 317 if you are not certain how to do this.

3. Fasten the bag with a snap fastener or with a button and buttonhole. If you use a snap fastener, sew on the top half of the snap, rub chalk on the knob, press the flap down on the bag to mark the place to sew the other half of the snap. Fasten an insignia or an old brooch or button on

the flap of the pocketbook to hide the stitching which holds the top of the snap in place. (Have you ever used the snap fasteners which are like grippers? They usually come in kits, with a handy tool for applying them.) If you use a button fastening for your bag, mark the size buttonhole you need, then stitch around this marked opening several times before you cut it. This will prevent the cut buttonhole from

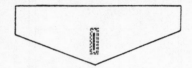

stretching. Sew the button directly beneath the cut buttonhole.

You can also make a loop buttonhole by cutting a strip of felt ½ inch wide and twice as long as the diameter of the button.

Fold the strip to ½-inch width. Stitch the raw edges together close to the edge.

Fasten the two ends of the loop to the point of the envelope flap with machine stitching.

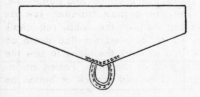

Sew the button below the flap, so that the loop will slip over the button.

TO CLOSE ENVELOPE BAG WITH A SLIDE FASTENER—Cut the bag in two pieces, as shown.

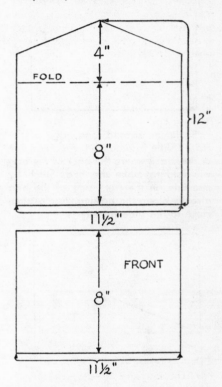

On the underside crease or mark with chalk or basting the line where the back piece will be folded to make the flap.

Baste one long edge of the closed slide fastener to one long edge of the bag front. Stitch by machine. If the machine has a cording foot—a presser foot with only one prong—use it. If it has no cording foot, use the regular presser foot with one of the prongs up on the ridge of the slide fastener, so you can stitch close to the metal. The length of the slide fastener will be determined by the size of the opening. Dress placket fasteners, 9 or 10 inch size, can sometimes be used on bags.

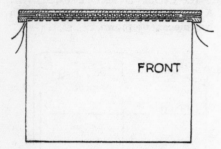

FRONT

Baste the second long edge of the closed slide fastener to the marked line at the place where the back of the bag will fold to make the flap. Stitch by machine on the right side of the bag directly along the basting. Again stitch close to the slide fastener.

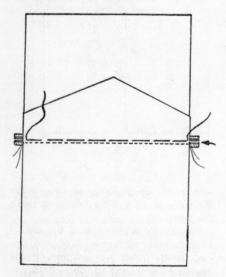

Fasten the threads of the machine stitching. Overcast the two separate ends of the tape at each end of the slide fastener, so the closing will be complete. The tape ends are tucked inside the bag.

Finish the bag by stitching down one side, across the bottom, then up the other side. Fasten all the threads. No snap is needed.

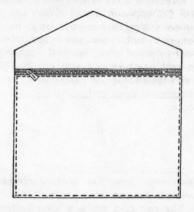

TO LINE AN ENVELOPE BAG—To line with felt cut a second bag, using the original pattern. Stitch the felt lining to the outside cover. You will also need to stitch around the flap, to hold the two thicknesses of felt together. Dark color lined with bright color is effective.

To line with material, cut the second bag like the original pattern. If the bag is to be closed with a slide fastener, however, do not cut a lining for the flap. Stitch the material together, on the wrong side, to make a separate

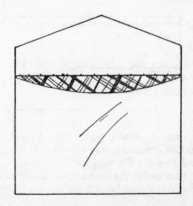

bag. Baste the lining in place in the bag, turn under the raw edges at the top and slip stitch to the bag.

ENVELOPE BAG WITH CHANGEABLE SLIP COVERS—If you already have a slip-cover bag, use the old cover as a pattern to make new covers. But if you want to make a slip-cover bag, make an envelope bag of felt or buckram— a stiff material which you can buy in a department store or from a mail-order house.

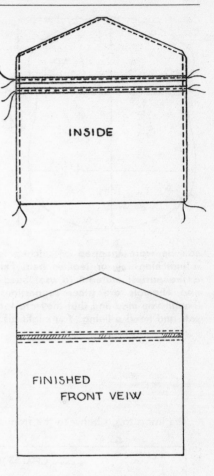

INSIDE

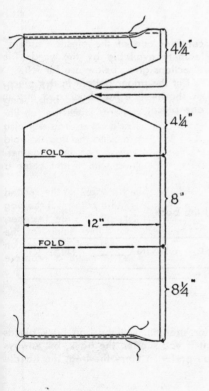

4¼"

4¼"

FOLD

8"

12"

FOLD

8¼"

FINISHED
FRONT VEIW

Line it. Make your slip cover a double envelope, one for the bag itself and one for the flap.

Turn under the raw edges of the two envelopes and hem them by machine.

Over-the-shoulder bag—This type of bag used to be considered a novelty, but it is now accepted as a proper bag style. However, the "over-the-shoulder" bag is not a good style for dressier occasions and should still be regarded for casual or sports clothes, for school, and of course business suits. For town or city wear this type of bag is not suited to the rounded or very short figure.

This bag requires about ⅔ of a yard of 36-inch felt. A small version

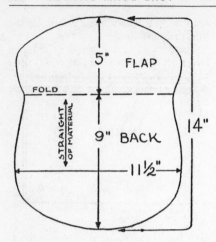

The bag front.

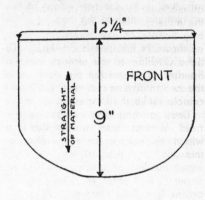

can be worn snapped or stitched to a matching felt or leather belt. Felt is the easiest material to use. Suède and chamois are other suggestions, though you may find that they are too soft and need a lining. You might also consider one of the plastic "patent" leathers available by the yard. The directions given below are for felt.

Cut the paper pattern in five pieces as shown—the bag back and flap in one piece.

The insert to go between the front and the back.

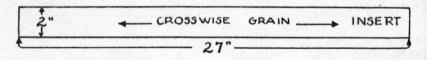

Two handles to be stitched together for strength. Cut the bag back pieces smaller if you wish. Shorten the bag front if you shorten the back, but always keep the front wider than the back. If you prefer to carry the bag, the handle can easily be shortened.

When you have your paper pattern all made up in the size you prefer, cut the material for the bag. Overlap the bag handle on the insert and stitch, as shown in the illustration. Then continue stitching all the way around the handle, ¼ inch from the edge, until the two thicknesses of the handle are completely stitched together.

Draw a chalk line across the bag front ¾ inch from the top and to within ½ inch of the sides. Measure this line, and then divide it into an equal number of spaces, each space about ½ inch apart. Mark these spaces on the line. Fold the front of the bag

drawstring that gathers the front of the bag to fit the back.

Pin and baste one edge of the side insert to the curved edge (sides and bottom) of the bag front. Stitch ¼ inch from the edge on the right side by machine.

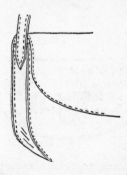

on this line, then cut the folded felt about ¼ inch deep at each mark. These are the slits which will hold the

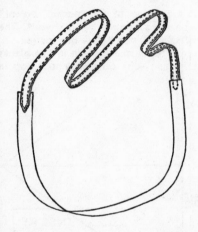

Pin and baste the other edge of the side insert to the back of the bag from the fold at the flap, down the side, around the bottom of the bag, and up the other side to the flap. This insert must not be stretched more on one edge than on the other, or the bag will appear twisted. Always pin and baste most carefully. Then stitch the insert to the back. Continue machine stitching around the flap for decoration.

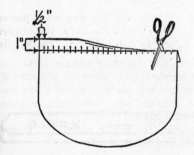

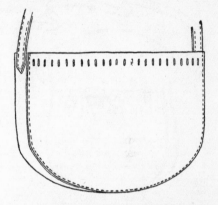

DRAWSTRINGS—a leather thong or bright, heavy cord does nicely—are

then firmly fastened to the inside of the bag with hand stitching. Drawstrings are woven in and out through slits, and fastened in a bow in the center front. The front of the bag is drawn up to fit the back.

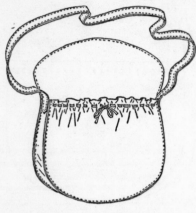

No fastening is used, but a heavy decorative emblem will hold down the

flap and will add to the effectiveness of the bag.

Envelope bag for evening wear— This clutch bag requires ½ yard of 36-inch heavy rayon slipper satin and ½ yard of 36-inch material—preferably satin—for lining. This type of bag is suitable for daytime dress-up or for evening. Black slipper satin is good for day wear, black or brilliant jewel tones, such as ruby or emerald, in satin, moiré, or brocade, for wear with formal evening clothes.

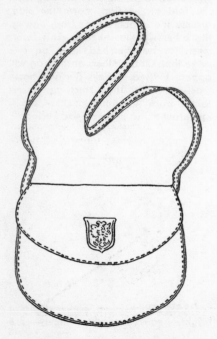

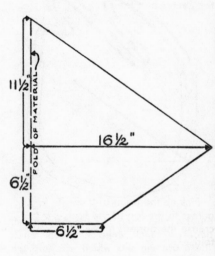

11½"

FOLD OF MATERIAL

16½"

6½"

6½"

The folded bag is made in one piece. Cut the paper pattern according to measurements given on diagram. If you fold the piece of paper when you cut the pattern, both sides will be exactly alike.

Open the paper pattern. It should look like the illustration.

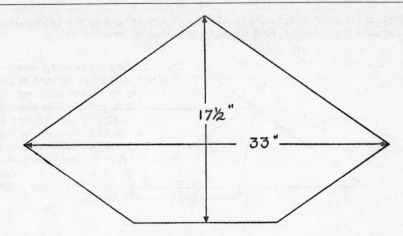

Make a fold all the way across the pattern 6½ inches from the bottom at the center and then mark off 9¾ inches at the center of this fold.

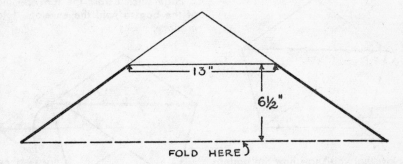

Pick up the point at the right end of the fold and bring this point forward and across to the top of the folded piece on the left side. To do this you will need to crease the pattern at the right end of the line you just marked along the bottom fold.

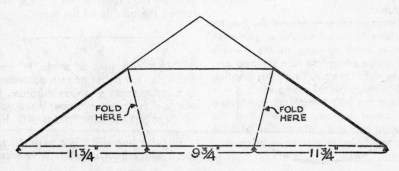

Pick up the point at the left end of the fold and bring it forward and across to complete the envelope. Fold the top point down to form the flap.

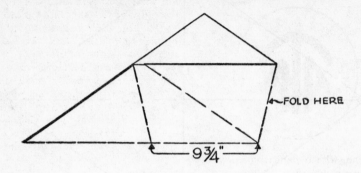

FOLD HERE

9¾"

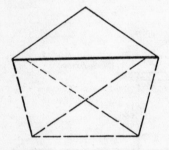

Now that you know how the pattern goes together, cut out the bag in your material. The lining is cut from the same pattern.

Pin and baste the lining to the bag with the two right sides of the material together.

Stitch all the way around the bag by machine ½ inch from the edge. Leave only a small opening at the 13-inch side large enough to turn the bag and lining right side out. Finish this opening with an invisible hemming stitch.

Fold the bag exactly as you folded the paper pattern. You will find the finished bag is slightly smaller than the pattern, because you have taken in a seam.

Edge stitch across the top opening of the bag to hold the envelope fold in place.

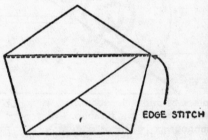

EDGE STITCH

Fasten the flap to the bag with a snap. As a finishing touch, put your loveliest old brooch or an antique button on the outside of the flap.

Circular bag—This is a perfect bag for a big felt monogram. It requires

½ yard of 36-inch felt. You can design the monogram yourself. Here is the way

it is done: with a pencil and piece of paper work your two or three initials into a circular motif, keeping the initial of your last name the largest. Cut out the letters and try them on a round

piece of paper the same size your bag will be when it is finished. Cut out the monogram in felt of a different color

than the bag. Baste the monogram in place on the front of the bag before any of the bag is stitched together. Stitch the monogram by machine, or

fasten it in place with tiny overhand hemming stitches. Be sure to use thread the same shade as the monogram, so the stitching will be inconspicuous.

The bag itself consists of a front, a back, an insert, and two handles stitched together for strength.

Fold a piece of paper (about 12 inches square) in four. Cut off the open corner and trim the open edges to make a pie-shaped piece. Retrim the curved edge until the piece when opened makes a perfect circle. The circle should be 9 inches in diameter.

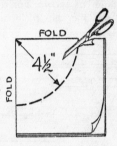

Next cut two of these circles from felt.

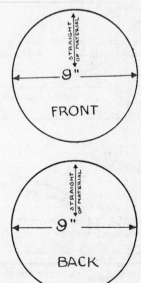

The 9-inch diameter will equal about 28 inches in circumference, and by adding allowance for a seam it will total 28½ inches. Cut a piece the same length and 2 inches wide to be used for the insert of the bag.

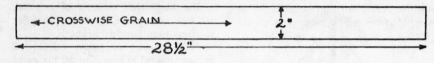

INSERT

Fold this long strip in half lengthwise and slit it down the middle to hold a slide fastener as shown. For a 12-inch fastener cut the slit 6 inches deep

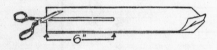

from the fold; 4½ inches deep for a

9-inch fastener. A 12-inch length is better, of course, as it provides a larger opening. A dress placket fastener is the best type to use.

Pin, baste, and machine stitch the slide fastener in place. You can conceal the opening by leaving the felt over the fastener, or you can trim away the felt neatly, allowing the slide fastener to show.

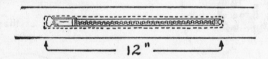

Stitch the handle ends to the insert beyond the slide fastener. See directions for the handle on the Over-the-Shoulder Bag.

HANDLE

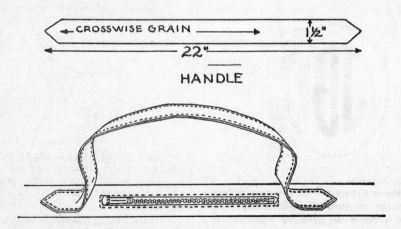

Baste the side insert to the bag front, so that the slide fastener comes across the top of the bag. Stitch by machine ¼ inch from the edge on the outside. Stitch two narrow ends of the insert together with a plain seam on the

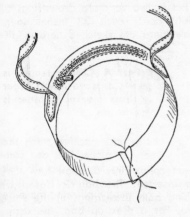

inside of the bag. Trim off the ends before stitching if necessary.

Pin and baste the insert to the back of the bag. Do not stretch or pull the insert. Stitch as you stitched the front.

Miser's pouch—This type of bag requires ½ yard of 36-inch felt. It is also suitable for dress-up when made

in heavy moiré or faille rayon or silk in dark colors. If desired, the bag can be made larger simply by changing the paper pattern. The directions given below are for felt.

Cut two circles 7 inches in diameter.

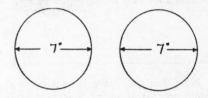

Cut a straight strip of material 22 ½ inches long and 8 ½ inches wide.

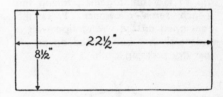

Fold over one long side of the strip 1 inch from the edge.

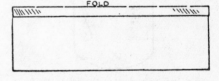

Mark off ¼ inch from each end on this fold for a seam allowance.

Make chalk marks 1 inch apart for the 22 inches between the end marks.

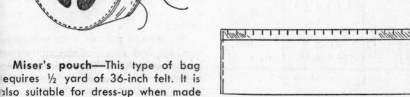

Cut a slit through the fold on each mark. Each cut should be about ¼ inch deep. When the fold is opened, the cuts will be ½ inch deep.

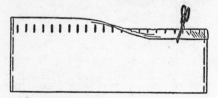

Now that you have completed the initial process of cutting your bag, you are ready to proceed with the next step and put it together.

Stitch the two 8½-inch edges of the strip of material together, taking the ¼-inch seam allowance. Press the seam open on the wrong side with a moderately hot iron placed on an almost dry pressing cloth.

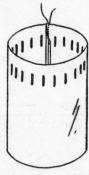

Pin the two circles together to form the bottom of the bag. Then turn the

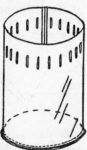

top or cylinder section of the bag to the right side and pin to the bottom, with the raw edge of the felt outside. Baste.

Stitch the three thicknesses of felt together by machine ¼ inch from the edge.

Put in two separate drawstrings of bright cord, each 33 inches long. Drawstrings are sketched here in dif-

ferent colors only to show how they are inserted. The bag is closed by pulling both drawstrings at the same time. For a dress-up bag, the drawstrings could be narrow grosgrain ribbon, velvet tubing, or a silk or rayon braid.

HATS—Every woman should own at least one giddy hat for the lift it gives to her spirit. If she can make it herself, so much the better! But do be certain that your lighthearted topper goes with your face, your figure, and your clothes.

The mature woman with soft gray hair will find swirls of veiling twisted around a bunch of flowers fastened to a circle of straw or felt cut from an old hat are especially becoming.

Head Bands—Cover a metal or plastic head band (commonly known as a "bicycle clip") with velvet or ribbon tubing. Sew on to the band a wreath or semicirclet of small flowers, feathers, ribbon, or velvet bows. Another idea is to sew on the clip a wide bow of velvet or dotted veiling as shown in the illustration. These are very good dress-up hats for both young and mature women. The latter should use subdued colors and velvet bows rather than fluffy flowerets.

Trimmed Veils—An inexpensive yet chic way of topping off a costume for women of all ages is to wear a trimmed veil which comes just over the forehead or part way over the face. You can buy it with bows or leaves right on it, or you can get a plain one and carefully sew on flat velvet or silk leaves, flower petals, or little velvet bows. These veiling dress-up hats are made in all colors, so you can match your costume. Black is, of course, classic and can be worn with any color.

The young woman will wear a flower hat only for dress-up occasions, while an older woman may find it looks well with an afternoon dress in a plain color and adds a touch of softness to a plain wool suit. Flower hats are easy to make. Flowers, pins, veiling, an old hat, a pair of scissors, needle, thread, and a mirror are all you need. Pin everything together for effect, then sew only enough to hold the pieces in place.

Turbans can be very attractive if they don't resemble kerchief-packaged heads. A turban can be made from any drapeable material—wool jersey is especially good and comes in wonderful colors. Experiment with a yard (more or less, whatever you have) of jersey, a piece of buckram or unbleached muslin for body, pins, and a mirror. Pin, twist, knot—do anything you want with that jersey. When it looks well from all angles, tack it where it is pinned.

If you want decoration on the turban, add your favorite clip. If it looks well without trimming, wear it plain. Velvet, satin, and tulle are suitable materials for dress-up turbans.

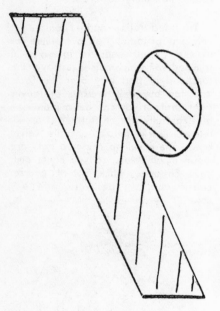

When you use jersey or other drapeable materials, it may be cut on the "straight." But if you use velvet or other nonstretchable material, cut the band for your turban on the bias as shown in the illustration.

Cut a simple lining, as shown in the sketch, or use a lining from an old hat, then slip stitch the lining to the turban.

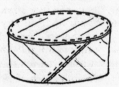

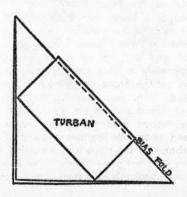

TURBAN

BIAS FOLD

If there is not enough material to go around your head with just a back seam, you can join the material with two seams—one at each side, to eliminate a front seam. However, there is a quick and simple turban you can make which lets you use a front seam if you need it. This model is gathered into a drape at the center front as well as at the back: see illustration. To make this, cut a band of material about 8 inches wide, and long enough to go around your head allowing 2 inches for the back seam. If you also need a front seam, allow 2 more inches to the length for that purpose. Turn the band to the wrong side and baste the back seam. Then turn the corner and continue basting the seam at the top of the band until it reaches the center front. If you are running a seam down the front, turn the corner and continue down. When turning the corners at back and front seams, do not make the turns sharp but round them off in a semicircle. Try this on, and if it fits well around your head, stitch the seams by machine or with very tiny hand stitches. Usually machine stitching is neater. Press the seams flat before proceeding to finish the turban.

Now make a separate front and back drape by sewing two rows of small gathering stitches, one on each side of the seam, using buttonhole twist or a heavy thread that matches the color of the material. Leave a few inches of thread loose. Try on the turban and pull up the loose threads, separately in front and in back, until you get the drape which best fits your head. With your needle, bring the four thread ends to the wrong side of the turban and tie them securely. Bend under the bottom edge of the turban and slip-stitch it to the lining to give your hat some "body." The lining is not absolutely necessary, but it does give your handiwork a more professional look.

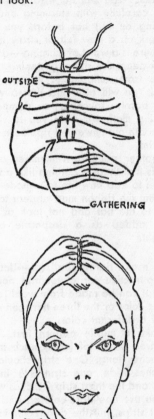

Felt or straw hats bought untrimmed are called shapes or bodies. When these shapes are steamed over the spout of a teakettle filled with boiling water, they can be stretched or shaped to fit your head in any current fashion. Many home "mad hatters" mold their creations of felt on saucepans and then allow the felt to dry. The milliner's name for this is blocking, and she has wooden shapes called "blocks." You will be wise to experiment carefully with steaming and reshaping an old hat before you start to work on a new felt or straw body. And here is a word of warning—do not try to steam the shiny, glistening braid made from cellophane. It just won't work! You will also find that a warm iron barely touching a dampened pressing cloth will help you to shrink or smooth out unwanted ripples in your hatbrim.

Another point to remember about hats is that there is nothing like a fresh ribbon to add new life to a made-over hat! But the ribbon must appear to belong to the hat and not look as if it were added as a desperate afterthought.

To make tiered skullcap—Unusual and attractive for a youthful person, this hat can be made from wool jersey in one color or the three tiers can each be of a different color.

Make a muslin pattern first. Then cut three pieces of jersey each about 21 inches long. One strip should be 5 inches wide, one strip 3½ inches wide, and the third strip 2 inches wide. (If you use one dark-colored and two bright strips, put the dark color in the middle.)

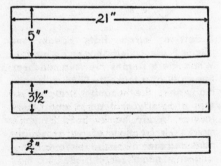

Make a circlet of each strip by sewing the two ends together on the wrong side of the material. Press open the seams, using a pressing cloth between the iron and the jersey.

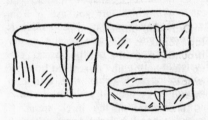

Pin the three circlets together at the top, right sides out. Keep the upper edges even, the bottom edges overlapping, the shortest layer on top.

Gather the three upper edges together ½ inch from the edge by hand or by machine.

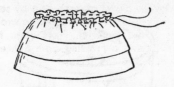

Draw the gathering thread until the top forms a circle about 8 inches around. Try on the hat. Loosen or draw up the gathering thread to get the proper size. Fasten the gathering thread.

Turn under the ½ inch above the gathering to the underside of the cap. Catch down by hand, so the stitching does not show on the right side.

Turn under the bottom edge of each layer of jersey about ¼ inch and baste.

Using pearl cotton thread or wool, stitch small beads around the bottom of each layer of jersey. The stitch which fastens the beads will also serve to hem the basted edge. Imitation gold or silver metal beads are effective.

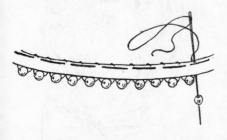

Berets—These caps are becoming to all faces of all ages. They are most flattering in smaller sizes to the youthful face and the small figure. If you are tall or if your figure is mature, cut a larger beret—one you can pull to the side and drape. Velveteen, lightweight woolens, soft felt, and crisp piqué may be used.

Cut the pieces out of muslin before you cut into your material. This muslin will be a "working pattern" which you can use for all the berets you will make. It is a good idea to cut a large size beret first, then cut it down if a smaller size is more becoming.

On the piece of muslin draw a circle 10 inches across and cut out the circle. Cut a strip of muslin for the lower crown 3½ inches wide by 25 inches long. Cut another strip for the hat band 1½ inches wide by 23½ inches long.

Mark off a dart on the circular piece. This will be the back of the beret. Make the dart 1 inch wide at the edge and then taper to a point 3 inches from the edge. Baste the dart, slash it, and press open for flatness.

Baste the seam of the lower crown strip. Match the seam to the dart and pin this strip to the upper crown (the circular piece) ¼ inch in from the edge all around, adjusting the two pieces of muslin for a good fit. Baste when properly fitted. Turn inside out, so that the seams are on the inside. It is not necessary to sew the hat band (the narrower strip) on the muslin.

Try the muslin form on as a last fit, and when it suits you rip it apart and cut the material for your beret from the three muslin pieces. Follow the sewing directions you used for the muslin model. Then prepare the hat band (the narrower strip) by first turning under one edge of the band ¼ inch. Baste that edge all around to the outside of the hat (starting at the back seam) over the raw edge of the lower crown ½ inch from the edge. Do not sew together narrow ends of the band. Turn the band under, lap one open narrow end over the other, and sew down the two ends.

To give the hat more body, if you use a material that is soft and floppy, use an interfacing for both the upper crown (circle) and the lower crown (the wider band). Baste the interfacings separately to the two pieces cut from the muslin pattern ⅛ inch from the edges. When joining the lower to the upper crown, baste through and then stitch through the four thicknesses of material.

INSIDE

BAND

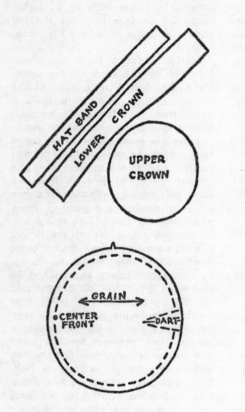

HAT BAND

LOWER CROWN

UPPER CROWN

GRAIN

CENTER FRONT

DART

The hat band (the narrower strip) can be grosgrain ribbon. Grosgrain will save turning under the edges and makes a good flat finish. Before turning under the band, trim the seams under the band to ¼ inch; then press the band on the wrong side of the beret to get a flat and neat finish.

Fur hats—To add distinction to your costume during the fall and winter months, you can make a dressy hat from a piece of luxury fur, or a sport or casual-wear hat out of inexpensive fur. You may have an unused fur collar, cuffs, muff, stole, or other article which you could use. Pill boxes, small berets, draped turbans, and even hats with brims can be made from fur.

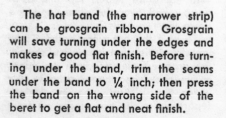

From a millinery supply house you can buy a ready-made buckram frame and use it as a base on which to sew your fur. Or you can cut a base for the hat out of a piece of muslin or other sturdy material, and after you have fitted, pinned, basted, and tried it on, you can rip apart the basting and use the muslin pieces as a pattern on which to cut your fur. Sew the muslin pieces together again for the foundation. Then sew the fur pieces. Finally sew the fur onto the muslin. Directions for cutting and sewing fur are given in Chapter 23.

A short-haired fur, such as mink or sealskin, is best to work with and the result is not too bulky. White fur hats that are extremely flattering can be made of ermine or bleached beaver. Leopard and broadtail are also good furs for hats. If you are tall and are able to wear a dramatic hat to advantage, you might make one of fox or other long-haired fur; but such a hat is not recommended for the person who has either a round face or a petite figure. The hat must not be top-heavy and it's best to practice wearing it in front of a full-length mirror so you may see how it balances with your face and figure. No trimming is needed for a fur hat although you can use an attractive hat pin with it.

If you have a tail from a mink or a strip of some other short-haired fur, you could make a head band of it. It is best not to have the band go all around the head as it creates a bulky look. The band should start about the middle of the top of your ear, go around the front of your head (set about an inch above the hairline on the forehead), and end at the same spot over the opposite ear. A metal or plastic "bicycle clip" which is covered with velvet or ribbon could be used, and all you need to do is to tack the fur onto it. If you do not like a clip, you could sew a matching color grosgrain ribbon band (plain or elasticized) to each end of the fur, to fit the band properly to the back of the head.

GLOVES—Do not attempt to make gloves without a pattern. Glove patterns usually come in whole sizes, or in small, medium, and large. The most attractive fabric gloves are those which are made to match a dress, such as print gloves to match a short-sleeved silk or rayon print summer dress.

Though there are exceptions to the rule, it is better not to trim ready-made gloves with cuffs to match your dress or other accessories. For some reason gloves with "accessoried" cuffs are just a little too fussy to be truly smart. Mitts can look very well with bridesmaids' dresses and full-skirted period evening gowns, but they are out of place when you are carrying groceries!

COLLARS OR CUFFS—Collars are a wonderful accessory. So are cuffs. But collars and cuffs together are usually too much of a good thing. They divide interest and make your outfit look "spotty." So make yourself an extra collar or dickey and also a pair of pretty or striking cuffs. But wear them at different times or with different outfits.

If you want to wear contrasting cuffs but your neckline also seems to look too bare, wear your pearl necklace. It is the one perfect piece of jewelry for any woman from the time she is ten until she is ten times a great-grandmother.

Collars, dickeys, and cuffs can all be made from cottons such as piqué, organdie, eyelet-embroidered fabrics, plaid or striped ginghams. Solid-color or printed silk or rayon crepes may also be used. Linen and plaid or striped taffetas are also good. Collars or cuffs made from plain material can be trimmed with embroidery, blanket stitching, or bound with bias of another color. Lace or ruffled edging can be stitched between the two thicknesses of a collar or cuffs.

Collars—A collar should fit the neckline of the dress or other garment with which it is to be worn.

If the dress has a collar, and you like the shape of it, use that as a pattern for the collar you intend to make. Cut the pattern in newspaper, allowing ½ inch of extra material on all seam edges.

If the dress does not have a collar, you can make a pattern from the collar of another dress by adjusting it to fit the neckline with which the collar is to be worn.

If you want to change the apparent shape of the neckline without cutting the dress, make a dickey to wear with the dress. A dickey is a collar and front together. It can have a high, round Peter Pan collar, or a straight convertible collar. This same straight collar, or Peter Pan collar, can also be made separately.

TO MAKE A STRAIGHT COLLAR— Measure the distance around the neck opening of the dress or other garment and cut the pattern as shown—half as long as the neck opening plus ½ inch for seam allowance. The paper pattern is cut only half as long as the neck opening because it will be placed on a fold of the material when you do the cutting.

Cut two pieces of material from this collar pattern, put the two right sides of the material face to face and stitch the two short ends and one long end together with a ½-inch seam. This will leave the fourth side open for turning the collar right side out. Press.

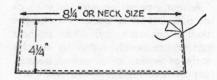

Stitch the open edge of the collar between the edges of folded bias tape. The bias tape should be long enough to extend 1 inch beyond each end of the collar.

Slip stitch the collar to the dress, so that it can be removed for frequent washing.

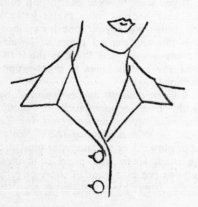

TO MAKE A PETER PAN COLLAR— This little, round, close-fitting collar is worn at the high neckline of a dress, suit, or sweater. A Peter Pan collar is stitched exactly like a straight collar but is a little more difficult to cut correctly, since the collar is curved to lie flat.

This curve can best be copied from a Peter Pan collar you may already have. Cut a pattern from a piece of newspaper.

If you do not have a collar of this type, measure the neckline of the dress for which you wish to make the collar. Then cut a paper pattern in the shape of a fourth of a circle. This pattern should measure half the distance around the neckline. Add ½ inch for a seam at the neck opening and cut the collar about 3 ½ inches wide.

TO MAKE A DICKEY—A good way to save money is by sewing your own dickeys. You will also have a much wider choice of color and material, since most of the dickeys which come ready made are not very "individual" in style or color, and when they are, the price is generally quite high.

The standard dickey requires about ½ yard of 35-inch material. You can

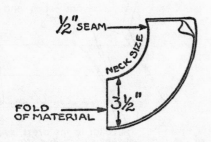

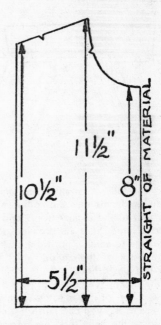

Cut the collar double thickness, place the right sides together, and stitch around the outside edge, allowing a ½-inch seam. Turn the collar right side out. Press.

A Peter Pan collar can be finished with a bias tape binding covering the raw edges of the neckline, or it can be stitched to a "front" and finished as described below.

make it from less by piecing the under section or lining of the collar. Be careful, however, to cut all the pieces on the straight grain of the material.

Cut the collar pattern out of paper in either a straight or Peter Pan style, as described above. Then cut a paper pattern for the dickey, as shown in the illustration, following measurements given.

Cut two collars and four dickey fronts. Put the pattern pieces on the straight lengthwise grain of the material, and be certain you have enough material for those six pieces needed for the dickey before you start cutting.

Place the two dickey fronts at opposite ends of one long side of the single collar, as shown. The right sides of the dickey front and collar will face together. Stitch. Put the other two dickey fronts and the single collar together in the same way. Press open all seams.

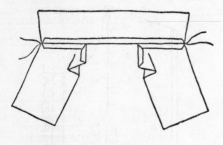

Pin carefully; then stitch one unit of the dickey fronts and the collar to the other unit of the dickey fronts and the collar. Dotted lines in drawing show you where to stitch. Turn right side out at the back of the collar, which has been left unstitched.

If the dickey is to be worn with a suit with a collar, or if it is to be worn with only one dress, you can finish it quickly by turning the unfinished neck edge to the inside of the dickey and edge stitching the open portion on the right side. When you put the dickey on the dress or suit, tack this back with a few hand stitches to keep it in place.

If you plan to change the dickey from dress to dress, you may want to cut a 2-inch-wide bias strip of the dickey material to hold the collar more firmly in place without tacking. Cut a bias strip 3 inches longer than the back collar opening, so the ends can slip in between the two pieces of the dickey front at either side of the collar opening. Fold the bias strip and baste it before stitching.

Try on the dickey and pin the ends

of the bias between the dickey fronts. Edge stitch across these places to hold the ends of the bias strip firmly in place.

Closing a Dickey—A dickey with a convertible collar may have snaps or small buttons at the bottom to fasten the two fronts together. The top is usually left open to show the becoming V neckline. A dickey with a Peter Pan collar can be fastened with small buttons and buttonholes made of thread loops, as shown in sketch.

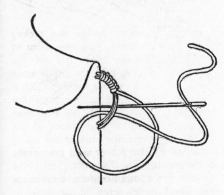

The following sketch shows a dickey with a Peter Pan collar. It is made in the same way as the dickey with a straight collar.

Wear a Scarf as a Dickey—Fold it into a triangle, as shown. This is an off-center fold, so the triangles will not overlap at the corners.

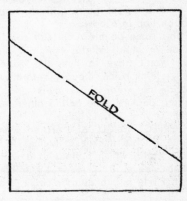

Fasten the two upper points at the back of the neck, then pull the two lower points to the back.

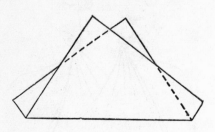

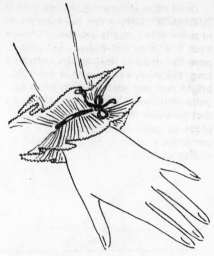

Use a hook and eye to fasten at the neck if a knot would be bulky or make the neckline too high. Another hook and eye, or tapes, can be used to fasten the scarf at the back waistline, depending on the scarf size.

Cuffs—Fresh, clean cuffs can make hands beautiful. Here are a few attention-getting, hand-prettying cuffs:

DOUBLE RUFFLE—Wear sheer white organdie cuffs on a dark crepe dress. Use two widths of ruffling and conceal the place where you join them together with a band of narrow black velvet ribbon tied in a bow.

This same double ruffle cuff can be made in plaid taffeta. Fringe it and you won't have to hem the edges. Better think twice, though, before you decide to wear these cuffs and a taffeta peplum. One or the other, not both, is your safest choice.

PERFECT CIRCLE of starched white piqué double thickness stitched to a plain band, which buttons to a wrist-fitting sleeve. It is made by folding each circle into a quarter circle, then trimming off the corner until the center circle exactly fits the wrist. Stitch the double circle together, turn, and apply the band as directed in Chapter 8. (See directions for making bound buttonholes, page 143.) Or use the buttonhole attachment on your machine. You may decide to use the buttons for trimming and fasten the cuffs to the dress with snaps.

Don't forget the plain SLIP-ON TURNBACK CUFF. It can be something to make your dress remembered if you treat it with an air. For example, suppose the dress is navy-blue wool with long, fairly loose sleeves. You can twist bright red and navy-blue rickrack together to form a solid row, and stitch that between two thicknesses of white piqué to make turnback cuffs. Or you can make a plain turnback cuff with a scalloped edge.

Have you seen bath towels and luncheon sets with cutout flowers hemmed on them by hand with invisible hemming stitches? Try an idea like that for cuffs. Use only a small flower or bunch for each cuff, though; don't overdo it.

The sizes are up to you. Know your wrist size, know your sleeve measurement, and do your experimenting in muslin until you have a pattern that is just right.

These cuffs are all "conversation pieces." They are not "made-over" ideas, though they could be used on old dresses to give them new life. Try these cuffs or the ones you dream up yourself—like cuffs from a lovely lace-trimmed handkerchief, or from an old Paisley scarf, or polka-dotted crepe with a sequin put on every other polka dot. These cuffs do not belong on a printed, striped, or figured dress. When your dress material has a design, let that design be the center of attention. Don't add trimming or you will be overdressed!

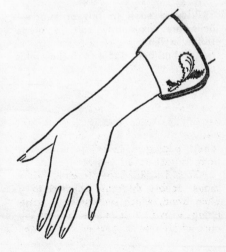

BELTS—A belt can be the difference between a so-so dress and an eye-catching dress. Women who know this will substitute a good belt for the cheap-looking one which so often comes with a ready-made dress.

You can make many exciting and unusual belts. There are only two precautions to remember: (1) Make your belt in a color and style which will look well with your dress, and (2) avoid wide, conspicuous belts unless you are tall enough or you have a small enough waistline to carry them. The short woman and the plump person can wear unusual and distinctive belts provided they keep them fairly narrow and wear them as single added decorations on each dress.

Here are suggestions for belts you can make. No exact measurements for length are given, since your own waist will determine the size. Make a pattern for yourself from unbleached muslin or any other medium-weight material in your scrap bag. A pattern made of material will be easier to work with than one of paper, since it can be crushed, drawn tight, fitted, tied in a bow or knot—just as your belt will be when it is finished.

Fringed sash in felt or suède— Belts are luxuriously soft in suède, stiffer in felt.

Cut the belt about 4 inches wide in felt, 5 inches wide in suède. It should be 15 inches longer than your waist measurement.

Fringe the ends by cutting slits along the edges 1½ inches deep and ⅛ of an inch apart. Fasten the belt by knotting it.

Make this two-color belt by cutting each half in a different color, joining the two pieces by a narrow seam on the wrong side down the center back. Be sure that the two colors are of the same texture of material (suède, felt, or any other material) to get the best results.

Plaited belt—This type of belt is attractive in rainbow colors on a solid-color pastel dress, or in a brilliant color combination on a plain dark dress. It looks as well on the gently rounded as on the tall, slender person.

Braid either 3 or 4 strips of felt, leather, or cord. You braid 3 strands as you would plait 3 strands of hair. The sketch shows how to do 4-strand braiding.

Cut 3 or 4 strands, each ½ inch wide. The length of each strand should measure one and a half times the distance around your waist plus 20 inches. For example, if your waist measures 26 inches, each strand will be 59 inches long.

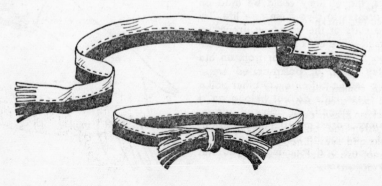

Lay the pieces side by side and fasten them together at a point 10 inches from one end before you begin braiding. Continue braiding until you are within 10 inches of the other ends of the pieces. Stitch across the braiding at each end, to hold it in place.

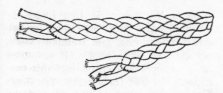

The ends of the strands can be left as is, knotted, or they can be rolled back and caught with a few stitches.

Scroll belt in felt—Cut double thicknesses of felt, as shown. Stitch the two thicknesses together 1/4 inch from the edge.

Fasten in front with a concealed hook and eye placed beneath the felt so it will not show.

Twisted belt in felt or suède—Cut the belt in two pieces as shown—each piece two thicknesses, stitched together along the edges to hold the belt in shape.

You may have each section of the belt in a different color if you wish. Color combinations, such as raspberry and jade green, worn on a plain navy, black or brown dress, will be stunning.

Fasten the belt in the back with hooks and eyes. (Snaps are not secure.) Do not use a buckle, for it makes the belt appear fussy.

Grosgrain ribbon belt—Stitch two thicknesses of heavy-ribbed grosgrain ribbon together with edge stitching. If you want additional stiffness, a piece of buckram or unbleached muslin can be cut about 1/8 inch narrower than the ribbon and stitched between the two thicknesses of ribbon.

This belt can be just long enough to have the ends turned under and fastened with a hook and eye, or it can have sash ends. Long ends can be fringed or cut in points and stitched like the rest of the belt.

If the belt of one color is lined in a contrasting or harmonizing color ribbon, the ends may be left free, so the two colors will show after the ends are knotted.

A grosgrain belt in a plain dark color, worn on a dark dress, is a perfect quick-change accessory. If the proportions are right, this belt will look well on most girls and women. Here are ways in which the belt can be decorated:

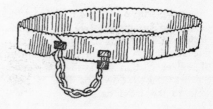

With a man's heavy gold watch chain and fobs looped part-way across the side front and fastened.

On a narrow grosgrain belt or any plain narrow belt which matches the dress, a loop of colored ribbon, fastened with any little old-fashioned pin. No old pin? Then wear a new one!

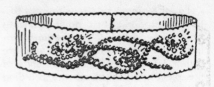

Make a border of small buttons across the top and the bottom of your belt. Small white pearl buttons with four holes, stitched on a black grosgrain belt with red thread, are effective.

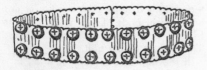

Two or three pretty buttons (old or new) can be stitched to the center front of a grosgrain belt.

For dress-up occasions a plain, dark dress can be given style by a grosgrain belt which has a design in beads and sequins. A belt can also be made of velvet ribbon with silk or rayon flowers tacked down as flat as possible to the front or side.

Make the grosgrain belt about 6 inches longer than the exact waist measurement and pull it through an old cut-steel shoe buckle, if you are lucky enough to have one. Snap the ends of the belt for security. You may also have an enamel belt buckle which can be used on a belt.

Shaped belts of felt—Belts of this type usually look best around a tiny waistline. They should be worn with sports clothes or wool dresses, but do not look well with rayon or silk crepes.

Cut the pattern carefully. Take a small dart at each side to shape the belt to the figure.

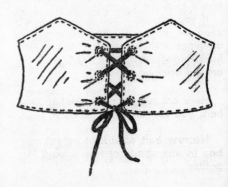

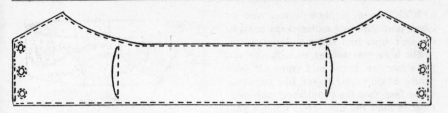

When the felt is cut, baste the darts, and try on the belt before stitching. The two fronts should not meet. This open space (about 1 or 2 inches) is laced together with strips of cord, leather, or ribbon. Felt may be used, but it is not so strong. You might also use fine quality shoe laces.

Mark the places, with pencil or chalk, where you want to punch openings for the lacings but do not punch through. Machine stitch around these marked-off circles. It is not hard to stitch these circles if you take only one stitch, leave the needle in the felt when you raise the presser foot of the machine, then turn the material slightly beneath the needle. Lower the presser foot, take the next stitch. Repeat until you have a completed circle, then punch a small hole in the center and trim it to make a round opening.

If you sew your belt by hand, proceed as above to mark places for openings with pencil or chalk. Punch hole through first, then blanket stitch around opening.

Here are two more suggestions for belts you can make at home.

Narrow belt of silk or velvet ribbon in one shade or two tacked together.

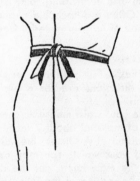

Self-fabric belt, muslin interlining, bias loop fastening tied in bows, ends of bias knotted. This belt can be made in felt, suède, or leather.

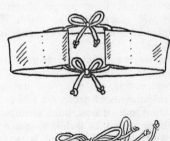

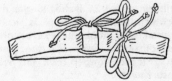

PEPLUMS—A peplum is a flared or gathered piece of material fastened to a belt and tied around the waist. If your hips are slender enough for you to wear one, it can add variety to your dark basic dress. If you like peplums, and feel that the usual short one ending around the hip line is not for you, you can still have the peplum effect by wearing a longer overskirt or apron with your dress. A black crepe basic dress with an overskirt of delicate black lace becomes a dressed-up outfit. It is not always necessary to have the peplum of a contrasting color and material. Often a detachable peplum can be made of leftover material from your dress.

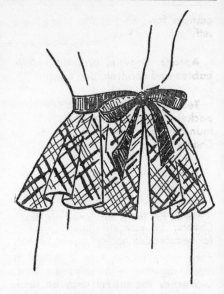

To make a gathered peplum—These directions are for a hip-length peplum:

Take your waist measurement. Cut a piece of material about 7 inches wide and about 1½ times the distance around your waist. You may need to piece the material to get the desired width. Be sparing of the fullness if you are using a stiff material, such as taffeta, which makes the figure appear much wider than it actually is.

Hem one long side and the two ends of the peplum. A flat seam binding stitched to the edge of the peplum by machine and then caught down by hand will make the best finish. See Chapter 8 for more complete directions on hems.

Gather the unfinished edge of the peplum to fit the waist. Adjusting the gathers evenly, pin this piece between two thicknesses of grosgrain ribbon. If you want to tie a bow, have each piece of ribbon about 24 inches longer than your waistline. If ribbon is to be fastened with hook-and-eye or given some other flat finish, cut the pieces cnly 2 inches longer than the waist measurement.

Edge-stitch the peplum between two ribbons. Edge-stitch the ribbons together at the top. Tie to form a bow at the front of the dress.

To make an overskirt or apron peplum—This is made like the hip-length peplum, but it is longer. Always adjust the length of a peplum so that it looks well in relation to the length of your dress and to your figure. The only way to find a becoming length is by experimenting. Tie any piece of material around your waist. Pin it up or let it down, to get the effect of the desired length, before you cut into good material.

GIFTS YOU CAN MAKE—The gift you make with your own hands receives a warmer welcome because of the thought and skill which went into its making.

All the accessories mentioned in this chapter are equally appropriate as gifts. In addition, here are more suggestions for gifts you can make yourself:

Aprons, lingerie, and clothes for babies and children. See Chapter 19.

Tea towels, luncheon sets, shoe pockets, lampshades, pot holders, laundry bags, garment covers. See Chapter 20.

Handkerchiefs made of fine linen, or napkins and tablecloths with hand-hemstitched hems or embroidered designs are good gift suggestions. In Chapter 18 you will find instructions for hemstitching and other fancy stitching.

Scarves for tables and dressers, made with unusual edgings, such as you will see in Chapter 17, make excellent gifts for someone who takes pleasure in her homemaking.

Scarves for dress wear or sportswear, for men and women and young folks, are simple to sew. For the man or boy a plaid, striped, or plain woolen material is suitable for ordinary wear, a white or light gray rayon or silk scarf for dress wear. For the woman or girl you are not so limited in materials. Her scarf can be made of silk, rayon, velvet, corduroy, or wool, and the colors and patterns in material can run riot.

Slippers are another welcome gift and can be made satisfactorily at home. Use an old felt hat or buy new felt by the yard. Make a paper pattern of the sole, using an old pair of slippers for measurement. Cut two soles of felt—and remember when sewing that one foot is right, the other left. If no felt is available, make soles of a few thicknesses of wool fabric. In the winter

make bedroom slippers out of wool for all the members of the family—the menfolk too. Undoubtedly you have some leftover pieces of wool material, or can cut up an old woolen coat which has outlived its usefulness.

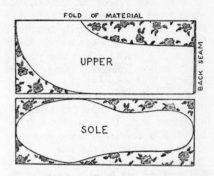

Cut a piece of paper the length of the foot, or you can use the sole pattern you cut for the purpose of measuring, and for the upper parts of the slippers cut four pieces alike, two for each foot. See illustration. Experiment first with a piece of extra material, until you get the right size and shape. Then keep it for future use, so that you won't need to make a new pattern each time you cut slippers.

Sew the front and the back seams, matching the two wrong sides of the material, so that the finished seams will

come on the right side. This is done because inside seams are uncomfortable. Now baste the uppers to the soles and stitch them down, also making the seam on the outside of the slippers. If you've made the whole slipper of felt, or even old pieces of leather, you won't need to worry about unfinished seams. Just trim them closely and they'll look fine. But if you use woolen material, or if it is summertime and you are using cotton material, then before stitching the uppers to the sole stitch binding (self color or contrasting) over the seams on the uppers to give them a finished look. The same binding can be used to cover the seam where the upper is stitched to the sole.

If you have a large piece of material and do not want a seam at the front of the slipper, fold the material in the center when you cut the uppers. When the material is cut and open, you'll have only to seam the back.

For women and children quilted cotton material makes an effective slipper. The sole can also be made of the same material, and if the binding is cotton and washable, you will have a slipper that can be laundered and will give long wear. Appliqué design or embroidery of animal heads or flowers can be put on the toes of a child's slippers.

Scuffs are made generally the same as slippers, except that they have no backs. Patterns may be bought for scuffs with full directions; but if you cut your own pattern, the sides of the front section should extend well back and under the instep. If you make the front too short, the scuff will slide off the foot. For a feminine touch, you might make the scuff with a cutout toe finished with the same bias tape as the rest of the scuff. Flat bows or amusing embroidered decoration may also be added as an extra fillip.

Toys to make—WASHABLE TOYS, which are soft and can neither hurt the child nor damage the furniture, are popular with parents as well as the tot. No child has too many toys, and to satisfy that constant urge for something new you can sew the toys at little or no expense. Leftover material, old Turkish towels, pieces of cotton fabric, or quilted chintz, can all be used. Make certain that the material is color fast, and launder it before you cut it up for toymaking. Also, use only materials that will stand hard wear, and are not so flimsy that they will come apart with rough handling.

You can simplify your sewing by buying patterns for stuffed toys which give specific directions. But if you want to design your own patterns, draw them on paper first before you cut the materials. Animals, such as rabbits, sheep, elephants, pandas, dogs, and cats as well as birds, barnyard chicks, and ducks, are all pleasing to the child. Cut out and seam on the wrong side, leaving the seam partly open on the underside of the body to turn the top inside out. For stuffing use cotton batting or silk floss. The latter has a tendency to get lumpy after laundering. You could also use a stuffing of foam rubber, cut up into tiny pieces, which bounces back into shape after laundering. Do not use sawdust, as it may come through the seams and it will not stand laundering.

With closely spaced overcast stitches close up the open seam. Apply the finishing touches by hand. Embroider the eyes, eyebrows, nose, and mouth, with colored wool or pearl cotton thread. If you have a pair of old washable kid gloves, you might cut out and sew a little tongue to protrude from the toy mouth. Or the tail and ears can be made of kid. Some toys have buttons for eyes; but it's better not to use them, as they may come loose and be swallowed by a baby.

A way to avoid laundering, and at the same time produce a strong stuffed toy, is to make it of oilcloth or plastic. This type of toy can be wiped off with a damp cloth.

The little girl's delight is her "rag" doll, which you can also sew and for which patterns and directions are available. Use the same principle as in making an animal or bird. You may make the doll in one piece or the body separate from the head, arms, and legs. Each one of them can be sewed and stuffed separately, then put together with strong hand stitching. Embroider the facial features and make the hair from strands of wool. And here is a chance for your ingenuity. You can provide the doll's clothes which you can cut and sew from patterns you buy or those you create yourself.

THE BEAN BAG is a perennial toy, used both by babies and by their bigger sisters and brothers. If you have some old felt hats, cut two pieces of the same size and shape. They don't need to be the same color—each side may be its own color—but be sure the thickness of the material is the same. If no felt is available, thick wool, heavy cotton fabric, or soft leather is suitable. The shape can be round or square, it can resemble a pear, an apple, or a heart.

Baste both pieces together 1/4 inch from the edge, leaving an opening 1 inch long. Stitch by machine. Using the small opening, fill the bag loosely with small dried beans—not too many,

as they make the bag too stiff and heavy to throw. Push the beans to one side, then machine stitch over the opening. Overcast the edges with bright-colored wool.

CHAPTER 23

Tailoring Suits, Coats, and Jackets

TAILORING is a skill that can be acquired by any seamstress who is willing to give her attention to the fine detail so essential in turning out a professional-looking garment. Making a suit or a coat is not nearly the difficult task that it might appear to be, and certainly the satisfaction of being able to turn out a smart-looking tailored garment at a fraction of its retail price is more than enough incentive to the average woman.

Patience and careful workmanship are the two basic requirements of learning to become your own tailor. The tailoring procedures themselves are not difficult; many of them are the same as those used in making any other garment.

HOW TO CHOOSE YOUR PATTERN AND MATERIAL—The things you learned about buying a pattern and choosing material in Chapter 2 and Chapter 3 also apply to tailored garments.

For your first tailoring job select a pattern which is simple—an unlined coat without a collar, for example.

In buying a coat pattern, buy the same size as you would for a dress,

since a coat pattern is cut with sufficient allowance for the clothes which are worn underneath it. In choosing a pattern select a style which will look well made up in the material you plan to use. For instance, thick wools or rough texture look best when made up in loosely fitted casual coats. The smooth-finished wools, such as gabardine, flannel, broadcloth, zibeline, men's-wear worsted, and coverts, are suitable for the more fitted styles and finer details of added trimming.

All woolens should be pre-shrunk before you begin to work with them. Ask the salesclerk to show you the label on the bolt. If the material is not guaranteed pre-shrunk, you can have it shrunk at a dry cleaner's, or you can do it yourself. For instructions, see Chapter 3.

If you are a beginner, select fabric that is not stretchy or loosely woven. If you are wise, you will not choose a plaid for a first tailoring venture, either. When you have become a little more experienced, you can try that Scotch-plaid suit you have always wanted.

Raincoats can also be made at

Corduroy and velveteen are attractive in certain types of coats and jackets. If you want to use these materials, choose a pattern which has as few pieces as possible and does not require a lot of outside stitching, for these materials do not stand pressing as well as wools. While corduroy and velveteen are usually cotton-backed, they can often be used for cold-weather coats if they are warmly interlined. Without the interlining they make good sports coats and suits, even evening coats, for milder climates.

Coats and suits and separate jackets

home. Water-repellent cotton broadcloth and twill are good materials for this purpose. If the coat is to be left unlined, make double-stitched seams; but if it is for use in colder weather, it should have a warm lining. You can also make a reversible raincoat by lining it with corduroy or smooth-textured wool suiting or coating. If you do this, make sure that both the outer and inner materials are pre-shrunk, so that there will be no possibility of having the coat shrink in a rain or in dry cleaning while the lining retains its original size.

can be made of washable cotton and linen for summer wear. For washable tailored clothes, select a pattern that is simple in construction so you will not

be faced with difficult pressing problems. Other materials for warm-weather coats and suits include silks, rayons, linens, and cotton coatings. In buying silk, get the pure-dye, unweighted type as it will wear longer. If you plan to use rayon, linen or cotton, try to get a material that will press easily.

Lining material is generally silk or rayon crepe or satin. The material chosen should be as fine in quality as the material of the coat or suit, for a cheap-looking lining can ruin the appearance of the entire garment. For the dressy coat or suit and for most tailored garments a pure-dye silk lining in a dark or matching color is the best choice.

Novel linings are sometimes used for effect. One example of this treatment is a plaid wool lining in a corduroy sports jacket. A lightweight coat of plain material is especially attractive when lined with the same silk or rayon print material that is used for the dress designed to be worn beneath the coat. In making a coat like this, however, remember that a coat with a printed lining will not look well worn over other clothes. Warm-weather coats and jackets of piqué, crash, or linen can be lined with rayon or smooth mercerized cotton.

In each case make sure that the lining material is also pre-shrunk, for a shrunken lining ruins the appearance of any garment.

Interlining—A heavy winter coat must be interlined. This interlining should be one of the lightweight woolen materials made especially for the purpose. Never buy anything but a wool interlining, since its primary purpose is to give warmth. Putting an interlining into a coat is a little tricky, and some home tailors prefer to avoid using two materials (interlining and lining) by using instead one fabric that acts as both interlining and lining. This could be satin or taffeta backed by a thin layer of foam rubber, or Milium, which is backed by an aluminum coating. There is also a quilted combination interlining and lining which is usually satin or crepe and thin wool. The fabrics are machine stitched together by square or diagonal quilting.

Interfacing and facing—Coats and jackets—even some which are unlined —require interfacing. This is a piece of pre-shrunk unbleached muslin, tailor's canvas, or a nonwoven interfacing which can be bought in various weights to suit different fabrics used for the garments. It is stitched between the jacket or coat fronts and the front facing. It gives firmness to the lapels so they will not sag and so that the weight of the buttons will not pull down the soft suit or coat material. Interfacing is also cut to fit between the two thicknesses of the collar when they are stitched together. The collar and the lapel of every well-made suit or coat are interfaced so that they will retain their clear, sharp lines.

A jacket or coat pattern will include a pattern piece for the facing. This facing is cut from a narrow piece of the garment material and shaped to fit the front of the garment. You will not need to buy additional material for this; your pattern allows for the facing.

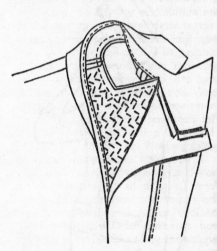

Tailoring supplies—In tailored coats and jackets many of the seams are taped—those at the armholes, the neck and shoulders, the front edges, and the lapels. This is particularly important if the material stretches easily. Buy tailor's tape (a twilled cotton tape) for the purpose; or, if that is not readily obtainable, use a heavy cotton bias binding. Like all other material used in the garment, the tape should be preshrunk.

For machine stitching, get mercerized cotton thread for the woolens of he same shade or a shade darker. For urning up hems and for silk linings, or outside stitching on some materials, silk hread is advised. All threads should be fast color, of course.

For an unlined coat or jacket, buy silk or rayon flat binding, matching the color as nearly as possible to the fabric. Use this to finish the seams and the hem. To finish curved seams around the armhole or neck facing, use a matching bias binding of silk or rayon. For a cotton unlined coat, buy a thin cotton bias binding.

Buy your buttons along with your other notions so that when you make the buttonholes you will be sure of the correct size. If you are making a suit, buy the slide fastener for the skirt placket, as well as any hooks and eyes or snaps you think you may need. If you are using ready-made shoulder pads, buy them now. If you are making your own, don't forget to get the material for them. Also buy your underarm shields in a thin rubberized material which you will cover later.

If you have not already done so, now is a good time to invest in a dress form. Dress forms are a great help to the woman who sews alone and are especially useful for tailoring jobs. If you assemble all the materials and equipment you need before you begin, you will find it much easier to concentrate on the interesting process of tailoring.

MAKING A TAILORED COAT OR JACKET—There are two general rules in which lie the secrets of all good tailoring:

Work carefully. Whether you are cutting, fitting, or sewing—even when you are basting—work as neatly as you can, for tailoring is largely a matter of fine workmanship.

Press as you go. The careful step-by-step pressing of your garment is essential for a crisp custom-made finish. The same results can never be achieved if all the pressing is left until last.

Cutting and fitting the pattern— Before you do anything with the pattern itself, study the directions which came with it. Don't overlook the layout pattern. Chapter 5 contains the information on laying out a pattern for cutting. Chapter 4 and Chapter 5 include instructions on making pattern alterations. The cutting and fitting procedures for tailored garments are the same as those for other articles of clothing, with one exception—professional tailors always work with a muslin pattern so that the garment can be fitted as smoothly as possible.

The muslin pattern should be cut from the paper pattern, basted together, and fitted. Baste the sleeve into place in the armhole. When all necessary alterations have been made and carefully marked, rip the pieces apart and press them. Then lay the pieces on the material and cut out your garment, paying special attention to any markings you may have made on the muslin pattern.

First tailoring steps—Baste the darts, the seams of the body of the coat, and the shoulder seams. If the material is very soft to handle, or if there is any easing in to be done, pin the pieces before you baste, putting the pins close together. The parts to be eased in will be shrunk and shaped in the pressing. Baste with small stitches. Press, then stitch on the machine, first the darts, then the side seams from the top down to the bottom. Stitch the shoulder seams last. Loosen the stitch on your machine if the material you are working with is heavy.

Then machine stitch the facing, interfacing, and coat together. If the coat material is soft, a strip of twilled cotton tape can also be stitched in with the seam for added firmness. Trim the seam to within ¼ inch of the stitching before turning the facing to the inside of the coat. Press.

Catch stitch the facing very lightly to the coat front, taking up only one thread of coat material in the stitch.

Interfacing and facing tailored jacket or coat—A jacket or a tailored coat with a collar and lapels requires a pre-shrunk muslin or tailor's canvas interfacing. This is fastened to the body of the jacket or coat with rows of loose diagonal basting stitches which catch only one thread of the jacket material.

These rows of hand tacking (sometimes called the padding stitch) start at the fold of the lapel at the point where it begins to roll back. They continue up and down, to cover the entire lapel. Baste this interfacing to the wrong side of the lapel, holding the

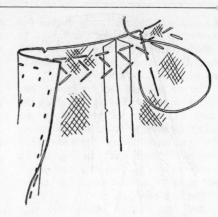

material over the hand so that the coat lapel will have the easy, unstrained roll that is a sign of fine tailoring.

Baste the collar interfacing to the underside of the collar, and tack the two pieces of material together, as shown in the illustration. Note the row of curved basting lines which connect the notches on the lower edge of the collar.

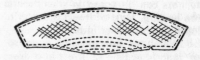

These lines must catch only one thread of the jacket material in each stitch, since they are to stay in place. Machine stitch the underside of the collar to the jacket, matching notches, and press open the seam.

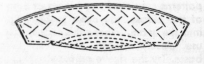

Join the upper side of the collar to the two front facings of the jacket. Clip the curved seams so they will lie flat when pressed. See page 76 for instructions.

tight or too loose, now is the time to make the adjustment. Remove the jacket and unpin the pads. For a smooth fit, tape the armholes. Since the armhole seam is circular and the tape is straight, have a hot iron ready. Lay a strip of tape on the ironing board, and with a damp cloth or brush dampen one half of the width of the

Place the facings on top of the jacket, with the right sides of the material together, and baste. The facing may be slightly larger than the jacket front to allow for turning the facing back over the interfacing. This extra fullness can be eased in when you do the basting. Most of it will come at the lapel. If your material is soft and lacks body, you may want to stitch a piece of tailor's tape into the seam which joins the facing to the jacket, so that the lapel will hold its shape.

Trim the seam to within ¼ inch of the stitching, then clip the edge of the seam at any curve or point so that it will lie flat when pressed.

Setting in the sleeves—Baste the sleeve seams. Some tailored sleeve patterns consist of two pieces and one of the pieces may need to be eased into the seam. Where this is the case, use closely spaced pins first, then baste. Try the sleeve on for size. Stitch the seams on the machine, and then press the seams flat, using a sleeve board.

Try the jacket on right side out. Pin in the shoulder pads to get the correct fit of the armholes. If they are too

tape. Then, while one hand runs the iron over the damp part, which will shrink, keep stretching the dry part of the tape with the other hand.

If the sleeve is larger than the armhole—and it generally is in coats and jackets—it will have to be eased in. Machine stitch over the top curved part of the sleeve before it is stitched into the armhole. Gather this stitching by pulling up the bobbin thread underneath until your sleeve is the correct size to fit into the armhole. Slip the gathered top of the sleeve over the end of the sleeve board and, using a slightly dampened pressing cloth, shrink in the top fullness.

For the next step you will need a little assistance.

Put the jacket on again and have someone pin both sleeves carefully into the armholes. Lift your arms up to make sure that the sleeves fit comfortably. While you have the jacket on, measure the length of the sleeve and pin up the sleeve hems. Take off the jacket, and with small stitches baste the sleeves into the armholes. The smaller the basting stitches are, the easier it will be to guide the machine stitching. Stitch the sleeves into the armholes, then press the armhole seams open to about four inches below the shoulder seam in the back and front. Press both sides of the seam together into the sleeve underarm.

To give more body at the wrist, a

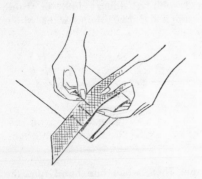

bias strip of muslin or wigan (a stiffening fabric) about 2 inches wide can be cut and the bottom of the strip placed along the hem line at the point where the sleeve will be turned up. Pin and baste the strip to the hem line, then attach both sides of the bias strip to the sleeve with a loose catch stitch. Turn the sleeve right side out, lay it on an ironing board, put a damp pressing cloth inside the sleeve, and press it flat, turning the sleeve round and round. This will shrink out any fullness by making the inside of the sleeve hem a little smaller than the outside. In an unlined sleeve, this bias strip should be the width of the hem; the hem is edged with flat seam binding before finishing.

Put the jacket on and pin the shoulder pads into place again. Remove the jacket. Tack the pads securely on the shoulder seam and around the armhole seam. If the jacket is unlined, the pads should be finished with an outer cover of self fabric or a piece of rayon or silk crepe to match in color. If lining is used, the pads can be covered with plain white muslin, since they will not be visible.

Buttonholes and pockets—This is the stage at which the buttonholes and pockets are made—before the coat is lined. See Chapter 10 for instructions on making buttonholes and pockets.

Interfacing and facing a casual topcoat—Cut the two interfacings from the pattern used for the front facings. Then cut the interfacing for the back of the neck from the pattern for the neck facing. If the coat has a collar, cut an interfacing for the collar as well.

Baste the facings flat to the inside fronts of the coat, matching all pattern markings or notches. Baste the neck interfacing to the inside of the neck, that is, to the wrong side of the coat.

Rip out all bastings. If there are any curved seams or points, clip them with the point of your scissors as described on page 76. Slit the darts, starting at the outer open end and cutting through very carefully with the point of scissors to the narrowest end at the bust line. Press the darts open. Press the side and shoulder seams open.

Next try on your coat or jacket, wrong side out, to see how the shoulder seams fit. They may have stretched a bit and will need to be adjusted. While you have the coat on, pin a strip of tailor's tape to the seam. Take off the coat and sew the tape to the shoulder seam with small running stitches or by machine. This will prevent any further stretching. You are now ready to put the interfacing in the garment.

Machine stitch the neck facing to the front facings. Then press the seams flat.

Baste the continuous front and neck facing to the right side of the coat, with the right sides of the materials together.

You may wonder why the interfacing is basted to the wrong side of the coat and the facing to the right side. This is because the facing is slightly larger than the coat front and must be gently

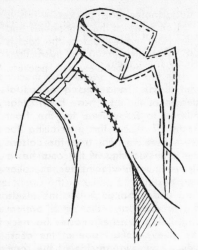

eased into the seams. The extra full-ness is taken by the interfacing and the roll of the coat fronts.

If the coat has a collar, it is attached in the same way as a jacket collar.

Finishing a lined coat or jacket— Measure the hem after your coat or jacket has hung for a day or two on a coat hanger or a dressmaking form if you have one. Wear a pair of shoes with the same heel height you plan to wear with the garment. Put on the coat or jacket, button it up, and turn up, pin, and baste the hem.

For a coat in which the lining will not be attached to the hem, and for an unlined jacket, the method of sewing the hem is the same. Press down the fold of the coat hem with your hand to test its bulkiness. Trim off as much material as you feel is necessary. If the fabric needs body, insert a bias strip of muslin or wigan, as explained above, for the sleeve hem. Baste the seam binding to the edge of the hem and machine stitch. Press the hem, easing in any excess fullness. Slip stitch or catch stitch the hem binding to the coat or jacket, using silk thread for strength.

If the lining is to be attached to the hem of the jacket, or if it is to be attached to a shortie coat, proceed as above, up to the point where the seam binding would be stitched to the hem. For an attached lining, omit the seam binding and catch stitch the raw edge of the hem to the jacket or coat. When the lining is sewed over it the raw edge will be hidden. For a firm edge that will not stretch, stitch a cotton twill tape under the raw edge of the hem. If the hem is circular, shrink the tape, as directed for the armhole.

Finishing an unlined coat or jacket— If your garment is to be unlined, all seams, the armholes, the front and the collar facing edges, the pocket edges extending on the inside of the jacket, and the bottom and the sleeves should be finished with matching seam binding so that no raw edges are left exposed.

Lining topcoat or jacket— A jacket is lined in the same way as a coat, up to the point where the garment is hemmed.

The lining is put in after you have fitted the garment and have given all seams a final pressing and sewn the shoulder pads in place.

If you are making a coat, cut out the lining, using the coat pattern. The front lining should not extend to the front edge of the coat, since the front facing is several inches wide. Make allowance for a 1-inch-wide pleat down the center fold of the lining material before you cut the lining for the back of the coat. This pleat allowance will give you greater freedom of shoulder movement. Allow for a ½-inch-wide pleat in the front lining pieces at the front shoulder.

Stitch the underarm seams of the lining and press the seams open.

Place the hemmed coat wrong side out on the dress form. A coat hanger will serve the purpose if you have no dress form. Pin the lining to the coat, matching the underarm seams. The lining should be right side out so that the two wrong sides of the material face each other. Pin the 1-inch pleat in place at the neck in the center back of the coat.

Baste the lining to the garment at both armholes; then, with long, loose basting stitches, tack it to the side seams of the coat and along the front facings.

Pin the seam of the front shoulder lining to the shoulder line of the coat, smooth out, and baste. Bring the edge

front to the front facing then to the neck facing. Catch stitch down the back pleat for about 2 inches from the top. Catch stitch down the shoulder pleats for 1 inch.

Join the sleeve sections by machine and press the seams open. If the sleeves of the coat have been greatly altered in fitting, you may prefer to baste the sleeve lining and slip it on the sleeve for fitting before making the final stitching. When complete, the sleeve lining is slipped over the sleeve and basted into place at the armhole. Turn under the edge of the lining at the armhole and slip stitch over the coat lining. Then attach the bottom of the sleeve lining to the hem of the sleeve by slip stitching. The lining should not be drawn tight but should be long enough to allow elbow room when the arm is bent.

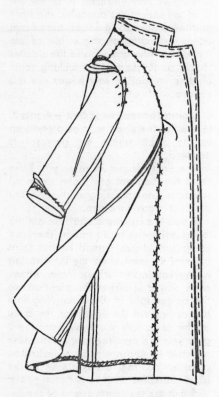

Turn up 1 inch of the lower edge of the lining and hem it by hand. The hem of the lining should be about 1 inch shorter than the hem of the coat. The side seams of the lining are fas-

of the back shoulder lining over the front section. Smooth out, baste, and slip stitch in place. Slip stitch the lining

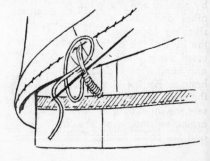

tened to the side seams of the coat with a bar tack, but the lining is left unattached at the bottom of the coat.

If you are making a jacket, the bottom of the lining is caught to the hem of the jacket and they are usually slip stitched together. The lining is not fitted too snugly at the bottom, but forms a little fold when it is pressed down. This conceals the slip stitching and at the same time prevents any strain on the lining.

Interlining coat—For cold weather, a wool interlining is a necessity in a winter coat. The jackets of winter suits may also have interlinings. Buying a fabric which already contains an interlining or a machine-quilted lining which is padded on the underside will minimize the work involved in interlining a child's coat or a sports coat, but in most cases fine tailoring calls for a separate interlining underneath the crepe or silk lining.

The interlining is put together separately and then put into the coat before the lining is tacked in place.

If the material used for the interlining is bulky, make very little allowance for seams and hems when cutting. If it is a lighter weight, pliable material, make the same seam allowances as you did for the lining. In both cases omit the pleat allowances at the center back and the shoulder line.

If a light material is used, open the darts after they have been stitched and press them flat. Overlap the seams by placing one raw edge on top of the other and catch stitching or machine stitching together. This will eliminate the bulk of the double thickness in the usual seam. Turn the coat inside out and hang it on a dress form or a coat hanger. Pin the interlining in place on the coat and with tiny running stitches sew the interlining in place around the armholes and over the front facing and the collar facing. Tack it at inter-

vals along the side seams of the coat. Set the sleeves into the interlining in the same way.

If you are using a bulky material, do not overlap the seam edges. Instead, bring the edges together at the seam line and tack them to the seams of the coat itself, or the lining. It is preferable to attach them to the lining seams, to prevent any bulky appearance in the coat itself. After they are tacked, join the interlining seams with a loose catch stitch where they meet, then adjust the lining over the coat, as explained above.

Sleeve interlining, as a rule, does not extend all the way to the wrist. In a tailored sleeve of two pieces, the interlining is usually cut for only the wider top piece and then caught down with running stitches to the two parallel seams in the sleeve. Interlining, as a rule, does not extend all the way underneath the front facing. It can extend about 1 inch under the facing to allow for sewing in place and then be cut off. Interlining reaches to about ½ inch or 1 inch above the fold of the hem of the lining. It is basted to the lining, and when the lining is hemmed, the slip stitch or catch stitch is caught into the interlining as well.

There are two methods of putting an interlining in a coat. In the first method it is attached directly to the coat and the lining placed over it and fastened to the side seams of the coat with bar tacks. The other method is to attach the interlining to the lining by basting the side seams of the interlining into the side seams of the lining. Machine stitch the seams together. The sleeve seams of the interlining and the lining are also basted and stitched together, then set into the sleeve, as described above, and fastened to the coat seams with bar tacks.

Underarm shields for coat or jacket—Underarm shields are sewed over the lining. For each shield cut two pieces of coat lining the shape of the shield, allowing for a hem on all edges. Seam the two crescent-shaped pieces together along the inside curve. Pin them to the shield. Turn under the hem allowance and baste together around the outside curves. Try on the coat and adjust each shield to the place where you want it to be. Pin them in place and remove the coat. Baste each shield to the lining inside the coat, turn the sleeve inside out, and baste that part of the shield which extends into the sleeve and then catch stitch or slip stitch the shield to the lining. Do not press.

MAKING THE SKIRT—The skirt of a suit is made in the same way as any other skirt. But since a suit skirt receives harder usage than other types of skirts, here is a hint that will insure longer wear.

If it is a slim skirt—and particularly if you expect to be sitting most of the time while you wear it—make a shield to hold the back of the skirt in shape. From a piece of leftover material from your jacket or coat lining, or from any extra piece of lining, cut a shield from the skirt back pattern. Make it long enough to reach about three or four inches above the bend of the the knee. Baste and stitch this shield into the side seams of your skirt in one operation. Stitch it in with the top of the skirt when you are attaching the waistband. Do not hem the shield; leave the bottom edge raw, or finish it by pinking.

To give your completed tailored garment that extra special look, have the final pressing done by a tailor.

WORKING WITH FUR—Coat collars and some jacket collars are sometimes made of fur, and handling fur is a special tailoring problem. Whether you have new fur, or want to use a piece

of fur which has previously been used on something else, the procedure is the same.

Cut a whole paper pattern of the collar or band you want to make. It is best not to cut a half pattern, since fur is never cut on a fold. No seam allowances are necessary. Determine how the fur runs—its direction should be straight up and down or toward the center back. You will want to know this if you have to piece the collar or band in one or in several places. It is a good idea to mark matching arrows

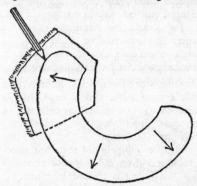

on the skin or back of the fur and then on the pattern, to enable you to lay out the fur properly before cutting. If you do have to piece the fur, lay the pieces side by side (do not overlap) and place the pattern over the skin side. With tailor's chalk or a white pencil draw the outline of your pattern.

RAZOR BLADE

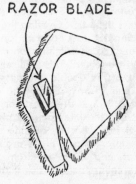

Cut the fur on this outline, using a single-edged razor blade or a very sharp knife. Cut only through the skin. Do not cut the hairs on the other side. If piecing is to be done, cut the pieces to meet evenly with no jagged edges.

To join the seams, put the fur sides together. Hold tightly, and with a strong needle and waxed thread sew the two edges with tiny overhand stitches. Be careful not to catch any of the fur in the stitches. The finished seam will not overlap—the two edges should meet each other and the seam should not be visible on the fur side.

Fur should be interlined. With the same tiny overcasting stitch sew a ½-inch cotton twill tape all around the fur piece. Hold the fur with the skin toward you, the tape folded over the fur side,

again being careful not to catch any of the hairs into your stitches. Cut the interlining on the same pattern from a piece of lamb's wool, flannel, or any

other soft piece of padding which will lie flat over the skin. Turn the tape back over the interlining, mitering the corners, and catch stitch the tape to the interlining.

If you're going to attach the fur collar to a coat, you have already allowed for material to line the fur, with turn-under allowance all around the piece. To hold the lining in place, sew

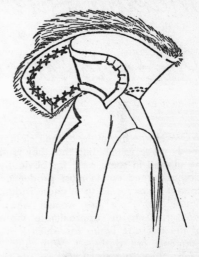

a line or two of running stitches at the back, catching the interlining of the fur into the stitches. When the fur collar is completed, slip stitch it in place, catching the stitches in the tape.

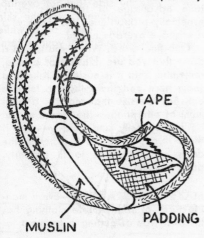

TAPE

MUSLIN   **PADDING**

Fur bands are interlined and taped in the same way. They are pinned flat in place on the garment and then slip stitched through the tape.

CHAPTER 24

Making Alterations in

Ready-to-Wear Clothing

WOMEN who buy many of their clothes ready made usually find that they must be altered in some way, for obviously clothes turned out in mass production cannot be expected to fit an individual figure. But there are women whose measurements do approximate those of the average figure for which these garments are designed. With a few minor alterations many of them can be made to fit properly, and when this is the case, carefully selected ready-made clothing becomes a time saver to the busy woman.

BUYING FOR SIZE—Since altering a finished garment is a different problem from making alterations in a garment as it is put together, it is always important to buy a dress in the size that requires a minimum of adjustment. For that reason it is wise not to acquire the habit of buying any one particular size, assuming that it will always be the best fit. A size 16, for example, may fit very well in one style and very badly or not at all in another.

There are tricks in shopping for clothing that will help you solve many of the problems of correct fitting. If you are short-waisted, try a half size or perhaps a petite size. Half sizes are no longer limited to matronly figures but come in almost every style. If your figure is slender and youthful, a junior size may be best for you. Although many of these junior-sized dresses are designed for the teen-age set, you will also find many styles that are meant to be worn by the older woman with the slender figure. You can also take advantage of tall sizes made especially proportioned for those who are above average height.

One final word: When you try on a dress that you are thinking of buying, remember that it is easier to take in a seam here and there than to let one out. Buy the size that requires a minimum of alterations—the type that can be made easily and quickly—and if there is any doubt as to whether the dress can be made to fit properly, don't buy it.

MAKING ALTERATIONS—Every manufacturer of ready-made clothing has his own way of putting a garment together, and the way you make an alteration may depend upon the method he has used in putting that particular garment together. The procedures for making the alterations listed below apply to most dresses. Any variations in the steps followed will be slight.

Shortening a skirt—This is a simple alteration. First rip the hem. If it is a colored dress, and you are not sure you will be able to match the color exactly, you may want to save the thread. If the hem is to be shortened only slightly, leave the tape or binding attached. If the hem must be shortened considerably, rip off the tape and save it to use in making the new hem. Rayon tape is usually weak in texture and is better replaced with new, but cotton tape is strong enough to be used again.

Press the hem on the wrong side, to eliminate the crease where the hem was originally turned up. To get an even hem line, try the dress on and mark, or have someone else mark, the line at which it is to be turned up. Pin and baste the new hem in place. Press. Then finish, using the type of hem that seems best for the garment.

Lengthening a skirt—Rip the hem and press out the crease of the old hem line. If there is enough material to turn up for the new hem, measure, pin, and baste it in place. Press the new fold flat and hem.

If you must use the full length of the letdown hem, rip or cut off the tape and attach a "false" hem as follows: Cut a 3-inch-wide bias band of material in a color and texture to match the material of the dress. If the two materials cannot be matched exactly, choose a lighter-weight material for the bias band.

Seam the bottom of the skirt and the new band together with the two right sides of the material facing. Turn the band under about ¼ inch above the seam so that the fold will not come at the seam line. When the skirt has been properly hung and you are sure that the hem line is even, pin and baste it in place. Press; then finish with any suitable type of hem.

Removing fullness at the hips—A bulky appearance at the hip line may actually be because of an excessive amount of fullness at the front or back waistline rather than at the curve of the hip line itself. The first thing to do, therefore, in making this alteration is to determine exactly where the bulkiness lies. Then rip out the hem, since you will be rehanging the skirt. Try on the dress or skirt and inspect it carefully in a full-length mirror. When you know the places that must be taken in, remove the dress and rip the seams where the alterations are to be made. Then ask someone to help with the refitting.

If the fullness lies at the waistline, rip the seam as well as any darts or tucks. Take these in as much as necessary to remove the extra fullness. Fullness in a gored skirt can be taken in evenly by making these seams deeper. In each case pin from the waistline down, tapering the seams back to the original seam line and the darts to nothing.

If the fullness must be removed at the hip line, take in the side seams evenly, trimming off the extra seam allowance.

When the skirt has been fitted, stitch the new seams and try on the dress again. Re-mark the hem, since the alteration may also have changed the hem line. Then pin, baste, press, and finish the new hem as for any dress.

Adding fullness to a garment—Before you buy a dress that fits too snugly in any part, be sure to look at the seams or darts to see whether they are wide enough to allow for ripping and letting out. Sometimes all that is necessary to add a quarter or an eighth of an inch is to let out the seam or a dart.

If you are adding width to a tight skirt with narrow seams, however, you will have to do it by raising the skirt at the waistline.

If you are altering a separate skirt, it will be necessary to rip off the waistband and slide fastener. If the skirt is part of a dress, rip the waist away from the skirt, but remove the slide fastener from the skirt part only, leaving the upper part of the fastener stitched to the waist. If the skirt is too long, leave the hem in for the time being, as it may be the proper length after the skirt has been altered. If the skirt length is correct before you begin the alterations, then rip out the hem, for you will have to re-mark the hem line after the skirt has been properly fitted.

When you have done all necessary ripping, try on the garment and raise the skirt until it fits comfortably across the hips. Mark the line where the waist is to be joined to the skirt, or where the waistband will be stitched, and remove the garment.

If you are making the alteration on a dress, the skirt waistline will be wider than the blouse waistline. Adjust the two waistlines to fit by taking in the darts in the skirt back or the seams in the skirt front. Try on the skirt again, and, when you are sure the skirt fits correctly, stitch the darts and press. Then baste the blouse to the skirt and stitch. Baste the slide fastener into the skirt and sew it in place. Then check the hemline, re-marking it if necessary. If the skirt is not long enough to allow for a hem, attach a false hem, as described on page 96.

When this alteration is made on a separate skirt, the waistline is fitted in the same way as above. Take up the added fullness by making the darts

and the skirt seams deeper. When the top of the skirt fits the waistband, it is set into place and restitched as for any skirt. See page 152 for directions.

Enlarging a waistline—If the dress is made with gathers or darts or pleats, this will be a simple operation. Rip apart the waist and the skirt, then rip out as much of the gathers, darts, or pleats as necessary to widen the waistline. Be sure that they are ripped out evenly on each side of the center front and the center back lines. Try on the waist and the skirt and pin them together at the waistline. When the gathers have been readjusted, baste, then stitch. If there is no place to add fullness except by letting out the seams, rip them and restitch, adding the same amount of fullness to each seam. A dress in which the waistline cannot be widened in either of these ways can be altered in the same way as a skirt that is too tight. After any of these alterations the hem line should be checked to see that it is still even.

Eliminating bagginess at the waistline of a dress—Bagginess in the blouse of a dress usually occurs at the back and may be owing to the fact that the dress has been purchased in a size to fit a full bosom.

If fullness must be removed from both the front and the back part of the blouse, it should be ripped completely apart from the skirt and refitted.

If the fullness is only at the back, rip the dress across the back waistline and refit the back of the blouse by drawing it under the skirt until the fullness disappears. It may also help to restitch the darts, taking them a little deeper.

In each case the slide fastener is ripped out of the blouse and left attached to the skirt, to be replaced after the blouse has been fitted properly. When the alteration has been made, recheck the hem line to be sure that it has not been affected by the adjustment.

Fitting heavy or round shoulders —There is no standard way to alter the back of a dress so that it fits smoothly over a heavy shoulder line. Much depends upon the style of the dress and the curve of the shoulders. The general procedure, however, is first to rip the side seams and then those across the back waistline. If there are darts at the waistline, they should be ripped also and pressed flat.

Try on the dress when you have completed the ripping and have someone fit the blouse to your shoulder line. In addition to the released darts some width can be gained from the side seams at the waistline.

Fitting thin shoulders—Correct excessive fullness across the shoulder blades by ripping the shoulder seams —and in most cases the underarm seams as well—and refitting the back of the blouse. The collar or binding around the neckline should also be ripped off, since this alteration will affect the neckline.

When the seams have been ripped, the dress or the blouse is tried on wrong side out and the blouse back raised so that the excessive fullness can be smoothed into the shoulder and underarm seams. The new seams are pinned in place and the new neckline remarked with chalk.

The garment is then removed and the new seams basted, stitched, and pressed. After this has been done, the neckline is recut and finished. In doing this, be particularly careful not to cut the neckline too deep. It is much wiser to cut out less than the allowance you feel necessary, even if it means cutting the neckline a second time.

Correcting tightness in the sleeves and underarm seams—A poor fit about the sleeve and the armhole can frequently be corrected by removal of some of the filling from the shoulder pad, or removal of the entire pad. In other cases it may be necessary to ease the strain by ripping the sleeve and the underarm seam. If there is sufficient seam allowance, the new seam lines can be marked and restitched. If there is not enough material to be taken from the seams, a gusset must be put under the arm.

From some inconspicuous place, such as the inside of the hem, cut two pieces of material large enough to fit under the arm. These pieces are usually wedge-shaped and are fitted and tapered into the sleeve and the underarm seams. Pin the pieces into place and try on the garment. When you have adjusted it to the best possible fit, baste and stitch the gussets.

You will usually have no difficulty in finding sufficient material for the gusset from some part of the garment. If it cannot be found elsewhere, it can be obtained by shortening the sleeve.

Correcting looseness at the sleeves and underarm seams—This can often be done by using a shoulder pad. If the looseness is mostly under the arm, the sleeve must be ripped out of the armhole, the underarm seam ripped apart for a few inches, and the sleeve reset into the armhole.

For best results this should be done with the help of an assistant. The garment is tried on wrong side out, the sleeve slipped into place and pinned. The underarm seam is then pinned and the garment removed. After the new seams have been basted, they are stitched and pressed.

Adjusting sleeve length—Sleeves can usually be made as long or as short as needed, but they should always be measured from the wrist up, since the right arm may not be exactly the same length as the left.

Shortening a sleeve consists merely of marking the new sleeve length and then rehemming a loose sleeve, or attaching the cuff of a fitted sleeve in the new position.

If the sleeve is being lengthened, the way it is finished may depend upon the type of sleeve. The hem of a loose sleeve can be taken out, pressed, and the sleeve finished with a faced hem. If there is not enough material to do this, it can be finished with a contrasting band of material.

A fitted sleeve can be lengthened by sewing an extension of material to the sleeve and hiding it with a cuff.

A sleeve which is gathered into a band cannot be lengthened in any way that retains the original style, but it is a simple matter to change the sleeve style to one suitable to the style of the dress. You will find information on finishing sleeves in Chapter 9.

POINTERS FOR LONGER WEAR—

Even when a ready-made garment does not need altering, it is always a good idea to examine the garment closely and make any minor repairs before it is worn. Doing this will save time and annoyance later as well as increase its life.

Check all seams for any breaks in the stitching. If you find any, restitch the seam in a matching thread, following the original seam line.

Inspect the seam edges for fraying. If there is sufficient seam allowance, frayed edges can be pinked to prevent their raveling further. If not, they should be overcast before the seam allowance ravels completely out. Very thin materials can be machine stitched close to the edge before being overcast.

Check the hem to be sure it is caught all the way around the skirt. If the turned-up edge has been bound with bias tape, be sure that it is not stitched so close to the edge that it will pull away from the material easily. Rip the binding and restitch any place where this seems likely to occur. For any other garment except cotton house dresses, a machine-stitched hem should be ripped out and done over by hand.

Examine all pockets, paying particular attention to the corners. If there are any loose, they should be tacked in place. For pockets which receive hard wear, such as those in play clothes or in children's clothes, reinforce them by stitching a piece of tape on the underside of the pocket at the top.

A slot pocket may be weak at the corners. It can be strengthened by machine stitching a small triangle over each corner with a matching thread. If the pocket is on a tailored garment, make an arrowhead as described on page 247.

Examine the placket. It may need a few stitches at either end to make it more secure.

Examine all snaps, hooks and eyes, buttons, buckles, and belt loops, and securely fasten any loose ones.

Check the buttonholes. There may be loose threads in a worked buttonhole. A bad break in the stitching can be remedied by machine stitching close to the edge all around the buttonhole, then reworking the buttonhole as described in Chapter 10.

Index

Abrasion, defined, 34
Absorbency, defined, 34
Accessories, 198–211, 328–60
 care of, 212–13
 closet, 299–301
 flexibility in, 184
 making, 328–60
  belts, 356–59
  collars and cuffs, 349–55
  gloves, 349
  handbags, 329–42
  hats, 342–49
  peplums, 360
 for plump women, 210–12
 for small women, 201–5
 for tall women, 205–9
 (See also specific items.)
Accordion pleats, 86
Acetate fabrics, 29
Acrilan fabric, 29
Adapting patterns, 164–83, 186–91
 dresses, 165–80, 186–88
  necklines, yokes, 172–74
  skirts, 165–72
  sleeves, 174–77
 suits, 180–82, 188–91
Allover embroidery, 236

Allover lace, edging, 233
Allover prints for first sewing, 25
Alterations,
 in fitting basted dresses, 114–20
  blouses of, 115–19
  skirts of, 114–15, 119–20
 in patterns, 44–57
  blouses, 47–49
  one-piece dresses, 52–54
  shorts and slacks, 54–56
  skirts, 49–52
  sleeves, 56–57
 in ready-to-wear clothes, 378–82
  adding fullness, 379–80
  at hipline, 379
  at shoulders, 381
  of skirt length, 379
  of sleeves, 381–82
  at waistline, 380–81
Altering, defined, 46
Animals, stuffed, 362–63
Anklets (jewelry), 201
Antique buttons, 141
Applied band for decoration, 101
Appliqué, 247–49
 on cuffs, 355
Apron peplums, 360

Aprons, 254–56
    lace, for evening, 93
    from men's shirts, 226
Armholes, setting sleeves into, 113,
    124–25
Armo, 34
Arms,
    altering patterns for various types,
        56–57
    (See also Sleeves.)
Arnel fabric, 29
Arrowheads, embroidered, 247
Austrian shades, 283–85
Average figures, styles for, 13

Baby clothes, 251
    bibs from towels, 318
    from men's shirts, 226
    tucks on, 83, 84
Back length, measuring, 12
Back-pleated skirts, 167–68
Backstitch, 70
Bagginess in dress bodices, 116,
    380
Bags,
    laundry, 300–1
    (See also Handbags.)
Ball buttons, 139
Band cuffs, 127
Bandings, 100–2
Bands, lace, 232
Bar fagoting, 246
Bar tacks, 155
Basic patterns, adapting, 164–83,
    186–91
Basic stitches, 69–71
Basket aprons, 254
Basting, 67–69
    (See also items to be basted.)
Bat-wing sleeve, 123
Bathing suit materials, 196

Bathrobes,
    make-over, 226
    trousseau, 258
Bathroom curtains, plastic, 277–78
Beach robe materials, 196
Beading with lace, 233
Bean bags, 363
Bed jackets in trousseau, 258, 260–
    61
Bedframes, slipcovering, 310
Bedspreads, 311–14
Belt loops, thread, 155
Belts,
    for expectant mothers, 323
    making, 329, 356–59
        matching dress, 155–56
    for thick waists, 18
Benches, dressing table, 298–99
Berets, 347–48
Bias-cut fabrics,
    basting to straight edge, 69, 77
    bindings, 102–4
        for collars, 132
        for hems, 94
        (See also other items to be
            bound.)
    cord for buttons, 139
    facings, 97, 127–28
    lingerie, 262
    for striped skirt, 62–63
    tape (see bindings, above)
Bib aprons, 254–55
Bibs, from towels, 318
Bicycle clips for hats, 343
Bindings, 102–4
    for collars, 132
    for hems, 94
Blanket stitch, 155, 239
Blankets, quilts from old, 316–17
Blind hems, 93
Blocking hats, 345–46

Blouses,
   dress bodices,
      altering basted, 115–19
      altering patterns, 47–49
      lining, 136
      (See also Dresses.)
   easy-to-make, 10, 163
   evening, 192
   from men's shirts, 219–20
   in planning wardrobe, 193–94
   (See also Necklines; Sleeves; etc.)
Bodices (see Blouses)
Boleros,
   with dolman sleeves, 177
   from jacket, 225
Bone buttons, 140
Border prints, use, 26
Bound buttonholes, 143–45
Bound seams, 73
Box pleats, 85
   in draperies, 289
Boys' clothing, 262
   (See also Children, sewing for.)
Braided (plaited) belts, 356–57
Braided leather buttons, 140
Braiding as trimming, 234–35
Brassieres in trousseau, 258
Bridesmaids' dresses, 187
Broad shoulders, 19, 48–49
   (See also Heavy shoulders; Square
      shoulders.)
Buckles,
   fabric-covered, 155
   on jackets, 181–82
Buckram-frame valance, 291
Bullion stitch, 242–43
Businesswoman's wardrobe, 185–86
Busts,
   measuring, 12
   patterns for large, 16

   patterns for small, 18
   (See also Alterations.)
Button-and-carpet thread, 36
Button loops, thread, 155
Buttoned-down-the-front dress,
      177–80
Buttonhole stitch, 147
Buttonhole twist, 36
Buttonholes, 143–48
   bound, 143–48
   machine attachment for, 7
   measuring, 143
   reinforcing, 382
   spacing, 143
   tailored, 148
   thread, 147–48
Buttons, 137–43
   on belts, 358
   buttonholes for, 143–48
   Chinese loop fastening, 143–44
   on jackets, 181
   sewing on, 141–42
   torn-off, replacing, 271

Café curtains, 281–82
Cap sleeves, 10, 123
Capes for expectant mothers, 327
Care of clothes, 212–17, 382
   pressing, 213–15
   repairing, 262–72, 382
   stain removal, 215–17
Care of fabrics, 29ff.
   (See also individual fabrics.)
Cascade draperies, 292–94
Casual clothes,
   topcoats, tailoring, 372–73
   in wardrobe, 184
   (See also Play clothes; Sports
      clothes.)
Catch stitch, 95, 241
Chain stitch, 242

Chairs, slip-covering, 301–9
Chamois accessories, 329
    gloves, 199–200
Chart, fabric, 29–33
Cheesecloth curtains, 277
Chewing gum, removing, 216
Chiffon,
    lining, 135
    seaming, 77
Children,
    sewing by, 250
        on machine, 7
    sewing for, 250–53, 262
        aprons, 256
        curtains, 277
        made-over bathrobes, 226
        made-over coats, 221–22
        made-over dresses, 220–21
        "practical tucks" in hems, 84
    (See also Baby clothes.)
Chinese loop fastenings, 142–43
Circular bags, 338–41
Circular flounces, 134
Circular skirts,
    altering length, 51
    facing hems, 96
    making patterns, 169–70
    rolled hems for, 93
    tucks on, 84
Circular ruffles, 230
Classic-style dresses (see Buttoned-
        down-the-front dresses)
Cleaning fluid, use, 215–16
Closet accessories, 299–301
Clutch bags (envelopes), 330–33
    for evening, 336–38
Coats,
    bias-bound hems, 94
    children's, 221–22
        from adults', 253
    for expectant mothers, 326

    fur collars for, 376–77
    repairing men's, 266–69
        collars, 267–68
        elbows, 266
        sleeves, 266–67, 268–69
    tailored, making, 369–77
        interfacing and facing, 370–
        71, 372–73
        interlining, 375
        lining, 373–74
        setting in sleeves, 371–72
Cobble stitch, 238
Coffee stains, 216
Collarless necklines, 10, 127–29
Collars, 130–33, 349–51
    bias binding for, 132
    fur, 376–77
    mending coat, 267–68
    separate, as accessories, 349–51
    on square necklines, 173
    turning shirt, 272
Colored shoes, 199
Colored stockings,
    for small women, 203
    for tall women, 205
Colors, becoming, 25
    (See also specific items of cloth-
        ings.)
Combination stitch, 71
Comforters, patchwork, 314–17
Contrasting-binding   buttonholes,
        145–46
Cording,
    in bound buttonholes, 146
    in headings, 231
    machine for, 7, 83
    in seams, 76
    in tucks, 83
Cording foot, 7, 83
    for zippers, 7, 149

Corduroy, 26
    cutting, 23–24
    in coats and jackets, 365
    pressing, 214, 215
    water spot removal, 217
Corner facings, 98–99
Corval fabric, 29
Cottage curtains, 281
Cotton fabric, 30
    pressing, 30, 215
    widths, 22, 60
Couching stitch, 238
Covered buttons, 137–39
Covers, mattress, 317
Cranes, drapery, 295
Creslan fabric, 30
Crisscross fagoting, 245
Crocheted buttons, 139
Cross-stitch 240–41
Cross-tucks, 83
Cuff links, button, 142
Cuffs, 126–27, 354–55
    repairing, 266–67, 272
    separate, as accessories, 349–50,
        354–55
    turning, 272
Curtains, 276–88
    café, 281–82
    cottage, 281
    fixtures for, 294–97
    hemming, 84, 274
    remodeling, 283
    ruffled, 280
    sash, 280–81, 283
    tailored, 279
    tucks in hem, practical, 84
    (See also Draperies.)
Curved tucks, 84
Curved yokes for skirts, 171
Custom dress-making, 106–11

Cut-steel buttons,141
Cutting,
    dress fabric, 23–24, 58–65
        in remodeling, 219
    fur, 376–77
    slip covers, 304–8
    (See also other items to be cut.)

Dacron fabric, 30
Damask hems, 96
Darning, 264–65
    by machine, 8, 264
Dart tucks, 79, 83
Darts, 78–82
    finishing, 82
Darvan fabric, 30
Decorative arrowhead, 247
Decorative darts, 82
Decorative seams, 74–76
Decorative stitches, 237–49
    blanket, 155, 239, 240
    bullion, 242–43
    buttonhole, 147
    catch, 241
    chain, 242
    cobble, 238
    couching, 238
    cross-, 240–41
    fagoting, 245–46
    feather, 241
    French knots, 242
    hemstitching, 243–44
    lazy-daisy, 241
    outline, 239
    saddle, 238
    satin, 239–40
    seed, 238–39
Decorative tucks, 83, 84
Deep overcasting, 70
Denim sports skirts, 196

Details,
   easy-to-make, 10
   hard-to-make, 11
   (See also Necklines; Sleeves; etc.)
Diagonal basting, 69
Diagonal hemstitching, 244
Diagonal yokes for skirts, 171
Dickeys, 349, 350, 351–54
   scarves as, 353–54
Dirndl sleeves, 124
Dishcloths from towels, 318
Doeskin gloves, 200
Dolls, rag, 363
Dolman sleeves, 123
   bolero with, 177
Door curtains, 281
Double-breasted blouses, 179
Double darts, 78, 82
Double hemstitching, 243
Double kick pleats, 87–88
Double ruffles, 230
   as cuffs, 354
Double sash curtains, 283
Double-woven fabric gloves, 199
Drapability, defined, 34
Draped fullness in skirts, 165, 166
Draped peplums, 172
Draped V necklines, 173
Draperies, 287–94
   fixtures for, 294–97
   swag and cascade, 292–94
   valances for, 290–92
Drawn work, 243–44
Dress forms, 5–6
Dresses,
   for expectant mothers, 322–24
   patterns for, 9–20
      adapting, 186–91
      cutting with, 58–65
      easy-to-make, 9–10, 162
      fitting and altering, 37–57

   hard-to-make, 11
   measuring for, 12
   for various figures, 13–20
   pointers for longer wear, 382
   putting together, 105–36
      alterations while, 114–20
      custom method, 105, 107–11
      factory method, 105–7
      lining while, 134–36
   ready-to-wear, altering, 378–82
   remodeling, 220–21, 223–24, 225
   styling and adapting, 163–80, 186–91
   (See also Buttons; Darts; Hems; etc.; Sleeves; etc.; Materials; Buttoned-down-the-front dresses; Sheath dresses; etc.)
Dressing-table skirts, 297–98
Dressmaker's seams, 71–73
Dynel fabric, 30

Earrings from old buttons, 141
Easy-to-make handbag, 330–33
Easy-to-make patterns, 9–10
Edge-stitched seams, 72
Edgings, 232–35
   (See also Embroidery; Lace; Ruffles; Scallops.)
Egg stains, 216
Elastic thread, 36, 228–29
Elbows,
   darts at, 80
   patches on, 226
   reinforcing, 264–65
Embroidery, 237–39
   allover, 236
   on buttons, 137–38
   on edgings, 235
   on inserts, 236

stitches, 237–39
    blanket, 155, 239, 240
    bullion, 242–43
    buttonhole, 147
    catch, 241
    chain, 242
    cobble, 238
    couching, 238
    cross-, 240–41
    fagoting, 245–46
    feather, 241
    French knots, 242
    hemstitching, 243–44
    lazy-daisy, 241
    outline, 239
    saddle, 238
    satin, 239–40
    seed, 238–39
Enameled buttons, 140
Enlarging waistlines in ready-to-wear garments, 380
Envelope handbags, 330–33
    for evening, 336–38
    slip covers for, 333
Equipment for sewing, 1–8
Even basting, 68
Evening wear, 192–93
    basic suit adapted for, 191
    envelope bag for, 336–38
    maternity, 325–26
    for plump women, 209, 210
    remodeling gowns, 223–24
    slips, 258, 259, 262
    for small women, 201, 202, 203, 204
    for tall women, 205, 208
Expectant mothers' clothes, 322–27
Extended bands, 101–2
Eyelet edging, 235
Eyelets, thread-loop, 155

Fabric-covered buttons, 137–39
Fabric (See Materials)
Face cloths from towels, 318
Facings, 96–100
    for corners, 98–99
    front, 97–98
    for necklines, 127–29
    for skirts, 96
    for sleeve openings, 126
    for tailored coats and jackets, 368, 370–71, 372–73
Factory method of dress-making, 105–6
Fagoting, 245–46
Family, sewing for, 250–72
    aprons, 254–56
    children's clothes (see Children, sewing for)
    house dresses, 254
    lingerie, 257–62
    mending, 262–72
    men's clothes, 262, 265–72
Fan pleats, 85–86
    in godet, 134
Fanlight window-curtain, 296
Fashion notes, 161–64
Fastening machine stitching, 67
Fastenings, 137–55
    buckles, 155, 181
    buttons and buttonholes, 137–49, 181
    hooks and eyes, 154–55
    slide fasteners, 149–51
    snaps, 153–54
    tape closures, 154
Feather stitch, 241
Felt accessories, 329 ff.
    bags, 329–36, 339–42
    belts, 356, 357, 358–59
    hats, 345–46

monogram, 339
slippers, 361–62
Fiber, defined, 34
Fiberglas, 31
Figure types,
  and pattern selection, 13–20
  (See also Plump women; Small
    women; Tall women)
Filling threads, 60
Finishing touches, 89–104
  (See also Darts; Seams; Sleeves;
    etc.)
Fitting,
  of basted dresses, 114–20
  defined, 46
  of patterns, 37–57
Fixtures, drapery, 294–97
Flared skirts, 133–34
  adjusting length, 51
  making pattern for, 169–70
  (See also Circular skirts.)
Flared sleeves, 176
Flat fell seams, 73
Flexibility in wardrobe, 184–85
Flounces, circular, 134
Flower hats, 343
Folding beds, slip-covering, 311
Formal wear (see Evening wear)
Formite, 35
Frayed cuffs, mending, 266–67
Frayed seam edges, repairing, 382
French knots, 242
French seams, 74
Fringe, 244–45
  on luncheon sets, 276
  on sash, 356
  on taffeta, 328–29
Frog fastenings, 142–43
Front facings, 97–98
Fruit stains, 216

Fullness in ready-to-wear garments,
  adding, 379–80
  removing, 379
Furs and fur pieces, 200, 376–77
  collars of, 376–77
  hats of, 348–49
  for plump women, 211
  for small women, 203
  for tall women, 208
Furniture, slip-covering, 301–11

Garment covers, 301
Gathers and gathering, 227–31
  for bench covers, 298–99
  for dressing-table skirts, 297–98
  headings, 231–32
  of lace, 232, 235
  by machine, 228–29
  for peplum, 360
  ruffles, 229–30 (See also Ruffles.)
  shirring, 228–29
Gifts, making, 360–63
  for men, 262
  (See also Aprons; Lampshades;
    Tea towels; etc.)
Girdle repairs, 263
Girls' clothing, 251–53
  aprons, 256
  made-over dresses, 220–21
  practical tucks in hems, 84
  (See also Children, sewing for;
    Teen-agers.)
Glacé gloves, 200
Glass buttons, 140
Gloves, 199–200
  making, 349
  for plump women, 210–11
  for small women, 204
  storing, 213
  for tall women, 207–8
Godets, 134

Gold-colored buttons, 140
Grain of fabric, 60
Grass stains, 216
Grease stains, 217
Gripper snaps, 154
Grosgrain ribbon belts, 357–58

Half sizes, ready-to-wear, 378
Hand (handle) defined, 34
Hand sewing,
    basting, 67–69
    gathering by, 227
    hemming, 91–94, 95–96
    seam finishing, 71–72, 75
    shirring by, 228
    stitches in,
    basic, 69–71
    decorative, 147, 237–49
    hemming, 92–94, 95–96
    padding, 370–71
    tying knot in thread, 66
    (See also Buttons; Facings; etc;
      Finishing touches.)
Hand-stitched buttons, 138–39
Handbags, 200
    making, 329–42
      circular, 339–41
      envelope, 330–33, 336–38
      miser's pouch, 341–42
      shoulder, 333–36
    for plump women, 211
    for small women, 203–4
    for tall women, 208
Handkerchiefs, aprons of, 256
Handling of fabrics (chart), 29–33
Hangers, use of, 114, 212
Hard-to-make patterns, 11
Hats, 198, 342–49
    for expectant mothers, 326–27
    for girls, 251
    making, 342–49

    berets, 347–48
    felt or straw, 345–46
    flower, 343
    fur, 348–49
    head bands, 343, 349
    tiered skullcaps, 346–47
    turbans, 343–45
    of veiling, 342, 343
    for plump women, 209
    for small women, 201
    storage of, 213
    for tall women, 205
Head bands, 343
    fur, 349
Headboards, slip-covering, 310–11
Headings, 230–31
    (See also Curtains.)
Heavy shoulders, 381
    (See also Broad shoulders; Square
      shoulders.)
Height (see Small women; Tall
    women)
Hem gauges, making, 91
Hems, 89–96
    facing, 96
    hand finishes, 92–94, 95–96
    machine finishes, 94–95
    marking, 90–91
    repair of, 382
Hemstitching, 243–44
Hips,
    fitting ready-to-wear garments,
      379
    measuring, 12
    (See also Alterations.)
Holdbacks, drapery, 295
Holes,
    darning, 263
    patching, 265–66
    reweaving, 262–63

Home, sewing for (see Household items)

Home dresses, 254
(See also House dresses.)

Hooks and eyes, 154–55

Hostess gowns in trousseau, 258–59, 261, 262

Hostess's wardrobe, 186

House coats in trousseau, 258–59,

House coats in trousseau, 258–59, 261, 262

House dresses, 254
for expectant mothers, 324

Household items, 273–321
bedspreads, 311–14
closet accessories, 299–301
curtains and draperies, 276–97
dressing-table skirts, 297–99
garment covers, 301
lampshades, 318–21
laundry bags, 300–1
mattress covers, pads, 317–18
pot holders, 318
quilts, 314–17
sheets (see Sheets)
shoe pockets, 299–300
slip covers, 301–11
table linens (see Table linens)
towels (see Towels)

Housewife's wardrobe, 185

Ink stains, 216

Inserts,
embroidered, 236
lace, 233
(See also Flares; Godets; etc.)

Interfacings, 34–35
in tailored clothes, 368
jackets, coats, 370
topcoats, 372–73

Interlinings,
in fur collars, 377
in winter coats, 367–68, 375

Interlon, 35

Inverted pleats, 85

Ironing (pressing), 213–15
darts, 82
in making tailored clothes, 369
pleats, 95
various fabrics, 214–15
on chart, 29 ff.

Ironing boards, 1, 213

Irons, 213

Jackets,
basic patterns, 164
bolero, 177, 225
fur collars for, 376–77
hemming unlined, 94
maternity, 326
remodelingold, 225
repairing, 266–67, 269–70
for sports, 196, 197
style variations, 180–82
tailoring of, 369–72, 373–76
interfacing and facing, 93, 368, 370–71

Jerkins from jackets, 225

Jersey,
lining for, 135
use of, 27

Jeweled buttons, 141

Jewelry, 200–1
on accessories, 329
on belts, 358
for plump women, 211
for small women, 204–5
for tall women, 208–9

Joining skirts and waists of dresses, 112–13

Jumpers from dresses, 225
Junior sizes, ready-to-wear, 378

Kayab, 35
Kick pleats, 86–88
Kid gloves, 200
Kimono sleeves, 10, 123
Knee patches, 266
Knees, reinforcing, 264–65
Knife pleats, 85
Knitting dress sleeves, 225–26
Knotted fringe, 244
Knotting thread,
    for hand sewing, 66
    in machine stitching, 67
Kodel fabric, 31

Lace, 232–34
    allover, edging of, 233
    appliqué, 248–49, 261
    aprons of, 193
    bands, 232, 261
    curtains, 278
    dress, lining for, 135
    as edging, 232–34
        for collars, 132
        for lingerie, 235, 261
    gathered, 232, 235
    inserts, 233
    joining, 232–33, 233–34
Lampshades, 318–21
    slip covers for, 320–21
Lapped seams, 75
Large busts, patterns for, 16
    widening blouse, 48
Laundry bags, making, 300–1
Lazy-daisy stitch, 241
Leather accessories,
    buttons, braided, 140
    handbags, 200, 329
    making, 329–30

Length,
    adjusting (see Lengthening; Shortening)
    of children's clothes, 251–52
    of skirts, "correct," 89
Lengthening,
    skirts, 379
        practical tucks for, 84
    sleeves, 381–82
    (See also Alterations.)
    pressing, 31, 214–15
    widths, 22, 60
Lingerie,
    handmade, 257–62
        materials for, 261–62
    remodeling, 226
Linings, 35, 134–36
    for draperies, 288
    for dresses, skirts, 134–36
    for envelope bags, 332–33
    for tailored garments, 135, 366–67, 373–75
Lipstick stains, 216
Looped self-bias cord, 235
Lounging pajamas in trousseau, 258
Luncheon sets, 274–76

Machine stitching, 7–8
    darning, 8, 264
    decorative, 237–38
    fastening, 67
    gathering, shirring, 227–29
    hemming, 94–95
    (See also Sewing machines.)
Make-overs, suggestions for, 218–26
Markings on patterns, 37–42, 63–65
Materials, 21–36
    chart of, 29–33
    cutting (see Cutting)

grain of, 60
placing pattern on, 23–24, 58–63
for pleating, 26–27
for plump women, 26
preparing for remodeling, 218–19
pressing various, 29 ff.
for softness, 27
sources of various, 29 ff.
(See also Cotton fabric; etc.; specific items to make.)
Measurements for patterns, 12
Maternity clothes, 322–27
coats, 327
dressy, 325
evening, 325–26
hats, 327–28
house dresses, 324
play clothes, 324–25
shoes, 327
suits, 327
Mattress covers and pads, 317–18
Mending, 262–72
darning, 264
girdle repairs, 263
men's clothes, 265–72
patching, 265–66, 271–72
reinforcing, 264–65
reweaving, 263–64
rips and tears, 263
Mending tape, 263
Men's clothing, 262
remodeling for women, 219–20, 222–23, 226
repairing, 265–72
frayed sleeves, collars, 266–68, 272
patching, 265–66, 271–72
of pockets, 269–71

sleeve relining, 268–69
torn-off buttons, 271
Metal buttons, 140
Mildew stains, 216
Mirror buttons, 141
Miser's pouch, 341–42
Mitered corner facings, 98–99
Mixing outfits, 184–86
Mocha gloves, 200
Molds for covered buttons, 138–39
Monk's cloth, 302
Monograms, felt, 339
Mother-and-daughter outfits, 253
Muslin patterns, 164–65, 369

Nail polish stains, 216–17
Nap, materials with (see Corduroy; Velvet; etc.)
Napkins, 274–76
damask hems for, 96
Narrow shoulders, 19–20, 118
(See also Thin shoulders.)
Necklines,
alterations in basted dresses, 116–17
darts at, 79
finishes for, 127–33, 172–73
collars, 130–33, 173
in maternity clothes, 323–24
slide fasteners at, 150–51
style changes in, 162
(See also Collars; Dickeys.)
Necks, long and short, patterns for, 18
Needle boards, 214
Needles, 2
Nightgowns, 258, 260
Net footing as edging, 235
Negligees in trousseau, 258, 262
slips made from, 226
Ninon curtains, 278

Notched collars with lapels, 131
Notches in patterns, 41
    cutting out, 63
Notions (see Buttons; Thread; etc.)
Nylon fabric, 31
    pressing, 31, 214

Odd-shaped buttons, 141
Oil stains, 217
One-piece dresses, altering, 52–53
Opera pumps, wearability, 199
Optical illusions with curtains, 296
Orlon fabric, 31
Outline stitch, 239
Over-the-shoulder bags, 333–36
Overalls, materials for, 197
Overblouses, 194
Overcasting, 70
    on seams, 71–72
Overhanding, 70–71
    for tucks, 84
Overskirts, 360
Oxfords, wearing, 199

Padding stitch, 370
Pads,
    mattress, 318
    shoulder, 121–23
    for stools, 298
Paint stains, 217
Painted buttons, 140
Pajamas,
    remodeling, 226
    in trousseau, 258
Panties in trousseau, 258
Passementeries, 234–35
Patch pockets, 156
Patching, 265–66
    elbow, 266
    underarm, 271–72

Patchwork quilts, comforters, 314–16
Patterns, 9–20
    adapting, 165–83, 186–91
    easy-to-make, 9–10
    fitting and altering, 37–57
        terms used, 46–47
        trying on, 43–44
    hard-to-make, 11
    markings on, 37–42, 63–65
    and materials,
        choosing, 21–23 ff.
        cutting, 58–65
    measurements for, 12
    for remodeling clothes, 218–26
    for various figure types, 13–20
    viscose acetate, 165
Pear-shaped figures, 17
Pearl buttons, 140
Peasant sleeves, 124
Pedal pushers, materials for, 197
Pellon, 35
Peplums, 360
    apron, 360
    gathered, 360
    side-draped, 172
Perfect circle cuffs, 354–55
Perforations in patterns, 42
Peter Pan collars, 351
Petticoats from slips, 226
Picot lace edging, 233
Picoted seams, 75
Picture windows, curtaining, 278
Piecing fabric,
    for remodeling, 219
    in skirt-making, 60
Pigskin gloves, 200
Pilling, defined, 34
Pillowcases out of torn sheets, 317
Pin tucks, 83
Pinch pleats in drapes, 289–90

Pincushions, 2
Pinking seams, 71
    to repair fraying, 382
Pinking shears, 5
Pins, 2
Piped seams, 75
Place mats, 274–76
Plackets, 151–53
    dress, 151–52
    reinforcing, 382
    skirt, 152–53
    in slashes, 153
Plaid fabrics, 23, 26
    cutting, 62–63
Plain seams, 71
Plaited belts, 356–57
Plastic, 33, 214
    aprons, 256
    curtains, 277–78
    handbags, 200
    slip covers, 308–9
    tablecloths, 274
Play clothes,
    for expectant mothers, 324–25
    patching elbows in, 266
    (See also Play suits; Sports clothes.)
Play suits, 196–97
    Turkish towel wraps, 256–57
Pleats, 84–88
    in draperies, 288–90
    materials for, 26–27
    in pattern alteration, 46
    in ruffles, 235
    in skirts, 85–88, 166–69, 170–71
        hemming, 95
    in skirts for dressing tables, 298
    in slip covers, 303–4
    types, 84–88

    accordian, 86
    box, 85, 289
    fan, 85–86
    inverted, 85
    kick, 86–88
    pinch, 289–90
    side, 85
Plump women,
    accessories for, 209–11
    fabrics for, 26, 194
Pockets, 156–60
    for jackets, 180–81
    reinforcing, 382
    repairing trouser, 269–71
Poles, drapery, 297
Pot holders, 318
Practical tucks, 84
Pre-shrinking fabrics, 58
Pressing, 213–15
    darts, 82
    in making tailored clothes, 369
    pleats, 95
    various fabrics, 214–15
    on chart, 29 ff.
Pressing cloths, 1, 5, 214
Pressing cushions (tailor's hams), 5, 214
Princess dresses, altering patterns, 52–53
Professional woman's wardrobe, 185–86
Puffed sleeves, 124
Pumps, 199
Putting dress together, 105–36

Quick hems, 92
Quick overcasting, 70
Quilts, 314–17
    from old blankets, 316–17
    patchwork, 314–16

Rag dolls, 363
Raglan sleeves, 123
Raincoats, 364–65
Raveled fringe, 244
Raveled seam edges, repairing, 382
Rayon fabric, 32
    pressing, 58, 214
    seam binding, 128
    widths, 22, 60
Razor blades, 2
Ready-to-wear clothing, 378–82
    altering, 378–82
    buying for size, 378
    pointers for longer wear, 382
Receptionist's wardrobe, 186
Reinforcing, 264–65
Relining sleeves, 269–70
Remodeling, 218–26
    coats, 221–22
    curtains, 283
    dresses, 218 ff.
    shirts, 219–20
    suits, 222–23
Repairing clothes, 262–72
    men's, 265–72
Resilience, defined, 34
Reversible raincoats, 365
Reversible skirts, 182–83
Reweaving, 263–64
Rhinestone buttons, 141
Ribbon belts, 357–58, 359
Ribbon silk seam binding, 128
Rickrack, 235
Right-side basting, 68
Ripping garments, to remodel, 218–19
Rips, mending, 263
Rods, drapery, 294–97
Rolled hems, 93
Rolled seams, 75

Round shoulders,
    altering patterns for, 49
    fitting dresses to, 381
Round yokes for blouses, 173–74
Ruffles, 227, 229–30
    on collars, 132
    for cuffs, 354
    on curtains, 280
    on sleeves, 175
Running stitch, 69
Runs in hose, darning, 264
Rust stains, 217

Saddle soap, use, 200
Saddle stitch, 238
Salesclerk's wardrobe, 186
Sash curtains, 280–83
Sashes, fringed, 356
Satin stitch, 239
Saw-tooth edges, facing, 100
Scallops,
    binding, 103–4
    embroidering, 240
    facing, 99–100
Scarves,
    aprons from, 256
    as dickeys, 353–54
    for gifts, 361
Scroll belts in felt, 357
Scuffs, making, 362
Seams, 71–77
    decorative, 74–76
    dressmaker, 71–73
    frayed, 382
    in tailored garments, 73–74, 368
    tricks with, 76–77
Seed stitch, 238
Separating slide fasteners, 150
Set-in kick pleats, 87–88
Set-in sleeves, 113, 124–25

adapting patterns, 174–77
in tailored garments, 371–72
Sewing machines, 6–8
  attachments, 7 (See also specific
     attachments.)
  slip-covering, 311
  stitching by, 7–8
    darning, 8, 264
    decorative, 237–38
    fastening, 67
    gathering, shirring, 227–29
    hemming, 94–95
Shades (see Lampshades; Window shades.)
Shanks, thread, for buttons, 141–42
Shaped belts of felt, 358
Shears, 1
  pinking, 5
Sheath dresses, 185
Sheets,
  hemming, 274
  pillowcases from old, 317
  repairing, 317
Shell tucks, 84
Shields, underarm, 375–76
Shirring, 228–29
Shirts, men's,
  remodeling, 219–20
  turning collars, cuffs, 272
  underarm patches, 271–72
Shirtwaist dresses, variations, 186–88
Shoe pockets, 299–300
Shoes, 198–99
  care of, 213
  for expectant mothers, 327
  for plump women, 209
  for small women, 202
  for tall women, 205
Short women,
  accessories for, 201–5

patterns for, 14
(See also Alterations; Shortening.)
Short-waisted women,
  overblouses for, 194
  (See also Alterations.)
Shortening,
  skirts, 379
  sleeves, 381–82
  (See also Alterations.)
Shortie coat materials, 196
Shorts,
  altering patterns for, 54–56
  materials for, 197
Shoulder bags, making, 333–36
Shoulders,
  darts at, 79–80
  fitting various types, 118–19, 381
  patterns for various types, 19–20
    altering, 48–49
  style changes in, 161
Shower curtains, 277–78
Shrinking fabrics before cutting, 58
Side-draped peplums, 172
Side pleats, 85
Silk fabric, 32
  pressing, 32, 214
  ribbon, uses, 128, 359
  widths, 22, 60
Silver-colored buttons, 140
Siri, 35
Sizes,
  in pattern measurement, 12, 21
  in ready-to-wear clothing, 378
  (See also Plump women; Small women; Tall women.)
Ski clothes, 197
Skirt markers, 5, 90
Skirts,
  basted, altering, 114, 119–20
  children's, 84
  darts in, 80, 81

evening, 192
for expectant mothers, 322, 325
facing, 96
flared (see Flared skirts)
joining to waist, 112–13
    binding top, 77
lengthening, 84, 379
lining, 134–36
patterns,
    adapting basic, 165–72
    altering and fitting, 39, 49–52
piecing bottoms, 60
plackets, 152–53
pleated, 85–88 (See also Pleats.)
remodeling, 224–25
reversible, 182–83
shortening, 379
for sportswear, 196
striped bias, cutting out, 62
suit, 182–83, 376
(See also Dressing-table skirts; Hems.)
Skullcaps, tiered, 346–47
Skyline shades, 285–87
Slacks,
    altering patterns for, 54–56
    materials for, 197
    reinforcing knees, 264–65
Slash plackets, 153
Slashed necklines, 129, 153
    with collars, 130–31
Sleeve boards, 213–14
Sleeveless jackets for sports, 196
Sleeves, 18, 123–27
    altering, 381
        in pattern, 56–57
    bishop, 225
    cap, 10, 123
    cutting out by pattern, 61–62
    darts at, 80

dolman, 123
flared, 176
godets for, 134
hard-to-make, 11
kimono, 10, 123
length, adjusting, 381–82
lining, 136
    relining, 269–70
measuring for pattern, 12
patterns,
    adapting, 174–77
    altering, 56–57
puffed, 124
raglan, 123
replacing woolen, 225–26
set-in, 113, 124–25
    adapting patterns, 174–77
    in tailored garments, 371–72
style changes in, 161
three-quarter draped, 175–76
(See also Cuffs; Elbows.)
Slide fasteners, 149–51
    avoiding trouble with, 263
    for handbags, 331–32
Slip basting, 68
Slip covers, 301–11
    for envelope bags, 333
    for lampshades, 320–21
    measuring for, 303–4
    plastic, 308–9
Slip-on turnback cuffs, 355
Slip-stitched hems, 93
Slippers, making, 361–62
Slips, 258, 259
    remodeling, 226
Slip openings,
    facings for, 99
    made like bound buttonholes, 146
Sloping shoulders, 118–19

Slot pockets, 157–58
  reinforcing, 382
Slot seams, 74
Small-busted figures,
  building up, 18
  (See also Alterations.)
Small women,
  accessories for, 201–5
  patterns for, 14
  (See also Alterations; Shortening.)
Smocking, 246–47
Snaps, 153–54
Socks,
  darning, 364
  for plump women, 210
  for small women, 203
  for tall women, 205
Sofas, slip-covering, 301–9
Spacing buttonholes, 143
Spectator pumps, 199, 202
Spoke fagoting, 246
Sponging woolens to shrink, 58
Sports clothes, 194–97
  patching elbows, 266
  (See also Play suits.)
Spreading, in pattern altering, 46
Sprinklers to dampen clothes, 214
Square necklines with collars, 173
Square shoulders, 119
  (See also Broad shoulders; Heavy
    shoulders.)
Stains, removing, 215–17
Sta-Shape, 35
Static-free, defined, 34
Stays, under shirring, 228
Stitching,
  hand (see Hand sewing)
  machine (see Machine stitching)
Stockings, 199
  care of, 213
  darning, 264

for plump women, 210
for small women, 203
for tall women, 205
Stoles, care of, 212
Stools, covering, 298–99
Straight of the goods, 60
Strap seams, 73–74
Straw hats, 345–46
Street accessories,
  for plump women, 209 ff.
  for small women, 201 ff.
  for tall women, 205 ff.
  (See also specific items.)
String gloves, 199
Striped fabrics, 23, 26
  cutting, 62–63
Stuffed toys, 362–63
Sturdy patches, 265–66
Studio-couch slip covers, 309
Styling clothes, 161–83
Suède accessories, 329
  fringed sash, 356
  gloves, 200
  twisted belt, 357
Sugar bags for towels, 273
Suits,
  boys', 262
  maternity, 326
  pattern variations, 180–83, 188–
    91
  play, 196–97
  tailoring of, 369–72, 373–76
  woman's made from man's, 222–
    23
  (See also Jackets.)
Sunback dresses, 197
Sunburst pleats, 85–86
Swag draperies, 292–94
Sweaters,
  care, 212, 213

evening, 192
for sports, 196
Synthetics (see specific fabrics)

Table linens, 274–76
hemming, 96
Tablecloths,
hemming, 96
plastic, 274
remodeling, 318
Tables, small, slip-covering, 311
Taffeta, fringing, 328–29
Tailored items, 364–77
buttonholes, 148
curtains, 278–79
coats, suits, jackets, 364–77
interlining of, 367–68, 375
interfacing and facing, 368,
370–71, 372–73
lining, 366–67, 373–75
dresses, lining, 135
lingerie, 258
seams, 73–74, 368
shirts, 194
skirts, 376
lining, 135
slot pockets, 158
in wardrobe, 185
Tailor's chalk, 5, 65
Tailor's hams (pressing cushions), 5,
214
Tailor's tacks, 64–65
Taking in ready-to-wear dresses,
379 ff.
Tall women,
accessories for, 205–8, 349
patterns for, 15
(See also Alterations; Lengthening.)
Tape (see Mending tape; etc.)
Tape closures, 154

Tape measures, 2
Tapering, in pattern altering, 47
Tar, removal of, 217
Tea towels, 273–74
Teacher's wardrobe, 186
Tearing fabric across grain, 59
Tears, mending, 263
Teen-agers,
colored stockings for, 203
curtains for, 277
formal wear, 203, 204
jewelry, 204
Tennis dresses, 187
Thin shoulders, fitting, 381
(See also Narrow shoulders.)
Thread, 2–3
for decorative stitches, 237
elastic, 36, 228–29
matching to fabrics, 35–36
sizes and types, 36
for tailoring, 369–69
Thread buttonholes, 147
Thread loops, 155
Thread shanks, 141–42
Three-quarter draped sleeves, 175–
76
Tiered skullcaps, 346–47
Top-heavy figures, 16
(See also Large busts.)
Top-stitched seams, 72–73
Topcoats, interfacing and facing,
372–73
Topel fabric, 32
Torn-off buttons, replacing, 271
Towels,
tea, 273–74
worn, remodeling, 318
wrap made of, 256–57
Toys, making, 362–63
Transfer embroidery patterns, 237

Transferring pattern markings, 63–64

Trimmed veils, 343

Trimmings, 232–36

(See also Embroidery; Lace; etc.)

Trouser knee patches, 266

Trouser pockets,

repairing, 270–71

replacing, 269–70

Trousseau lingerie, 257–62

Trying on patterns, 43–44

Tucks, 82–84

dart tucks, 79

in pattern alterations, 46

Turbans, 343–45

Turkish towel wraps, 256–57

Turnback cuffs, 126

slip-on, 355

Turning collars and cuffs, 272

"Tweedy" clothes (see Casual clothes)

Twisted belts in felt or suède, 357

Two-color belts, felt or suède, 356

Two-piece dresses, suits as, 189–91

Tying knots for hand sewing, 66

Underarms,

darts at, 80

patches on, 271–72

reinforcing, 264–65

shields for, 375–76

tightness at, correcting, 381

wrinkles at, correcting, 115

Underlinings, types of, 35

(See also Linings.)

Uneven basting, 68

Unlined garments, finishing, 94, 373

Upholstered furniture, slip-covering, 301–9

Upholsterer's seams, 76

V necklines,

bias-faced, 127–28

draped, 173

Valances, 290–92

Veiling for hats, 342, 343

Velcro tape closures, 154, 183

Velvet,

cutting, 23–24

pressing, 214, 215

ribbon belt of, 359

water spot removal, 217

Velveteen for coats and jackets, 217, 365

Vestees, tucks on, 83

Vicara fabric, 32

Vinyl plastic, 33

(See also Plastic.)

Visible slide fasteners, 150

Waistlines,

alterations in,

in basted dresses, 117–18

in patterns, 48, 52

in ready-to-wear garments, 380–81

concealing heavy, 18

darts at, 80–82

measuring for patterns, 12

style changes in, 162

Waists (see Blouses; Waistlines.)

Wallpaper-covered valances, 290

Walnut-shell buttons, 139

Wardrobe planning, 184–97

activities and, 185–86

adapting patterns in, 186–91

evening clothes in, 192–93

flexibility in, 184–85

sports clothes in, 194–97

Warp threads, 60

Washability of various fabrics, 29 ff.

Washable toys, 362–63

Water spots, removing, 217
Welt pockets, 159–60
Welt seams, 73
Whipped hems, 93–94
Widths of various materials, 22, 60
Window shade,
    Austrian, 283–85
    skyline, 285–87
Wooden buttons, 140
Wool fabric, 33
    lining for, 135
    pressing, 33, 214
    reinforcing, 265
    taping seams, 77
    widths, 22, 60

Worked buttonholes, 147
Worn coat collars, 267–68
Wraps, Turkish towel, 256–57

Yardsticks, 2
Yarns, for decorative stitches, 237
Yokes,
    for blouses, 133, 173–74
    for skirts, 170, 171

Zefran fabric, 33
Zigzag attachments, 8, 238, 249
Zippers (slide fasteners), 149–51
    avoiding trouble with, 263
    for handbags, 331–32